ADMINISTRATIVE LAW IN CANADA

FIFTH EDITION

ADMINISTRATIVE LAW
IN CANADA

FIFTH EDITION

Sara Blake

Administrative Law in Canada, Fifth Edition

Library and Archives Canada Cataloguing in Publication

Blake, Sara, 1956
Administrative law in Canada/Sara Blake. — 5th ed.

Includes index.
ISBN 978-0-433-45840-1

1. Administrative law — Canada. I. Title.

KE5015.B53 2006   342.71'06   C2006-900980-5

Published by LexisNexis Canada, a member of the LexisNexis Group
LexisNexis Canada Inc.
123 Commerce Valley Dr. E., Suite 700
Markham, Ontario
L3T 7W8

Customer Service
Telephone: (905) 479-2665 • Fax: (905) 479-2826
Toll-Free Phone: 1-800-668-6481 • Toll-Free Fax: 1-800-461-3275
Email: customerservice@lexisnexis.ca
Web Site: www.lexisnexis.ca

Printed and bound in Canada.

ABOUT THE AUTHOR

Since 1997, Sara Blake has been practising general civil litigation. She is a civil litigation lawyer with the Ontario Ministry of the Attorney General, Crown Law Office — Civil Law, where she acts for government ministries and agencies in appeals, civil actions, applications for judicial review and tribunal hearings. She has argued cases before all levels of court including the Supreme Court of Canada, the Ontario Court of Appeal and the Federal Court of Appeal. Previously, she was Senior Litigation Counsel of the Ontario Securities Commission where she conducted numerous investigations and proceedings before the Commission and the Courts.

Blake is a recipient of the 2009 SOAR Medal, awarded by the Society of Ontario Adjudicators and Regulators to recognize an outstanding contribution to the administrative justice system in Ontario. She is a Past Chair of the Administrative Law Section of the Ontario Bar Association. She served as a member of the SOAR Model Rules Committee who drafted model procedural rules for all Ontario tribunals. She attended Osgoode Hall Law School and was called to the bar in Ontario in 1985.

Sara Blake is frequently invited to speak on the subject of Administrative Law.

PREFACE

The aim of this book is to unravel the mysteries and complexities of Administrative Law so that they may be understood by all. The cloud of legalese, which has made the subject difficult to understand, is dispersed and the sunlight of plain English shows it not to be quite so complex a subject as it has been made out to be. The rules of the game are explained in a straightforward manner but without oversimplification. The subject is discussed plainly yet comprehensively with all the essential details. Extensive footnotes provide references for those who wish to explore any subject in greater depth.

Participants in proceedings before any tribunal will find answers to their questions on what procedure the tribunal is supposed to follow, on the extent of the powers of the tribunal and on questions about the exercise of discretion and on bias. Where do I find the rules of the game? What kind of notice or disclosure should be given to the parties? What types of evidence can the tribunal consider in making its decision? How does the tribunal make its decision? Does the tribunal really have the power to do that? I think the tribunal may be biased against me! These issues, and others, are fully explored.

The methods for challenging the decision are explained for parties who are dissatisfied with the decision of a tribunal or the manner in which the tribunal proceeded. The tests and factors that are considered by a court when deciding whether to interfere with a tribunal proceeding or decision are fully set out.

This book will be useful to tribunal members, parties to tribunal proceedings, lawyers, judges and law students. It is written to assist both non-lawyers and lawyers in understanding the process.

For readers who use this book as the starting point for research, the research is up to date as of the end of December 2010. For those who do not have access to QuickLaw, many of the cases can be found on the free website of the Canadian Legal Information Institute: www.canlii.org.

Sara Blake
Toronto
August 2011

TABLE OF CONTENTS

TABLE OF CASES

E

I

J

L

N

Q

R

S

T

W

TABLE OF STATUTES

A

J

L

O

P

R

S

PART I

PROCEEDINGS BEFORE THE TRIBUNAL

Chapter 1

INTRODUCTION

Legislatures enact laws to deal with a wide variety of societal concerns. A legislature cannot do everything itself. It cannot anticipate every situation or nuance. Often statutes are worded in general terms, delegating authority to tribunals and public officials to fill in the details and to deal with individual situations.

> Administrative boards play an increasingly important role in our society. They regulate many aspects of our life, from beginning to end. Hospital and medical boards regulate the methods and practice of the doctors that bring us into this world. Boards regulate the licensing and the operation of morticians who are concerned with our mortal remains. Marketing boards regulate the farm products we eat; transport boards regulate the means and flow of our travel; energy boards control the price and distribution of the forms of energy we use; planning boards and city councils regulate the location and types of buildings in which we live and work. In Canada, boards are a way of life. Boards and the functions they fulfil are legion.[1]

Every tribunal that exercises statutory powers acts as an arm of government with a mandate to implement the policy of the government as it is expressed in the statute. Unlike courts, they are not independent of government but, instead, are a part of government.[2]

One reason for delegating powers of decision to a tribunal is to provide an expeditious and inexpensive method of settling disputes with less formality than found in court proceedings. A tribunal may inexpensively process a high volume of cases or process and decide applications for statutory benefits or licences. Others may have a mandate to protect the public from harm by regulating those who carry on a particular type of trade, business or profession. The discipline of wayward professionals may be better done by their peers who can evaluate professional conduct against the accepted standards of the profession. Powers may be conferred on experts to decide complex or technical issues. A sector of society may be governed by persons with accumulated years of experience and a specialized understanding of the activities they supervise.[3] Power may be

---

[1] *Newfoundland Telephone Co. v. Newfoundland (Board of Commissioners of Public Utilities)*, [1992] S.C.J. No. 21 at para. 17.

[2] *Ocean Port Hotel Ltd. v. British Columbia (General Manager, Liquor Control and Licensing Branch)*, [2001] S.C.J. No. 17 at para. 24.

[3] *National Corn Growers Assn. v. Canada (Import Tribunal)*, [1990] S.C.J. No. 110 at para. 9.

conferred on elected officials in the expectation that they will act in accordance with prevailing political, economic and social views.[4]

Administrative law is the law that governs how these decisions are made in individual cases. It is more concerned with how a decision is reached than with the result.[5] For those dissatisfied with a decision, it sets out the complaint procedure and the remedies.

This book is, therefore, divided into two parts. The first part (chapters 2 to 5) describes the rules by which tribunals are expected to operate. (The generic term "tribunal" is used to include all public officials, boards and agencies who exercise statutory authority.)

Chapter 2 describes the procedure that tribunals may be expected to follow when exercising decision-making authority. Typically the procedure is prescribed by statutes and rules that are specific to each tribunal. Where there is a gap in these statutory rules, the basic rule to follow is that of fairness. Any procedure adopted by a tribunal must be fair to the parties affected by its decisions.

Tribunals are usually accorded some degree of discretion in the exercise of their powers. How this discretion may and may not be exercised is discussed in chapter 3. Also discussed in that chapter is the related topic of bias. Decision makers are expected to be impartial. The chapter explains what is regarded as unacceptable bias.

No tribunal has unlimited powers. Tribunal powers are granted by statute and defined and limited by statute. A tribunal may make a decision or rule only if authorized by statute to do so.[6] Chapter 4 discusses the scope of tribunals' decision-making powers while chapter 5 discusses their rule-making powers.

What if a tribunal has failed to comply with the rules described in the first part of this book? The second part (chapters 6 to 9) explains the types of redress that are available and how they may be obtained. Chapter 6 describes rights of appeal while chapter 7 explains how to apply to a court for judicial review of a tribunal decision. Generally, parties should take advantage of rights of appeal that are available and should not turn to the courts for judicial review unless rights of appeal have been exhausted or are not available. Chapter 8 describes the extent to which a court may scrutinize the activities of tribunals while chapter 9 describes the judicial remedies that may be awarded and judicial discretion to refuse a remedy.

---

[4]   *Canada (Attorney General) v. Inuit Tapirisat of Canada*, [1980] S.C.J. No. 99; *Chamberlain v. Surrey School District No. 36*, [2002] S.C.J. No. 87 at paras. 10, 12, 191, 193, 201.

[5]   *Sobeys Inc. v. Charlottetown (City)*, [1996] P.E.I.J. No. 11 at para. 37 (P.E.I.S.C.).

[6]   *ATCO Gas and Pipelines Ltd. v. Alberta (Energy and Utilities Board)*, [2006] S.C.J. No. 4 at para. 2.

Chapter 2

TRIBUNAL PROCEDURE

A. INTRODUCTION

The focus of this chapter is on how tribunals and public officials go about exercising the powers of decision that have been granted to them by statute. How must they deal with the persons who will be affected by their decisions? How do they notify those persons of the tribunal's intention to decide a matter? What rights do those persons have to influence the decision and what steps must they take to persuade the tribunal to decide in their favour? What type of audience must the decision maker offer? How should the tribunal manage the interactions among persons who advocate different positions?

The procedures that are followed in making a decision vary considerably from one type of decision to another. The procedure must be flexible but with the goal of accomplishing the statutory mandate while dealing fairly with the parties concerned. Tribunals should adopt procedures that enable them to consider each case on its merits. They should avoid becoming bogged down with procedural formalities and technicalities as these may cause unnecessary delay and expense and may defeat the statutory purpose.[1] This is especially true of lay tribunals whose members are drawn from the community with an expectation that they will apply their judgment acquired through knowledge and experience.[2] Some procedural formality may be necessary to ensure that the public feel that they have been fairly treated. Fairness is the essential purpose of all procedural rules. Common sense should prevail over legal formalism.[3]

B. WHERE ARE THE RULES?

While most tribunals are required, by common law or statute, to follow some basic rules of procedure, there is no set code that applies to all. Procedure may vary greatly from one tribunal to another. To find out what rules a particular tribunal must abide by, one must first look to the tribunal's

---

[1] *Toronto (City) v. Canadian Union of Public Employees, Local 79*, [1982] O.J. No. 222 (Ont. C.A.).

[2] *Preston Crossing Properties Inc. v. Saskatoon (City)*, [2006] S.J. No. 335 at para. 46 (Sask. C.A.).

[3] *Saleh v. Canada (Minister of Employment and Immigration)*, [1989] F.C.J. No. 1015 at para. 23 (F.C.T.D.).

enabling statute, which might prescribe these rules. But many statutes set out the tribunal's powers only. Even statutes that prescribe procedure often leave gaps. Enabling statutes rarely provide comprehensive codes of procedure.

Typically it is necessary to look further. Regulations enacted pursuant to the enabling statute, and rules and guidelines promulgated by the tribunal may describe the procedure. Often a telephone call to the tribunal registrar will elicit a wealth of information concerning the tribunal's procedures. However, a tribunal is not obliged to provide advice on procedure.[4] Parties are expected to read the prescribed requirements.

C. GENERAL PROCEDURAL CODES

British Columbia, Alberta, Ontario and Quebec have enacted general procedural statutes that apply to some, not all, tribunals. The B.C. Act focuses on empowering the tribunal to enact its own rules of procedure in contrast to the statutes of the other provinces which prescribe minimum rules of procedure, though the Ontario Act is moving towards empowering the tribunal but still contains many mandatory requirements.

1.   British Columbia

Many B.C. statutes, which grant authority to tribunals to adjudicate and make decisions that directly affect individual rights, state that all or part of the *Administrative Tribunals Act* ("*ATA*")[5] applies to certain of the proceedings before the tribunal. The starting point is the tribunal's enabling statute to determine what sections, if any, of the *ATA* apply to the tribunal.[6] The *ATA* applies primarily to the hearing of applications, appeals and complaints, and contains only a few procedural requirements such as the right of a party to be represented and to summons and examine witnesses at the hearing and the duty of the tribunal to give reasons for its decision. The Act grants to these tribunals a wide range of powers to control their proceedings. Most procedures are prescribed by rules enacted by the tribunal pursuant to s. 11 and practice directives issued pursuant to ss. 12 and 13. The Lieutenant Governor in Council may make regulations prescribing procedure for a tribunal and repealing or amending any rule made by a tribunal.[7]

---

[4]   *Sundaram v. Canada (Minister of Citizenship and Immigration)*, [2006] F.C.J. No. 366 (F.C.); *Engineering Students Society, University of Saskatchewan v. Saskatchewan (Human Rights Commission)*, [1983] S.J. No. 274 at para. 17 (Sask. Q.B.).

[5]   S.B.C. 2004, c. 45.

[6]   *Administrative Tribunals Act*, S.B.C. 2004, c. 45, s. 1 "tribunal".

[7]   *Administrative Tribunals Act*, S.B.C. 2004, c. 45, s. 60.

2.   Alberta

Some Alberta tribunals that exercise statutory powers must comply with the procedures prescribed by the *Administrative Procedures and Jurisdiction Act ("APJA")*.[8] The Act defines "statutory power" to mean a power conferred by statute other than a power conferred on a court or a power to make regulations,[9] including power to make a decision affecting a person's rights, licence or status. By regulation the Act is deemed to apply to specified tribunals.[10] The Act prescribes minimum requirements for notice to parties, disclosure of the case to be met, the right to make representations, and the tribunal's duty to furnish written reasons. These procedural rules are in addition to any rules prescribed by the tribunal's enabling statute.[11] The *Alberta Bill of Rights*[12] also prescribes a right to "due process of law" when a decision is made that affects an individual's right to liberty, security of the person and enjoyment of property.[13]

3.   Ontario

Every Ontario tribunal that exercises a statutory power of decision and is required by its enabling statute or "otherwise by law" to hold a hearing must follow the procedures prescribed by the *Statutory Powers Procedure Act ("SPPA")*.[14] "Statutory power of decision" is defined to mean a power conferred by statute to make a decision affecting a person's rights, privileges, liabilities, or benefits.[15] The phrase "otherwise by law" recognizes that the common law may require an oral hearing in some situations. Many Ontario statutes expressly state whether the Act applies to the exercise of a specific statutory power of decision. A tribunal that is exempted from the *SPPA* by its enabling statute or by s. 3(2) of the *SPPA*, must still comply with the common law requirement of procedural fairness.[16] The Act prescribes minimum procedural rules concerning a party's right to notice, to be represented, to cross-examine witnesses and to request reasons for

---

[8]   R.S.A. 2000, c. A-3; as am. S.A. 2005, c. 4.

[9]   *Administrative Procedures and Jurisdiction Act*, R.S.A. 2000, c. A-3; as am. S.A. 2005, c. 4, s. 1(*c*).

[10]   *Authorities Designation Regulation*, Alta. Reg. 64/2003.

[11]   *Administrative Procedures and Jurisdiction Act*, R.S.A. 2000, c. A-3; as am. S.A. 2005, c. 4, s. 8.

[12]   R.S.A. 2000, c. A-14.

[13]   *Lavallee v. Alberta (Securities Commission)*, [2009] A.J. No. 21 at paras. 166-207 (Alta. Q.B.), affd [2010] A.J. No. 144 (Alta. C.A.), leave to appeal to S.C.C. refused.

[14]   R.S.O. 1990, c. S.22, s. 3(1) [as. am.], (the *"SPPA"*).

[15]   *SPPA*, s. 1(1) [as am.]. See also s. 1 of the *Judicial Review Procedure Act*, R.S.O. 1990, c. J.1, which contains the same definition.

[16]   *Downing v. Graydon*, [1978] O.J. No. 3539 at para. 9 (Ont. C.A.).

decision. Additional procedures may be prescribed by rules enacted by the tribunal.

Ontario has also enacted the *Adjudicative Tribunals Accountability, Governance and Appointments Act*,[17] most of which is not yet proclaimed in force. It concerns appointments and a code of conduct for adjudicative tribunal members.

4.   Quebec

The Quebec *Administrative Justice Act*[18] establishes general rules of procedure applicable to all decisions affecting individuals. A hearing is required for all adjudicative decisions. Where there is no duty to hold a hearing, it incorporates the common law duty of fairness. The Act establishes the Administrative Tribunal of Quebec to hear appeals from these administrative decisions. It also establishes the Administrative Justice Council, which deals with complaints and questions of ethics.

The Quebec *Charte des droits et libertés de la personne*[19] provides that every person whose rights and duties may be affected has a right to an impartial hearing by an independent tribunal and a right to be represented by counsel at such a hearing.

5.   Public Inquiries Procedures

Every jurisdiction has a Public Inquiries Act that prescribes procedure to be followed by special inquiries and commissions. In Newfoundland, all tribunals are vested with the powers and procedure prescribed by the *Public Inquiries Act*.[20] The Administrative Tribunal of Quebec also has the powers of public inquiry commissions.[21] In other jurisdictions, some tribunals are granted Public Inquiries Act powers and procedures.

6.   *Charter of Rights and Freedoms* and *Bill of Rights*

The *Canadian Charter of Rights and Freedoms*[22] applies to proceedings of statutory tribunals but many of its provisions do not apply because their

---

[17]   *Adjudicative Tribunals Accountability, Governance and Appointments Act, 2009*, S.O. 2009, c. 33, Sch. 5; O. Reg. 126/10 designates "adjudicative tribunals".

[18]   R.S.Q. c. J-3.

[19]   *Charter of human rights and freedoms*, R.S.Q. c. C-12, arts. 23 [as am.] and 34.

[20]   See the *Interpretation Act*, R.S.N.L. 1990, c. I-19, s. 24.

[21]   *Administrative Justice Act*, R.S.Q. c. J-3, s. 74.

[22]   Hereinafter "*Charter*".

application is restricted to criminal prosecutions. Few tribunals have authority to make decisions affecting liberty or security of the person.[23] Neither livelihood nor economic, commercial, or property rights are included in the "right to life, liberty and security of the person" protected by s. 7 of the *Charter*.[24] The procedural rules set out in s. 11 of the *Charter* regarding "Proceedings in Criminal and Penal Matters" do not apply to tribunal proceedings.[25] Likewise, s. 13 of the *Charter*, which prohibits the use of a witness' prior testimony to incriminate the witness in subsequent proceedings, does not prevent the use of prior testimony in administrative proceedings. This is because it is not a purpose of administrative proceedings to incriminate a person, that is, to prove guilt in a criminal proceeding.[26]

The *Canadian Bill of Rights*[27] applies only to federal tribunals. It grants a right to a fair hearing in accordance with the principles of fundamental justice. This right applies to decisions that affect property rights, which are not protected by the *Charter*.[28]

D.   COMPLIANCE WITH PRESCRIBED RULES

The procedure followed by a tribunal may be found in a statute or regulation, or in rules, guidelines, or directives issued by the tribunal. It may be set out in a notice issued for a particular proceeding. It may be a matter of unwritten tribunal policy and practice. Some procedural rules must be followed strictly while others are flexible depending on the circumstances. The courts distinguish between rules that are mandatory, which must be followed, and those which are directory and may be waived where to do so does not cause prejudice to a party.[29] Which

---

[23]   Examples of those that do have this authority: *R. v. Conway*, [2010] S.C.J. No. 22; *Wareham v. Ontario (Minister of Community and Social Services)*, [2008] O.J. No. 4598 (Ont. C.A.).

[24]   *Mussani v. College of Physicians and Surgeons of Ontario*, [2004] O.J. No. 5176 (Ont. C.A.); *Nisbett v. Manitoba (Human Rights Commission)*, [1993] M.J. No. 160 (Man. C.A.), leave to appeal refused [1993] S.C.C.A. No. 232; *R.V.P. Enterprises Ltd. v. British Columbia (Minister of Consumer and Corporate Affairs)*, [1988] B.C.J. No. 520 (B.C.C.A.), leave to appeal refused [1988] S.C.C.A. No. 263; *Malartic Hygrade Gold Mines (Canada) Ltd. v. Ontario (Securities Commission)*, [1986] O.J. No. 206 (Ont. Div. Ct.).

[25]   *R. v. Wigglesworth*, [1987] S.C.J. No. 71; *Law Society of Manitoba v. Savino*, [1983] M.J. No. 206 at para. 20 (Man. C.A.); *Re Petroleum Products Act*, [1986] P.E.I.J. No. 118 (P.E.I.S.C.); *Fang v. College of Physicians and Surgeons (Alberta)*, [1985] A.J. No. 1080 (Alta. C.A.).

[26]   *Knutson v. Saskatchewan Registered Nurses Association*, [1990] S.J. No. 603 (Sask. C.A.).

[27]   S.C. 1960, c. 44.

[28]   *Sam Lévy and Associés Inc. v. Mayrand*, [2005] F.C.J. No. 882 (F.C.), affd [2006] F.C.J. No. 867 (F.C.A.), leave to appeal refused [2006] C.S.C.R. no 317; *Air Canada v. Canada (Attorney General)*, [2003] J.Q. no 21, 222 D.L.R. (4th) 385 (Que. C.A.), leave to appeal refused [2003] C.S.C.R. no 111.

[29]   *Potter v. Halifax Regional School Board*, [2002] N.S.J. No. 297 at paras. 117-120, 139 (N.S.C.A.), leave to appeal refused [2002] S.C.C.A. No. 306.

procedural rules are mandatory? This is not an easy question to answer. Interpretation Acts state that "may" is to be construed as permissive while "shall" must be construed as imperative. However, the courts sometimes construe "shall" as being merely directory, not mandatory.[30]

How do you determine which rules are fixed and which are not? Generally, the word "shall" is mandatory but the interpretation of what must be done in a specific case should reflect common sense and relate to the statutory purpose.[31] If non-compliance with a procedural rule is likely to cause prejudice to a party's right to be heard, compliance with the rule may be mandatory, particularly if important interests of the party are at stake.[32] Prejudice must be proven with evidence. It will not be assumed simply from proof of non-compliance with the rule.[33] In addition, the public interest and statutory purposes should not be defeated by overly strict adherence to procedural rules.[34]

Sometimes the statute may simply state that the tribunal is to "hear and decide" or that it may act only "after investigation and inquiry" or "for cause". Such words have usually been held to require an oral hearing.[35] A statute may permit a decision to be made "after consultation". A consultation should involve interaction between the decision maker and parties, with the exchange of information, so that the decision maker is informed of the parties' positions.[36] The procedural details of a hearing or consultation are informed by the common law rules of procedural fairness.

A party must comply with any procedural obligation that the tribunal cannot waive.[37] Even when a tribunal does have the power to grant relief from a procedural rule, its power is discretionary.[38] A tribunal must exercise its

---

[30]   *Oates v. Newfoundland and Labrador (Royal Newfoundland Constabulary Public Complaints Commissioner)*, [2003] N.J. No. 190 (N.L.C.A.).

[31]   *Lavallee v. Alberta (Securities Commission)*, [2010] A.J. No. 144 (Alta. C.A.).

[32]   *1657575 Ontario Inc. (c.o.b. Pleasures Gentlemen's Club) v. Hamilton (City)*, [2008] O.J. No. 3016, 92 O.R. (3d) 374 (Ont. C.A.).

[33]   *Society Promoting Environmental Conservation v. Canada (Attorney General)*, [2003] F.C.J. No. 861 at para. 46 (F.C.A.).

[34]   *Potter v. Halifax Regional School Board*, [2002] N.S.J. No. 297 at paras. 117-120, 139 (N.S.C.A.), leave to appeal refused [2002] S.C.C.A. No. 306; *Society Promoting Environmental Conservation v. Canada (Attorney General)*, [2003] F.C.J. No. 861 (F.C.A.); *Oates v. Newfoundland and Labrador (Royal Newfoundland Constabulary Public Complaints Commissioner)*, [2003] N.J. No. 190 (N.L.C.A.).

[35]   *Harelkin v. University of Regina*, [1979] S.C.J. No. 59.

[36]   *Lakeland College Faculty Assn. v. Lakeland College*, [1998] A.J. No. 741 (Alta. C.A.).

[37]   *Upper Lakes Shipping Ltd. v. Sheehan*, [1979] S.C.J. No. 15; *Towers Department Stores Ltd. v. Nadeau* (1978), 97 D.L.R. (3d) 266 (Que. S.C.); *Ali v. Canada (Minister of Manpower and Immigration)*, [1977] F.C.J. No. 243 (F.C.A.); *DBC Marine Safety Systems Ltd. v. Canada (Commissioner of Patents)*, [2007] F.C.J. No. 1500 (F.C.).

[38]   *Al's Towing Service Ltd. v. Manitoba (Highway Transport Board)*, [1978] M.J. No. 96 (Man. C.A.); *Fréchette v. Canada (Minister of Labour)*, [1984] F.C.J. No. 533 (F.C.A.).

discretion reasonably and not decide against a party solely because it did not strictly follow every minor procedural rule, without considering the merits.[39] A tribunal should not arbitrarily require strict compliance from some parties but not others.[40] A tribunal should not enforce compliance with an unpublished procedural rule without first advising the parties of it.[41]

E. COMMON LAW PROCEDURAL RULES: THE DUTY TO BE FAIR

In the absence of prescribed procedural rules, the courts require that a decision made pursuant to statutory authority, which affects the rights of an individual person, be made following fair procedures.[42] This requirement is called the "doctrine of fairness" or the "duty to act fairly".[43]

At a minimum, the duty to act fairly requires that, before a decision adverse to a person's interests is made, the person should be told the case to be met and be given an opportunity to respond.[44] The purpose is twofold. First, it gives the person to be affected an opportunity to influence the decision. Second, the information received from that person should assist the decision maker to make a rational and informed decision.[45] A person is more willing to accept an adverse decision if the process has been fair.

The right to be heard is not a right to the most advantageous procedure[46] nor a right to have one's views accepted[47] nor a right to be granted the remedy sought.[48] It is only a right to have one's views heard and considered by the decision maker.

---

[39] *Communications Union Canada v. Bell Canada*, [1976] O.J. No. 2254 (Ont. Div. Ct.); *Fisher v. Hotels, Clubs, Restaurants, Tavern Employees Union, Local 261*, [1980] O.J. No. 3590 (Ont. Div. Ct.); *R. v. Zeidler Forest Industries Ltd.*, [1978] A.J. No. 545 at paras. 11-12 (Alta. T.D.).

[40] *Apotex Inc. v. Ontario (Attorney General)*, [1984] O.J. No. 3272 (Ont. H.C.J.).

[41] *Butler Metal Products Co. v. Canada (Employment and Immigration Commission)*, [1982] F.C.J. No. 181 (F.C.A.).

[42] *Martineau v. Matsqui Institution Disciplinary Board (No. 2)*, [1979] S.C.J. No. 121.

[43] It has been variously expressed as "the right to be heard", "the rules of natural justice", "the duty to act judicially" and "*audi alterem partem*" (the duty to hear both sides).

[44] *Nicholson v. Haldimand-Norfolk (Regional) Police Commissioners*, [1978] S.C.J. No. 88.

[45] *Gallant v. Canada (Deputy Commissioner Correctional Service)*, [1989] F.C.J. No. 70 (F.C.A.), leave to appeal refused [1989] S.C.C.A. No. 215; *Haghighi v. Canada (Minister of Citizenship and Immigration)*, [2000] F.C.J. No. 854 (F.C.A.).

[46] *Ironside v. Alberta (Securities Commission)*, [2009] A.J. No. 376 at para. 107 (Alta. C.A.).

[47] *Papin-Shein c. Cytrynbaum*, [2008] J.Q. no 12176 (Que. C.A.); *Nova Scotia (Attorney General) v. Ultramar Canada Inc.*, [1995] F.C.J. No. 1160 at para. 52 (F.C.T.D.).

[48] *Enterlake Air Services Ltd. v. Bissett Air Services Ltd.*, [1991] M.J. No. 382 (Man. Q.B.).

A variety of procedural options are available to meet the duty to be fair. What is "fair" in a given case depends on the circumstances.[49] An oral hearing is not always necessary. The flexible nature of the duty of fairness recognizes that meaningful participation can occur in different ways in different situations.[50] Sometimes, all that is required is that the person be advised verbally of the gist of the proposed decision and the reasons for it and be permitted to respond verbally.[51] In some cases written notice and an opportunity to make written submissions will suffice. The extent of written submissions may vary from the completion of a standard-form question-naire,[52] the delivery of a single letter stating one's position through the exchange of correspondence in which the issues are fully discussed[53] to a formal application supported by documentary evidence and the reports of experts. Sometimes a person cannot adequately answer the case without an oral hearing. The nature of the oral hearing required may vary from an informal interview with an agent of the decision maker to a round table discussion with the tribunal[54] or a formal proceeding similar to a civil trial or an inquisitorial process. A party may be entitled to see documents relied on by the decision maker and to cross-examine witnesses. In certain circum-stances, a decision maker may be permitted to refer the fact-finding process to a committee or to an agent for investigation and report. The main consideration, in choosing the appropriate procedure, is whether the procedure is fair to the parties.

The same procedure is not expected of all tribunals. There is great variety in the types of tribunals and in the types of decisions made by them. The concept of procedural fairness is not a fixed concept. It varies with the context and the interests at stake.[55] "At the heart of this analysis is whether, considering all the circumstances, those whose interests were affected had a meaningful opportunity to present their case fully and

---

[49] *Canada (Attorney General) v. Mavi*, [2011] S.C.J. No. 30.

[50] *Baker v. Canada (Minister of Citizenship and Immigration)*, [1999] S.C.J. No. 39 at para. 32.

[51] *B. (K.) (Litigation guardian of) v. Toronto District School Board*, [2008] O.J. No. 475 (Ont. Div. Ct.).

[52] *Cannella v. Toronto Transit Commission*, [1999] O.J. No. 2282 (Ont. Div. Ct.), leave to appeal refused November 19, 1999 (Ont. C.A.), leave to appeal refused [2000] S.C.C.A. No. 31.

[53] *McLeod v. Alberta Securities Commission*, [2006] A.J. No. 939 at para. 39 (Alta. C.A.), leave to appeal refused [2006] S.C.C.A. No. 380.

[54] Round table discussion met duty of fairness: *Atlantic Collection Agency Ltd. v. Nova Scotia (Service Nova Scotia and Municipal Relations)*, [2006] N.S.J. No. 204 (N.S.S.C.); did not: *Kelly v. New Brunswick (Provincial Planning Appeal Board)*, [1984] N.B.J. No. 291 (N.B.Q.B.).

[55] *Chiarelli v. Canada (Minister of Employment and Immigration)*, [1992] S.C.J. No. 27 at paras. 45-46.

fairly." The Supreme Court of Canada has identified the following five factors to be considered in determining what is appropriate.[56]

1. The Nature of the Decision and the Process Followed in Making it

This factor appears to be two quite different factors. The first part refers to whether the decision is legislative or political in nature and affects the community as a whole or is an adjudicative decision that turns on questions of fact and law and affects the interests of a single individual. The other part concerns the statutorily prescribed process for making the decision. Sometimes the prescribed process is an indication of the nature of the decision. That is, the closer the prescribed procedure is to the trial model, the greater the duty of fairness.

As a discretionary decision based on the consideration of policy is quite different from an adjudicative decision based on the facts of the case, a court-type procedure will not be required.[57] Many statutes confer political decision-making powers on Cabinet, Ministers and other public officials to enable them to respond to the political, economic, and social concerns of the moment. These types of decisions do not attract a duty of fairness and are subject only to statutorily prescribed procedural re-quirements.[58] These decision makers may consult anyone and are not obliged to make disclosure of the "case to be met".[59] Even where the decision affects the interests of only one person, the duty of fairness may be met by giving notice and permitting the person to make written submissions to a lower official who must ensure that the person's position is put before the Minister or Cabinet. There is no right to an oral hearing.[60]

---

[56] *Baker v. Canada (Minister of Citizenship and Immigration)*, [1999] S.C.J. No. 39 at paras. 21-28.

[57] *Baker v. Canada (Minister of Citizenship and Immigration)*, [1999] S.C.J. No. 39 at para. 23; *Imperial Oil Ltd. v. Quebec (Minister of the Environment)*, [2003] S.C.J. No. 59.

[58] *Canada (Attorney General) v. Inuit Tapirisat of Canada*, [1980] S.C.J. No. 99; *Idziak v. Canada (Minister of Justice)*, [1992] S.C.J. No. 97; *Canadian Assn. of Regulated Importers v. Canada (Attorney General)*, [1994] F.C.J. No. 1 (F.C.A.), leave to appeal refused [1994] S.C.C.A. No. 99; *Imperial Oil v. Quebec (Minister of the Environment)*, [2003] S.C.J. No. 59; *Dairy Farmers of Ontario v. Denby*, [2009] O.J. No. 4474 (Ont. Div. Ct.); *Newfoundland and Labrador (Consumer Advocate) v. Newfoundland and Labrador (Public Utilities Board)*, [2005] N.J. No. 83 (N.L.T.D.).

[59] *Pembroke Civic Hospital v. Ontario (Health Services Restructuring Commission)*, [1997] O.J. No. 3142 (Ont. Div. Ct.), leave to appeal refused September 10, 1997 (Ont. C.A.); *Newfound-land and Labrador (Consumer Advocate) v. Newfoundland and Labrador (Public Utilities Board)*, [2005] N.J. No. 83 (N.L.T.D.).

[60] *Chiarelli v. Canada (Minister of Employment and Immigration)*, [1992] S.C.J. No. 27; *Whitley v. United States of America*, [1994] O.J. No. 2478 (Ont. C.A.), affd [1996] S.C.J. No.

Some decisions of other elected bodies such as municipal councils and school boards may be legislative and free of the duty to act fairly.[61] A by-law is legislative if it is of general application and based on policy. However, if the elected council's decision will adversely affect the interests of one individual more than others, there may be a duty to act fairly, even though the decision is based primarily on public interest concerns.[62] Often school board or municipal decision making commences with the identification of a problem followed by an assessment of policy approaches to solving the problem. Once the policy issues are settled, the application of the policy decisions may impact certain individuals more directly. As the decision-making process moves along the continuum from the legislative to the particular, procedural rights may arise for those directly affected.[63] In this context, the duty to act fairly does not require trial-type procedures but rather the gathering of information and recommendations from a variety of sources and the consultation of persons who may be interested.[64] Where public hearings or consultation are mandated, meaningful public participation may require that any reports that are to be tabled be made available in advance.[65]

As the nature of the decision becomes less political and more concerned about individual rights and duties, the more likely that more procedural requirements may be imposed. See the third factor below.

Where a decision-making power is conferred on a government official, the procedural requirements should be consistent with the bureaucratic model of decision making which is characterized by expertise, teamwork and the division of labour.[66]

25; *Al Yamani v. Canada (Solicitor General)*, [1995] F.C.J. No. 1453 (F.C.T.D.); *Sovereign Life Insurance Co. v. Canada (Minister of Finance)*, [1997] F.C.J. No. 1022 (F.C.T.D.).

[61]   *Friends of the Regina Public Library Inc. v. Regina (Public Library Board)*, [2004] S.J. No. 250 (Sask. C.A.); *Potter v. Halifax Regional School Board*, [2002] N.S.J. No. 297 (N.S.C.A.), leave to appeal refused [2002] S.C.C.A. No. 306; *Maple Ridge (District) v. Thornhill Aggregates Ltd.*, [1998] B.C.J. No. 1485 at paras. 29-30 (B.C.C.A.), leave to appeal refused [1998] S.C.C.A. No. 407; *Vanderkloet v. Leeds and Grenville County Board of Education*, [1985] O.J. No. 2605 (Ont. C.A.), leave to appeal refused [1986] 1 S.C.R. xv.

[62]   *Congrégation des témoins de Jéhovah de St-Jérôme-Lafontaine v. Lafontaine (Village)*, [2004] S.C.J. No. 45; *Homex Realty and Development Co. v. Wyoming (Village)*, [1980] S.C.J. No. 109.

[63]   *Canadian Pacific Railway Co. v. Vancouver (City)*, [2006] S.C.J. No. 5; *Elliott v. Burin Peninsula School Board District No. 7*, [1998] N.J. No. 128 (N.L.C.A.); *Potter v. Halifax Regional School Board*, [2002] N.S.J. No. 297 (N.S.C.A.), leave to appeal refused [2002] S.C.C.A. No. 306.

[64]   *Gardner v. Williams Lake (City)*, [2006] B.C.J. No. 1389 (B.C.C.A.); *Potter v. Halifax Regional School Board*, [2002] N.S.J. No. 297, 215 D.L.R. (4th) 441 (N.S.C.A.), leave to appeal refused [2002] S.C.C.A. No. 306.

[65]   *Canadian Pacific Railway Co. v. Vancouver (City)*, [2006] S.C.J. No. 5 at paras. 55-57.

[66]   *Haghighi v. Canada (Minister of Citizenship and Immigration)*, [2000] F.C.J. No. 854 at para. 28 (F.C.A.).

The procedural requirements are usually higher with respect to a final decision than with respect to an interim decision. There may be no procedural constraints on an interim decision, especially if there is a right to a hearing before a final decision.[67] For example, where protection of the public requires an interim suspension of a licence, a requirement to hold a prior hearing, or even to notify the licensee in advance, may frustrate the need for prompt action.[68] If an interim decision has serious consequences for the party affected, a hearing should be convened as soon as possible.[69]

In an emergency there may be no duty to be fair. A prison warden may act immediately to avert a disturbance among the inmates.[70] Environment officials may move swiftly to clean up a gas leak without first finding out who is responsible.[71] A dangerous driver's licence may be suspended summarily to protect the public.[72] In volatile labour disputes, a labour relations board may move quickly.[73] Usually there is a statutory right to a hearing soon after an emergency order has been made.

Where the authority granted is to investigate and report but not decide, there may be a limited duty to act fairly. The extent of the duty turns on the role of the investigation in the decision-making process and on the degree that the rights of a person may be finally decided.[74] An investigation that cannot result in a decision, other than a decision to commence proceedings in court or before a tribunal, attracts the fewest procedural requirements because the subsequent proceeding will provide the opportunity to be heard.[75] In these investigations, fairness may require no more

---

[67] *Canada (Minister of National Revenue) v. Coopers and Lybrand Ltd.*, [1978] S.C.J. No. 97; *Pintendre Autos Inc. c. Québec (Procureur général)*, [1998] J.Q. no 2184 (Que. C.A.).

[68] *Farbeh v. College of Pharmacists of British Columbia*, [2009] B.C.J. No. 1640 (B.C.S.C.); *Re Petroleum Products Act*, [1986] P.E.I.J. No. 118 (P.E.I.C.A.).

[69] *Menon v. College of Physicians and Surgeons (New Brunswick)*, [2007] N.B.J. No. 270 (N.B.Q.B.).

[70] *Cardinal v. Kent Institution*, [1985] S.C.J. No. 78; *Morin v. Saskatchewan (Director of Corrections)*, [1982] S.J. No. 547 (Sask. C.A.); *Bruce v. Canada (Commissioner of Corrections)*, [1979] F.C.J. No. 185 (F.C.T.D.).

[71] *Mac's Convenience Stores Inc. v. Ontario (Minister of Environment)*, [1984] O.J. No. 3338 (Ont. Div. Ct.).

[72] *Hundal v. British Columbia (Superintendent of Motor Vehicles)*, [1985] B.C.J. No. 3046 (B.C.C.A.).

[73] *Tomko v. Nova Scotia (Labour Relations Board)*, [1975] S.C.J. No. 111; *Amalgamated Transit Union, Local 113 v. Ontario (Labour Relations Board)*, [2007] O.J. No. 3907 (Ont. Div. Ct.); *International Brotherhood of Electrical Workers, Local 1739 v. International Brotherhood of Electrical Workers*, [2007] O.J. No. 2460 (Ont. Div. Ct.).

[74] *Irvine v. Canada (Restrictive Trade Practices Commission)*, [1987] S.C.J. No. 7 at para. 80; *Seaway Trust Co. v. Ontario (No. 2)*, [1983] O.J. No. 257 (Ont. H.C.J.); *Haber v. Wellesley Hospital (Medical Advisory Committee)*, [1986] O.J. No. 857 (Ont. Div. Ct.), affd [1988] O.J. No. 3023 (Ont. C.A.), leave to appeal refused April 26, 1988.

[75] *Egerton v. Appraisal Institute of Canada*, [2009] O.J. No. 1880 (Ont. C.A.); *Partington v. Complaints Inquiry Committee*, [2005] A.J. No. 787 (Alta. C.A.); *Economic Development Edmonton v. Wong*, [2005] A.J. No. 1051 (Alta. C.A.); *Comité de déontologie policière c.*

than that a person to be questioned be permitted to be accompanied by counsel and be told the subjects on which questions will be asked.[76] A suspect is not entitled to be present when other witnesses are questioned.[77] However, where an adverse decision may result from the investigator's recommendation with no opportunity to make representations to the ultimate decision maker, a higher level of disclosure by the investigator and an opportunity to make submissions to the investigator may be required[78] and the investigator's report should fairly and accurately set out the facts and the representations of the parties to facilitate an informed decision.[79] If the decision maker chooses not to act in accordance with the investigator's recommendation, the parties affected should be advised of the reasons and given an opportunity to respond.[80] In Ontario, an investigator, whose recommendation does not bind the decision maker, need not comply with the *SPPA*.[81]

There is no right to be heard before a decision is made to hold a hearing. A proposed respondent need not be given an opportunity to respond to allegations prior to the issuance of a notice of hearing.[82]

A tribunal that decides a dispute between two parties is expected to accord both parties equivalent procedural rights. It must "hear both sides" before deciding. However, a tribunal whose primary duty is to mediate rather than decide a dispute, though it is expected to act fairly between the parties, may be permitted more procedural leeway.[83]

Dechenault, [2005] J.Q. no 9801 (Que. C.A.), leave to appeal refused [2005] C.S.C.R. no 438; *Doyle v. Canada (Restrictive Trade Practices Commission)*, [1983] F.C.J. No. 81, [1983] 2 F.C. 867 (F.C.A.).

[76] *Ontario (Securities Commission) v. Biscotti*, [1988] O.J. No. 1115 (Ont. H.C.J.).

[77] *Irvine v. Canada (Restrictive Trade Practices Commission)*, [1987] S.C.J. No. 7 at para. 96.

[78] *Fraternité Inter-Provinciale des Ouvriers en Électricité v. Quebec (Office de la Construction)*, [1983] J.Q. no 394, 148 D.L.R. (3d) 626 at 640 (Que. C.A.); *Abel v. Ontario (Advisory Review Board)*, [1980] O.J. No. 3878 (Ont. C.A.); *Canada (Attorney General) v. Canadian Tobacco Manufacturers' Council*, [1986] F.C.J. No. 155 (F.C.A.); *Saskatchewan Teachers' Federation v. Munro*, [1992] S.J. No. 675 (Sask. C.A.).

[79] *Braeside Farms Ltd. v. Ontario (Treasurer)*, [1978] O.J. No. 3458 at para. 33 (Ont. Div. Ct.).

[80] *Cardinal v. Kent Institution*, [1985] S.C.J. No. 78; *Al Yamani v. Canada (Solicitor General)*, [1995] F.C.J. No. 1453 at paras. 75-77 (F.C.T.D.).

[81] *Statutory Powers Procedure Act*, R.S.O. 1990, c. S.22, s. 3(2)(*g*); See *Emerson v. Law Society of Upper Canada*, [1983] O.J. No. 3287 (Ont. H.C.J.).

[82] *Puar v. Assn. of Professional Engineers and Geoscientists*, [2009] B.C.J. No. 2186 (B.C.C.A.); *Bailey v. Saskatchewan Registered Nurses' Assn.*, [1994] S.J. No. 462 (Sask. Q.B.), vard [1995] S.J. No. 755 (Sask. C.A.); *Kindler v. MacDonald*, [1987] F.C.J. No. 507 (F.C.A.); *Varity Corp. v. Ontario (Director of Employment Standards Branch)*, [1989] O.J. No. 1837 (Ont. Div. Ct.); No procedural rights before a decision to reconsider: *Barnes v. Ontario (Social Benefits Tribunal)*, [2009] O.J. No. 3096 (Ont. Div. Ct.).

[83] *Tomko v. Nova Scotia (Labour Relations Board)*, [1975] S.C.J. No. 111; *Turbo Resources Ltd. v. Rotchell*, [1985] S.J. No. 121 (Sask. Q.B.).

If a decision is based entirely on material and information supplied by the person subject to it, there may be no duty to notify that person and invite submissions before an adverse decision is made.[84] Typically, this situation involves an application for a benefit or licence and usually there is nothing to preclude re-application with more information. However, if the subsequent application shows no change in circumstances, it may be dismissed without the procedural formalities followed when a new application is received.[85] Before revoking the benefit, there may be a duty to state the grounds and provide an opportunity to respond.[86] If the statute grants an applicant an opportunity to be heard before an application for a benefit is refused, a similar opportunity must also be offered before the benefit is revoked.[87]

In cases involving animal health and food safety, the requirement of fairness may be met by conducting proper tests or inspections.[88] In some cases, the person affected may present submissions as to the adequacy of the testing procedures or the conclusions to be drawn from the test results.[89]

2.   The Nature of the Statutory Scheme

The common law right to procedural fairness cannot override procedure prescribed by statute. In the case of conflict, the statutory procedure governs. The common law duty to be fair may be applied only where the statute is silent as to the procedure to be followed.[90]

The duty of fairness is not a stand-alone proposition to be universally applied. It is informed by the institutional constraints on the tribunal (such as heavy case loads) and must be consonant with the statutory objectives and

---

[84]   *Scarborough Community Legal Services v. Canada (Minister of National Revenue)*, [1985] F.C.J. No. 166 (F.C.A.); *Windsor v. Nova Scotia (Teachers' Pension Commission)*, [1980] N.S.J. No. 614 (N.S.S.C.).

[85]   *Pugliese v. British Columbia (Registrar of Mortgage Brokers, Financial Services Tribunal)*, [2008] B.C.J. No. 503 (B.C.C.A.); *Bonavista (Town) v. Bonavista Local Board of Appeal*, [1995] N.J. No. 212 (Nfld. C.A.).

[86]   *Renaissance International v. Canada (Minister of National Revenue)*, [1982] F.C.J. No. 187 (F.C.A.); *Webb v. Ontario Housing Corp.*, [1978] O.J. No. 3378 (Ont. C.A.); *Mercer v. Newfoundland and Labrador Housing Corp.*, [1984] N.J. No. 189 (Nfld. T.D.).

[87]   *Desjardins v. Bouchard*, [1982] F.C.J. No. 238 (F.C.A.).

[88]   *Miel Labonté Inc. v. Canada (Attorney General)*, [2006] F.C.J. No. 247 (F.C.); *Bevan v. Ontario Society for the Prevention of Cruelty to Animals*, [2007] O.J. No. 645 (Ont. C.A.); *Barcrest Farms Inc. v. Canada (Minister of Agriculture)*, [1982] F.C.J. No. 79 (F.C.T.D.); *River Valley Poultry Farm Ltd. v. Canada (Attorney General)*, [2009] O.J. No. 1605 (Ont. C.A.), leave to appeal refused [2009] S.C.C.A. No. 259.

[89]   *Griffin v. Canada (Agriculture Canada, Inspections Division)*, [1989] F.C.J. No. 300 (F.C.T.D.); *Archer (c.o.b. Fairburn Farm) v. Canada (Canadian Food Inspection Agency)*, [2001] F.C.J. No. 46 (F.C.T.D.).

[90]   *Ocean Port Hotel Ltd. v. British Columbia (General Manager, Liquor Control and Licensing Branch)*, [2001] S.C.J. No. 17.

the role of the particular decision within the statutory scheme.[91] The procedural requirements may be elevated where the function of the decision maker, within the statutory context as a whole, is to adjudicate disputes. They may be reduced where the function is primarily one of managing competing interests in the regulatory field or developing regulatory policy, even though the decision affects one person more than others.[92] Where the essential purpose is to serve the public interest, even though the decision may be directed at an individual, the procedural requirements may be lower.[93]

Procedural constraints should not frustrate a tribunal's attempts to carry out its statutory mandate.[94] Before a new procedural requirement is imposed, its impact on cost, on delay in the decision-making process and any resulting diversion of resources should be considered when determining whether it is necessary or whether the duty of fairness can be met in a less expensive or time-consuming way.[95]

However, in the few administrative proceedings to which s. 7 of the *Charter* applies, expediency is not a reasonable limit on a *Charter*-protected right.[96] The principles of fundamental justice prescribed by s. 7 of the *Charter* are substantially the same as the common law duty of fairness, with one notable exception. While the common law rules may not be used to frustrate the objects of a statute, the principles of fundamental justice prevail over the statutory objects subject to the reasonable limits test in s. 1 of the *Charter*.[97] Similarly, the *Canadian Bill of Rights*

---

[91] *Fortis Properties Corp. v. United Steelworkers of America, Local 1-306*, [2007] N.B.J. No. 68 at paras. 5-6 (N.B.C.A.).

[92] *Imperial Oil Ltd. v. Quebec (Minister of the Environment)*, [2003] S.C.J. No. 59; *Society Promoting Environmental Conservation v. Canada (Attorney General)*, [2003] F.C.J. No. 861 (F.C.A.); *Canadian Restaurant and Foodservices Assn. v. Canadian (Dairy Commission)*, [2002] O.J. No. 3685 (Ont. Div. Ct.).

[93] *British Columbia (Securities Commission) v. Pacific International Securities Inc.*, [2002] B.C.J. No. 1480 (B.C.C.A.).

[94] *TELUS Communications Inc. v. Telecommunications Workers Union*, [2005] F.C.J. No. 1253 at para. 42 (F.C.A.); *Mensinger v. Canada (Minister of Employment and Immigration)*, [1987] 1 F.C. 59 (F.C.T.D.); *Khan v. Canada (Minister of Citizenship and Immigration)*, [2001] F.C.J. No. 1699 at para. 32 (F.C.A.).

[95] *Haghighi v. Canada (Minister of Citizenship and Immigration)*, [2000] F.C.J. No. 854 at para. 28 (F.C.A.); *Canada (Attorney General) v. Mavi*, [2011] S.C.J. No. 30 at para. 40.

[96] *Singh v. Canada (Minister of Employment and Immigration)*, [1985] S.C.J. No. 11 at paras. 70-73.

[97] *Singh v. Canada (Minister of Employment and Immigration)*, [1985] S.C.J. No. 11, at paras. 25, 33, 56; *Gallant v. Canada (Deputy Commissioner Correctional Service)*, [1989] F.C.J. No. 70 (F.C.A.), leave to appeal refused [1989] S.C.C.A. No. 215; *Pearlman v. Manitoba Law Society Judicial Committee*, [1991] S.C.J. No. 66; *R. v. Cadeddu*, [1982] O.J. No. 3593 (Ont. H.C.J.); *Hundal v. British Columbia (Superintendent of Motor Vehicles)*, [1985] B.C.J. No. 3046 (B.C.C.A.).

may be applied to declare inoperative a statutory procedural rule in a federal statute which is contrary to the duty of fairness.[98]

Where there is a right to a full oral hearing, the right is to one hearing. If the statute provides for several levels of appeal or review by different decision makers, the full oral hearing need only be granted once. The other decisions, either before or after the oral hearing, may be made on the written record, supplemented as appropriate in the circumstances.[99]

The B.C. *ATA* authorizes any combination of written, electronic and oral hearings.[100] The Ontario *SPPA* grants tribunals the option of holding an oral hearing, a written hearing (unless there is good reason for not holding the hearing in writing) or an electronic hearing (unless it would cause a party significant prejudice).[101] An electronic hearing may be held by teleconference or videoconference.

Some regulatory functions, such as inspections, have been privatized by statute or by contract. To the extent that a private entity exercises statutory powers so as to affect the rights of an individual, the duty of fairness applies. When the Crown is dissatisfied with the performance of regulatory functions by a contractor, the Crown cancels or refuses to renew the contract and takes the position that the dispute is governed by the law of contract. One exception has been carved out where a key term of the contract is that the regulatory functions be performed by an accredited person and the contract is cancelled because of dissatisfaction with the performance of that accredited person. The accredited person has a right to procedural fairness before the accreditation is cancelled.[102] In contrast, the dismissal of a government employee is governed by the law of contract.[103] The extent to which the Crown's exercise of a contractual right is governed by the duty of fairness turns on the extent to which the contractual obligations are governed by statute.[104]

---

[98] *Air Canada v. Canada (Attorney General)*, [2003] J.Q. no 21, 222 D.L.R. (4th) 385 (Que. C.A.), leave to appeal refused [2003] C.S.C.R. no 111. The court, without discussion, granted a corporation the benefit of a right which the *Canadian Bill of Rights* grants only to individuals.

[99] *St-Pie (Municipalité de) c. Commission de protection du territoire agricole du Quebec*, [2009] J.Q. no. 15512 (Que. C.A.), leave to appeal refused [2010] S.C.C.A. No. 54.

[100] *Administrative Tribunals Act*, S.B.C. 2004, c. 45, s. 36.

[101] *Statutory Powers Procedure Act*, R.S.O. 1990, c. S.22, s. 5.1 and s. 5.2 [as am.].

[102] *Société de l'assurance automobile du Quebec v. Cyr*, [2008] S.C.J. No. 13. As the Court found the duty of fairness in a statutory requirement, it is not clear whether it would be imposed in other jurisdictions.

[103] *Dunsmuir v. New Brunswick*, [2008] S.C.J. No. 9 at paras. 74, 81-84, 117, 119.

[104] *Canada (Attorney General) v. Mavi*, [2011] S.C.J. No. 30.

3.   The Importance of the Decision to the Person Affected

Where the statutory purpose is to decide the rights of an individual and the decision may have serious adverse consequences for that individual, procedural protections may be greater.

A decision to deprive an individual of liberty may be made only after an oral hearing,[105] even if the deprivation of liberty is indirect.[106] There are degrees of liberty. Segregation of an inmate from the general prison population is a further restriction on liberty, and the inmate is entitled to a hearing that may be informal but must be fair.[107] However, in prison emergencies, an inmate may be segregated from other inmates without prior notice or an oral hearing. Once the emergency has passed, the inmate should be advised of the reasons for segregation and be given an opportunity to make representations before a decision is made to continue the segregation.[108] In an emergency there may be no duty to act fairly before transferring an inmate from one prison to another.[109] A deprivation of a conditional liberty such as parole is accorded greater procedural rights than a discretionary refusal to grant parole. A parolee may be entitled to an oral hearing when parole is revoked, but an applicant for parole may not.[110]

A child should not be permanently removed from parental custody without giving the parents reasons and an opportunity to respond.[111]

Property interests are highly regarded. The prescribed statutory procedure for expropriation is comprehensive, leaving little room for the common law. A person whose property is being expropriated has greater rights than do objecting neighbours.[112] Notice and a hearing may be required before a decision is made restricting the subdivision and use of a parcel of land.[113]

---

[105] *R. v. Cadeddu*, [1982] O.J. No. 3593 (Ont. H.C.J.).

[106] *Singh v. Canada (Minister of Employment and Immigration)*, [1985] S.C.J. No. 11 at paras. 58-59.

[107] *Cardinal v. Kent Institution*, [1985] S.C.J. No. 78; *Martineau v. Matsqui Institution Disciplinary Board*, [1979] S.C.J. No. 121.

[108] *Cardinal v. Kent Institution*, [1985] S.C.J. No. 78; *Martineau v. Matsqui Institution Disciplinary Board*, [1979] S.C.J. No. 121.

[109] *Morin v. Saskatchewan (Director of Corrections)*, [1982] S.J. No. 547 (Sask. C.A.); *Gallant v. Canada (Deputy Commissioner Correctional Service)*, [1989] F.C.J. No. 70 (F.C.A.), leave to appeal refused [1989] S.C.C.A. No. 215.

[110] *MacDonald v. Canada (National Parole Board)*, [1986] 3 F.C. 157 at 174-75 (F.C.T.D.).

[111] *Beson v. Newfoundland (Director of Child Welfare)*, [1982] S.C.J. No. 95.

[112] *Society Promoting Environmental Conservation v. Canada (Attorney General)*, [2003] F.C.J. No. 861 (F.C.A.).

[113] *Homex Realty and Development Co. v. Wyoming (Village)*, [1980] S.C.J. No. 109; *Kelly v. New Brunswick (Provincial Planning Appeal Board)*, [1984] N.B.J. No. 291 (N.B.Q.B.).

A full oral hearing has been required when expelling a member from a profession[114] or a union.[115] A professional discipline proceeding, however, is not a criminal trial and rigid criminal procedure is not appropriate.[116] Before membership in a profession is refused on the grounds of lack of good character, the applicant need only be informed of the concerns and given an opportunity to respond in writing.[117] Not all licensed employment attracts the same procedural rights. Persons who have spent many years training to qualify to practice a profession are entitled to greater procedural protections than licensees with fewer educational qualifications.[118]

The only procedural right afforded an applicant for a licence may be the right to submit an application and have it considered.[119] Most licences are issued for a fixed term and the licensee must apply for renewal and pay a prescribed fee. The licensing body need not give notice of the expiry of a licence or of the non-receipt of an application for renewal[120] or of revocation for non-payment of fees.[121] Before revoking a licence for cause, advance notice of the issues and a meeting to fully discuss them may be required.[122] Where the purpose of licensing is public safety, there may be fewer procedural rights.[123]

Expulsion of an individual from membership in a voluntary association attracts no duty of fairness unless the individual's livelihood or property rights are affected. If these rights are affected, the individual must be given advance notice of the cause for the proposed expulsion and an opportunity to respond to the allegations.[124]

---

[114] *Emerson v. Law Society of Upper Canada*, [1983] O.J. No. 3287 (Ont. H.C.J.).

[115] *Rees v. United Association of Journeymen and Apprentices of the Plumbing and Pipe Fitting Industry of the United States and Canada, Local 527*, [1983] O.J. No. 3152 (Ont. Div. Ct.).

[116] *Béliveau v. Barreau du Quebec*, [1992] A.Q. no 1208, 101 D.L.R. (4th) 324 (Que. C.A.), leave to appeal refused [1992] S.C.C.A. No. 343.

[117] *Simlote v. Assn. of Professional Engineers, Geologists and Geophysicists Alberta*, [1983] A.J. No. 810 (Alta. Q.B.).

[118] *British Columbia (Securities Commission) v. Pacific International Securities Inc.*, [2002] B.C.J. No. 1480 (B.C.C.A.).

[119] *Motta v. Canada (Attorney General)*, [2000] F.C.J. No. 27 (F.C.T.D.).

[120] *Eiba v. Canada (Attorney General)*, [2004] F.C.J. No. 288 (F.C.); *Hoffman-La Roche (F.) AG v. Canada (Commissioner of Patents)*, [2003] F.C.J. No. 1760 (F.C.).

[121] *Gelineau v. Canadian Board for Certification of Prosthetists and Orthotists*, [2003] M.J. No. 162 (Man. Q.B.).

[122] *Baiton Enterprises Ltd. v. Saskatchewan (Liquor Licensing Commission)*, [1984] S.J. No. 871 (Sask. Q.B.).

[123] *Thomson v. Alberta (Transportation and Safety Board)*, [2003] A.J. No. 1115 (Alta. C.A.), leave to appeal refused [2003] S.C.C.A. No. 510; *Green v. Manitoba (Registrar of Motor Vehicles)*, [1992] M.J. No. 259 (Man. C.A.); *Edwards (c.o.b. Seleh Special Care Home) v. New Brunswick (Minister of Health and Community Services)*, [2000] N.B.J. No. 217 (N.B.Q.B.), affd [2000] N.B.J. No. 438 (N.B.C.A.).

[124] *Lakeside Colony of Hutterian Brethren v. Hofer*, [1992] S.C.J. No. 87.

4.   The Legitimate Expectations of the Parties

Fairness may require consistency in procedure. A tribunal may reasonably be expected to follow the same procedures it has followed in the past,[125] provided the evidence of past practice is clear and unequivocal.[126] Similarly, clear and unequivocal promises should be kept. If a tribunal has promised that it will consult certain persons before making its decision, those persons have a legitimate expectation that they will be consulted, even if there is no statutory or other right to be consulted.[127] However, the existence of a past procedural practice or policy does not give rise to a legitimate expectation unless it reflects the tribunal's common practice, it is directly applicable in the circumstances and the persons seeking to enforce it knew of it and relied on it.[128] In addition, to be legitimate, the expected procedure must not conflict with statutory requirements.[129]

A tribunal is not expected to state in advance how it intends to rule on specific procedural or evidentiary questions that may arise at a hearing[130] but, if it does specifically state the procedure that it intends to follow and the parties have relied on that representation, it would be unfair to follow a different procedure.[131] The parties have a legitimate expectation that the stated procedure will be followed,[132] but they cannot expect more. An offer to hear a party orally, when not required, does not confer a right to a full oral hearing with witnesses but only a right to make verbal submissions.[133]

---

[125] *Congrégation des témoins de Jéhovah de St-Jérôme-Lafontaine v. Lafontaine (Village)*, [2004] S.C.J. No. 45 at para. 10.

[126] *Canadian Union of Public Employees (C.U.P.E.) v. Ontario (Minister of Labour)*, [2003] S.C.J. No. 28 at para. 133.

[127] *Old St. Boniface Residents Assn. Inc. v. Winnipeg (City)*, [1990] S.C.J. No. 137 at paras. 73-75.

[128] *Attaran v. University of British Columbia*, [1998] B.C.J. No. 115 at paras. 60-91 (B.C.S.C.); *Humber Heights of Etobicoke Ratepayers Inc. v. Toronto District School Board*, [2003] O.J. No. 1381 (Ont. Div. Ct.).

[129] *Canadian Union of Public Employees v. Ontario (Minister of Labour)*, [2003] S.C.J. No. 28 at para. 131; *dela Fuente v. Canada (Minister of Citizenship and Immigration)*, [2006] F.C.J. No. 774 at paras. 19-20 (F.C.A.), leave to appeal refused [2006] S.C.C.A. No. 291; *DBC Marine Safety Systems Ltd. v. Canada (Commissioner of Patents)*, [2007] F.C.J. No. 1500 (F.C.), affd [2008] F.C.J. No. 1268 (F.C.A.).

[130] *Engineering Students Society, University of Saskatchewan v. Saskatchewan (Human Rights Commission)*, [1983] S.J. No. 274 (Sask. Q.B.).

[131] *Bendahmane v. Canada (Minister of Employment and Immigration)*, [1989] F.C.J. No. 304 (F.C.A.); *Gaw v. Canada (Commissioner of Corrections)*, [1986] F.C.J. No. 63 (F.C.T.D.).

[132] *Furey v. Conception Bay Centre Roman Catholic School Board*, [1993] N.J. No. 170 (Nfld. C.A.).

[133] *Wood v. Wetaskiwin (County)*, [2003] A.J. No. 239 (Alta. C.A.).

5.   The Procedure Chosen by the Tribunal

Tribunals are given latitude in setting their own procedure. The courts are careful not to place decision makers in a procedural straitjacket. As long as the procedure adopted by a tribunal treats those who come before it fairly, a court will not intervene.[134]

Tribunals that process a high volume of cases may have screening procedures and production targets. Efficient processing, by itself, is not procedurally unfair. There is a public interest in containing administrative costs and in expeditious decision making.[135] A tribunal may manage a case so as to make the parties focus on the essential issues[136] or it may conduct a hearing where none is required if it believes this is necessary to make a decision in a difficult case.[137] A tribunal may deal with many similar cases by first adjudicating a "test case" and then applying in subsequent cases the same analytical approach and findings of general facts, subject to a right of the parties in the subsequent cases to dispute the analysis and findings and provided that the analysis and findings are not binding on a panel assigned to hear subsequent cases.[138]

A requirement to hold a hearing does not mandate the adversarial process except where required by statute.[139] A tribunal may choose an adversarial or an inquisitorial process or something in between. An inquisitorial process may be appropriate to process efficiently and fairly a high volume of cases in which parties are often unrepresented, and may be used even if they are represented.[140]

---

[134] *Baker v. Canada (Minister of Citizenship and Immigration)*, [1999] S.C.J. No. 39 at para. 27; *Council of Canadians with Disabilities v. Via Rail Canada Inc.*, [2007] S.C.J. No. 15 at paras. 230-231; *Prassad v. Canada (Minister of Employment and Immigration)*, [1989] S.C.J. No. 25; *Downing v. Graydon*, [1978] O.J. No. 3539 at para. 48 (Ont. C.A.).

[135] *Khan v. Canada (Minister of Citizenship and Immigration)*, [2001] F.C.J. No. 1699 at para. 32 (F.C.A.); *Irripugge v. Canada (Minister of Citizenship and Immigration)*, [2000] F.C.J. No. 29 (F.C.T.D.).

[136] *James v. British Columbia (Labour Relations Board)*, [2007] B.C.J. No. 217 (B.C.C.A.).

[137] *Joshi v. British Columbia Veterinary Medical Assn.*, [2010] B.C.J. No. 422 (B.C.C.A.).

[138] *Geza v. Canada (Minister of Citizenship and Immigration)*, [2004] F.C.J. No. 1401 (F.C.), appeal allowed for other reasons [2006] F.C.J. No. 477 (F.C.A.).

[139] *Nova Scotia (Director of Assessment) v. Knickle*, [2007] N.S.J. No. 449 (N.S.C.A.); *Aurora College v. Niziol*, [2010] N.W.T.J. No. 86 (N.W.T.S.C.); *Universal Workers Union, Labourers' International Union of North America, Local 183 v. Ontario (Human Rights Commission)*, [2006] O.J. No. 50 (Ont. Div. Ct.).

[140] *Benitez v. Canada (Minister of Citizenship and Immigration)*, [2007] F.C.J. No. 735 (F.C.A.), leave to appeal refused [2007] S.C.C.A. No. 391; *Thamotharem v. Canada (Minister of Citizenship and Immigration)*, [2007] F.C.J. No. 734 (F.C.A.), leave to appeal refused [2007] S.C.C.A. No. 394.

F. WERE PROCEDURAL DEFICIENCIES REMEDIED LATER IN THE PROCEEDING?

To determine whether fair procedure has been followed, one must examine the entire proceeding. Although procedural irregularities at one stage may appear to have prejudiced a party's rights, they may diminish in significance if the party has been accorded a full and fair hearing at a later stage in the proceeding. A tribunal may cure its procedural defaults. In the end, the party may be seen not to have suffered any prejudice.

In considering whether a procedural defect has been cured, a number of factors should be considered: the nature of the dispute before the tribunal, the nature and gravity of the procedural defect, the likelihood that the prejudicial effect of that failure may permeate any re-hearing, review or appeal process, the procedural nature of the review, re-hearing or appeal and the significance of the decision to the aggrieved party.[141]

Accordingly, if, at the commencement of a hearing, it is discovered that a party has not been given adequate notice of the proceeding or of the case to be met, the tribunal may adjourn the proceeding to permit adequate notice to be given in order to cure that default. If a decision on the merits of a case, though rendered in violation of a party's procedural rights, has been reconsidered by the same tribunal or upheld by an appellate tribunal, after a full and fair hearing, the procedural defects of the first hearing may be cured.[142] If, at the first hearing, the party was permitted to present all of his or her evidence but was precluded from making oral argument, an appeal on the record that permits full argument may cure this defect.[143] However, an appeal on the record may not be adequate to cure a breach of the duty of fairness that can be corrected only by a full hearing.[144] Failure to follow proper procedure at the complaint and investigation stage is not a roadblock to subsequent discipline proceedings.[145]

---

[141] *International Union of Operating Engineers, Local 882 v. Burnaby Hospital Society*, [1997] B.C.J. No. 2775 (B.C.C.A.).

[142] *McNamara v. Ontario (Racing Commission)*, [1998] O.J. No. 3238 (Ont. C.A.); *Taiga Works Wilderness Equipment Ltd. v. British Columbia (Director of Employment Standards)*, [2010] B.C.J. No. 316 (B.C.C.A.).

[143] *Doucette v. Nova Scotia (Police Commission)*, [1980] N.S.J. No. 465 (N.S.C.A.).

[144] *Khan v. University of Ottawa*, [1997] O.J. No. 2650 (Ont. C.A.); *Melanson v. New Brunswick (Workers' Compensation Board)*, [1994] N.B.J. No. 160 (N.B.C.A.), leave to appeal refused [1994] S.C.C.A. No. 266.

[145] *Histed v. Law Society of Manitoba*, [2006] M.J. No. 290 (Man. C.A.), leave to appeal refused [2006] S.C.C.A. No. 436; *Bechamp v. Assn. of Registered Nurses*, [1994] M.J. No. 281 (Man. C.A.).

G. IS THE TRIBUNAL RELIEVED BY STATUTE FROM COMPLIANCE WITH PROCEDURAL REQUIREMENTS?

A statute may relieve a tribunal of procedural duties that would otherwise be required by common law. The common law requirements of procedural fairness cannot override statutorily prescribed procedure. The statute governs unless it specifically grants discretion to vary the prescribed procedure.[146]

A statute may confer power on a tribunal to decide "with or without a hearing". Such words may not completely free the tribunal of procedural duties; they merely relieve it from holding an oral hearing. The tribunal must still follow fair procedure.[147]

Some statutes authorize tribunals to screen out complaints that, on their face, are not within their jurisdiction or are more appropriately within the jurisdiction of another forum, or that are frivolous, vexatious, or trivial or made in bad faith or are an attempt to re-litigate a matter that has been finally decided. To some extent, all tribunals may refuse to hear cases on these grounds. A complaint that is frivolous lacks legal merit; one that is vexatious lacks factual merit or is harassing or annoying; one that is trivial is too minor to warrant invoking the process.[148]

H. HAS THE PARTY WAIVED PROCEDURAL RULES?

Persons may waive procedural rules that exist for their benefit.[149] For example, a person may agree to proceed on short notice, even though entitled to more time to prepare a case.[150] Parties may submit an agreed statement of facts to obviate the necessity of presenting evidence and to

---

[146] *Ocean Port Hotel Ltd. v. British Columbia (General Manager, Liquor Control and Licensing Branch)*, [2001] S.C.J. No. 17; *Horsefield v. Ontario (Registrar of Motor Vehicles)*, [1999] O.J. No. 967 at paras. 63-65 (Ont. C.A.).

[147] *R. v. Cadeddu*, [1982] O.J. No. 3593 (Ont. H.C.J.); *Hundal v. British Columbia (Superintendent of Motor Vehicles)*, [1985] B.C.J. No. 3046 (B.C.C.A.); *International Brotherhood of Electrical Workers, Local 1739 v. International Brotherhood of Electrical Workers*, [2007] O.J. No. 2460 (Ont. Div. Ct.).

[148] *Milner Power Inc. v. Alberta (Energy and Utilities Board)*, [2010] A.J. No. 866 (Alta. C.A.).

[149] See generally the *Statutory Powers Procedure Act*, R.S.O. 1990, c. S.22, s. 4 and s. 4.1; *Administrative Justice Act*, R.S.Q. c. J-3, s. 100.

[150] Acknowledgement of service is not waiver of short notice: *Ans v. Paul*, [1980] N.S.J. No. 492 (N.S.S.C.).

expedite the proceeding.[151] A party may, for tactical reasons, choose not to take advantage of the full opportunity to be heard.[152]

If there is any doubt whether a procedural rule has been waived, the waiver should not be accepted. A waiver must be "informed"; one must know what one is waiving for it to be effective.[153] The important question is whether the person is aware of the consequences of their choice.[154] This may make it impossible for a party to waive a right to a hearing with respect to incidents that have not yet occurred.[155] Waiver may be inferred where a party has knowledge of a procedural irregularity but does not state any objection. This is discussed in chapter 9, as it is one of the discretionary grounds on which a reviewing court may refuse to grant relief.

I.   SPECIFIC PROCEDURAL RULES

The remainder of this chapter concerns specific procedural rules that some tribunals may be required to apply when adjudicating cases that directly affect important individual rights and interests. These rules generally do not apply to legislative and policy decisions. Many of these rules apply only to tribunals that are required to hold oral hearings.

J.   STATUS: WHO MAY BE A PARTY?

Who may participate in a tribunal's decision-making process? A person who will be directly affected by a decision may participate.[156] Under the Alberta *APA*, a person whose rights will be "varied or affected" may participate.[157] Other statutes state that persons with a "substantial interest in the proceedings" or "all interested parties" may participate. The Ontario *SPPA* and the Quebec *AJA* both state that any person "entitled by law" or

---

[151] *Emerson v. Law Society of Upper Canada*, [1983] O.J. No. 3287 (Ont. H.C.J.); *Samson v. Sisters of Charity of Immaculate Conception*, [1985] B.C.J. No. 2021 (B.C.C.A.), leave to appeal refused (1985), 67 B.C.L.R. xl.

[152] *Council of Canadians with Disabilities v. Via Rail Canada Inc.*, [2007] S.C.J. No. 15 at paras. 235-245.

[153] *392014 Alberta Ltd. v. Canal Flats (Village)*, [2008] B.C.J. No. 1470 at paras. 18-25 (B.C.S.C.); *R. v. Conroy*, [1983] O.J. No. 3089 (Ont. H.C.J.).

[154] *La Presse c. Bouchard*, [2001] J.Q. no 2501 (Que. S.C.).

[155] *Amerato v. Ontario (Motor Vehicle Dealers Act, Registrar)*, [2005] O.J. No. 3713 (Ont. C.A.).

[156] Interpretation of statutory words "directly affected": *Corp. of the Canadian Civil Liberties Assn. v. Ontario (Civilian Commission on Police Services)*, [2006] O.J. No. 4699 (Ont. C.A.), leave to appeal refused [2007] S.C.C.A. No. 40; of statutory word "aggrieved": *Newfoundland (Office of the Citizen's Representative) v. Newfoundland and Labrador Housing Corp.*, [2009] N.J. No. 208 (N.L.T.D.).

[157] *Administrative Procedures and Jurisdiction Act*, R.S.A. 2000, c. A-3, s. 1(*b*).

"designated by law" may participate.[158] Many statutes do not define the parties with precision, leaving it up to the tribunal, and ultimately to the courts, to define who may participate in a particular proceeding. However, where the statute does clearly define the parties and does not grant express authority to add any other party, the tribunal has no authority to do so.[159]

Factors that may be considered include the statutory purposes, the subject matter of the proceeding, a person's interest in the subject and the effect that the decision might have on that interest. It may be more difficult to demonstrate an interest if the subject matter concerns high-level policy development rather than a fact-specific inquiry into the property or individual rights of a person. A mere academic interest may not be sufficient. The extent to which the result may affect the person's legal interests is important. The issue may be viewed differently where the rights of one person may be affected than if many persons may be similarly affected, though status should not be denied solely because there may be other people with similar interests who may also be entitled to status, nor because the participation of many people will lengthen the proceedings and result in additional expense. A person who has vital information to give or has made the allegations that are the subject of the inquiry may be considered to have an interest. All of these factors and others may be considered but no one factor should be determinative. They should be considered in the context of each inquiry after examining all of the circumstances. Essentially, what is required is evidence that the subject-matter of the inquiry may seriously affect an individual.[160]

In discipline proceedings, the complainant has no procedural rights except those granted by statute because most licensing regulators do not have authority to grant remedies to complainants.[161] The licensee whose conduct is complained about is necessarily a party to the discipline proceeding, but not necessarily to the prior inquiry into the complaint.[162] In contrast, a

---

[158] *Statutory Powers Procedure Act*, R.S.O. 1990, c. S.22, s. 5; Quebec *Administrative Justice Act*, R.S.Q. c. J-3, s. 101.

[159] *Canadian Union of Public Employees, Local 394 v. Crozier*, [2001] B.C.J. No. 195 (B.C.C.A.).

[160] *Re Ontario (Royal Commission on the Northern Environment)*, [1983] O.J. No. 994 (Ont. Div. Ct.); *Kelly v. Alberta (Energy Resources Conservation Board)*, [2009] A.J. No. 1161 (Alta. C.A.), leave to appeal granted [2010] A.J. No. 1187 (Alta. C.A.); *McFadyen v. Ontario (Mining and Lands Commissioner)*, [2007] O.J. No. 4875 (Ont. Div. Ct.).

[161] *Friends of the Oldman River Society v. Alberta (Assn. of Professional Engineers, Geologists and Geophysicists)*, [2001] A.J. No. 568 (Alta. C.A.), leave to appeal refused [2001] S.C.C.A. No. 366; *Berg v. British Columbia (Police Complaint Commissioner)*, [2006] B.C.J. No. 1027 (B.C.C.A.), leave to appeal refused [2006] S.C.C.A. No. 300; *Walker v. Health Professions Appeal and Review Board*, [2008] O.J. No. 661 (Ont. Div. Ct.); *Graywood Investments Ltd. v. Ontario (Energy Board)*, [2005] O.J. No. 345 (Ont. Div. Ct.).

[162] *Comité de déontologie policière c. Dechenault*, [2005] J.Q. no 9801 (Que. C.A.), leave to appeal refused [2005] C.S.C.R. no 438.

human rights complainant has procedural rights at both stages, reflecting the authority of human rights tribunals to grant remedies to complainants.[163]

In labour relations matters, the union has the exclusive right to represent employees and an employee may not participate separately.[164]

A party whose sole interest is in how the decision will affect their contract with a regulated party does not have standing because their contractual interest is too indirect.[165]

A person may be added as a respondent if there is some reliable evidence that may support an order against them.[166] However, mere knowledge or involvement in the subject matter of the inquiry may make a person a witness but not a respondent.[167]

A directly affected party, who is granted standing, should be permitted to present evidence as well as argument. The tribunal may, however, restrict each added party's evidence and arguments to matters relevant to the proceeding and that party's specific interest in those matters.[168]

Public interest standing is sometimes granted to public interest groups that specialize in advocacy on specific issues such as the environment. These groups often have greater resources and expertise than do individuals who are more directly affected. However, if the statute permits only persons who are "directly affected" to participate in the proceeding, the tribunal has no authority to grant public interest standing, even where the public interest is a significant issue in the proceeding.[169] The B.C. *ATA* explicitly authorizes tribunals to which it applies to admit intervenors and prescribe the scope of their participation.[170] A party who chose to participate only as an intervenor,

---

[163] *Sketchley v. Canada (Attorney General)*, [2005] F.C.J. No. 2056 (F.C.A.); *McKenzie Forest Products Inc. v. Ontario (Human Rights Commission)*, [2000] O.J. No. 1318 (Ont. C.A.), leave to appeal refused [2000] S.C.C.A. No. 285; but no rights after death of complainant: *British Columbia v. Gregoire*, [2005] B.C.J. No. 2593 (B.C.C.A.), leave to appeal refused [2006] S.C.C.A. No. 23.

[164] *Noël v. Société d'énergie de la Baie James*, [2001] S.C.J. No. 41.

[165] *Telecommunications Workers Union v. Canada (Radio-television and Telecommunications Commission)*, [1995] S.C.J. No. 55; *Syndicat du transport de Montréal c. Métromédia CMR Plus inc.*, [2010] J.Q. no 306 (Que. C.A.).

[166] *University of Prince Edward Island v. Nilsson*, [2009] P.E.I.J. No. 2 (P.E.I.S.C.).

[167] *United Food and Commercial Workers International Union v. Rol-Land Farms Ltd.*, [2008] O.J. No. 682 at paras. 50-60 (Ont. Div. Ct.).

[168] *American Airlines Inc. v. Canada (Competition Tribunal)*, [1988] F.C.J. No. 1049 (F.C.A.), affd [1989] S.C.J. No. 12; *Re Ontario (Royal Commission on the Northern Environment)*, [1983] O.J. No. 994 (Ont. Div. Ct.); *Henderson v. Ontario (Securities Commission)*, [1976] O.J. No. 2342 (Ont. H.C.J.).

[169] *Friends of the Athabasca Environmental Assn. v. Alberta (Public Health Advisory and Appeal Board)*, [1996] A.J. No. 47 (Alta. C.A.).

[170] *Administrative Tribunals Act*, S.B.C. 2004, c. 45, s. 33.

not as a full party, may not later complain that the scope of its participation was restricted.[171]

A tribunal that has express or implied statutory authority to intervene in the proceedings of another tribunal, may do so. The latter tribunal may permit such intervention, in accordance with the criteria applied to private intervenors.[172] A city wishing to intervene in proceedings before a tribunal should pass a resolution authorizing the intervention and should ensure that its governing statute grants authority to pass such a resolution.[173]

Questions of standing should be decided at the outset prior to the start of the hearing on the merits.[174] A hearing cannot proceed fairly while a person's right to participate remains uncertain. Persons requesting to participate should describe their interest and state the purpose of their intervention to the tribunal with sufficient particularity so as to enable other parties to make representations and to enable the tribunal to decide whether to grant status and to define the scope of participation. They may be expected to prove their interest with evidence[175] and opposing parties may provide evidence that they do not have sufficient interest.[176] One cannot expect to be granted status on a vague request to intervene and on an assurance that one's position will be fully disclosed at the hearing.[177]

A recent strategy of some regulated entities for dissuading the public from participating in regulatory proceedings has been to sue those who have been granted standing. The courts may be receptive to a preliminary motion to dismiss such actions as an abuse of process.[178]

K. NOTICE

1. Purpose

Before a decision is made, notice must be given to all persons who may be affected by it (except in cases of emergency). Failure to give notice will likely be fatal to any decision. The purpose of notice is to alert persons whose interests may be affected so that they may take steps to protect

---

[171] *Telus Communications Co. v. Canada (Canadian Radio-Television and Telecommunications Commission)*, [2010] F.C.J. No. 927 (F.C.A.).

[172] *Newfoundland Telephone Co. v. TAS Communications Systems Ltd.*, [1987] S.C.J. No. 79.

[173] *Rowand v. Edmonton (City)*, [1983] A.J. No. 843 (Alta. C.A.).

[174] *Court v. Alberta (Environmental Appeal Board)*, [2003] A.J. No. 662 (Alta. Q.B.).

[175] *Court v. Alberta (Environmental Appeal Board)*, [2003] A.J. No. 662 (Alta. Q.B.).

[176] *Cheyne v. Alberta (Utilities Commission)*, [2009] A.J. No. 1160 (Alta. C.A.).

[177] *Allied Auto Parts Ltd. v. Canada (Transport Commission)*, [1982] F.C.J. No. 230 (F.C.A.).

[178] Colloquially known as "strategic litigation against public participation (SLAPP)": *Hunt Oil Co. of Canada, Inc. v. Galleon Energy Inc.*, [2010] A.J. No. 348 (Alta. Q.B.).

their interests.[179] It also informs affected persons, as well as the decision maker, of the matters in issue and the proposed action to be taken.[180] Fairness requires that the hearing and decision be restricted to the matters set out in the notice.[181] If other matters are to be considered, additional notice should be given and an adjournment may be required. Disclosure of the case to be met is further discussed in the next section.

It may not be sufficient to invite persons for informal discussions about their affairs without advising them that the result of these discussions may be a decision adverse to their interests.[182] A tribunal should not assume, simply because it has been having discussions with a party about a matter, that the party knows a decision will be made.[183] It should still tell the party that it intends to make a decision determining the matter. However, if the explicit purpose of the discussions was to provide an opportunity to have input into the decision, a decision may be made without further notice.[184] It may not be sufficient to summon a person to a meeting without informing them of the purpose of the meeting.[185] A subpoena requiring a person to attend a proceeding as a witness is not notice that a decision affecting that person's interests may be made.[186]

Notice given to a community of a pending decision that may affect property rights must describe the geographical area to be affected so that property owners may ascertain whether their property is within it.[187]

A notice of an oral hearing must state the time and place so that recipients may attend if they wish. Parties must also be notified of any change in the time or place for the hearing.[188]

---

[179]   *Sinkovich v. Strathroy (Town) Commissioners of Police*, [1988] O.J. No. 1212 (Ont. Div. Ct.), leave to appeal refused (1988), 33 Admin. L.R. xliv (Ont. C.A.); *Collins v. Ontario (Pension Commission)*, [1986] O.J. No. 769 (Ont. Div. Ct.).

[180]   *Kenney v. College of Physicians and Surgeons*, [1991] N.B.J. No. 915 (N.B.C.A.).

[181]   *Entrop v. Imperial Oil Ltd.*, [2000] O.J. No. 2689 (Ont. C.A.).

[182]   *Baiton Enterprises Ltd. v. Saskatchewan (Liquor Licensing Commission)*, [1984] S.J. No. 871 (Sask. Q.B.); *Weston v. Chiropody (Podiatry) Review Committee*, [1980] O.J. No. 3643 (Ont. C.A.); *Wagner v. College of Physicians and Surgeons*, [1984] S.J. No. 391 (Sask. Q.B.).

[183]   *Homex Realty and Development Co. v. Wyoming (Village)*, [1980] S.C.J. No. 109.

[184]   *Halfway River First Nation v. British Columbia (Ministry of Forests)*, [1999] B.C.J. No. 1880 at paras. 76-80 (B.C.C.A.).

[185]   *Alberta (Funeral Services Regulatory Board) v. Strong*, [2006] A.J. No. 1558 (Alta. Q.B.); *Murphy v. Newhook*, [1984] N.J. No. 152 (Nfld. T.D.).

[186]   *Elson v. St. John's (City) Residential Tenancies Board*, [1980] N.J. No. 87 (Nfld. Dist. Ct.); *Honkoop v. Summerside Raceway Presiding Judge*, [1984] P.E.I.J. No. 50 at para. 17 (P.E.I.S.C.).

[187]   *Central Ontario Coalition Concerning Hydro Transmission Systems v. Ontario Hydro*, [1984] O.J. No. 3253 (Ont. Div. Ct.); *Ontario (Joint Board under the Consolidated Hearings Act) v. Ontario Hydro*, [1985] O.J. No. 2551 (Ont. C.A.); *Basic Management Ltd. v. Saskatoon (City)*, [1983] S.J. No. 196 (Sask. Q.B.).

The Alberta *APA* requires that all parties be given "adequate" notice.[189] The Ontario *SPPA* and Quebec *AJA* require that the parties to any proceeding be given "reasonable notice".[190] What is "adequate" or "reasonable" depends on the circumstances and will be determined by the application of common law principles of fairness. The *SPPA* and *AJA* further require that the notice state the time, place and purpose of the hearing and that, if the party notified does not attend, the tribunal may proceed in the party's absence.[191]

2. Delivery of Notice

May notice be given orally or must it be in writing? In most cases, written notice is advisable so that there can be no dispute as to whether notice was given. Where no oral or written hearing is required, oral notice that a decision will be made may be sufficient. If a hearing is required, written notice is usually also required. Many statutes require a tribunal to give advance written notice to all who may be affected by a proposed decision.

How ought written notice be delivered to the parties? The B.C. *ATA* permits service of a party by ordinary mail, electronic transmission or any other method that allows proof of receipt.[192] Most other statutes, including the *SPPA*, *AJA* and *APA*, are silent on this point. It is usually acceptable to send notice by ordinary mail. To be certain the party received it, it may be advisable to send it by registered mail or to deliver the notice physically into the person's hands. A party who provides an email address consents to notice being given by email and should ensure that tribunal emails are not blocked or diverted.[193] If the recipient proves that an email notification was not received and was not blocked or diverted, proof that an email was sent may be difficult as computer-generated proofs tend only to show that it was relayed to the recipient's server.[194] Where the number of parties is not too great, each party should receive personal notice. However, where the proposed decision concerns many people, an advertisement in a local

---

[188] *Supermarchés Jean Labrecque Inc. v. Flamand*, [1987] S.C.J. No. 54; *De Wolfe v. Canada (Correctional Service)*, [2003] F.C.J. No. 1475 (F.C.).

[189] *Administrative Procedures and Jurisdiction Act*, R.S.A. 2000, c. A-3, s. 3.

[190] *Statutory Powers Procedure Act*, R.S.O. 1990, c. S.22, s. 6(1); *Administrative Justice Act*, R.S.Q. c. J-3, s. 129.

[191] *Statutory Powers Procedure Act*, R.S.O. 1990, c. S.22, s. 6(2) and (3) [as am.]; *Administrative Justice Act*, R.S.Q. c. J-3, s. 129.

[192] *Administrative Tribunals Act*, S.B.C. 2004, c. 45, ss. 19-20.

[193] *Golden Win Investments Ltd. v. British Columbia (Assessor of Area No. 15 – Fraser Valley)*, [2010] B.C.J. No. 2683 (B.C.S.C.); *Zhang v. Canada (Minister of Citizenship and Immigration)*, [2010] F.C.J. No. 65 (F.C.).

[194] *Yazdani v. Canada (Minister of Citizenship and Immigration)*, [2010] F.C.J. No. 1071 (F.C.); *Alavi v. Canada (Minister of Citizenship and Immigration)*, [2010] F.C.J. No. 1197 (F.C.).

newspaper may be all that is required.[195] Sometimes a combination of service by mail and newspaper advertisement may be expected, particularly in matters affecting many property interests in a locality.[196]

A failure to comply with a statutory requirement to give notice may be forgiven if the persons otherwise received notice and were not prejudiced in their ability to respond.[197]

In some circumstances, constructive notice may be sufficient. For example, newspaper articles in a local newspaper, although not published at the instance of the tribunal, may be regarded as sufficient.[198] Likewise, notice given to an association may be adequate service on the members,[199] and vice versa.[200] However, constructive notice may not be sufficient if the decision affects an important legal interest.[201]

3.   Notified Party Fails to Attend or Respond to Notice

Where a party who has been given proper notice fails to respond or attend, the tribunal may proceed in the party's absence and the party is not entitled to further notice.[202] All that the tribunal need establish, before proceeding in the absence of the party, is that the party was given notice of the date and place of the hearing. The tribunal need not investigate the reasons for the party's absence.[203] A tribunal may assume that notice sent to an address given by the party was received because the onus is on the party to inform the tribunal of changes of address.[204] If the tribunal has

---

[195] See *Little v. Cowichan Valley (Regional District)*, [1978] B.C.J. No. 1293 (B.C.C.A.), and *Caddy Lake Cottagers Assn. v. Florence-Nora Access Road Inc.*, [1998] M.J. No. 315 (Man. C.A.), for discussions of the type of newspaper that is acceptable. *Administrative Tribunals Act*, S.B.C. 2004, c. 45, s. 21.

[196] *Ontario (Joint Board under the Consolidated Hearings Act) v. Ontario Hydro*, [1985] O.J. No. 2551 (Ont. C.A.).

[197] *Society Promoting Environmental Conservation v. Canada (Attorney General)*, [2003] F.C.J. No. 861 (F.C.A.); *Administrative Tribunals Act*, S.B.C. 2004, c. 45, s. 20.

[198] *Arts v. London and Middlesex (County) Roman Catholic Separate School Board*, [1979] O.J. No. 4508 (Ont. H.C.J.).

[199] *Arts v. London and Middlesex (County) Roman Catholic Separate School Board*, [1979] O.J. No. 4508 (Ont. H.C.J.).

[200] *Mechanical Contractors Assn. of Alberta v. Alberta (Industrial Relations Board)*, [1978] A.J. No. 582 (Alta. S.C.).

[201] *St. Peter's Evangelical Lutheran Church v. Ottawa (City)*, [1982] S.C.J. No. 90; *Wassenaar v. Scarborough (City)*, [1985] O.J. No. 2288 (Ont. H.C.J.).

[202] *Statutory Powers Procedure Act*, R.S.O. 1990, c. S.22, s. 7; *Administrative Justice Act*, R.S.Q. c. J-3, s. 100; *Deslauriers c. Ordre des arpenteurs-géométres du Quebec*, [1998] A.Q. no 443 (Que. C.A.), leave to appeal refused [1998] C.S.C.R. no 175.

[203] *Aubut v. Canada (Minister of National Revenue)*, [1990] F.C.J. No. 1100 (F.C.A.), leave to appeal refused [1991] S.C.C.A. No. 31.

[204] *Toronto (City) v. Wolf*, [2008] O.J. No. 3061 (Ont. Div. Ct.); *Wilks v. Canada (Immigration and Refugee Board)*, [2009] F.C.J. No. 354 (F.C.).

information to suggest that the party may not have received it or if notice is returned undelivered, a tribunal should not proceed without making further efforts to locate and serve the party.[205] If, a tribunal is aware that a party's absence is the result of a misunderstanding,[206] or a failure to serve proper notice,[207] or for some other valid reason, the proceeding should, if possible, be adjourned to a later date on proper notice.

If a new issue concerning the absent party is added to the notice of hearing, the absent party should be notified of the new issue before the tribunal proceeds to hear and decide the issue. As a party's conscious decision not to attend is based on the issues listed in the notice of hearing, it cannot be presumed that the party is not interested in responding to any new issues that arise subsequently.[208] Likewise, failure to attend does not amount to a waiver of bias. A conscious decision not to attend means only that the party trusts an impartial tribunal to render a decision on the merits.[209] However, a party who is absent by choice does waive all procedural and evidentiary objections that could be made at the hearing and the right to challenge the decision on the merits.[210]

If, after a decision has been made, the tribunal learns that a party did not receive proper notice, the matter may be re-heard on proper notice to all parties.[211] If the absent party presents medical evidence of inability to attend, the matter should be re-heard.[212] If the failure to attend was due to the party's own negligence or choice, a re-hearing may be refused.[213]

4.   Timeliness of Notice

Sufficient time should elapse between the receipt of notice and the commencement of the hearing to enable a party to prepare. Matters which are complex or which may significantly affect the party's interests may require more time. A tribunal should not insist on proceeding on short

---

[205] *Hopper v. Foothills (Municipal District No. 31)*, [1976] A.J. No. 548 (Alta. C.A.); *Haugen v. Camrose (County)*, [1979] A.J. No. 543 (Alta. C.A.); *Keymanesh v. Canada (Minister of Citizenship and Immigration)*, [2006] F.C.J. No. 804 (F.C.).

[206] *Rayonnier Quebec Inc. v. Quebec (Tribunal du Travail)*, [1976] C.A. 748 (Que. C.A.).

[207] *Hopper v. Foothills No. 31 (Municipal District)*, [1976] A.J. No. 548 (Alta. C.A.).

[208] *IMP Group Ltd. v. Dillman*, [1995] N.S.J. No. 326 (N.S.C.A.); *Alberta v. Alberta (Labour Relations Board)*, [1998] A.J. No. 936 (Alta. Q.B.).

[209] *Chipman Wood Products (1973) Ltd. v. Thompson*, [1996] N.B.J. No. 395 (N.B.C.A.).

[210] *Violette v. New Brunswick Dental Society*, [2004] N.B.J. No. 5 (N.B.C.A.).

[211] *Di Leo v. Hétu*, [1982] C.S. 442 (Que. S.C.).

[212] *Toronto Housing Co. v. Sabrie*, [2003] O.J. No. 652 (Ont. Div. Ct.); *Ahamad v. Canada (Minister of Citizenship and Immigration)*, [2000] F.C.J. No. 289 (F.C.T.D.).

[213] *Wayzhushk Onigum Nation v. Kakeway*, [2001] F.C.J. No. 1167 (F.C.T.D.); *Schuit Plastering and Stucco Inc. v. Ontario (Labour Relations Board)*, [2009] O.J. No. 2082 (Ont. Div. Ct.); *Tomaszewska v. College of Nurses (Ontario)*, [2007] O.J. No. 1731 (Ont. Div. Ct.).

notice of a few hours or a few days over the objection of a party who has not had time to prepare,[214] except in emergencies.[215] A party may waive short notice, but a time limit prescribed by statute or regulation cannot be unilaterally shortened by the tribunal without express authority to do so.[216]

5.   Delays and Time Limits

A proceeding must be commenced within the time limit prescribed by statute.[217] For the purpose of time limits, a proceeding is commenced when the notice of hearing is issued or the complaint or other notice is filed, whichever is the initiating document under the statutory process.[218] So long as the proceeding is commenced within the statutory time limit, delays prior to the commencement are immaterial.[219] Limitation periods prescribed by general statutes do not apply to tribunal proceedings.[220] Most limitation periods start when the subject event occurs. The tort concept of "discoverability" does not apply.[221] Some tribunals are required by statute to commence proceedings within a specified time after the facts first came to their knowledge. This test is difficult to apply because facts are rarely learned and analyzed all at once. To turn suspicion into "knowledge", sufficient credible and persuasive information must be gathered about the

---

[214] *Davidson v. Bagla*, [2006] O.J. No. 4044 (Ont. Div. Ct.); *Clouâtre v. Hosie*, [2008] S.J. No. 249 (Sask. Q.B.).

[215] *Amalgamated Transit Union, Local 113 v. Ontario (Labour Relations Board)*, [2007] O.J. No. 3907 (Ont. Div. Ct.).

[216] *Costello v. Calgary (City)*, [1983] S.C.J. No. 4; *Hopper v. Foothills (Municipal District No. 31)*, [1976] A.J. No. 548 (Alta. C.A.); *Hoffbeck v. British Columbia (Superintendent of Motor Vehicles)*, [1985] B.C.J. No. 2832 (B.C.S.C.); *Lightfoot v. Gerecke*, [1983] S.J. No. 25 (Sask. Q.B.).

[217] Time limits for filing complaints: *Burns v. United Assn. of Journeymen of the Plumbing and Pipe Fitting Industry, Local 170*, [1977] B.C.J. No. 1262 (B.C.S.C.); *Upper Lakes Shipping Ltd. v. Sheehan*, [1979] S.C.J. No. 15; *Towers Department Stores Ltd. v. Nadeau* (1978), 97 D.L.R. (3d) 266 (Que. S.C.) (strict compliance required); *Manitoba (Human Rights Commission) v. Winnipeg (City)*, [1982] M.J. No. 316 (Man. Q.B.), affd [1983] M.J. No. 112 (Man. C.A.); *R. v. Zeidler Forest Industries Ltd.*, [1978] A.J. No. 545 (Alta. S.C.) (strict compliance not required). Time limits for giving notice: *Perrott v. Storm*, [1985] N.S.J. No. 467 (N.S.C.A.) (strict compliance required). Time limits for commencing proceedings: *Vialoux v. Registered Psychiatric Nurses Assn.*, [1983] M.J. No. 215 (Man. C.A.) (strict compliance required); *Police Assn. (Metro Toronto) v. Toronto (Metro) Commissioners of Police*, [1978] O.J. No. 3496 (Ont. H.C.J.) (strict compliance not required).

[218] *Smolensky v. British Columbia (Securities Commission)*, [2004] B.C.J. No. 298 at paras. 27-28 (B.C.C.A.), leave to appeal refused [2004] S.C.C.A. No. 274.

[219] *British Columbia (Securities Commission) v. Cicci*, [1993] B.C.J. No. 2823 (B.C.C.A.).

[220] *West End Construction Ltd. v. Ontario (Ministry of Labour)*, [1989] O.J. No. 1444 (Ont. C.A.); *Colledge v. Niagara (Region) Police Commission*, [1983] O.J. No. 3265 (Ont. C.A.), leave to appeal refused (1984), 3 O.A.C. 319n; *Hanson v. Selinger*, [1979] S.J. No. 468 (Sask. Q.B.), leave to appeal refused [1980] S.J. No. 198 (Sask. C.A.).

[221] *Engel v. Edmonton (City) Police Service*, [2008] A.J. No. 422 (Alta. C.A.), leave to appeal refused [2008] S.C.C.A. No. 284.

events and those involved.[222] Tribunals to which the BC *ATA* applies must issue practice directives respecting the time by which an application, complaint or appeal must be perfected.[223] Where statute permits the tribunal to grant an extension of time, it may do so where there are good reasons for the extension and the responding party will not suffer prejudice to its ability to respond caused by the loss of evidence.[224]

A requirement that a hearing be held within a prescribed time after the delivery of a complaint or notice encourages the timely hearing of cases but failure to comply is not fatal to the proceeding.[225] If the tribunal has authority to extend this time limit, it may do so without notice to the parties,[226] but only to ensure a fair process, not to permit a complainant to bolster inadequate proof.[227] Where the statute requires officials to act "forthwith", failure to do so is not grounds to stay the proceeding.[228]

Where no time limit is prescribed by statute, a proceeding will not usually be dismissed for delay, no matter how tardy the complainant was in bringing the matter to the tribunal's attention.[229] Likewise, failure of the tribunal to investigate and commence proceedings with dispatch after receipt of the complaint is not grounds to stay the proceeding, unless the respondent can demonstrate prejudice of such a kind and degree as to significantly impair the right to a fair hearing. There must be evidence that the delay has affected the respondent's ability to respond to the allegations. Such evidence would include the death or disappearance of important witnesses or the loss of important evidence because of the lapse of time. In the absence of evidence of prejudice to the right to a fair hearing, a proceeding is unlikely to be stayed for delay. It is not enough to show that the respondent has been living under a cloud of suspicion that negatively affects the respondent's reputation, career prospects and relationships unless the delay was inordinate and directly

---

[222] *Thériault v. Royal Canadian Mounted Police*, [2006] F.C.J. No. 169 (F.C.A.); *Smart v. Canada (Attorney General)*, [2008] F.C.J. No. 1167 (F.C.A.); *Erikson v. Ontario (Securities Commission)*, [2003] O.J. No. 593 at paras. 49-53 (Ont. Div. Ct.).

[223] *Administrative Tribunals Act*, S.B.C. 2004, c. 45, s. 12.

[224] *Halifax Employers Assn. v. International Longshoremen's Assn., Local 269*, [2004] N.S.J. No. 316 (N.S.C.A.), leave to appeal refused [2004] S.C.C.A. No. 464; *Canada (Attorney General) v. Somwaru*, [2010] F.C.J. No. 1584 (F.C.A.); *Richard v. Canada (Attorney General)*, [2010] F.C.J. No. 1370 (F.C.A.), leave to appeal refused [2010] S.C.C.A. No. 461.

[225] *Nova Scotia (Minister of Finance) v. Nova Scotia Teachers Union*, [1995] N.S.J. No. 122 (N.S.C.A.); *Rahman v. College and Assn. of Respiratory Therapy*, [2001] A.J. No. 343 (Alta. Q.B.); *Edmonton Police Service v. Alberta (Information and Privacy Commissioner)*, [2009] A.J. No. 488 (Alta. Q.B.); *contra: Kellogg Brown and Root Canada v. Alberta (Information and Privacy Commissioner)*, [2007] A.J. No. 896 (Alta. Q.B.).

[226] *Vanovermeire v. Edmonton (City) Police Commission*, [1993] A.J. No. 347 (Alta. Q.B.).

[227] *Canadian National Railway Co. v. Paterson Grain*, [2010] F.C.J. No. 1231 (F.C.A.).

[228] *Rankel v. Psychologists Assn. Alberta*, [1993] A.J. No. 345 (Alta. C.A.), leave to appeal refused [1993] S.C.C.A. No. 319.

[229] *Pearlman v. Manitoba Law Society Judicial Committee*, [1991] S.C.J. No. 66.

caused significant psychological harm to the respondent or attached a stigma to the respondent's reputation such that the system of adjudication will be brought into disrepute.[230] A party who requests or agrees to an adjournment waives delay.[231] A complaint of delay should be submitted to the tribunal before applying to a court for relief.[232] A tribunal may justify its own delay in deciding an application by showing evidence of ongoing investigation to gather relevant facts.[233] Statutory authority to take action "at any time" precludes a challenge on the ground of delay.[234]

Where the onus is on a party to prosecute its application or grievance, unreasonable delay by the party may be regarded as an abandonment of the claim and the application or grievance may be dismissed.[235]

If a proceeding commenced within the prescribed time limit is aborted or quashed by a court because of an irregularity, the proceeding may be resumed, even though out of time, because it is regarded as a continuation of the failed proceeding.[236]

L. DISCLOSURE OF THE CASE TO BE MET

Fairness requires that a party who will be affected by a decision must first be informed of the case to be met. Without knowledge of the matters in issue one cannot effectively exercise one's right to be heard. Disclosure enables a party to review the alleged facts, to prepare to challenge them with evidence that rebuts them or reduces their impact and to prepare submissions explaining how they should be weighed and analyzed.

Generally, the obligation to disclose is on the one who has the information. In proceedings initiated by the tribunal it is usually the tribunal who has gathered the information and has the obligation to disclose it, though responding parties may also be required to make disclosure. Many tribunals have discretion as to how they acquire information for use in a proceeding. It does not matter how the information is obtained as long as

---

[230] *Blencoe v. British Columbia (Human Rights Commission)*, [2000] S.C.J. No. 43; *Stinchcombe v. Law Society*, [2002] A.J. No. 544 (Alta. C.A.); *Grover v. Canada (Attorney General)*, [2010] F.C.J. No. 370 (F.C.).

[231] *Stinchcombe v. Law Society*, [2002] A.J. No. 544 (Alta. C.A.); *Huot c. Pigeon*, [2006] J.Q. no 965 (Que. C.A.).

[232] *Comité de déontologie policière du Quebec v. Bourdon*, [2000] J.Q. no 2963 (Que. C.A.).

[233] *Chong v. Canada (Minister of Citizenship and Immigration)*, [2001] F.C.J. No. 1817 (F.C.T.D.).

[234] *Addison & Leyen Ltd. v. Canada*, [2007] S.C.J. No. 33.

[235] *Fraternité des Policiers de Communauté Urbaine de Montréal Inc. v. Beaulieu*, [1978] C.S. 406 (Que. S.C.); B.C. *Administrative Tribunals Act*, S.B.C. 2004, c. 45, s. 12.

[236] *Nicholson v. Haldimand-Norfolk (Regional) Police Commissioners*, [1980] O.J. No. 3845 (Ont. C.A.), leave to appeal refused [1981] S.C.C.A. No. 254; *Webb v. Ontario (Securities Commission)*, [1987] O.J. No. 161 (Ont. Div. Ct.).

it is disclosed.[237] In cases initiated by a party, the tribunal may have the statutory power to require parties to make pre-hearing disclosure to each other and to the tribunal.[238] A party who initiates a proceeding may not keep relevant information confidential.[239]

The extent of disclosure varies along a spectrum. At one end is simply a requirement that the person be told verbally the gist of the factual subject and the nature of the decision to be made. Further along the spectrum is the requirement to give advance written notice of the nature of the decision to be made and the key facts upon which it will be based. To that requirement may be added the requirement to disclose the evidence to be presented to the decision maker. At the far end of the spectrum, the party may be entitled to review all relevant information (except privileged material) including material which will not be submitted to the decision maker.

Relevance is the essential criterion. Irrelevant information need not be disclosed.[240] There are degrees of relevance. The more important the information is to a central issue to be decided, the more likely it should be disclosed, in contrast to information that is repetitive or relevant only to a peripheral issue. It is appropriate to ask: if the information is put before the decision maker, what is the likelihood that it will influence the result? If it is not likely, then it is not probative and need not be disclosed.

The objectives of the statute and the nature and function of the powers assigned to the tribunal influence the extent of disclosure. More disclosure may be expected where the mandate is to adjudicate disputes or discipline wrongdoers; less where the mandate is to manage competing interests or to decide what is in the public interest when making regulatory or policy decisions.[241] A body that decides policy questions is entitled to hear from anyone but is not obliged to make any disclosure.[242] However, where a public hearing is mandated, interested members of the public may be entitled to review reports that will be considered in making the decision,

---

[237] *Board of Education v. Rice*, [1911] A.C. 179 at 182 (H.L.); *Downing v. Graydon*, [1978] O.J. No. 3539 (Ont. C.A.); *Pierre-Pierre v. Finlay*, [1991] R.J.Q. 1947 (C.S.).

[238] E.g., *Statutory Powers Procedure Act*, R.S.O. 1990, c. S.22, s. 5.4; *Canadian Pacific Airlines Ltd. v. Canadian Air Line Pilots Assn.*, [1993] S.C.J. No. 114.

[239] *Bank of Nova Scotia Properties Inc. v. Winnipeg (City) Assessor*, [2006] M.J. No. 40 (Man. Q.B.).

[240] *Woolley v. College of Physicians and Surgeons*, [1996] B.C.J. No. 184 (B.C.S.C.).

[241] *Imperial Oil Ltd. v. Quebec (Minister of the Environment)*, [2003] S.C.J. No. 59; *Canada (Attorney General) v. Inuit Tapirisat of Canada*, [1980] S.C.J. No. 99; *Newfoundland and Labrador (Consumer Advocate) v. Newfoundland and Labrador (Public Utilities Board)*, [2005] N.J. No. 83 (N.L.T.D.); *United States of America v. Kavaratzis*, [2006] O.J. No. 1661 (Ont. C.A.), leave to appeal refused [2006] S.C.C.A. No. 252.

[242] *Pembroke Civic Hospital v. Ontario (Health Services Restructuring Commission)*, [1997] O.J. No. 3142 at paras. 16-19 (Ont. Div. Ct.), leave to appeal to C.A. refused Sep. 10, 1997.

in order to be able to intelligently participate in the debate of the issues,[243] but not a subsequent report clarifying issues debated at the meeting.[244] If the statutory mandate is to provide an expeditious and inexpensive forum to adjudicate disputes or process applications, the disclosure requirements should not be so onerous as to defeat this purpose.[245]

The extent of legal formality prescribed for the proceedings may indicate the extent and nature of disclosure required. A tribunal, which does not have the power to summons witnesses, conducts less formal proceedings and need not require disclosure to as great an extent as a tribunal subject to more formal procedural requirements.[246] It may be sufficient if the allegations are orally summarized for the party.[247] A summary may be more useful than full documentary disclosure because it identifies what is important.[248]

Where a party has a right to call and cross-examine witnesses, the party may be entitled to the disclosure necessary to exercise those rights meaningfully.[249] This may include some disclosure of information relevant to credibility, but only to the extent it is probative of key factual issues.[250] Credibility is such an amorphous issue that caution should be exercised so as to protect against endless demands for disclosure by a party wanting to derail the proceeding.

In investigations where no decision will result, witnesses subpoenaed to give evidence should be advised of the general nature of the matters on which they are to be questioned. They need not be given particulars nor shown documents even though they may be suspects.[251]

Some statutes prescribe disclosure requirements. The Ontario *SPPA* requires disclosure of reasonable information of any allegations concerning

---

[243] *Pitt Polder Preservation Society v. Pitt Meadows (District)*, [2000] B.C.J. No. 1305 (B.C.C.A.); but see *Williams Lake Conservation Co. v. Chebucto Community Council of Halifax (Regional Municipality)*, [2004] N.S.J. No. 232 (N.S.C.A.).

[244] *Hubbard v. West Vancouver (District)*, [2005] B.C.J. No. 2769 (B.C.C.A.); *Heritage Trust of Nova Scotia v. Halifax (Regional Municipality)*, [2007] N.S.J. No. 79 (N.S.S.C.).

[245] *Haghighi v. Canada (Minister of Citizenship and Immigration)*, [2000] F.C.J. No. 854 (F.C.A.); *Khan v. Canada (Minister of Citizenship and Immigration)*, [2001] F.C.J. No. 1699 at para. 32 (F.C.A.).

[246] *Pierre-Pierre v. Finlay*, [1991] R.J.Q. 1947 (C.S.).

[247] *550551 Ontario Ltd. v. Framingham*, [1991] O.J. No. 1035 (Ont. Div. Ct.); *Desjardins v. Bouchard*, [1982] F.C.J. No. 238 (F.C.A.); *Scott v. Nova Scotia (Rent Review Commission)*, [1977] N.S.J. No. 571 at para. 43 (N.S.C.A.).

[248] *Léonard v. Canada (Attorney General)*, [2003] F.C.J. No. 954 (F.C.T.D.).

[249] *People First of Ontario v. Ontario (Niagara Regional Coroner)*, [1992] O.J. No. 3 (Ont. C.A.).

[250] *Emery v. Alberta (Workers' Compensation Bd., Appeals Commission)*, [2000] A.J. No. 1189 (Alta. Q.B.).

[251] *Ontario (Securities Commission) v. Biscotti*, [1988] O.J. No. 1115 (Ont. H.C.J.); *Samuel, Son and Co. v. Canada (Restrictive Trade Practices Commission)*, [1987] F.C.J. No. 1027 (F.C.T.D.).

the good character, propriety of conduct or competence of a party.[252] It also authorizes tribunals to order the parties to make pre-hearing disclosure.[253] The Alberta *APA* requires a tribunal to inform a party of the facts or allegations that are contrary to the party's interests in sufficient detail so as to permit the party to understand them and to contradict or explain them.[254]

The extent of disclosure may turn on what is at stake for a party. A person whose interests will be directly affected by the tribunal's decision is entitled to greater disclosure than an intervenor. A complainant is entitled to greater disclosure than an intervenor or objector.[255] Objectors and members of the public who attend licensing or rate hearings may not always be entitled to receive copies of the material submitted by the applicant.[256] A business that intervenes in a competitor's hearing may not be entitled to detailed disclosure because their interests are not at stake in the proceeding.[257]

As the right to liberty or security of the person may be affected in cases involving denial of parole or refugee status, disclosure must be made in accordance with the principles of fundamental justice prescribed by s. 7 of the *Charter*.[258] These principles appear to be the same as administrative law principles.

As the focus of the issues turns from policy to questions of individual fault or liability, the disclosure requirements may increase. One who alleges that a party engaged in misconduct or is liable to pay compensation may be required to make disclosure to that party of all evidence and information that they have with respect to the events, acts or words at issue. In most cases, all information that will be put before the decision maker should be disclosed but there is no requirement to disclose information that was gathered but will not be put before the decision maker.[259] It is especially important that disclosure be made of any information which may be prejudicial to the party's interests and which will be put before the decision

---

[252] *Statutory Powers Procedure Act*, R.S.O. 1990, c. S.22, s. 8.

[253] *Statutory Powers Procedure Act*, R.S.O. 1990, c. S.22, s. 5.4.

[254] *Administrative Procedures and Jurisdiction Act*, R.S.A. 2000, c. A-3, s. 4(*b*).

[255] *Stumbillich v. Ontario (Health Disciplines Board)*, [1984] O.J. No. 3309 (Ont. C.A.), leave to appeal refused (1985), 6 O.A.C. 399n; *Downing v. Graydon*, [1978] O.J. No. 3539 (Ont. C.A.).

[256] *Temple v. Ontario (Liquor Licence Board)*, [1982] O.J. No. 3632 (Ont. Div. Ct.); *Seafarers International Union of Canada v. Canadian National Railway Co.*, [1976] F.C.J. No. 42 (F.C.A.).

[257] *All Ontario Transport Ltd. v. Ontario (Highway Transport Board)*, [1979] O.J. No. 4381 (Ont. Div. Ct.).

[258] *Charter*, s. 7; *Singh v. Canada (Minister of Employment and Immigration)*, [1985] S.C.J. No. 11; *Cadieux v. Mountain Institution*, [1984] F.C.J. No. 253 (F.C.T.D.).

[259] *Hutchinson v. Canada (Minister of the Environment)*, [2003] F.C.J. No. 439 at para. 49 (F.C.A.); *Harris v. Barristers' Society*, [2004] N.S.J. No. 463 (N.S.C.A.).

maker.[260] Actual prejudice need not be established. If there is a reasonable likelihood of prejudice, the information must be disclosed.[261] While failure to disclose may be fatal to a decision if the party's right to a fair hearing was prejudiced,[262] failure to disclose non-prejudicial information may not.[263] In some cases, exculpatory information should also be disclosed.[264]

The most complete and detailed disclosure is required in cases involving the discipline of professionals, because a discipline proceeding jeopardizes a vocation that may be practised only after extensive training to qualify and because the allegations often impugn the individual's good character and reputation. (A licence to engage in a business or trade is not a right of the same order and does not attract the same standards of procedural fairness.[265]) In professional discipline, factual particulars should be described in the notice of hearing[266] or in a supplementary document.[267] Both the client and the specific misconduct should be identified.[268] However, a notice should not read like an Information in a criminal proceeding.[269] How detailed it should be depends on the complex-

---

[260] *United Food and Commercial Workers Union, Local 401 v. Westfair Foods Ltd.*, [2010] A.J. No. 386 (Alta. C.A.); *Downing v. Graydon*, [1977] O.J. No. 2357 (Ont. C.A.).

[261] *Kane v. University of British Columbia*, [1980] S.C.J. No. 32.

[262] In *Kane v. University of British Columbia*, [1980] S.C.J. No. 32, the fact that the non-disclosure gave rise to a reasonable likelihood of prejudice proved fatal to the decision. However, the Alberta Court of Appeal has said that the party must satisfy a reviewing court that it could have answered or blunted prejudicial statements for the court to set aside the tribunal's decision for non-disclosure: *United Association of Journeymen and Apprentices of the Pipefitting Industry of the United States and Canada, Local 488 v. Alberta (Industrial Relations Board)*, [1976] A.J. No. 355 (Alta. C.A.).

[263] *Canadian Cable Television Assn. v. American College Sports Collective of Canada, Inc.*, [1991] F.C.J. No. 502 (F.C.A.).

[264] *Mason v. British Columbia (Securities Commission)*, [2003] B.C.J. No. 1438 (B.C.C.A.); *Stevens v. Canada (Restrictive Trade Practices Commission)*, [1979] F.C.J. No. 24 (F.C.T.D.).

[265] *British Columbia (Securities Commission) v. Pacific International Securities Inc.*, [2002] B.C.J. No. 1480 at paras. 11-13 (B.C.C.A.); *Genex Communications Inc. v. Canada (Attorney General)*, [2005] F.C.J. No. 1440 (F.C.A.), leave to appeal refused [2005] C.S.C.R. no 485; *1657575 Ontario Inc. v. Hamilton (City)*, [2008] O.J. No. 3016 at para. 29 (Ont. C.A.).

[266] *Bateman v. Assn. of Professional Engineers*, [1984] M.J. No. 391 at paras. 17-22 (Man. Q.B.); *Baiton Enterprises Ltd. v. Saskatchewan (Liquor Licensing Commission)*, [1984] S.J. No. 871 (Sask. Q.B.); *Aamco Automatic Transmissions Inc. v. Simpson*, [1980] O.J. No. 3695 (Ont. Div. Ct.); *contra: MacDonald v. Windsor-Essex County Real Estate Board*, [1982] O.J. No. 3459 (Ont. H.C.J.).

[267] *Cwinn v. Law Society of Upper Canada*, [1980] O.J. No. 3548 (Ont. Div. Ct.), leave to appeal refused (1980), 28 O.R. (2d) 61*n*; *Herman Motor Sales Inc. v. Ontario (Registrar of Motor Vehicle Dealers and Salesmen)*, [1980] O.J. No. 3680 (Ont. Div. Ct.); *Collins v. Estevan Roman Catholic Separate School Division No. 27*, [1988] S.J. No. 476 (Sask. C.A.).

[268] *Finch v. Assn. of Professional Engineers and Geoscientists*, [1994] B.C.J. No. 930 (B.C.C.A.).

[269] *Violette v. New Brunswick Dental Society*, [2004] N.B.J. No. 5 at para. 38 (N.B.C.A.); *Histed v. Law Society of Manitoba*, [2006] M.J. No. 290 at para. 67 (Man. C.A.), leave to appeal refused [2006] S.C.C.A. No. 436; *Béliveau v. Barreau du Quebec*, [1992] J.Q. no 1208 (Que. C.A.),

ity and seriousness of the case. A failure to provide details in the notice of hearing can be cured by full disclosure of the evidence to be filed at the hearing.[270] The tribunal is not restricted to considering only the facts alleged in the notice of hearing, but should make its decision in light of all of the facts adduced at the hearing.[271] The notice is merely an outline of the alleged facts.[272]

Criminal law rules do not apply because the stakes are not as high.[273] Even though regulation may have very serious financial consequences for a party, these consequences are not as serious as the potential loss of liberty which is at stake in a criminal proceeding.[274] Also, the proceedings have different purposes. The purpose of criminal proceedings is to punish wrongdoers. The purpose of disciplinary proceedings is to protect the public. Even the most formal tribunal hearings tend to be more like civil trials than criminal proceedings. However, even in civil proceedings full disclosure is required. The main difference between civil and criminal proceedings is that, in civil proceedings, the disclosure is reciprocal in that all parties make full disclosure to all other parties. In criminal proceedings only the prosecution is obliged to make full disclosure. The defence is not required to make any disclosure (except in special circumstances such as alibi evidence) because, in criminal cases, an accused person has a right to remain silent. As there is no right to remain silent in administrative proceedings, there is a trend towards reciprocal disclosure even in discipline proceedings. The B.C. *ATA* and Ontario *SPPA* empower tribunals to make rules requiring parties to exchange documents and other evidence.[275]

---

leave to appeal refused [1992] S.C.C.A. No. 343; *Datta v. Saskatchewan (Medical Care Insurance Commission)*, [1986] S.J. No. 726 (Sask. C.A.), see Issue IV.

[270] *S. (A.B.) v. Manitoba (Director of Child and Family Services)*, [1995] M.J. No. 52 (Man. C.A.).

[271] *Compagnie de taxi Laurentides inc. c. Commission des transports du Quebec*, [2009] J.Q. no 1872 at paras. 46-56 (Que. C.A.); *Incorporated Synod of the Diocese of Toronto v. Ontario (Human Rights Commission)*, [2008] O.J. No. 1692 at para. 15 (Ont. Div. Ct.).

[272] *Quebec (Sa Majesté du Chef) v. Ontario (Securities Commission)*, [1992] O.J. No. 2232 at para. 27 (Ont. C.A.), leave to appeal refused [1992] S.C.C.A. No. 580.

[273] *May v. Ferndale Institution*, [2005] S.C.J. No. 84 at para. 91; *Blencoe v. British Columbia (Human Rights Commission)*, [2000] S.C.J. No. 43; *Genex Communications Inc. v. Canada (Attorney General)*, [2005] F.C.J. No. 1440 (F.C.A.), leave to appeal refused [2005] C.S.C.R. no 485; *Nova Scotia (Minister of Community Services) v. M. (D.J.)*, [2002] N.S.J. No. 368 (N.S.C.A.), leave to appeal refused [2002] S.C.C.A. No. 473; *Violette v. New Brunswick Dental Society*, [2004] N.B.J. No. 5 at para. 38 (N.B.C.A.). A tribunal may choose to make disclosure in accordance with the criminal law standards: *Deloitte and Touche LLP v. Ontario (Securities Commission)*, [2003] S.C.J. No. 62.

[274] *CIBA-Geigy Canada Ltd. v. Canada (Patented Medicine Prices Review Board)*, [1994] F.C.J. No. 884 (F.C.A.).

[275] *Administrative Tribunals Act*, S.B.C. 2004, c. 45, s. 11; *British Columbia (Assessor of Area No. 1 – Capital) v. Lehigh Portland Cement Ltd.*, [2010] B.C.J. No. 244 (B.C.S.C.); *Statutory Powers Procedure Act*, R.S.O. 1990, c. S.22, s. 5.4 [as am.]; *Ontario (Human Rights Commission) v. Dofasco Inc.*, [2001] O.J. No. 4420 (Ont. C.A.).

The names of witnesses who will testify should be disclosed. Witnesses statements should be disclosed if they exist.[276] Complainants do not have a right to confidentiality. It is assumed that they will take greater care to provide accurate information if they know it will be disclosed.[277] However, the importance of personal information to a central issue in the case should be weighed against the right to privacy of individuals who are not parties to the proceeding.[278] Notes of an interview of a party by a tribunal investigator should be provided.[279]

If the tribunal intends to rely on publicly available information in making its decision, the disclosure obligation may be met by identifying the information and the public location where it may be viewed.[280]

A tribunal need not disclose uncontested general and background information of which it takes official notice or which is derived from its own expertise.[281] However, specific information known by the tribunal as a result of past experience with similar cases should be disclosed if it will be relied upon.[282] If a substantive issue turns on an internal policy guideline, it should be disclosed to the parties, so that they may make submissions on the application of the policy to the factual circumstances.[283]

The obligation to disclose applies only to evidence and does not require disclosure of the investigation report or other report prepared by staff of the tribunal,[284] unless the report is to be relied upon by the tribunal when making

---

[276] *Hudson Bay Mining and Smelting Co. v. Cummings*, [2006] M.J. No. 304 (Man. C.A.).

[277] *Lycka v. Alberta (Information and Privacy Commissioner)*, [2009] A.J. No. 439 (Alta. Q.B.); *Bergwitz v. Fast*, [1980] B.C.J. No. 1565 (B.C.C.A.); *Napoli v. British Columbia (Workers' Compensation Board)*, [1981] B.C.J. No. 972 (B.C.C.A.); *Ontario (Human Rights Commission) v. House*, [1993] O.J. No. 3380 (Ont. Div. Ct.).

[278] *Deloitte and Touche LLP v. Ontario (Securities Commission)*, [2003] S.C.J. No. 62; *Canada (Minister of Public Safety and Emergency Preparedness) v. Kahlon*, [2005] F.C.J. No. 1335 (F.C.); *Mason v. British Columbia (Securities Commission)*, [2003] B.C.J. No. 1438 (B.C.C.A.).

[279] *Nrecaj v. Canada (Minister of Employment and Immigration)*, [1993] F.C.J. No. 699 (F.C.T.D.).

[280] *Mancia v. Canada (Minister of Citizenship and Immigration)*, [1998] F.C.J. No. 565 (F.C.A.).

[281] *Seafarers International Union of Canada v. Canadian National Railway Co.*, [1976] F.C.J. No. 42 (F.C.A.). Ontario tribunals are specifically empowered to take notice of facts that may be judicially noticed as well as generally recognized scientific or technical facts, information or opinions within its scientific or specialized knowledge: *Statutory Powers Procedure Act*, R.S.O. 1990, c. S.22, s. 16. See also *Administrative Justice Act*, R.S.Q. c. J-3, ss. 140, 141, 142.

[282] *Champlin Canada Ltd. v. Calco Ranches Ltd.*, [1986] A.J. No. 620 (Alta. Q.B.).

[283] *Dale Corp. v. Nova Scotia (Rent Review Commission)*, [1983] N.S.J. No. 427 at para. 31 (N.S.C.A.).

[284] *CIBA-Geigy Canada Ltd. v. Canada (Patented Medicine Prices Review Board)*, [1994] F.C.J. No. 884 (F.C.A.); *Edworthy v. Saskatchewan (Water Appeal Board)*, [1992] S.J. No. 476 (Sask. Q.B.); *Batson v. Ontario (Human Rights Commission)*, [2007] O.J. No. 2233 (Ont. Div. Ct.).

its decision.[285] Staff memoranda and investigator's reports which merely recommend proceedings may be privileged.[286]

Information acquired after the hearing should be disclosed to the parties if it is to be taken into account in the decision, and the parties should be given an opportunity to make representations on it.[287]

In addition to the evidence, the essential issues to be considered should be identified.[288] A party should not be left in the position of discovering, upon receipt of the tribunal's decision, that it turned on a matter on which the party had not made representations because the party was not aware it was in issue.[289] Nor is it fair to have an important issue sprung on a party during a hearing without prior notice or an adjournment.[290] This does not require explicit disclosure of applicable statutory provisions or case law, unless the decision may turn on law that has been overlooked by the parties. A tribunal need not disclose additional authority on a point that has been argued nor authority for a general proposition.[291]

The tribunal should advise the party of the types of disciplinary orders being contemplated and give an opportunity to make representations as to the appropriate order and extenuating circumstances.[292] It is sufficient to identify the statutory provision which prescribes the types of orders that may be made. In contrast, there may be no duty to forewarn an applicant for a licence of the conditions that may be attached to the licence if granted.[293]

A tribunal may take into account the knowledge and expertise of a party when determining how much disclosure is necessary to make the party

---

[285] *Markwart v. Prince Albert (City)*, [2006] S.J. No. 676 at para. 34 (Sask. C.A.); *Bhagwandass v. Canada (Minister of Citizenship and Immigration)*, [2001] F.C.J. No. 341 (F.C.A.).

[286] *Idziak v. Canada (Minister of Justice)*, [1992] S.C.J. No. 97.

[287] *Salinas v. Canada (Minister of Employment and Immigration)*, [1992] F.C.J. No. 559 (F.C.A.); *Kannata Highlands Ltd. v. Kannata Valley (Village)*, [1987] S.J. No. 719 at § 5 (Sask. C.A.).

[288] *Gratton-Masuy Environmental Technologies Inc. v. Building Materials Evaluation Commission*, [2002] O.J. No. 4252 (Ont. Div. Ct.).

[289] *Danakas v. Canada (War Veterans Allowance Board)*, [1985] F.C.J. No. 32 (F.C.A.); *McAllister v. Veterinary Medical Assn.*, [1985] N.B.J. No. 167 (N.B.C.A.), leave to appeal refused [1985] S.C.C.A. No. 8.

[290] *Morgan v. Canada (National Parole Board)*, [1982] F.C.J. No. 47 (F.C.A.); *Chowdhury v. Canada (Minister of Citizenship and Immigration)*, [2006] F.C.J. No. 187 (F.C.).

[291] *Diavik Diamond Mines Inc. v. Northwest Territories (Director of Human Rights)*, [2007] N.W.T.J. No. 89 at paras. 54-55 (N.W.T.S.C.); *Knoll North America Corp. v. Adams*, [2010] O.J. No. 5611 (Ont. Div. Ct.).

[292] *Cymbalisty v. Chiropractors' Assn.*, [1985] S.J. No. 222 (Sask. Q.B.).

[293] *CTV Television Network Ltd. v. Canada (Canadian Radio-television and Telecommunications Commission)*, [1982] S.C.J. No. 24.

aware of the case to be met.[294] If there have been ongoing discussions and the issues have been clearly defined, a tribunal may assume that the parties know what matters are in issue, but if the discussions have not specifically identified which issue will be considered when the decision is made, it should be identified to the parties.[295]

There are exceptions to the disclosure requirement. Lack of full disclosure in an emergency may be excused.[296] A tribunal may refuse to disclose confidential information such as information involving national security,[297] prison security,[298] the identity of informers,[299] business secrets,[300] medical files of psychiatric patients[301] or privileged communications.[302] A decision to withhold disclosure should be based on a concern about harm that may result from disclosure of the specific information, rather than because it is of a class of information that is generally regarded as confidential, and only to the extent necessary to avoid the harm.[303] The substance of information may sometimes be revealed without disclosing the identity of informers.[304] A disclosure order may not be restricted to counsel; parties are entitled to see everything disclosed to their counsel.[305]

---

[294] *Violette v. New Brunswick Dental Society*, [2004] N.B.J. No. 5 at para. 37 (N.B.C.A.); *Re Cardinal Insurance Co.*, [1982] F.C.J. No. 516 (F.C.A.), leave to appeal refused [1982] S.C.C.A. No. 104.

[295] *Fredericks v. Essex (Town) Commissioners of Police*, [1983] O.J. No. 3220 (Ont. Div. Ct.).

[296] *Tomko v. Nova Scotia (Labour Relations Board)*, [1975] S.C.J. No. 111.

[297] *Chiau v. Canada (Minister of Citizenship and Immigration)*, [2000] F.C.J. No. 2043 (F.C.A.); *Al Yamani v. Canada (Solicitor General)*, [1995] F.C.J. No. 1453 at paras. 111-113 (F.C.T.D.); *Sogi v. Canada (Minister of Citizenship and Immigration)*, [2004] F.C.J. No. 947 (F.C.A.), leave to appeal refused [2004] S.C.C.A. No. 354.

[298] *Gaudet v. Marchand*, [1994] A.Q. no 375 (Que. C.A.); *Cadieux v. Mountain Institution*, [1984] F.C.J. No. 253 (F.C.T.D.); *Latham v. Canada (Solicitor General)*, [1984] F.C.J. No. 177 (F.C.T.D.); *Couperthwaite v. Canada (National Parole Board)*, [1982] F.C.J. No. 99 (F.C.T.D.); *Wilson v. Canada (National Parole Board)*, [1985] F.C.J. No. 1188 (F.C.T.D.).

[299] *Chiarelli v. Canada (Minister of Employment and Immigration)*, [1992] S.C.J. No. 27 at paras. 48-50; *Gallant v. Canada (Deputy Commissioner Correctional Service)*, [1989] F.C.J. No. 70 (F.C.A.); *Ruiperez v. Lakehead University*, [1983] O.J. No. 3013 (Ont. C.A.); *Fraternité Inter-Provinciale des Ouvriers en Electricité v. Quebec (Office de la Construction)*, [1983] J.Q. no 394, 148 D.L.R. (3d) 626 at 632, 641 (Que. C.A.).

[300] *Sarco Canada Ltd. v. Canada (Anti-Dumping Tribunal)*, [1978] F.C.J. No. 127 (F.C.A.); *Citizens' Health Action Committee Inc. v. Manitoba (Milk Control Board)*, [1979] M.J. No. 220 (Man. Q.B.).

[301] *Toronto Police Assn. v. Toronto Police Services Board*, [2008] O.J. No. 4380 (Ont. Div. Ct.); *Egglestone v. Ontario (Advisory Review Board)*, [1983] O.J. No. 3076 (Ont. Div. Ct.).

[302] *Idziak v. Canada (Minister of Justice)*, [1992] S.C.J. No. 97; *Pritchard v. Ontario (Human Rights Commission)*, [2004] S.C.J. No. 16; *York Region District School Board v. Ontario College of Teachers*, [2007] O.J. No. 286 (Ont. Div. Ct.).

[303] *Cadieux v. Mountain Institution*, [1984] F.C.J. No. 253 (F.C.T.D.).

[304] *Demaria v. Regional Classification Board*, [1986] F.C.J. No. 493 (F.C.A.).

[305] *British Columbia v. British Columbia Government and Service Employees' Union*, [2005] B.C.J. No. 17 (B.C.C.A.).

Disclosure should be timely. There should be sufficient time after disclosure to permit the party to review the information and to prepare to respond to it.[306] An adjournment may be necessary for this purpose.[307]

The disclosure obligation is ongoing. It is not uncommon for investigations to continue after the issuance of a notice of hearing or for new witnesses to come forward upon learning of the proceedings. This new information, if relevant, should be disclosed as soon as practicable. The only requirement is that the disclosure be made sufficiently in advance of the hearing, to enable the respondent to prepare to respond to it.[308]

Disclosure should be made to each party directly, not just to some parties with a hope that they will pass it along to other parties.[309]

If, at the hearing, it becomes apparent that insufficient disclosure has been made, the proceeding should not be dismissed. A tribunal may order further disclosure and adjourn the hearing to allow a party time to review it and respond.[310] A proceeding should not be stayed because of non-disclosure due to loss or destruction of evidence. Deliberate destruction may warrant an adverse inference when making findings of fact.[311]

A party must request disclosure. Failure to make disclosure does not violate the duty of fairness unless the party requested disclosure and did not receive it.[312] A declaration by tribunal counsel that disclosure has been made must be accepted in the absence of evidence to the contrary.[313]

M. ADJOURNMENTS

A tribunal's choice of date for a hearing prevails unless a party can demonstrate that to proceed on that date would result in a denial of

---

[306] *Friends of the Public Gardens v. Halifax (Planning Advisory Committee)*, [1984] N.S.J. No. 83 at paras. 63-74 (N.S.T.D.); *Noormohamed v. Canada (Minister of Employment and Immigration)*, [1993] F.C.J. No. 926 (F.C.T.D.).

[307] *Edmonton (City) v. Edmonton (City) Assessment Review Board*, [2010] A.J. No. 1192 (Alta. Q.B.).

[308] *Yerxa v. Canada*, [1993] F.C.J. No. 715 (F.C.T.D.).

[309] *Lewis v. Canada (Employment and Immigration Commission)*, [1985] F.C.J. No. 169 (F.C.A.), leave to appeal refused (1985), 63 N.R. 317*n*.

[310] *Cascades Conversion inc. c. Yergeau*, [2006] J.Q. no 3120 (Que. C.A.).

[311] *Genex Communications Inc. v. Canada (Attorney General)*, [2005] F.C.J. No. 1440 (F.C.A.), leave to appeal refused [2005] C.S.C.R. no 485; *Ontario (Ministry of Community, Family and Children's Services) v. Ontario (Crown Employees Grievance Settlement Board)*, [2006] O.J. No. 2517 (Ont. C.A.), leave to appeal refused [2006] S.C.C.A. No. 367.

[312] *Johnston v. Lac Ste. Anne (County) Subdivision and Development Appeal Board*, [2007] A.J. No. 1218 (Alta. C.A.); *Siad v. Canada (Secretary of State)*, [1996] F.C.J. No. 1575 (F.C.A.), leave to appeal refused [1997] S.C.C.A. No. 47.

[313] *Quebec (Procureur général) v. Bouliane*, [2004] J.Q. no 4883 at paras. 168-73 (Que. C.A.), leave to appeal refused [2004] C.S.C.R. no 290.

procedural fairness.[314] No one has a right to an adjournment. Adjournments are within the discretion of the tribunal. Every tribunal has an inherent power to adjourn a proceeding to ensure that parties are dealt with fairly, except where precluded by statute. A requirement to make a decision within a specified time limit does not prevent a tribunal from adjourning to be fair.[315] Some statutes expressly grant authority to adjourn a proceeding.[316] Even if the parties agree to adjourn, the tribunal may refuse to do so.[317] Conversely, a tribunal should not use its power to adjourn as a tactic to avoid or delay making a decision[318] nor adjourn to await the outcome of policy development or the enactment of legislation.[319]

Various factors may be considered when deciding whether to adjourn. The most important is the requirement of a fair hearing.[320] This requirement must be balanced against the tribunal's statutory duty[321] and the need to resolve disputes expeditiously and to avoid delay.[322]

An adjournment is typically granted where a party has received short notice[323] or late disclosure of the case to be met.[324] It is only late or inadequate disclosure of key evidence that would justify an adjournment.[325] Late or non-disclosure of supplementary evidence containing no new material information may not be grounds for an adjournment.[326] An

---

[314] *Hanley v. Eden*, [2005] O.J. No. 55 (Ont. Div. Ct.); *Butterfield v. Canada (Attorney General)*, [2006] F.C.J. No. 1132 (F.C.), affd [2007] F.C.J. No. 1235 (F.C.A.).

[315] *Loomis Armored Car Service Ltd. v. Manitoba Food and Commercial Workers, Local 832*, [1982] M.J. No. 430 (Man. Q.B.); *Japan Electrical Manufacturers Assn. v. Canada (Anti-Dumping Tribunal)*, [1986] F.C.J. No. 652 (F.C.A.); *Municipal Contracting Ltd. v. International Union of Operating Engineers, Local 721*, [1988] N.S.J. No. 274 (N.S.T.D.).

[316] *E.g.*, *Administrative Tribunals Act*, S.B.C. 2004, c. 45, s. 39; *Statutory Powers Procedure Act*, R.S.O. 1990, c. S.22, s. 21.

[317] *Rathé v. Quebec (Ministre de l'Environnement et de la Faune)*, [2000] J.Q. no 5077 (Que. S.C.).

[318] For example, see *Yasin v. Psychological Assn.*, [1979] B.C.J. No. 1451 (B.C.S.C.); *Sterzik v. Beattie*, [1985] A.J. No. 686 (Alta. Q.B.), vard [1986] A.J. No. 1103 (Alta. C.A.).

[319] *Regroupement national des Conseils régionaux de l'environnement du Quebec v. Quebec (Régie de l'énergie)*, [2001] J.Q. no 2183 (Que. C.A.).

[320] *Flamboro Downs Holdings Ltd. v. Teamsters, Local 879*, [1979] O.J. No. 4199 (Ont. Div. Ct.); *Pierre v. Canada (Minister of Manpower and Immigration)*, [1978] F.C.J. No. 70 (F.C.A.).

[321] *Prassad v. Canada (Minister of Employment and Immigration)*, [1989] S.C.J. No. 25.

[322] *Flamboro Downs Holdings Ltd. v. Teamsters, Local 879*, [1979] O.J. No. 4199 (Ont. Div. Ct.); *Morgan v. Ontario Land Surveyors Assn.*, [1980] O.J. No. 3544 (Ont. Div. Ct.); *Windsor Airline Limousine Services Ltd. v. Ontario Taxi Assn., Local 1688*, [1980] O.J. No. 3815 (Ont. Div. Ct.).

[323] *Clouâtre v. Hosie*, [2008] S.J. No. 249 (Sask. Q.B.).

[324] *Edmonton (City) v. Edmonton (City) Assessment Review Board*, [2010] A.J. No. 1192 (Alta. Q.B.).

[325] *Haydon v. Canada (Attorney General)*, [2003] F.C.J. No. 957 (F.C.T.D.).

[326] *Richmond Square Development Corp. v. Middlesex Condominium Corp. No. 134*, [1993] O.J. No. 997 (Ont. Div. Ct.).

adjournment may also be granted if a new issue or new evidence that might affect the decision is raised for the first time during the hearing.[327]

As a party is expected to take reasonable steps to retain a lawyer who is available, a request for an adjournment because counsel has other commitments on the date fixed for the hearing may be denied,[328] especially if the party did not retain counsel until just before the hearing date.[329] A party who dismisses counsel just before the hearing may be denied an adjournment to find new counsel.[330] A party who makes reasonable efforts to retain counsel who is available should be accommodated,[331] especially if the time is short between when notice was given and the hearing.[332]

An adjournment should be granted if a party submits medical evidence of an illness that prevents the party from attending the hearing.[333] However, ill health is not grounds to stay the proceeding altogether.[334]

The interests of the parties should be balanced. Greater weight may be given to the interests of a party whose livelihood is at stake than to those of an intervenor.[335] If other parties are in attendance and ready to proceed with witnesses, the tribunal may refuse an adjournment unless the requesting adjournment party requesting adjournment undertakes to pay their costs thrown away.[336] An adjournment may be refused if previous adjournments have been granted.[337]

A tribunal should not adjourn its proceeding to await the outcome of a civil proceeding. The public have an interest in the prompt and just

---

[327] *Morgan v. Canada (National Parole Board)*, [1982] F.C.J. No. 47 (F.C.A.); *Cascades Conversion inc. c. Yergeau*, [2006] J.Q. no 3120 (Que. C.A.).

[328] *Flamboro Downs Holdings Ltd. v. Teamsters, Local 879*, [1979] O.J. No. 4199 (Ont. Div. Ct.).

[329] *Gosselin v. Canada (Attorney General)*, [1998] F.C.J. No. 854 (F.C.T.D.); *Ochnik v. Ontario Securities Commission*, [2007] O.J. No. 1730 (Ont. Div. Ct.); *Krebs v. Canada (Minister of National Revenue)*, [1977] F.C.J. No. 134 (F.C.A.).

[330] *Flamboro Downs Holdings Ltd. v. Teamsters, Local 879*, [1979] O.J. No. 4199 (Ont. Div. Ct.); *Pierre v. Canada (Minister of Employment and Immigration)*, [1978] F.C.J. No. 70 (F.C.A.), affg [1977] F.C.J. No. 132 (F.C.T.D.).

[331] *Law Society of Upper Canada v. Igbinosun*, [2009] O.J. No. 2465 (Ont. C.A.).

[332] *Markwart v. Prince Albert (City)*, [2006] S.J. No. 676 (Sask. C.A.).

[333] *Olech v. Royal College of Dental Surgeons*, [1994] O.J. No. 520 (Ont. Div. Ct.); *Kampman v. Canada*, [1993] F.C.J. No. 66 (F.C.A.); *Howatt v. College of Physicians and Surgeons*, [2003] O.J. No. 138 (Ont. Div. Ct.).

[334] *Canada (Ministre de la Citoyenneté et de l'Immigration) v. Obodzinsky*, [2000] F.C.J. No. 1675 (F.C.T.D.).

[335] *Morgan v. Ontario Land Surveyors Assn.*, [1980] O.J. No. 3544 (Ont. Div. Ct.); *Wigby v. Pearson*, [1977] Y.J. No. 5 (Y.T.S.C.); *Consumers' Assn. v. Canada (Transport Commission)*, [1979] F.C.J. No. 52 (F.C.T.D.).

[336] *Morgan v. Ontario Land Surveyors Assn.*, [1980] O.J. No. 3544 (Ont. Div. Ct.).

[337] *Prassad v. Canada (Minister of Employment and Immigration)*, [1989] S.C.J. No. 25; *Iwasyk v. Saskatchewan (Human Rights Commission)*, [1977] S.J. No. 353 (Sask. Q.B.), revd on another ground [1978] S.J. No. 210 (Sask. C.A.).

exercise by the tribunal of its powers. The tribunal's procedures, unlike those of the court, are expected to be simple, summary and expeditious.[338] Likewise, a tribunal should not adjourn its hearing to await the outcome of a criminal proceeding because the two proceedings have different purposes and different burdens of proof. The respondent's right to remain silent in respect of the criminal proceeding is not infringed by the administrative hearing because testimony given at the administrative hearing cannot be used to incriminate the respondent in the criminal proceeding.[339]

As the price of an adjournment, a tribunal may demand an undertaking to comply with reasonable conditions or suspend the requesting party's licence.[340] To protect the public, a licensee facing discipline proceedings who requests an adjournment may be required to undertake not to practise the profession or licensed activity.[341]

Before adjourning, the tribunal should fix the time and place for the resumption of the hearing. As a fixed time to resume the hearing grants a party a legitimate expectation that the hearing will continue, a decision should not be rendered without further hearing, even if it is unable to proceed at the scheduled time.[342] If the tribunal fails to reconvene the hearing at the time and place to which it has been adjourned, it does not lose power to continue the proceeding,[343] but must notify the parties of the time and place for the continuation of the proceeding. If, at the time of the adjournment, no date is fixed, parties should be given notice before the hearing is reconvened. If a date but no place is fixed, parties may assume that the hearing will be reconvened in the same place.[344]

---

[338] *Anheuser-Busch Inc. v. Carling O'Keefe Breweries of Canada Ltd.*, [1982] F.C.J. No. 191 (F.C.A.); *Howe v. Institute of Chartered Accountants*, [1994] O.J. No. 2907 (Ont. Gen. Div.), affd [1995] O.J. No. 2496 (Ont. C.A.); *Carleton Condominium Corp. No. 441 v. Ontario (New Home Warranty Program)*, [1996] O.J. No. 1345 (Ont. Div. Ct.); *contra: Curtis v. Manitoba (Securities Commission)*, [2006] M.J. No. 490 (Man. C.A.).

[339] *Phillips v. Nova Scotia (Commission of Inquiry into the Westray Mine Tragedy)*, [1995] S.C.J. No. 36; *Thomson v. Alberta (Transportation Safety Board)*, [2003] A.J. No. 1115 (Alta. C.A.), leave to appeal refused [2003] S.C.C.A. No. 510; *Seth v. Canada (Minister of Employment and Immigration)*, [1993] F.C.J. No. 540 (F.C.A.).

[340] *St. Margaret's Bayshore Inn Ltd. v. Nova Scotia (Attorney General)*, [1987] N.S.J. No. 452 (N.S.T.D.), affd [1988] N.S.J. No. 392 (N.S.C.A.).

[341] *Amourgis v. Law Society of Upper Canada*, [1984] O.J. No. 3345 (Ont. Div. Ct.).

[342] *Albarahmeh v. Canada (Minister of Citizenship and Immigration)*, [2010] F.C.J. No. 1437 (F.C.).

[343] *Mavour v. Canada (Minister of Employment and Immigration)*, [1984] F.C.J. No. 87 (F.C.A.).

[344] *MacAuley v. Penkala*, [1985] S.J. No. 727 (Sask. C.A.).

N. EFFECTIVE PARTICIPATION

1. Right of a Party to be Present throughout Hearing

If an oral hearing is held, a party is entitled to be present at all times while evidence and submissions are being presented to the tribunal. This is the best way to ensure full disclosure of the case to be met. Only by being present while all evidence is heard can a party be certain of having all of the information possessed by the tribunal. A tribunal should not hear evidence in the absence of a party whose conduct is impugned and under scrutiny.[345] It may not be sufficient to summarize matters that were discussed in a party's absence because of the possibility that something will be omitted.[346] However, if a party disrupts the proceeding, the party may, after being given a warning and an opportunity to behave appropriately, be expelled.[347]

An order excluding witnesses from the hearing room should not be applied to individual parties.[348] If the party is a corporation, so long as its counsel is present, its officers may be excluded while its employees testify. This does not exclude the corporate party who continues to be represented by its counsel.[349] A need to keep information confidential may be grounds for exclusion of a party.[350]

If there is no right to an oral hearing, the decision maker may gather and review documents and interview witnesses, without inviting the party to attend the interviews. The party's only right is to be shown the evidence and to file responding evidence and submissions.[351]

---

[345] *Kane v. University of British Columbia*, [1980] S.C.J. No. 32.

[346] *Couperthwaite v. Canada (National Parole Board)*, [1982] F.C.J. No. 99 (F.C.T.D.).

[347] *Gioris v. Ontario (Disability Support Program)*, [2002] O.J. No. 2416 (Ont. Div. Ct.).

[348] *Syndicat des salariés de béton St-Hubert-CSN c. Béton St-Hubert inc.*, [2010] J.Q. no 13493 (Que. C.A.); *Canadian Union of Public Employees, Local 2404 v. Grand Bay-Westfield (Town)*, [2006] N.B.J. No. 512 at para. 9 (N.B.C.A.); *Homelite v. Canada (Import Tribunal)*, [1987] F.C.J. No. 537 (F.C.T.D.); *Fooks v. Assn. of Architects*, [1982] A.J. No. 707 (Alta. Q.B.).

[349] *N.W. Construction (1993) Ltd. v. British Columbia (Workers' Compensation Board)*, [2004] B.C.J. No. 714 (B.C.C.A.).

[350] *Couperthwaite v. Canada (National Parole Board)*, [1982] F.C.J. No. 99, [1983] 1 F.C. 274 at 286 (F.C.T.D.); *Egglestone v. Ontario (Advisory Review Board)*, [1983] O.J. No. 3076 (Ont. Div. Ct.).

[351] *Pierre-Pierre v. Finlay*, [1991] R.J.Q. 1947 (C.S.).

In an investigation that will not result in a decision (except to commence proceedings) a party has no right to be present when witnesses are examined or at any other time during the investigation.[352]

2.   Right to be represented by Counsel or an Agent

The right to be represented by counsel before a tribunal is part of the right of a party to be present at an oral hearing. If there is a right to one, there may be a right to the other.[353] This right arises from the requirement that the tribunal afford a party an opportunity to present its case.[354] Adequate presentation may require the talents of a lawyer, particularly if the issues are complex or involve questions of law. Since it is difficult to assess, in advance, a party's ability to present a case adequately, an impression that the party has the ability should not be the sole ground for refusing a request to be represented by counsel.[355] Other factors to be considered include the nature of the proceeding, the extent of formality in the proceeding, the seriousness of its consequences for the party, the complexity of the issues, whether any questions of law are at issue, the party's experience with that type of proceeding and whether the proceeding affords subsequent opportunities to correct errors.[356]

Where s. 7 of the *Charter* applies, it does not create an absolute right to counsel unless some of the other factors also call for representation by counsel.[357] The right to counsel provided by s. 10(*b*) of the *Charter* applies

---

[352] *Irvine v. Canada (Restrictive Trade Practices Commission)*, [1987] S.C.J. No. 7; *North American Van Lines Canada Ltd. v. Canada (Director of Investigation and Research, Competition Act)*, [1997] F.C.J. No. 1314 (F.C.T.D.).

[353] In *Guay v. Lafleur*, [1964] S.C.J. No. 49, the S.C.C. treated these rights as equivalent.

[354] *Howard v. Stony Mountain Institution*, [1985] F.C.J. No. 56 (F.C.A.), leave to appeal refused [1987] S.C.J. No. 91.

[355] *Howard v. Stony Mountain Institution*, [1985] F.C.J. No. 56 (F.C.A.), leave to appeal refused [1987] S.C.J. No. 91.

[356] *Howard v. Stony Mountain Institution*, [1985] F.C.J. No. 56 (F.C.A.), leave to appeal refused [1987] S.C.J. No. 91; *Ha v. Canada (Minister of Citizenship and Immigration)*, [2004] F.C.J. No. 174 (F.C.A.); *Joplin v. Vancouver (City) Police Department*, [1985] B.C.J. No. 2311 (B.C.C.A.); *Engen v. Canada (Kingston Penitentiary)*, [1987] F.C.J. No. 641 (F.C.T.D.); *Re Parrish*, [1993] F.C.J. No. 22 (F.C.T.D.); *Ahvazi c. Concordia University*, [1992] J.Q. no 832 (Que. C.A.).

[357] *Christie v. British Columbia (Attorney General)*, [2007] S.C.J. No. 21; *Dehghani v. Canada (Minister of Employment and Immigration)*, [1993] S.C.J. No. 38; *Howard v. Stony Mountain Institution*, [1985] F.C.J. No. 56 (F.C.A.), leave to appeal refused [1987] S.C.J. No. 91. See also *Engen v. Canada (Kingston Penitentiary)*, [1987] F.C.J. No. 641 (F.C.T.D.); *MacInnis v. Canada (Attorney General)*, [1996] F.C.J. No. 1117 (F.C.A.).

only if the party is detained.[358] For some proceedings, the right to counsel is granted by statute or regulation.[359]

A right to counsel does not include a right to have counsel fees paid out of public funds unless a legal aid statute or the tribunal's enabling statute expressly so provide.[360]

Where there is a right to be represented by counsel, a tribunal should allow a party sufficient time to find available counsel.[361] However, the right to be represented by counsel of one's choice does not permit a party to delay the proceeding by selecting counsel who is not available on the dates fixed for hearing.[362] Likewise, the right to be represented by counsel does not permit a party to attend with an army of lawyers. A tribunal may restrict a party to representation by a single counsel.[363]

The tribunal is not obliged to inform a party of the right to be represented by counsel, unless required to do so by statute, regulation, or its own rules.[364] Where required, the tribunal should not inform the party in such a way as to influence the party to waive the right to counsel.[365] If a party for whom a proceeding may entail serious consequences decides to proceed without counsel, the tribunal should ensure that the party understands the seriousness of the proceeding and its potential outcome.[366]

---

[358] *Dehghani v. Canada (Minister of Employment and Immigration)*, [1993] S.C.J. No. 38.

[359] See generally: *Administrative Tribunals Act*, S.B.C. 2004, c. 45, s. 32; *Statutory Powers Procedure Act*, R.S.O. 1990, c. S.22, ss. 10 [as am.], 11 [as am.], 23(3); *Charte des droits et libertés de la personne*, R.S.Q. c. C-12, art. 34, and *Administrative Justice Act*, R.S.Q. c. J-3, ss. 102 [as am.], 103 [as am.].

[360] *Christie v. British Columbia (Attorney General)*, [2007] S.C.J. No. 21; *Winters v. Legal Services Society*, [1999] S.C.J. No. 49; *Berg v. British Columbia (Police Complaint Commissioner)*, [2006] B.C.J. No. 1027 at para. 73 (B.C.C.A.), leave to appeal refused [2006] S.C.C.A. No. 300; *Berg Estate v. British Columbia*, [2006] B.C.J. No. 616 (B.C.C.A.), leave to appeal refused [2006] S.C.C.A. No. 200; *Robertson v. Edmonton Police Service*, [2002] A.J. No. 1366 (Alta. Q.B.); *A.B. v. Canada (Minister of Citizenship and Immigration)*, [1997] F.C.J. No. 1528 (F.C.T.D.).

[361] *McCarthy v. Canada (Minister of Employment and Immigration)*, [1978] F.C.J. No. 84 (F.C.A.); *Sewjattan v. Canada (Minister of Employment and Immigration)*, [1979] F.C.J. No. 34 (F.C.A.); *Halm v. Canada (Minister of Employment and Immigration)*, [1995] F.C.J. No. 303 (F.C.T.D.).

[362] *Pierre v. Canada (Minister of Manpower and Immigration)*, [1978] F.C.J. No. 70 (F.C.A.); *Ruiz v. Canada (Minister of Citizenship and Immigration)*, [2008] F.C.J. No. 1131 (F.C.).

[363] *Re Parrish*, [1993] F.C.J. No. 22 (F.C.T.D.).

[364] *Morgan v. Canada (National Parole Board)*, [1982] F.C.J. No. 47 (F.C.A.); *Jekula v. Canada (Minister of Citizenship and Immigration)*, [1998] F.C.J. No. 1503 (F.C.T.D.).

[365] *Swan v. Canada (Minister of Manpower and Immigration)*, [1975] F.C.J. No. 809 (F.C.A.).

[366] *Dakota Ojibway Tribe v. Bewza*, [1985] M.J. No. 172 at para. 16 (Man. C.A.), leave to appeal refused [1986] S.C.C.A. No. 194.

A party who expressly chooses to proceed without counsel may not later have the decision quashed for lack of representation.[367] A tribunal should assist an unrepresented party by explaining the process and the tests to be applied to the issues and may encourage the party to focus on the important issues, but should not advise the party on tactical questions such as which witnesses to call.[368] A tribunal may also be expected to alert an unrepresented party to a procedural option, such as a right to request an adjournment, if this option appears to be necessary to ensure that they receive a fair hearing in the circumstances.[369]

A party may not complain if counsel chosen by the party failed to present the case competently.[370] In these situations the tribunal is not at fault. The tribunal is not obliged to ensure competent representation.[371]

A tribunal may use its power to prevent abuse of its processes to preclude a lawyer from representing parties whose interests may conflict.[372] However, it appears that this power may not be used to exclude a lawyer who misbehaves. The tribunal may only state a case to the court for contempt and complain to the Law Society.[373]

The power to prevent abuse of process may be used to exclude agents who are not lawyers. Counsel before tribunals need not be lawyers (subject to legislation governing the practice of law). An agent may act,[374] but a tribunal may limit participation to those agents who will facilitate, rather than hinder, the adjudicative process.[375] The tribunal may exclude an agent if it is concerned that the agent will not act with honesty and integrity,[376] if the

---

[367]   *College of Optometrists of Ontario v. SHS Optical Ltd.*, [2008] O.J. No. 3933 (Ont. C.A.), leave to appeal refused [2008] S.C.C.A. No. 506.

[368]   *Kelly v. Nova Scotia (Police Commission)*, [2006] N.S.J. No. 78 (N.S.C.A.); *Kamtasingh v. Canada (Minister of Citizenship and Immigration)*, [2010] F.C.J. No. 45 (F.C.).

[369]   *Audmax Inc. v. Ontario (Human Rights Tribunal)*, [2011] O.J. No. 210 (Ont. Div. Ct.).

[370]   *Man Yee So. v. Canada (Minister of Employment and Immigration)*, [1979] F.C.J. No. 174 (F.C.A.); *Ursulescu v. Chomicki*, [1995] S.J. No. 656 (Sask. Q.B.).

[371]   *Cyrus v. Canada (Minister of National Health and Welfare)*, [1992] F.C.J. No. 471 (F.C.A.), leave to appeal refused [1992] S.C.C.A. No. 399. More recently judicial review has been granted because of a lawyer's incompetence: *Memari v. Canada (Minister of Citizenship and Immigration)*, [2010] F.C.J. No. 1493 (F.C.); and an agent's incompetence: *Rodrigues v. Canada (Minister of Citizenship and Immigration)*, [2008] F.C.J. No. 108 (F.C.).

[372]   *Booth v. Hunter*, [1994] O.J. No. 52 (Ont. Div. Ct.); *Universal Workers' Union, Labourers' International Union of North America, Local 183 v. Ontario (Labour Relations Board)*, [2007] O.J. No. 1048 (Ont. Div. Ct.).

[373]   *Sternberg v. Ontario (Racing Commission)*, [2008] O.J. No. 3864 (Ont. Div. Ct.).

[374]   *Law Society of British Columbia v. Mangat*, [2001] S.C.J. No. 66; *Thomas v. Assn. of New Brunswick Registered Nursing Assistants*, [2003] N.B.J. No. 327 (N.B.C.A.).

[375]   *Thomas v. Assn. of New Brunswick Registered Nursing Assistants*, [2003] N.B.J. No. 327 (N.B.C.A.).

[376]   *Royal & SunAlliance Insurance Co. of Canada v. Volfson*, [2005] O.J. No. 4523 (Ont. Div. Ct.); *Codina v. Law Society of Upper Canada*, [1996] O.J. No. 3348 (Ont. Div. Ct.); *Ontario Securities Commission v. Robinson*, [2009] O.J. No. 5632 (Ont. S.C.J.).

issues are so complex that participation of the agent will cause confusion, or if there is a need to ensure confidentiality of information.[377] A tribunal may permanently bar an agent from representing any party where necessary to preserve the integrity of its proceedings.[378] An agent may not be excluded solely because the tribunal is overwhelmed by the great number of applications filed on behalf of many clients, for which the agent is to be paid on a contingency fee basis if successful, provided the agent satisfies the tribunal that each client has authorized the application filed on its behalf.[379]

Some tribunals prefer to exclude lawyers, but to permit parties to be represented by agents, where statute permits them to do so.[380] Some believe that, without lawyers, the tribunal and parties may focus on the merits of the case and avoid being diverted by arguments on questions of law, procedure and evidence. However, because corporations and unions may appear only by agent, a tribunal may not restrict such party's choice of agent to non-lawyers. It follows that individuals' choice of representative may not be restricted.[381]

Sometimes the choice of representative of an employee or union member facing discipline may be restricted to another employee or member, who may be a lawyer, but not an outsider. This is acceptable if it permits the party to present the case adequately.[382] In New Brunswick a union may not preclude a member facing discipline from being represented by a lawyer[383] but, in non-disciplinary matters, representation may be restricted to union members.[384]

Persons under investigation and witnesses may be represented by counsel when they are questioned, but their counsel may not be present when other witnesses are questioned. Their counsel may put questions to them to clarify and explain the evidence given but may not cross-examine them.[385] An employer's counsel may be excluded when employees are

---

[377] *Thomas v. Assn. of New Brunswick Registered Nursing Assistants*, [2003] N.B.J. No. 327 (N.B.C.A.)

[378] *Rezaei v. Canada (Minister of Citizenship and Immigration)*, [2002] F.C.J. No. 1721 (F.C.T.D.).

[379] *van Beek and Associates v. Ontario (Regional Assessment Commissioner, Region No. 14)*, [1994] O.J. No. 394 (Ont. Div. Ct.).

[380] But the *Statutory Powers Procedure Act*, R.S.O. 1990, c. S.22, s. 23(3), permits a tribunal to exclude unlicensed agents, but does not permit the exclusion of lawyers or licensed agents.

[381] *Ontario Men's Clothing Manufacturers Assn. v. Arthurs*, [1979] O.J. No. 4359 (Ont. Div. Ct.), leave to appeal refused [1979] O.J. No. 2008 (Ont. C.A.). The N.B.C.A. questions whether this case might be decided differently today: *Thomas v. Assn. of New Brunswick Registered Nursing Assistants*, [2003] N.B.J. No. 327 (N.B.C.A.). See also: *Christie v. British Columbia (Attorney General)*, [2007] S.C.J. No. 21.

[382] *Laroche v. Beirsdorfer*, [1981] F.C.J. No. 1108 at paras. 39-41 (B.C.C.A.).

[383] *Wark v. Green*, [1985] N.B.J. No. 300 (N.B.C.A.).

[384] *Thomas v. Assn. of New Brunswick Registered Nursing Assistants*, [2003] N.B.J. No. 327 (N.B.C.A.).

[385] *Irvine v. Canada (Restrictive Trade Practices Commission)*, [1987] S.C.J. No. 7.

questioned.[386] There is no right to have an agent present when questioned in an investigation.[387]

A tribunal should give reasons for denying a request to be represented by counsel, so that the party and a court reviewing the matter may determine whether the exclusion of counsel was justified.[388]

3.   Right to an Interpreter

The right to be present at proceedings is of little use if a party is unable to understand what is said. Section 14 of the *Canadian Charter of Rights and Freedoms* provides:

> A party or witness in any proceedings who does not understand or speak the language in which the proceedings are conducted or who is deaf has the right to the assistance of an interpreter.

Section 2(*g*) of the *Canadian Bill of Rights* provides a similar right. It is not clear who is to pay for an interpreter under these provisions. Generally, where a party bears the cost of participating in a proceeding, that cost includes the cost of interpretation if required.[389]

A party who requires an interpreter should make this need known as early as possible in the proceeding.[390] The party should not wait to learn the outcome and, if adverse, complain that he or she did not understand what took place at the hearing. Failure to object promptly constitutes waiver of the right to translation.[391]

The right to an interpreter arises only when the party "does not understand or speak the language in which the proceedings are conducted". If an opposing party submits that the requestor can understand the language in which the proceedings are conducted, the tribunal may permit cross-examination of the requestor to ascertain the latter's facility in the language.[392] Mere comprehension of the words of a language is different from the full ability to express oneself so as to advance a persuasive case and may not be sufficient. Evidence as to a person's facility with a language includes the

---

[386]   *Royal Bank of Canada v. Bhagwat*, [2009] F.C.J. No. 1465 (F.C.).

[387]   *Ontario Securities Commission v. Robinson*, [2009] O.J. No. 4515 (Ont. S.C.J.).

[388]   *Howard v. Stony Mountain Institution*, [1985] F.C.J. No. 56 (F.C.A.), leave to appeal refused [1987] S.C.J. No. 91.

[389]   *Lapointe v. Canada (Treasury Board)*, [2004] F.C.J. No. 283 at para. 44 (F.C.).

[390]   *Taire v. Canada (Minister of Citizenship and Immigration)*, [2003] F.C.J. No. 1128 (F.C.).

[391]   *Diallo v. Canada (Minister of Citizenship and Immigration)*, [2004] F.C.J. No. 1756 (F.C.).

[392]   *Roy v. Hackett*, [1987] O.J. No. 933 (Ont. C.A.).

extent to which they make errors of spelling and grammar.[393] When in doubt, a tribunal should err on the side of permitting interpretation. A tribunal should assume that a request for an interpreter is made in good faith and is not made to delay the proceedings or to frustrate cross-examination.

A party who does not understand the notice of hearing bears the onus of seeking assistance to find out what it is about.[394] A blind party may be entitled to notice in braille or an audio-recording.[395]

The Immigration Regulations expressly require an adjudicator to determine at the outset, whether the party is able to understand and communicate in the language in which the proceeding is conducted. If an interpreter is required, the inquiry must be adjourned until one is provided, at no cost to the party, even when no interpreter can be found because the party speaks an uncommon language.[396]

An interpreter must interpret *verbatim* everything that is said throughout the proceedings. Nothing may be summarized.[397] The interpretation must be continuous, precise, competent, impartial and contemporaneous but need not be perfect. Complaints about the adequacy of interpretation must be made at the first opportunity. A party may not wait to see if the decision is adverse before complaining.[398]

Most people in Canada have some facility in one of Canada's official languages and may find it easier to express some matters in that language rather than their own. For this reason, a tribunal may not require the person to speak exclusively through the translator.[399]

The right to an interpreter does not include the right to have documentary evidence translated, provided the documents are in one of Canada's official languages. It is for the party's counsel to review the documents, to assess their impact and evidentiary force and to discuss them with the client. If any passage in a document is quoted during the hearing, the translator should translate that passage.[400]

---

[393] *Beaudoin v. Canada (Minister of National Health and Welfare)*, [1993] F.C.J. No. 505 (F.C.A.).

[394] *Quebec (Commission de contrôle des permis d'alcool) v. Muro*, [1976] C.A. 297 (Que. C.A.).

[395] *Matthews v. Board of Directors of Physiotherapy*, [1990] O.J. No. 1167 (Ont. Div. Ct.).

[396] *Faiva v. Canada (Minister of Employment and Immigration)*, [1983] F.C.J. No. 41 (F.C.A.).

[397] *Weber v. Canada (Minister of Manpower and Immigration)*, [1976] F.C.J. No. 194 (F.C.A.).

[398] *Mohammadian v. Canada (Minister of Citizenship and Immigration)*, [2001] F.C.J. No. 916 (F.C.A.), leave to appeal refused [2001] S.C.C.A. No. 435.

[399] *Chapagain v. Canada (Minister of Citizenship and Immigration)*, [2010] F.C.J. No. 1104 (F.C.).

[400] *Szczecka v. Canada (Minister of Employment and Immigration)*, [1993] F.C.J. No. 934 (F.C.A.).

Unless expressly required by statute,[401] the tribunal may choose to conduct its proceeding in either English or French and cannot be required to hold the hearing in the other official language. The right of a party is to an interpreter, not to dictate the language of the proceeding.[402] The right to an interpreter is also available to a party's counsel who speaks the other official language[403] but a party would be better represented by hiring counsel who understands and can speak persuasively in the language in which the proceeding is conducted.

4.   Right of a Party to Discontinue the Proceedings

A person who initiated a proceeding by filing a complaint or an application, may not have a unilateral right to cause the proceeding to end before it has run its course. The premature termination of a proceeding may be within the discretion of a tribunal. The primary consideration is whether it would be in the public interest to continue the proceeding. In addition, other parties may have a right to have the issues determined.[404] A party, whose request to end the proceeding is refused, may choose not to participate any further.[405]

However, where the sole authority of the tribunal is to decide the complaint or application, the withdrawal of the complaint or application removes that authority.[406] Where the complainant has the onus of proving the complaint, the refusal of the complainant to do so may effectively end the proceeding.[407] Similarly, death of the complainant may preclude proof of the complaint.[408] A commission that referred a complaint to a hearing, after screening it, may have authority to withdraw the complaint and stop

---

[401] *Landry v. Law Society of Upper Canada*, [2010] O.J. No. 2696 (Ont. Div. Ct.). All federal tribunals are required to hold hearings in the official language of Canada chosen by the party: *Beaudoin v. Canada (Minister of National Health and Welfare)*, [1993] F.C.J. No. 505 (F.C.A.).

[402] *Northwest Child and Family Services Agency v. L. (E.)*, [1992] M.J. No. 8 (Man. Q.B.).

[403] *Canadian Javelin Ltd. v. Canada (Restrictive Trade Practices Commission)*, [1980] F.C.J. No. 237 (F.C.).

[404] *Palacios c. Comité de déontologie policière*, [2007] J.Q. no 3630 (Que. C.A.); *Carfrae Estates Ltd. v. Stavert*, [1976] O.J. No. 2244 (Ont. Div. Ct.); *McIntosh v. College of Physicians and Surgeons*, [1998] O.J. No. 5222 (Ont. Div. Ct.). Except in B.C., *Administrative Tribunals Act*, S.B.C. 2004, c. 45, s. 17(1).

[405] *McKenzie Forest Products Inc. v. Ontario (Human Rights Commission)*, [2000] O.J. No. 1318 (Ont. C.A.), leave to appeal refused [2000] S.C.C.A. No. 285.

[406] *McKeown v. Royal Bank of Canada*, [2001] F.C.J. No. 231 (F.C.T.D.); *St. Basil's Parish Centre Bingo v. Saskatchewan Liquor and Gaming Authority*, [1994] S.J. No. 445 (Sask. Q.B.).

[407] *Aylward v. McMaster University*, [1991] O.J. No. 230 (Ont. Div. Ct.).

[408] *Kellogg Brown and Root Canada v. Alberta (Information and Privacy Commissioner)*, [2008] A.J. No. 1252 (Alta. C.A.).

the hearing as part of its authority to decide whether a hearing of the complaint would be in the public interest.[409]

5.   Minors and Incapable Adults

With the exception of immigration, minors are rarely involved in adminis-trative law matters. If a minor's interests may be affected, the minor should be represented by a parent or guardian or it may be prudent to notify the official guardian of the matter. In immigration matters a minor must be represented by a parent or legal guardian.[410] This requirement is not waived where the minor is represented by counsel.[411]

A tribunal does not have authority to determine whether an adult party has mental capacity.[412] Capacity should be presumed unless lack of capacity has been determined by the appropriate authority. If a party has been found to be mentally incapable, a tribunal should ensure that the party is repre-sented[413] by a competent representative.[414] Notice of the proceeding should be given to a person authorized to act on behalf of the mentally incapable person or to the official guardian.[415]

O.   HEARING IN PUBLIC

It is a basic principle that all hearings should be held in public. The public has an interest in seeing that proceedings are properly conducted and that parties are treated fairly. Public hearings are a safeguard against covert dealing beyond the scrutiny of the public or the press. In the absence of express statutory authority to exclude the public, they must be admitted.[416] A blanket statutory prohibition on public proceedings may violate the *Charter* right to freedom of the press.[417] A tribunal that has discretion

---

[409] *British Columbia (Police Complaint Commissioner) v. Vancouver (City) Police Department*, [2003] B.C.J. No. 399 (B.C.S.C.); *contra: Canadian Museum of Civilization Corp. v. Public Service Alliance of Canada, Local 70396*, [2006] F.C.J. No. 884 (F.C.).

[410] *Azdo v. Canada (Minister of Employment and Immigration)*, [1980] F.C.J. No. 72 (F.C.A.).

[411] *Kissoon v. Canada (Minister of Employment and Immigration)*, [1978] F.C.J. No. 130 (F.C.A.).

[412] *Blass v. University of Regina Faculty Assn.*, [2007] S.J. No. 649 (Sask. Q.B.).

[413] *Blanchard v. Millhaven Institution*, [1982] F.C.J. No. 136 (F.C.T.D.).

[414] *Black v. Canada (Minister of Citizenship and Immigration)*, [2009] F.C.J. No. 872 (F.C.).

[415] *L.L.B. (Guardian ad litem of) v. Canadian Union of Public Employees*, [1999] N.J. No. 341 (Nfld. T.D.); *Da Costa v. Canada (Minister of Citizenship and Immigration)*, [1997] F.C.J. No. 1262 (F.C.T.D.).

[416] *Vancouver (City) v. British Columbia (Assessment Appeal Board)*, [1996] B.C.J. No. 1062 (B.C.C.A.).

[417] *Canadian Broadcasting Corp. v. Summerside (City)*, [1999] P.E.I.J. No. 3 (P.E.I.S.C.); *Southam Inc. v. Canada (Attorney General)*, [1997] O.J. No. 4533 (Ont. Gen. Div.).

should exercise it in favour of public hearings unless there is good reason to exclude the public.[418] The onus is always on the person requesting privacy who must establish the claim with evidence of the harm that could result from permitting the public to attend. The onus is not on the person requesting that the hearing be open to the public.[419]

A hearing should be held in a facility that is open to the public. If it is necessary to hold the hearing in a secure facility because a party is in detention, the tribunal should ensure that members of the public wishing to attend the hearing have appropriate access to the proceeding.[420]

A tribunal that has authority to exclude the public should endeavour to minimize the scope of the exclusion. Confidentiality concerns rarely require that the public be excluded from the entire hearing. One option is to exclude public access only to specific confidential exhibits and testimony while permitting public access to the remainder of the hearing. Another is to hold the hearing in public, but prohibit the press from publishing specified information. A tribunal may have power to issue a publication ban as part of its inherent power to control its proceedings.[421] The most common purposes are to protect national security or to protect an important privacy interest of a non-party witness. These factors should be weighed against the important interest of the public in seeing how tribunals exercise their powers.[422]

It may be appropriate to exclude the public from a hearing or to order a publication ban to protect the right to a fair trial of a witness who faces criminal charges that are to be tried before a jury, and that relate to the same matter on which the witness is required to testify, especially where a publication ban has been ordered at the witness' preliminary inquiry. This is to ensure that the jury is not influenced by pre-trial publicity. The party

---

[418]   *R. v. Tarnopolsky; Ex parte Bell*, [1969] O.J. No. 1603 at para. 16 (Ont. C.A.), revd on other grounds [1971] S.C.J. No. 66; *Ottawa (City) Commissioners of Police v. Lalande*, [1986] O.J. No. 1382 (Ont. Dist. Ct.); *Southam Inc. v. Canada (Minister of Employment and Immigration)*, [1987] F.C.J. No. 658 (F.C.T.D.).

[419]   *Phillips v. Nova Scotia (Commission of Inquiry into the Westray Mine Tragedy)*, [1995] S.C.J. No. 36; *Pacific Press Ltd. v. Canada (Minister of Employment and Immigration)*, [1991] F.C.J. No. 313 (F.C.A.); *Blackwood v. Canada (Minister of Employment and Immigration)*, [1991] F.C.J. No. 407 (F.C.T.D.).

[420]   *Gervasoni v. Canada (Minister of Citizenship and Immigration)*, [1995] F.C.J. No. 979 (F.C.T.D.).

[421]   *Phillips v. Nova Scotia (Commission of Inquiry into the Westray Mine Tragedy)*, [1995] S.C.J. No. 36; *contra: Canadian Newspapers Co. v. Law Society of Upper Canada*, [1986] O.J. No. 1304 (Ont. Div. Ct.).

[422]   *Re Suazo*, [1996] A.Q. no 3893, 142 D.L.R. (4th) 313 (Que. C.A.), leave to appeal refused [1997] C.S.C.R. no 64; *Fraternité Inter-Provinciale des Ouvriers en Électricité v. Quebec (Office de la Construction)*, [1983] J.Q. no 394, 148 D.L.R. (3d) 626 at 634, 642 (Que. C.A.); *Ottawa (City) Commissioners of Police v. Lalande*, [1986] O.J. No. 1382 (Ont. Dist. Ct.); *Petro-Canada Inc. v. Nova Scotia (Public Utilities Board)*, [1987] N.S.J. No. 114 (N.S.T.D.); *A.B. v. Investment Dealers Association of Canada*, [2007] B.C.J. No. 1007 (B.C.S.C.).

requesting the exclusion of the public must show that the effect of publicizing the evidence will be to leave potential jurors irreparably prejudiced, or so impair the presumption of innocence that a fair trial is impossible. There must be proof of the link between publicity and its adverse effect. Where the trial will be before a judge alone, there is no need to exclude the public from the tribunal hearing because judges are able to disregard pre-trial publicity.[423] If the criminal proceeding is concluded, a publication ban is unnecessary.[424]

A fear that another tribunal may take discipline proceedings against the witness, if they learn of the witness' evidence through publicity, is not grounds for the public to be excluded.[425]

The issuance of a confidentiality order protects the information from public disclosure but does not seal it against compelled disclosure pursuant to subpoena or search warrant issued by another authority.[426]

Section 41 of the B.C. *ATA* and s. 9(1) of the Ontario *SPPA* require that a hearing be open to the public, unless the desirability of avoiding disclosure outweighs the purposes of open hearings. Section 42 of the B.C. *ATA* permits the tribunal to receive evidence in confidence to the exclusion of a party. Article 23 of the Quebec *Charte des droits et libertés de la personne* guarantees to every person, the right to a public hearing before every quasi-judicial tribunal. Section 10 of the Quebec *AJA* requires hearings to be held in public but permits the tribunal to hold them *in camera* where necessary to maintain public order. Section 131 provides for publication bans and s. 130 admits journalists to *in camera* hearings (unless the journalist's presence is prejudicial to a party) but prohibits the journalists from identifying the party.

A statutory requirement that hearings be open to the public does not require tribunals to give advance notice of their hearings to the press[427] but a tribunal may choose to extend this courtesy to the press.

An investigation need not be conducted in public,[428] but the extent to which witnesses and their counsel may be restricted from disclosing what they know about the investigation is under debate.[429]

---

[423] *Phillips v. Nova Scotia (Commission of Inquiry into the Westray Mine Tragedy)*, [1995] S.C.J. No. 36; *Southam Inc. v. LaFrance*, [1990] A.Q. no 498 (Que. C.A.).

[424] *Episcopal Corp. of the Diocese of Alexandria-Cornwall v. Ontario (Cornwall Public Inquiry, Commissioner)*, [2007] O.J. No. 100 (Ont. C.A.).

[425] *C.D. v. Canada (Minister of National Revenue)*, [1991] F.C.J. No. 227 (F.C.A.).

[426] *AGT Ltd. v. Canada (Attorney General)*, [1997] F.C.J. No. 398 (F.C.A.), leave to appeal refused [1997] S.C.C.A. No. 314.

[427] *Canadian Newspapers Co. v. Law Society of Upper Canada*, [1986] O.J. No. 1304 (Ont. Div. Ct.).

P.   EVIDENCE

Adjudicative decisions concern fact situations within the tribunal mandate. A decision cannot be made in the absence of facts. A tribunal must find the facts and these findings must be based on evidence. The requirement for evidence promotes accurate fact finding. A party is more willing to accept an adverse decision if it is factually sound. A tribunal need not accept counsel's assertions as to facts and may require proof.[430]

Unless expressly prescribed, court rules of evidence do not apply to proceedings before an administrative tribunal.[431] This reflects the public interest mandate of many tribunals and the fact that tribunal members, being lay people, are not schooled in the rules of evidence and are expected to apply common sense to their consideration of evidence.

However, the tribunal should maintain control over the admission of evidence. Not all facts are of equal importance. There may be several important facts on which the decision turns. Other facts may provide context or contribute to a deeper understanding. Not all evidence is equally probative and reliable. Essentially, there are two questions that should be asked. First, what evidence should be admitted and considered in the fact-finding process? Second, how reliable is it? The purpose of the first question is to keep the hearing focused on the matters to be decided, while the purpose of the second question is to improve accuracy in fact finding.

The basic criterion for the admissibility of evidence is relevance.[432] Relevant evidence is admissible; irrelevant evidence is inadmissible. Relevance is determined by the purpose and subject matter of the proceeding described in the notice of hearing or written allegations. Evidence relevant to those matters is admissible. A decision may be quashed if a failure to admit relevant evidence affected a party's right to a fair hearing.[433] Not all relevant evidence is, however, of equal probative value. Some facts are more important than others. As the most important evidence is that which

---

[428] *Dragun v. Law Society of Manitoba*, [1998] M.J. No. 75 (Man. C.A.); *Midgley v. Law Society of Alberta*, [1980] A.J. No. 608 (Alta. Q.B.); *Gordon v. Canada (Minister of National Defence)*, [2005] F.C.J. No. 409 (F.C.).

[429] *Shapray v. British Columbia (Securities Commission)*, [2009] B.C.J. No. 1358 (B.C.C.A.).

[430] *Forbes v. Canada (Minister of Employment and Immigration)*, [1984] F.C.J. No. 408 (F.C.A.).

[431] *Toronto (City) v. Canadian Union of Public Employees, Local 79*, [1982] O.J. No. 222 (Ont. C.A.); *Canadian Recording Industry Assn. v. Society of Composers, Authors and Music Publishers of Canada*, [2010] F.C.J. No. 1533 (F.C.A.); *Administrative Procedures and Jurisdiction Act*, R.S.A. 2000, c. A-3, s. 9 [as am.].

[432] See generally *Administrative Tribunals Act*, S.B.C. 2004, c. 45, s. 40; *Statutory Powers Procedure Act*, R.S.O. 1990, c. S.22, s. 15; *Administrative Justice Act*, R.S.Q. c. J-3, s. 139.

[433] *Université du Quebec à Trois-Rivières v. Larocque*, [1993] S.C.J. No. 23.

concerns the key facts on which the decision will turn, the key factual issues should be identified so as to avoid straying too far from the central purpose of the inquiry.[434] When in doubt as to relevance, evidence may be admitted, leaving its probative value to be decided later.[435]

Relevant hearsay should be admitted but, as it cannot be challenged by cross-examination, it may be given less weight than direct evidence.[436] Even in those proceedings where the rules of evidence apply, hearsay is admissible if it is necessary to the determination of the issues in the proceeding and it is reliable.[437] A tribunal may accept unchallengeable hearsay evidence over direct evidence provided it explains why it did so.[438] The credibility of hearsay from the Internet may turn on the reliability of the website host.[439]

When faced with contradictory or implausible evidence, a tribunal may have to assess the credibility of witnesses and documents to make findings of fact. Factors that may be considered in assessing credibility include witnesses' appearance, demeanour and manner when testifying, their ability to observe and describe the events about which they are testifying, a motivation to fabricate their evidence, partiality towards one of the parties and inconsistencies in their evidence and between their evidence and earlier statements.[440] Evidence as to the bad character of a party is not probative of credibility.[441] Evidence of a witness who refuses to be cross-examined is admissible but may be given less weight.[442] Polygraph evidence should not be admitted.[443] Fairness requires that, if

---

[434] *Ontario (Provincial Police) v. Cornwall (Public Inquiry)*, [2008] O.J. No. 153 at para. 61 (Ont. C.A.).

[435] *Kelly v. Nova Scotia (Police Commission)*, [2006] N.S.J. No. 78 at para. 36 (N.S.C.A.).

[436] *Cambie Hotel (Nanaimo) Ltd. v. British Columbia (Liquor Control and Licensing Branch, General Manager)*, [2006] B.C.J. No. 501 (B.C.C.A.); *Pitts v. Ontario (Ministry of Community and Social Services, Director of Family Benefits Branch)*, [1985] O.J. No. 2578 (Ont. Div. Ct.); *Canada (Attorney General) v. Mills*, [1984] F.C.J. No. 917 (F.C.A.); *Canada (Attorney General) v. Basra*, [2010] F.C.J. No. 76 (F.C.A.).

[437] *Khan v. College of Physicians and Surgeons*, [1992] O.J. No. 1725 (Ont. C.A.).

[438] *Siad v. Canada (Secretary of State)*, [1996] F.C.J. No. 1575 (F.C.A.), leave to appeal refused [1997] S.C.C.A. No. 47; *Pitts v. Ontario (Ministry of Community and Social Services, Director of Family Benefits Branch)*, [1985] O.J. No. 2578 (Ont. Div. Ct.); *International Brotherhood of Electrical Workers, Local 435 v. Manitoba Telecom Services Inc.*, [2002] M.J. No. 472 (Man. Q.B.).

[439] *Jahazi v. Canada (Minister of Citizenship and Immigration)*, [2010] F.C.J. No. 271 at paras. 59-61 (F.C.).

[440] *College of Nurses v. Quiogue*, [1993] O.J. No. 1121 (Ont. Div. Ct.).

[441] *Saint John (City) v. New Brunswick (Workplace Health, Safety and Compensation Commission)*, [2008] N.B.J. No. 440 (N.B.C.A.).

[442] *Wuziuk v. Manitoba (Director of Social Services)*, [1980] M.J. No. 79 at para. 36 (Man. C.A.).

[443] *Re Stonechild* (2003), 7 Admin. L.R. (4th) 284 (Commr. of Inquiry).

a witness' evidence is rejected as not credible, the reasons for disbelief should be given,[444] unless the evidence is inherently improbable.[445]

A certificate that a person has been convicted of a criminal offence, if relevant, is admissible as conclusive proof that the person did the acts for which the conviction was entered. The facts may not be re-litigated before the tribunal.[446] However, an acquittal or stay of the criminal proceeding is not proof that the person did not commit the alleged acts and the factual allegations may be re-litigated in the tribunal proceeding.[447] Findings of fact supporting the acquittal are admissible but are not binding on the tribunal[448] because of the different standards of proof and different rules on admissibility of evidence as between the criminal proceeding and the administrative proceeding.

A transcript of the testimony of a person given in any prior proceeding is admissible against that person in a subsequent tribunal hearing, unless the witness, when testifying, claimed the protections of the provincial Evidence Act and that Act applies to the proceedings in which the testimony is tendered in evidence. Neither s. 13 of the *Charter* nor s. 5 of the *Canada Evidence Act*[449] applies because they preclude only the subsequent use of testimony to incriminate the witness, *i.e.*, to prove their guilt in a criminal proceeding. They do not prevent the use of testimony against the witness in tribunal proceedings.[450] In a re-hearing of a matter after a court has quashed the tribunal decision, the transcript of the first hearing is admissible unless the court quashed findings of credibility.[451]

A tribunal may admit evidence that would not be admitted in a criminal proceeding having been obtained in violation of the *Charter*, if it

---

[444] *Law Society of Upper Canada v. Neinstein*, [2010] O.J. No. 1046 (Ont. C.A.); *Pitts v. Ontario (Ministry of Community and Social Services, Director of Family Benefits Branch)*, [1985] O.J. No. 2578 (Ont. Div. Ct.); *Maldonado v. Canada (Minister of Employment and Immigration)*, [1979] F.C.J. No. 248 (F.C.A.).

[445] *McDonald v. Canada (Employment and Immigration Commission)*, [1991] F.C.J. No. 533 (F.C.A.).

[446] *Toronto (City) v. Canadian Union of Public Employees, Local 79*, [2003] S.C.J. No. 64.

[447] *Haché v. Lunenburg County District School Board*, [2004] N.S.J. No. 120 (N.S.C.A.); *Bennett v. British Columbia (Securities Commission)*, [1992] B.C.J. No. 1655 (B.C.C.A.), leave to appeal refused [1992] 6 W.W.R. lvii; *Amalgamated Transit Union, Local 279 v. Ottawa (City)*, [2007] O.J. No. 3780 (Ont. Div. Ct.).

[448] *Bennett v. British Columbia (Securities Commission)*, [1992] B.C.J. No. 1655 (B.C.C.A.), leave to appeal refused [1992] 6 W.W.R. lvii.

[449] R.S.C. 1985, c. C-5, s. 5 [as am.].

[450] *Knutson v. Saskatchewan Registered Nurses Assn.*, [1990] S.J. No. 603 (Sask. C.A.); except in Ontario where consent of the party is required before transcripts from another proceeding may be admitted in evidence: *Statutory Powers Procedure Act*, R.S.O. 1990, c. S.22, s. 15.1 [as am.].

[451] *Taire v. Canada (Minister of Citizenship and Immigration)*, [2003] F.C.J. No. 1128 (F.C.); *Badal v. Canada (Minister of Citizenship and Immigration)*, [2003] F.C.J. No. 440 (F.C.T.D.).

is satisfied that the information is reliable and persuasive.[452] A confession that has been ruled inadmissible in criminal proceedings may be admitted in tribunal proceedings,[453] because the reason for inadmissibility is often a violation of the right to remain silent, which does not apply in administrative proceedings.[454] The circumstances in which the confession was made may affect the weight accorded it. A confessor who is available to testify may be cross-examined to test the credibility of the confession.[455] However, a tribunal may refuse to admit illegally obtained evidence if its use would tend to bring the administration of justice into disrepute and if it is not of a nature likely to further the interests of justice.[456] A prior interview of a party by the regulator's investigator is admissible.[457]

A tribunal that is called on to interpret a contract may admit evidence considered helpful to the task. The parol evidence rule, which restricts the admissibility of extrinsic evidence to aid in the interpretation of contracts, is not applicable in administrative proceedings.[458]

Relevant expert evidence is admissible. Any frailties in the facts or hypotheses upon which an opinion is based, or in the qualifications of the expert, affect the weight of the evidence but not its admissibility,[459] but an opinion of an expert who is biased and not objective may be rejected.[460] The facts upon which an opinion is based should be revealed so that the validity of the opinion may be tested. A tribunal may use its own expertise to assess whether to accept or reject the opinion.[461] If appropriate, the opinions of lay people may also be admitted.[462] Any lack of qualifications goes to the weight to be accorded the opinions and not to its admis-

---

[452] *Mooring v. Canada (National Parole Board)*, [1996] S.C.J. No. 10; *Thomson v. Alberta (Transportation and Safety Board)*, [2003] A.J. No. 1115 (Alta. C.A.), leave to appeal refused [2003] S.C.C.A. No. 510.

[453] *Greater Niagara Transit Commission v. Amalgamated Transit Union, Local 1582*, [1987] O.J. No. 835 (Ont. Div. Ct.).

[454] *P. (D.) v. Wagg*, [2004] O.J. No. 2053 (Ont. C.A.).

[455] *United Glass and Ceramic Workers of North America v. Pilkington Brothers (Canada) Ltd.*, [1978] O.J. No. 3533 (Ont. Div. Ct.).

[456] *Houle v. Mascouche (Ville)*, [1999] J.Q. no 2652, 179 D.L.R. (4th) 90 (Que. C.A.).

[457] *Alberta (Securities Commission) v. Brost*, [2008] A.J. No. 1071 (Alta. C.A.); *Scott v. Ontario (Racing Commission)*, [2009] O.J. No. 2858 (Ont. Div. Ct.); *Ontario (Racing Commission) v. Hudon*, [2008] O.J. No. 5313 (Ont. Div. Ct.).

[458] *United Brotherhood of Carpenters and Joiners of America, Local 579 v. Bradco Construction Ltd.*, [1993] S.C.J. No. 56.

[459] *Alberta (Workers' Compensation Board) v. Alberta (Appeals Commission)*, [2005] A.J. No. 1012 at paras. 62-68 (Alta. C.A.); *Canadian Recording Industry Assn. v. Society of Composers, Authors and Music Publishers of Canada*, [2010] F.C.J. No. 1533 (F.C.A.); *Ontario (Minister of Municipal Affairs and Housing) v. Ontario Municipal Board*, [2001] O.J. No. 922 (Ont. Div. Ct.); *Khan v. College of Physicians and Surgeons*, [1992] O.J. No. 1725 (Ont. C.A.).

[460] *Deemar v. College of Veterinarians of Ontario*, [2008] O.J. No. 3322 (Ont. C.A.).

[461] *NSP Investments Ltd. v. Ontario (Joint Board)*, [1990] O.J. No. 411 (Ont. Div. Ct.).

[462] *Lariviere v. Millhaven Institution*, [1986] F.C.J. No. 644 (F.C.T.D.).

sibility. A tribunal may consider relevant expert evidence recycled from previous cases involving different parties, provided disclosure is made.[463] This contributes to the goal of being an inexpensive forum accessible to the public.

A tribunal may use its own expertise in assessing the evidence. Expertise is one of the reasons for conferring decision-making powers upon tribunals. A panel of doctors is better able to understand medical evidence. Professionals are disciplined by their fellow professionals because they know the standards demanded of responsible professionals. A discipline panel may apply its expertise in assessing the evidence and in determining whether the conduct in question met the standards of the profession.[464] Expertise may assist a tribunal in drawing inferences from primary facts. However, the expertise of the tribunal should not be the basis of an essential finding of fact upon which a decision turns. Evidence tending to prove essential facts should be adduced.[465] If necessary, a tribunal may retain an expert at its own expense to provide evidence.[466]

A tribunal may take notice of commonly accepted facts and generally recognized facts within its specialized knowledge.[467] Facts that are generally recognized within the field regulated by the tribunal need not be proven.[468] Basic anatomy and common medical terms need not be proven before a discipline committee of doctors.[469] A local tribunal may take notice of facts known to all who live in the area; for example, local weather conditions and the peculiarities of local travel.[470] However, a tribunal should not rely on its ability to take notice of common facts as the basis of its finding on an important disputed fact.[471]

A tribunal may visit a site that is the subject matter of the proceeding but, before doing so, it should notify the parties and give them an

---

[463] *Alberta Report v. Alberta (Human Rights and Citizenship Commission)*, [2002] A.J. No. 1539 (Alta. Q.B.).

[464] *Huerto v. College of Physicians and Surgeons*, [1994] S.J. No. 390 (Sask. Q.B.), affd [1996] S.J. No. 56 (Sask. C.A.).

[465] *Reddall v. College of Nurses*, [1983] O.J. No. 3100 (Ont. C.A.); *Fletcher Challenge Energy Canada Inc. v. Sulz*, [2001] S.J. No. 86 at para. 59 (Sask. C.A.); *Nova Scotia (Director of Assessment) v. Knickle*, [2007] N.S.J. No. 449 at para. 45 (N.S.C.A.).

[466] *Ontario (Attorney General) v. Ontario (Review Board)*, [2010] O.J. No. 207 (Ont. C.A.).

[467] All tribunals have inherent authority, which is enacted in *Statutory Powers Procedure Act*, R.S.O. 1990, c. S.22, s. 16; *Administrative Justice Act*, R.S.Q. c. J-3, ss. 140-42.

[468] *Knoll North America Corp. v. Adams*, [2010] O.J. No. 5611 (Ont. Div. Ct.).

[469] *Ringrose v. College of Physicians and Surgeons (No. 2)*, [1978] A.J. No. 961 (Alta. C.A.).

[470] *Western Memorial Hospital Assn. v. Newfoundland Assn. of Public Employees*, [1986] N.J. No. 53 (Nfld. T.D.).

[471] *Dennis v. British Columbia (Superintendent of Motor Vehicles)*, [2000] B.C.J. No. 2447 (B.C.C.A.); *contra: Knoll North America Corp. v. Adams*, [2010] O.J. No. 5611 (Ont. Div. Ct.).

opportunity to attend.[472] Provided the parties had an opportunity to be present at the viewing and to see what the tribunal saw, the tribunal need not disclose its observations to the parties.[473] A tribunal is not obliged to visit a site and may instead expect a party to prove with evidence what would be seen. The purpose of the inspection should be to better appreciate the evidence and not to gather evidence. By gathering evidence the tribunal members become witnesses whom parties may desire to cross-examine. To gather evidence, an expert should be appointed to inspect the site and report and be available for cross-examination.[474]

Testimony given by witnesses over the telephone is admissible.[475]

Q. WITNESSES

1. Right of a Party to Call Evidence

The right to present one's case necessarily includes the right to present evidence. A tribunal that is not required to hold an oral hearing need not hear witnesses orally, but should permit a party to present evidence in written form.[476] It may be presented in the form of statutory declarations, affidavits, signed statements or letters from the witnesses, as appropriate.

A tribunal may require parties to request permission to call witnesses and to indicate the names of the witnesses, the nature of their evidence, and its relevance.[477] A tribunal may refuse permission to call witnesses if parties do not indicate what facts they seek to prove by the witness' testimony,[478] or if the evidence appears to be irrelevant or repetitive.[479] If a party's credibility is in issue, that party should be heard

---

[472] *Carrières P.C.M. (1994) Inc. v. Baker*, [1999] J.Q. no 518 (Que. S.C.); *Batten v. Newfoundland Light and Power Co.*, [1978] N.J. No. 137 at para. 118 (Nfld. T.D.).

[473] *Jaworski v. Canada (Attorney General)*, [1998] F.C.J. No. 824 (F.C.T.D.), affd [2000] F.C.J. No. 643 (F.C.A.), leave to appeal refused [2000] S.C.C.A. No. 348.

[474] *Murray v. Rockyview (Municipal District No. 44)*, [1980] A.J. No. 649 at paras. 49-52 (Alta. C.A.).

[475] *Holoboff v. Alberta (Securities Commission)*, [1991] A.J. No. 465 (Alta. C.A.).

[476] *Young v. Powell River School District No. 47*, [1982] B.C.J. No. 1967 (B.C.C.A.); *International Brotherhood of Electrical Workers, Local 1739 v. International Brotherhood of Electrical Workers*, [2007] O.J. No. 2460 (Ont. Div. Ct.). See also *Administrative Justice Act*, R.S.Q. c. J-3, s. 5(3).

[477] *Carter v. Phillips*, [1988] O.J. No. 1833 (Ont. C.A.); *Fraternité Inter-Provinciale des Ouvriers en Electricité v. Quebec (Office de la Construction)*, [1983] J.Q. no 394, 148 D.L.R. (3d) 626 at 642 (Que. C.A.). Except in B.C. where parties have a right to summons witnesses: *Administrative Tribunals Act*, S.B.C. 2004, c. 45, s. 34.

[478] *Cotroni v. Quebec (Police Commission)*, [1977] S.C.J. No. 101.

[479] *Tse v. Canada (Secretary of State)*, [1993] F.C.J. No. 1396 (F.C.T.D.).

orally, even though the rest of the hearing may be conducted in writing.[480] Issues relating to summonsing witnesses are discussed below in § 2.19, "Power of Tribunal to Obtain Evidence by Compulsion". If necessary to proceed expeditiously, time limits may be imposed on the oral presentation of evidence provided parties have an opportunity to present written evidence.[481] Otherwise, a tribunal should not discourage a party from calling relevant evidence simply to shorten the hearing.[482]

If one party is permitted to call witnesses, all parties should be accorded the same right.[483] A party who fails to take advantage of the opportunity granted to present evidence may not later complain.[484] If the statute mandates an adversarial process, rather than an inquisitorial process, the right to call witnesses includes the right not to call witnesses, even if the tribunal would like to hear their evidence.[485] However, where the tribunal has evidence of misconduct by a party, an adverse inference may be drawn from the party's failure to testify or refusal to submit to cross-examination.[486]

If a party is permitted to testify orally, there is no right to be questioned first by the party's own counsel. The tribunal may commence the examination so as to focus at the outset on key facts and points that are of concern, rather than sit through the lengthy and unfocused examination that counsel sometimes conduct before getting to the point.[487]

2. Cross-Examination of Witnesses

A tribunal may refuse to permit cross-examination of witnesses unless necessary for a fair hearing or required by statute.[488] This refusal does not constitute a denial of fairness if there is sufficient uncontradicted evidence

---

[480] *Khan v. University of Ottawa*, [1997] O.J. No. 2650 (Ont. C.A.).

[481] *Amalgamated Transit Union, Local 113 v. Ontario (Labour Relations Board)*, [2007] O.J. No. 3907 (Ont. Div. Ct.).

[482] *Kamtasingh v. Canada (Minister of Citizenship and Immigration)*, [2010] F.C.J. No. 45 (F.C.).

[483] *Canada (Attorney General) v. Leclerc*, [1979] F.C.J. No. 45 (F.C.A.).

[484] *Pugliese v. North York (Borough)*, [1978] O.J. No. 3706 (Ont. Div. Ct.).

[485] *Universal Workers Union, Labourers' International Union of North America, Local 183 v. Ontario (Human Rights Commission)*, [2006] O.J. No. 50 (Ont. Div. Ct.).

[486] *Canada (Minister of Citizenship and Immigration) v. Malik*, [1997] F.C.J. No. 378 (F.C.T.D.); *Norway House Indian Band v. Canada (Adjudicator, Labour Code)*, [1994] F.C.J. No. 3 (F.C.T.D.).

[487] *Benitez v. Canada (Minister of Citizenship and Immigration)*, [2007] F.C.J. No. 735 (F.C.A.), leave to appeal refused [2007] S.C.C.A. No. 391; *Thamotharem v. Canada (Minister of Citizenship and Immigration)*, [2007] F.C.J. No. 734 (F.C.A.).

[488] For example see *Administrative Tribunals Act*, S.B.C. 2004, c. 45, s. 38; *Statutory Powers Procedure Act*, R.S.O. 1990, c. S.22, s. 10.1 [as am.]; *Administrative Justice Act*, R.S.Q. c. J-3, s. 5(3), s. 132 [as am.].

on which to base the decision or if other effective methods of responding are available.[489] There are two purposes of cross-examination: to challenge a witness' credibility or to obtain evidence from the witness to prove the cross-examining party's case. Where issues of credibility arise with respect to a key witness whose evidence is of vital significance, fairness may require the tribunal to permit some cross-examination.[490] Similarly, if a party needs evidence from a witness of another party, some questioning should be permitted either orally or in writing.[491]

A tribunal may require the party seeking to cross-examine a witness to state what evidence the party hopes to gain and, if no useful purpose will be served, may refuse permission.[492] A tribunal may, with advance notice, impose time limits on cross-examination, provided it is willing to grant extensions of time where necessary for a fair hearing.[493] This may have the salutary effect of encouraging counsel to focus the cross-examination on matters that are truly important.

In multifaceted and multiparty public hearings into questions of policy and the public interest, cross-examination may be unsuitable, unwieldy and lead to disturbance, disruption and delay. The tribunal may refuse to permit cross-examination.[494] Similarly, in a proceeding which is informal in nature and is conducted before a tribunal of non-lawyers, a request to cross-examine witnesses may be refused because the use of cross-examination techniques by counsel may lead to a process which a lay tribunal may have difficulty controlling.[495]

If cross-examination is desirable but the witness to be examined is not present, a tribunal may compel the attendance of the witness if it has

---

[489] *Armstrong v. Canada (Commissioner of Royal Canadian Mounted Police)*, [1998] F.C.J. No. 42 (F.C.A.); *Grain Services Union (ILWU-Canada) v. Friesen*, [2010] F.C.J. No. 1677 (F.C.A.); *Gerle Gold Ltd. v. Golden Rule Resources Ltd.*, [1999] F.C.J. No. 269 (F.C.T.D.), vard [2000] F.C.J. No. 1650 (F.C.A.); *Payne v. Peel (Regional Municipality) Police Services Board*, [2003] O.J. No. 340 (Ont. Div. Ct.); *Genex Communications Inc. v. Canada (Attorney General)*, [2005] F.C.J. No. 1440 at paras. 163-175 (F.C.A.), leave to appeal refused [2005] C.S.C.R. no 485; *Nuosci v. Canada (Attorney General)*, [1994] F.C.J. No. 293 (F.C.A.); *Everett v. Canada (Minister of Fisheries and Oceans)*, [1994] F.C.J. No. 418 (F.C.A.); *MacDonald v. Canada (National Parole Board)*, [1986] 3 F.C. 157 at 173 (F.C.T.D.).

[490] *Emery v. Alberta (Workers' Compensation Board, Appeals Commission)*, [2000] A.J. No. 1189 (Alta. Q.B.); *Cashin v. Canadian Broadcasting Corp.*, [1984] F.C.J. No. 93 (F.C.A.).

[491] *Attorney General of New Brunswick v. Dominion of Canada General Insurance Company*, [2010] N.B.J. No. 413 (N.B.C.A.).

[492] *Tandy Electronics Ltd. v. United Steelworkers of America*, [1979] O.J. No. 4367 (Ont. Div. Ct.).

[493] *Imperial Oil Ltd. v. Alberta (Minister of the Environment)*, [2003] A.J. No. 721 at para. 70 (Alta. Q.B.).

[494] *Unicity Taxi Ltd. v. Manitoba (Taxicab Board)*, [1992] M.J. No. 381 (Man. Q.B.), affd [1992] M.J. No. 608 (Man. C.A.).

[495] *MacInnis v. Canada (Attorney General)*, [1996] F.C.J. No. 1117 (F.C.A.).

power to do so.[496] A tribunal that does not have the power to subpoena witnesses need not produce a witness for cross-examination.[497] However, if a witness voluntarily testifies, opposing parties may be permitted to test that witness' evidence by cross-examination.[498]

Where a statute expressly permits a party to cross-examine witnesses, a tribunal may limit cross-examination only if satisfied that the cross-examination of the witness has been sufficient to disclose the facts fully and fairly.[499] Cross-examination may be restricted to relevant facts[500] but a tribunal cannot altogether prevent a party from exercising a statutory right to cross-examine.[501] Cross-examination on matters of doubtful relevance need not be permitted and repetitive cross-examination may be curtailed.[502] To protect witnesses privacy, a tribunal should prohibit cross-examination on personal matters that are collateral to the subject of the hearing.[503] The right to cross-examine appears not to include a right to have witnesses subpoenaed for the purpose of cross-examination.[504] Where there are grounds to refuse to disclose the identity of informers and other confidential sources, the tribunal may refuse to produce the informers for cross-examination.[505]

Parties who represent themselves sometimes use their right to cross-examine to make speeches and provide additional information. The tribunal should endeavour to curtail the speeches and should disregard this information unless the opposing party is given an opportunity to challenge it.[506]

---

[496] *Willette v. Royal Canadian Mounted Police Commissioner*, [1984] F.C.J. No. 255 (F.C.A.).

[497] *Semchuk v. Regina School Division No. 4*, [1987] S.J. No. 233 (Sask. C.A.); *Pierre-Pierre v. Finlay*, [1991] R.J.Q. 1947 (C.S.).

[498] *Sorobey v. Canada (Public Service Commission Appeal Board)*, [1986] F.C.J. No. 616 (F.C.A.).

[499] *Administrative Tribunals Act*, S.B.C. 2004, c. 45, s. 38(2); *Statutory Powers Procedure Act*, R.S.O. 1990, c. S.22, s. 23(2) [as am.]; *Administrative Justice Act*, R.S.Q. c. J-3, s. 132 [as am.]; *Innisfil (Township) v. Vespra (Township)*, [1981] S.C.J. No. 73.

[500] *Henderson v. Ontario (Securities Commission)*, [1976] O.J. No. 2342 (Ont. H.C.J.).

[501] *Henderson v. Ontario (Securities Commission)*, [1976] O.J. No. 2342 (Ont. H.C.J.); *Innisfil (Township) v. Vespra (Township)*, [1981] S.C.J. No. 73.

[502] *Kirchmeir v. Boulanger*, [2000] A.J. No. 1563 at para. 21 (Alta. C.A.).

[503] *College of Physicians and Surgeons v. Deitel*, [1997] O.J. No. 1866 at para. 229 (Ont. Div. Ct.), leave to appeal refused Sep. 17, 1997 (Ont. C.A.); *Ursulescu v. Chomicki*, [1995] S.J. No. 656 at para. 29 (Sask. Q.B.).

[504] *Ellis v. Ontario (Ministry of Community and Social Services)*, [1980] O.J. No. 3582 at para. 20 (Ont. Div. Ct.). Except in B.C. where the party may serve a summons on the witness: *Administrative Tribunals Act*, S.B.C. 2004, c. 45, s. 34.

[505] *Gaudet v. Marchand*, [1994] Q.J. No. 375 (Que. C.A.).

[506] *MacEwan (Grant) Community College v. Alberta (Human Rights Commission)*, [2000] A.J. No. 241 (Alta. Q.B.).

3.   Exclusion of Witnesses

Where witness credibility is an issue and cross-examination is permitted, an order may be made, if requested by a party, excluding witnesses from the hearing room until after they have testified.[507] This avoids the risk that some witnesses may alter their testimony on hearing the testimony of others. Many hearings are fairly conducted without excluding witnesses. Whether to make an order is within the discretion of the tribunal, but should not be refused without good reason. Failure to exclude a witness, whose credibility is in issue, during the testimony of prior witnesses may affect the weight to be given to that witness' testimony.[508]

Expert witnesses are usually permitted to hear testimony of other parties' experts so they can advise counsel with respect to cross-examination of those experts and as to evidence to be called in response.[509]

Parties ought not to be excluded, because they have a right to be present throughout the hearing.[510] If a party is a corporation, its representative who instructs its counsel ought not to be excluded. An employee whose conduct is the subject of the proceeding should not be excluded.[511] However, if credibility is an issue in a hearing into complaints made by several grievors, each may be excluded while the others testify.[512]

4.   Transcripts

Testimony need not be transcribed, unless required by statute, though it may be desirable to have it recorded to facilitate resolution of later disputes as to whether there was evidence to support the tribunal's findings. Where a transcript or recording of the hearing is required, failure of the recording

---

[507] *Wiebe v. Canada*, [1992] F.C.J. No. 308 (F.C.A.); *Homelite v. Canada (Import Tribunal)*, [1987] F.C.J. No. 537 (F.C.T.D.).

[508] *Canada (Canadian Radio-television and Telecommunications Commission) v. Canada (Human Rights Tribunal)*, [1990] F.C.J. No. 819 (F.C.T.D.).

[509] *Richmond v. College of Optometrists*, [1995] O.J. No. 2621 (Ont. Div. Ct.).

[510] A B.C. tribunal may exclude a party when necessary to maintain order at the hearing: *Administrative Tribunals Act*, S.B.C. 2004, c. 45, s. 48. Query whether s. 9(2) [as am.] of *Statutory Powers Procedure Act*, R.S.O. 1990, c. S.22, s. 23(2) [as am.], gives Ontario tribunals similar authority.

[511] *Canada (Canadian Radio-television and Telecommunications Commission) v. Canada (Human Rights Tribunal)*, [1990] F.C.J. No. 819 (F.C.T.D.).

[512] *United Brotherhood of Carpenters and Joiners of America, Local 1985 v. Graham Construction and Engineering Ltd.*, [2002] S.J. No. 518 (Sask. Q.B.).

device or gaps in the transcript are not fatal unless they raise a serious possibility of the denial of a ground of appeal or review.[513]

Generally, a tribunal may not prevent a party from having someone attend the hearing to take notes.[514] However, in cases where there are public policy reasons for not recording the proceedings, a party may be prohibited from transcribing or recording it. This prohibition may be appropriate in cases where mediation and resolution of disputes between parties is the goal and participation in the proceeding by the parties (who are not lawyers) is encouraged.[515]

R.   PROOF

1.   Onus of Proof

Which party presents their case to the tribunal first? The party with the burden of proof should go first. If no party has a burden of proof, the order of presentation does not matter, provided that the parties are accorded a fair hearing.[516] As onus of proof is concerned with who bears the risk of a gap in the evidence, a party who advocates a particular position bears the onus of producing the evidence in support.[517] An applicant has the onus of proving entitlement to the permit or other relief claimed.[518] An exemption must be proven by the party who claims to be within it.[519]

In proceedings concerning allegations of professional misconduct or violations of human rights, the onus of proof is on the complainant[520] or, more often, on counsel employed or retained by tribunals to present the case. Legally the burden of proof never shifts to the respondent. However, in practice, if the complainant establishes a *prima facie* case that the alleged

---

[513] *Canadian Union of Public Employees, Local 301 v. Montreal (City)*, [1997] S.C.J. No. 39. Tribunals in B.C., see *Administrative Tribunals Act*, S.B.C. 2004, c. 45, s. 35.

[514] *Mroszkowski v. Ontario (Director of Vocational Rehabilitation Services Branch)*, [1978] O.J. No. 3481 (Ont. Div. Ct.).

[515] *Alberta (Labour Relations Board) v. International Brotherhood of Electrical Workers (IBEW), Local 1007*, [1991] A.J. No. 896 (Alta. Q.B.).

[516] *Denby v. Agriculture, Food and Rural Affairs Appeal Tribunal*, [2006] O.J. No. 1968 at para. 45 (Ont. Div. Ct.).

[517] *Chopra v. Canada (Attorney General)*, [2007] F.C.J. No. 1134 at para. 42 (F.C.A.); *R. v. Peckham*, [1994] O.J. No. 1995 at para. 26 (Ont. C.A.), leave to appeal refused [1994] S.C.C.A. No. 471; *Nova Scotia (Director of Assessment) v. Knickle*, [2007] N.S.J. No. 449 (N.S.C.A.).

[518] *Law Society of Upper Canada v. Evans*, [2008] O.J. No. 2729 (Ont. Div. Ct.).

[519] *Koressis v. Turner*, [1986] O.J. No. 287 (Ont. Div. Ct.).

[520] *Floris v. Nova Scotia (Director of Livestock Services)*, [1986] N.S.J. No. 399 (N.S.T.D.); *Ontario (Liquor Control Board) v. Karumanchiri*, [1988] O.J. No. 167 (Ont. Div. Ct.).

conduct was committed, a respondent who desires a favourable decision would be wise to adduce evidence to rebut the complainant's case.[521]

In court trials, a party with the burden of proof may not split its case by holding back evidence to be presented after other parties have presented their evidence. This rule does not apply to tribunal hearings, but the procedure is considered orderly. If new evidence is presented, responding parties should have an opportunity to respond, except to evidence tendered solely to rebut evidence presented by them.[522]

In inquisitorial proceedings, there may be an onus on the tribunal to obtain relevant evidence.[523]

2.   Non-Suit

A party with the burden of proof, who fails to lead sufficient evidence to establish the case, runs the risk of having the case dismissed without the other parties being called upon to respond. The other parties may bring a "motion for non-suit". The motion should be granted only if a *prima facie* case has not been made out. This is a lower standard than the balance of probabilities applied when finally deciding whether the burden of proof has been met. If there is some evidence, however weak and viewed in a light most favourable to the party with the burden of proof, a *prima facie* case has been made out. Credibility of witnesses and weight of evidence is not considered at this stage. Evidence omitted through inadvertence may be admitted before the motion is decided. The party moving for dismissal is usually required to elect to call no evidence before the motion will be considered by the tribunal.[524]

3.   Standard of Proof

When are facts proven? In tribunal proceedings, the standard of proof is the balance of probabilities. This standard is less onerous than the standard imposed in criminal cases where, to succeed, the Crown must

---

[521]   *Base-Fort Patrol Ltd. v. Alberta (Human Rights Commission)*, [1982] A.J. No. 687 (Alta. Q.B.); *United Assn. of Journeymen and Apprentices of the Pipefitting Industry of the United States and Canada, Local 488 v. Alberta (Industrial Relations Board)*, [1976] A.J. No. 355 at 97 (Alta. C.A.).

[522]   *Sood v. College of Physicians and Surgeons*, [1995] S.J. No. 721 (Sask. Q.B.).

[523]   *R. v. LePage*, [2006] O.J. No. 4486 (Ont. C.A.).

[524]   *Merchant v. Law Society of Saskatchewan*, [2002] S.J. No. 288 (Sask. C.A.); *Ontario v. Ontario Public Service Employees Union*, [1990] O.J. No. 635 (Ont. Div. Ct.); *International Brotherhood of Electrical Workers, Local 348 v. AGT Ltd.*, [1997] A.J. No. 1004 (Alta. Q.B.); *Northern Lights Health Region v. United Nurses of Alberta, Local 124*, [2007] A.J. No. 366 (Alta. Q.B.); *Filgueira v. Garfield Container Transport Inc.*, [2006] F.C.J. No. 1005 (F.C.).

prove that an offence was committed "beyond a reasonable doubt". If on all the reliable evidence, it has been proven that the events alleged probably occurred, they have been proven.[525] Even in disciplinary proceedings this standard of proof prevails.[526] Allegations of criminal conduct do not require stricter proof. Regardless how serious the allegations, the standard of proof does not change. It remains a single standard, a simple balance of probabilities.[527] A statutory standard of "reasonable grounds" is lower than the standard of balance of probabilities.[528]

The quality of evidence required to establish a fact on a balance of probabilities depends on the circumstances, including the nature of the facts to be proved. An unlikely fact may require more reliable evidence than does a likely fact.[529] More reliable evidence may be required to prove serious allegations of wrongdoing than other types of facts.[530] A statutory test requiring proof of future risk is met by proof of past and present circumstances from which future risk may be inferred. Predictions based on such evidence may not be dismissed as speculative.[531]

Standards of proof are concerned with establishing what happened. They do not apply to policy questions such as those that require the balancing of factors to determine what is in the public interest.[532]

S.   EVIDENCE GATHERING POWERS

Essentially three types of compulsory powers are used to obtain evidence. The first is the subpoena or summons requiring a person to testify or to produce documents or things. The second permits an inspector to inspect premises and to request the production of business records. This power

---

[525] *Newfoundland and Labrador (Mineral Claims Recorder) v. Vinland Resources Ltd.*, [2008] N.J. No. 48 (Nfld. C.A.).

[526] *Stetler v. Ontario (Agriculture, Food and Rural Affairs Appeal Tribunal)*, [2005] O.J. No. 2817 (Ont. C.A.); *Beaini v. Assn. of Professional Engineers*, [2003] N.S.J. No. 229 (N.S.S.C.), affd [2004] N.S.J. No. 383 (N.S.C.A.); *Rak v. British Columbia (Superintendent of Brokers)*, [1990] B.C.J. No. 2383 (B.C.C.A.); *Cambie Hotel (Nanaimo) Ltd. v. British Columbia (General Manager, Liquor Control and Licensing Branch)*, [2006] B.C.J. No. 501 (B.C.C.A.).

[527] *V. (K.) v. College of Physicians and Surgeons*, [1999] A.J. No. 440 (Alta. C.A.), leave to appeal refused [1999] S.C.C.A. No. 331; *Shalala v. Law Society (N.B.)*, [1994] N.B.J. No. 473 (N.B.C.A.); *Bradley Air Services Ltd. (c.o.b. First Air) v. Chiasson*, [1995] F.C.J. No. 343 (F.C.T.D.), affd [1996] F.C.J. No. 818 (F.C.A.).

[528] *Mendoza v. Canada (Minister of Public Safety and Emergency Preparedness)*, [2007] F.C.J. No. 1204 at para. 25 (F.C.).

[529] *Carrillo v. Canada (Minister of Citizenship and Immigration)*, [2008] F.C.J. No. 399 (F.C.A.).

[530] *Newfoundland (Treasury Board) v. Newfoundland and Labrador Assn. of Public and Private Employees, Local 6206*, [2006] N.J. No. 380 (N.L.T.D.).

[531] *Martin v. Canada (Attorney General)*, [2005] F.C.J. No. 752 (F.C.A.).

[532] *R. v. Peckham*, [1994] O.J. No. 1995 (Ont. C.A.).

also allows for spot audits of regulated businesses to ensure compliance with regulations. For example, a farm may be inspected for compliance with health regulations and quotas, or a tavern may be inspected for compliance with its liquor licence. The third type of power is the search and seizure power. When contravention of a statute is suspected, this power permits authorized persons to pay a surprise visit to premises and to search for and seize evidence of the contravention.

Since a tribunal derives all of its powers from statute and has no inherent powers, it has no powers to obtain evidence except those expressly granted by statute.[533] Express grants of power are subject to limitations. The power may be used only to obtain relevant evidence.[534] The power to compel evidence to be produced at a hearing may not be used to order disclosure prior to the hearing.[535] Tribunals that need compulsory powers to conduct effective investigations have statutory investigation powers in addition to the power to compel evidence at a hearing. Tribunal powers may be used to gather evidence for regulatory purposes only. They may not be used to gather evidence to be used in criminal proceedings.[536] Tribunals should rely on their statutory evidence gathering powers rather than apply to a court for a mandatory injunction.[537]

Any tribunal may hear testimony and other evidence given voluntarily regardless whether it has compulsory powers.[538] A tribunal may gather evidence without resorting to its compulsory powers.[539]

1.   Search and Seizure Powers

A search and seizure provision authorizes the gathering of evidence of the commission of an offence for possible use in a prosecution.

---

[533] In B.C., Ontario and Newfoundland, general summons powers are conferred on all tribunals: *Administrative Tribunals Act*, S.B.C. 2004, c. 45, s. 34; *Statutory Powers Procedure Act*, R.S.O. 1990, c. S.22, s. 12 [as am.]; *Interpretation Act*, R.S.N.L. 1990, c. I-19, s. 24 [as am.].

[534] *Ontario Assessment Commissioner District No. 9 v. Seachel Accommodations Ltd.*, [1979] O.J. No. 4310 (Ont. Div. Ct.).

[535] *Canadian Pacific Airlines Ltd. v. Canadian Air Line Pilots Assn.*, [1993] S.C.J. No. 114. But see: *Nova Scotia (Attorney General) v. Bishop*, [2006] N.S.J. No. 411 (N.S.C.A.).

[536] *R. v. Jarvis*, [2002] S.C.J. No. 76; *British Columbia (Securities Commission) v. Branch*, [1995] S.C.J. No. 32; *Phillips v. Nova Scotia (Commission of Inquiry into the Westray Mine Tragedy)*, [1995] S.C.J. No. 36; *O'Hara v. British Columbia*, [1987] S.C.J. No. 69; *Starr v. Houlden*, [1990] S.C.J. No. 30.

[537] *Cambie Surgeries Corp. v. British Columbia (Medical Services Commission)*, [2010] B.C.J. No. 1766 (B.C.C.A.).

[538] *Dupras v. Mason*, [1994] B.C.J. No. 2456 at para. 22 (B.C.C.A.).

[539] *Rassouli-Rashti v. College of Physicians and Surgeons of Ontario*, [2009] O.J. No. 4762 at para. 41 (Ont. Div. Ct.)

Section 8 of the *Charter* provides that everyone has the right to be secure against unreasonable search or seizure. This protects a person's right to privacy. To be characterized as reasonable under s. 8 of the *Charter*, the statutory provision must require prior authorization of the search by a person who is able to assess the evidence in a neutral and impartial manner. The authorizing person need not be a judge, but must be capable of acting judicially, must not have an interest in the proceedings, and must be satisfied on reasonable and probable grounds established upon oath, that there is evidence to be found at the place of the search.[540] The authorizing person must have discretion whether to issue the search warrant and cannot be required to issue it on certain conditions being met.[541] In exercising this discretion, the authorizing person should balance the interests of the individual to be free from intrusions of the state and that of the state to intrude on the privacy of the individual for the purpose of law enforcement. The factors to be weighed include the nature of the offence alleged, the nature of the intrusion sought including the place to be searched, the time of the search and the persons who are the subject of the search. Residences have a higher protection than business premises. The authorizing person also has discretion to impose conditions and restrictions on the search. The search and seizure authorization must not be so broad as to permit a general search for any evidence that a person has committed any offence. A search and seizure may be authorized only in respect of a specific offence, and only documents and things relevant to that offence may be searched for and seized.[542]

A statutory power that permits a regulator to seize a licensee's business records when suspending its licence does not offend s. 8 of the *Charter* because those who choose to engage in a regulated industry have a low expectation of privacy. This power may be used even though the regulator suspects that the licensee has committed a criminal offence.[543]

2.   Inspection Powers

Spot audits and inspections of premises by regulators comply with s. 8 of the *Charter*. The purpose of these inspections is not to detect criminal activity, but rather to ensure compliance with rules that are designed to protect the public. Persons who engage in regulated businesses have a lower expectation of privacy. Inspection, or the threat of it, is an effective means of ensuring

---

[540] *Canada (Director of Investigation and Research, Combines Investigation Branch) v. Southam Inc.*, [1984] S.C.J. No. 36.

[541] *Baron v. Canada*, [1993] S.C.J. No. 6.

[542] *Kruger Inc. v. Canada (Minister of National Revenue)*, [1984] F.C.J. No. 174 (F.C.A.).

[543] *Prime Realty Ltd. v. British Columbia (Superintendent of Real Estate)*, [1993] B.C.J. No. 1920 (B.C.S.C.).

compliance with standards. Inspections are usually conducted during reasonable hours at business premises. Although inspections are intrusions or searches, without prior judicial authorization, they are not regarded as unreasonable pursuant to s. 8 of the *Charter*. Inspection powers do not authorize inspectors to force entry. They are enforced by way of proceedings for obstruction or to compel compliance. Powers of inspection are usually circumscribed, permitting inspection only of regulated entities for the purpose of ensuring compliance with regulatory requirements. The documents to be inspected are often those that are required by law to be kept by persons engaged in that type of business. They may be examined and copied by the inspector.[544] An inspector may observe the regulated person while engaged in the regulated activity.[545] Regulated persons have a duty to co-operate with an inspector.[546] The use of a power to compel a regulated person to submit to a medical examination does affect the right to privacy, and may attract a right to procedural fairness before the order is made.[547]

Inspection powers may be used even though the inspector suspects or has reasonable grounds to believe that the law has been violated. The right to use inspection powers is determined, not by the knowledge or suspicions of the inspector, but by the purpose of the inspection. An inspection power may be used for purposes related to regulatory compliance but not to gather evidence for a criminal prosecution. If, after or during an inspection, a criminal investigation is commenced, the evidence already gathered in the inspection may be used in the criminal investigation and proceeding but, if the inspection continues (for valid regulatory purposes), information subsequently gathered in the inspection should not be shared with those conducting the criminal investigation.[548] Information gathered in the inspection may be used in regulatory proceedings.[549]

A power to seize and destroy diseased plants and animals and contaminated food does not offend s. 8. The public interest in protecting health and the environment competes successfully against a person's interest in being secure against unreasonable seizure of property, especially as this situation often presents an emergency requiring quick action by officials. A seizure of this type does not involve an invasion of privacy or suggestion of criminal misconduct. As long as there are

---

[544] *R. v. Potash*, [1994] S.C.J. No. 7.

[545] *Gore v. College of Physicians and Surgeons of Ontario*, [2009] O.J. No. 2833 (Ont. C.A.).

[546] *Artinian v. College of Physicians and Surgeons*, [1990] O.J. No. 1116 (Ont. Div. Ct.).

[547] *Cotton v. College of Nurses of Ontario*, [2008] O.J. No. 2172 (Ont. Div. Ct.).

[548] *R. v. Jarvis*, [2002] S.C.J. No. 76; *R. v. Sandhu*, [2011] O.J. No. 619 (Ont. C.A.).

[549] *Osif v. College of Physicians and Surgeons of Nova Scotia*, [2009] N.S.J. No. 111 (N.S.C.A.).

reasonable grounds to believe that the seizure is necessary to protect against a threat to health or to the environment, it is not unreasonable.[550]

3.   Subpoena Powers

Administrative Law does not recognize any right to remain silent. Any person may be compelled to testify before a tribunal that has the power to subpoena witnesses, even respondents and other persons who may be adversely affected by the resulting decision of the tribunal. Section 11(c) of the *Charter* protects only a person charged with an offence from being compelled to testify at their criminal trial. It does not apply to administrative proceedings, not even to disciplinary proceedings because they are not penal in nature. A person accused of professional misconduct may be compelled to testify at their own disciplinary hearing, even if the alleged conduct is criminal in nature,[551] unless a statute expressly states that they are not compellable.[552] They may be required to testify before the testimony of other witnesses is heard[553] and they may be cross-examined from the outset.[554]

Section 7 of the *Charter* does not extend the right to remain silent to regulatory proceedings. There is a presumption that all witnesses, other than those accused at their own criminal trials, are compellable witnesses. Although the liberty interest is engaged by the testimonial compulsion, a summons issued for regulatory purposes does not violate the principles of fundamental justice. Participants in a regulated field expect to be questioned by the regulators and, when summoned to testify, they know the subject of the inquiry and can prepare themselves for questions and they may be accompanied by counsel.[555]

A tribunal may not issue a subpoena for the primary purpose of gathering evidence for a criminal prosecution. A subpoena is enforceable so long as the tribunal proceeding has a valid regulatory purpose, and the purpose of the subpoena is to gather evidence relevant to that purpose. One asks, what is the predominant purpose for which the evidence is sought? If the purpose is

---

[550] *R. v. Bertram S. Miller Ltd.*, [1986] F.C.J. No. 404 (F.C.A.), leave to appeal refused [1986] S.C.C.A. No. 351.

[551] *Belhumeur v. Barreau du Quebec*, [1988] A.Q. no 905, 54 D.L.R. (4th) 105 (Que. C.A.); *Fang v. College of Physicians and Surgeons*, [1985] A.J. No. 1080 (Alta. C.A.); *R. v. Wigglesworth*, [1987] S.C.J. No. 71.

[552] *Police Complaints Commissioner v. Kerr*, [1997] O.J. No. 42 (Ont. C.A.), leave to appeal refused [1997] S.C.C.A. No. 133.

[553] *Quebec (Procureur général) v. Bouliane*, [2004] J.Q. no 4883 at paras. 174-177 (Que. C.A.), leave to appeal refused [2004] C.S.C.R. no 290.

[554] *Real Estate Council of Alberta v. Henderson*, [2007] A.J. No. 1068 (Alta. C.A.), leave to appeal refused [2007] S.C.C.A. No. 588.

[555] *British Columbia (Securities Commission) v. Branch*, [1995] S.C.J. No. 32; *Phillips v. Nova Scotia (Commission of Inquiry into the Westray Mine Tragedy)*, [1995] S.C.J. No. 36.

solely to gather evidence to incriminate the witness, that is to prove their guilt in a criminal proceeding, and not to gather evidence for regulatory purposes, the subpoena is not enforceable.[556] To challenge a subpoena, the witness must show that the tribunal is acting in bad faith, using its powers to gather evidence to be used against the witness in criminal proceedings. It would be a highly unusual case in which this is found to be the purpose of a subpoena issued by a tribunal.

A concurrent criminal prosecution against a witness arising out of the same conduct does not give grounds to refuse to testify. Testimonial compulsion by a tribunal for regulatory purposes does not violate a witness' right to remain silent in respect of outstanding criminal charges because s. 13 of the *Charter* provides that the testimony given before the tribunal is not admissible in the criminal proceeding. The right to remain silent in respect of the criminal charges is not grounds for a stay of the tribunal proceeding.[557] Likewise, being compelled to testify before the tribunal does not violate an accused's right to a fair trial. Pre-trial publicity arising from the tribunal proceedings is a concern only if the witness' criminal charges are to be tried before a jury. Even in these circumstances, the fact of publicity alone is not sufficient to raise concern. If the effect of the publicity will leave potential jurors so irreparably prejudiced that a fair trial is impossible, the tribunal may prohibit publication of the witness' testimony.[558] The *Charter* does not protect against the loss of a tactical advantage in being made to reveal one's defence prior to the criminal trial.[559] However, a tribunal's subpoena powers may not be used to obtain disclosure of evidence gathered by police in a criminal investigation, except on notice to the Attorney General.[560]

A witness who is concerned about subsequent use of testimony given before the tribunal to prove liability in a civil proceeding may claim the protection of the provincial Evidence Act provision. This protection should be granted by the tribunal if requested by the witness.[561]

---

[556] *British Columbia (Securities Commission) v. Branch*, [1995] S.C.J. No. 32; *Phillips v. Nova Scotia (Commission of Inquiry into the Westray Mine Tragedy)*, [1995] S.C.J. No. 36; *O'Hara v. British Columbia*, [1987] S.C.J. No. 69; *Starr v. Houlden*, [1990] S.C.J. No. 30.

[557] *Phillips v. Nova Scotia (Commission of Inquiry into the Westray Mine Tragedy)*, [1995] S.C.J. No. 36.

[558] *Phillips v. Nova Scotia (Commission of Inquiry into the Westray Mine Tragedy)*, [1995] S.C.J. No. 36. If the press violate the publication ban, application may be made to a Superior Court for an order punishing the press for contempt: *Canadian Broadcasting Corp. v. Quebec (Police Commission)*, [1979] S.C.J. No. 60.

[559] *Thomson v. Alberta (Transportation and Safety Board)*, [2003] A.J. No. 1115 at para. 42 (Alta. C.A.), leave to appeal refused [2003] S.C.C.A. No. 510.

[560] *College of Physicians and Surgeons of Ontario v. Peel Regional Police*, [2009] O.J. No. 4091 (Ont. Div. Ct.).

[561] The *Statutory Powers Procedure Act*, R.S.O. 1990, c. S.22, s. 14 [as am.] has obviated the need for the witness to request this protection when testifying in a hearing before an Ontario tribunal, making the protection automatic.

A witness, who is concerned about the use that may be made in another country of testimony compelled in Canada, must rely on the laws of the foreign jurisdiction regarding the subsequent use that may be made of testimony in that country. In a Canadian proceeding, a witness may not plead the Fifth Amendment of the American Constitution to avoid the use of the testimony in proceedings in the United States.[562]

A power to subpoena documents for regulatory purposes complies with section 8 of the *Charter*.[563] Usually only business records are demanded. These attract only a limited expectation of privacy, especially those kept by participants in a regulated industry. If a witness does not comply with a subpoena, the issuing tribunal can enforce compliance only by commencing contempt proceedings in a Superior Court where the subpoena is reviewed by a judge who exercises an independent discretion whether to order the witness to comply. As this procedure gives the witness an opportunity to dispute the subpoena before it is enforced, the seizure of records by summons is not regarded as unreasonable (no search is involved).[564] The use of computer passwords, revealed by the seized documents, to access further information does not violate section 8.[565]

Exceptions to the compellability of witnesses are few. Judges and tribunal members cannot be compelled and are not competent to testify with respect to what happened during a trial or hearing, or with respect to their reasons for decision.[566] They can be compelled to testify as to events witnessed in a non-judicial capacity. Jurors cannot be compelled to testify.[567] Crown Attorneys may not be compelled to testify with respect to their exercise of prosecutorial discretion.[568] A provincial tribunal may not compel a federal agent to testify or to produce documents concerning matters within federal jurisdiction[569] and *vice versa*. However, a provincial tribunal may compel members and employees of another tribunal of the

---

[562] *Campbell v. Bell*, [1979] B.C.J. No. 1505 (B.C.C.A.); *United States v. Pressey*, [1988] O.J. No. 446 (Ont. C.A.).

[563] *British Columbia (Securities Commission) v. Branch*, [1995] S.C.J. No. 32.

[564] *Thomson Newspapers Ltd. v. Canada (Director of Investigation and Research, Restrictive Trade Practices Commission)*, [1986] O.J. No. 1066 (Ont. C.A.), affd [1990] S.C.J. No. 23.

[565] *McEwan v. British Columbia (Securities Commission)*, [2006] B.C.J. No. 3060 (B.C.C.A.).

[566] *MacKeigan v. Hickman*, [1989] S.C.J. No. 99; *Agnew v. Assn. of Architects*, [1988] O.J. No. 1181 (Ont. Div. Ct.); *Clendenning v. Belleville Commissioners of Police*, [1976] O.J. No. 2383 (Ont. Div. Ct.); *Allan v. Ontario (Attorney General)*, [1984] O.J. No. 3270 (Ont. Div. Ct.); *Ermina v. Canada (Minister of Citizenship and Immigration)*, [1998] F.C.J. No. 1785 (F.C.T.D.); *Administrative Tribunals Act*, S.B.C. 2004, c. 45, s. 55.

[567] *Re Morin*, [1997] O.J. No. 4526 (Ont. Div. Ct.).

[568] *Picha v. Lee Inquest (Coroner of)*, [2009] B.C.J. No. 1461 (B.C.C.A.).

[569] *Quebec (Attorney General) v. Canada (Attorney General)*, [1978] S.C.J. No. 84; *Canada (Attorney General) v. Saskatchewan (Commission of Inquiry into the investigation of the death of Gail Miller and the wrongful conviction of David Edgar Milgaard)*, [2006] S.J. No. 523 (Sask. Q.B.).

same province to testify.[570] A Minister is compellable, except when the legislature is in session, but may claim Crown privilege with respect to specific questions.[571] Counsel for an opposing party may not be compelled to testify, except where the party seeking to compel the testimony can persuade the tribunal that it is relevant and necessary.[572]

Privileged information may not be compelled. Questions of privilege may be resolved by a court on an application to enforce the subpoena or on judicial review of an order to disclose privileged information.[573] Communications between client and lawyer for the purpose of obtaining legal advice are privileged.[574] Cabinet and ministerial communications are immune from disclosure that would be prejudicial to the public interest.[575] The test to determine whether any other communications are privileged is:

(1)   The communications must originate in a *confidence* that they will not be disclosed.

(2)   This element of *confidentiality must be essential* to the full and satisfactory maintenance of the relation between the parties.

(3)   The *relation* must be one that, in the opinion of the community, ought to be sedulously fostered.

(4)   The *injury* that would enure to the relation by the disclosure of the communications must be *greater than the benefit* thereby gained for the correct disposal of litigation.[576]

---

[570]   A statutory provision making them non-compellable in civil proceedings may be of no avail: *Prince Edward Island (Workers' Compensation Board) v. Queens Regional Authority*, [1999] P.E.I.J. No. 40 (P.E.I.C.A.); *contra*: *Task Specific Rehabilitation Inc. (c.o.b. TSR Clinics) v. Steinecke*, [2004] O.J. No. 3159 (Ont. C.A.). In B.C. see *Administrative Tribunals Act*, S.B.C. 2004, c. 45, s. 55.

[571]   *Sparling v. Smallwood*, [1982] S.C.J. No. 93.

[572]   *Cannon v. Canada (Assistant Commissioner, RCMP)*, [1997] F.C.J. No. 1552 at para. 23 (F.C.T.D.).

[573]   *Canada (Privacy Commissioner) v. Blood Tribe Department of Health*, [2008] S.C.J. No. 45; *Canada (Royal Canadian Mounted Police Public Complaints Commission) v. Canada (Attorney General)*, [2005] F.C.J. No. 1011 (F.C.A.).

[574]   J. Sopinka, S. Lederman and A.W. Bryant, *The Law of Evidence in Canada*, 3d ed. (Markham, ON: LexisNexis Canada, 2009). Chapter 14 contains a comprehensive discussion of issues relating to privilege.

[575]   *Carey v. Ontario*, [1986] S.C.J. No. 74; *Sparling v. Smallwood*, [1982] S.C.J. No. 93. With respect to federal Crown privilege see ss. 37 [as am.], 38 [as am.] and 39 [as am.] of the *Canada Evidence Act*, R.S.C. 1985, c. C-5, which protects federal government information in both federal and provincial proceedings; *Quebec (Attorney General) v. Canada (Attorney General)*, [1978] S.C.J. No. 84. Quebec Crown privilege is governed by art. 308 of the *Code of Civil Procedure*, R.S.Q. c. C-25.

[576]   *Slavutych v. Baker*, [1975] S.C.J. No. 29; *Moysa v. Alberta (Labour Relations Board)*, [1989] S.C.J. No. 54; *University of Guelph v. Canadian Assn. of University Teachers*, [1980] O.J. No. 3665 (Ont. H.C.J.).

Information that is confidential but not privileged is not protected[577] but tribunals should endeavour to avoid compelling disclosure of confidential information unless the information is necessary. Protection of a witness' privacy may prevail.[578]

A tribunal may not use information against a person who provided the information under the promise that it would not be so used.[579]

The power of a provincial tribunal to compel witnesses to testify stops at the provincial border. Witnesses who are outside the province cannot be compelled to testify without express provision that would enable the tribunal to obtain the assistance of a court or tribunal in the jurisdiction in which the witness is located. The commission evidence provisions of the provincial Evidence Acts cannot be used for this purpose, because a tribunal is not a court of competent jurisdiction for the purposes of those provisions.[580] The Interprovincial Summonses Acts cannot help as their application is restricted to civil proceedings.[581] Without express statutory authority, a provincial tribunal may not travel to a location outside the province for the purpose of hearing the voluntary testimony of witnesses in that jurisdiction,[582] but this does not prevent the tribunal from hearing the out-of-province witness by telephone or video.

Parties who cannot compel the attendance of witnesses[583] depend on the tribunal to require unwilling witnesses to testify. A tribunal has discretion whether to subpoena witnesses but should issue subpoenas where necessary to ensure a fair hearing. If a party shows that the witness' evidence is reasonably relevant to the subject matter of the proceeding and can be obtained in no other way, that witness should be summoned.[584] Some tribunals screen requests by parties for witness subpoenas to prevent

---

[577] *Canada (Director of Investigation and Research) v. Canada (Restrictive Trade Practices Commission)*, [1985] F.C.J. No. 232 (F.C.A.); *MacMillan Bloedel Ltd. v. West Vancouver Assessment Areas Assessors*, [1981] B.C.J. No. 1890 (B.C.S.C.).

[578] *Canada (Minister of Public Safety and Emergency Preparedness) v. Kahlon*, [2005] F.C.J. No. 1335 (F.C.).

[579] *Slavutych v. Baker*, [1975] S.C.J. No. 29.

[580] *Ontario (Securities Commission) v. Bennett*, [1990] O.J. No. 140 (Ont. H.C.J.), affd [1991] O.J. No. 253 (Ont. C.A.). However, tribunals may be able to obtain evidence from witnesses in the United States: *Penty v. Law Society of British Columbia*, [1999] B.C.J. No. 2447 (B.C.C.A.), leave to appeal refused [1999] S.C.C.A. No. 616.

[581] Except Ontario tribunals whose witness summonses may be enforced in other provinces: *Interprovincial Summonses Act*, R.S.O. 1990, c. I.12, as am. in 2009.

[582] *Ewachniuk v. Law Society of British Columbia*, [1998] B.C.J. No. 372 (B.C.C.A.).

[583] Only in B.C. can parties compel the attendance of witnesses without the assistance of the tribunal: *Administrative Tribunals Act*, S.B.C. 2004, c. 45, s. 34.

[584] *United Brotherhood of Carpenters and Joiners of America, Local 1338 v. MacLean Construction Ltd. (Employees of)*, [1984] P.E.I.J. No. 34 (P.E.I.S.C.); *Carter v. Phillips*, [1988] O.J. No. 1833 (Ont. C.A.).

abuse[585] of the subpoena power by ensuring that subpoenas are issued only to witnesses who have relevant evidence to give. Other tribunals issue all subpoenas requested by parties and address questions of relevance at the time each witness attends in response to a subpoena.[586] Whether to screen requests for subpoenas is at the discretion of the tribunal.

What can a tribunal do if a witness does not comply with a subpoena? Tribunals have no inherent power to punish for contempt of their processes or orders. Most statutory subpoena powers provide for an application to court for an order requiring compliance, or a prosecution for contempt of the tribunal's order.[587] If there is no prescribed procedure, the tribunal may apply to a Superior Court for an injunction to enforce a subpoena.[588] Before applying to court, the tribunal must issue an order clearly stating what is to be done and, then, non-compliance with that order must be proven. No application may be made in respect of a witness who testifies voluntarily, but who refuses to answer certain questions. A tribunal must formally order the witness to attend and to answer questions before applying to court.[589] Contempt must be proven beyond a reasonable doubt. The evidence usually includes certified copies of the tribunal notice of hearing, the summons to witness, an affidavit of service of the summons, and the transcript of the questions asked, the witness' refusal to answer and the tribunal's order to answer. If an affidavit is filed in support of the application, cross-examination is not permitted without leave of the court, in order to protect the confidentiality of investigative information.[590] If the witness had a right to refuse to answer the question, a court will not find contempt.[591] On a first finding of contempt, the typical court order requires the witness to attend before the tribunal and to answer ques-

---

[585] The most common abuse is the harassment of politicians and public officials by in-person litigants.

[586] *Wal-Mart Canada Corp. v. Saskatchewan (Labour Relations Board)*, [2004] S.J. No. 704 at paras. 32-37 (Sask. C.A.), leave to appeal refused [2005] S.C.C.A. No. 13; *Strofolino v. Helmstadter*, [2001] O.J. No. 2791 at paras. 42-45 (Ont. S.C.J.).

[587] See generally *Administrative Tribunals Act*, S.B.C. 2004, c. 45, ss. 34, 49; *Statutory Powers Procedure Act*, R.S.O. 1990, c. S.22, ss. 12 [as am.], 13 [as am.]; *McNaught v. Toronto Transit Commission*, [2005] O.J. No. 224 (Ont. C.A.); *United Steelworkers of America v. Citron*, [1989] O.J. No. 749 (Ont. Div. Ct.), leave to appeal refused (1989) 69 O.R. (2d) 115*n* (Ont. C.A.). If there is a prescribed procedure, the court has no authority to deal with a witness who does not co-operate except pursuant to the prescribed procedure: *Marlatt v. Woolley*, [2000] O.J. No. 192 (Ont. Div. Ct.).

[588] *Pharmascience Inc. v. Binet*, [2006] S.C.J. No. 48.

[589] *Alberta (Board of Arbitration) v. Kakuschke*, [1985] A.J. No. 653 (Alta. Q.B.).

[590] *British Columbia (Securities Commission) v. S. (B.D.)*, [2003] B.C.J. No. 979 (B.C.C.A.), leave to appeal refused [2003] S.C.C.A. No. 341; *Alberta (Market Surveillance Administrator) v. Enmax Energy Corp.*, [2007] A.J. No. 744; [2008] A.J. No. 1375 (Alta. Q.B.); *Canada (Commissioner of Competition) v. Toshiba of Canada Ltd.*, [2010] O.J. No. 311 (Ont. S.C.J.), leave to appeal refused [2011] O.J. No. 2032 (Ont. Div. Ct.).

[591] *Couture v. Hewison*, [1979] B.C.J. No. 1312 (B.C.S.C.).

tions.[592] If the witness fails to comply with the court order, the court may punish the witness for contempt.[593]

Instead of contempt proceedings, a regulator may discipline a licensee who fails to respond to the regulator's inquiries.[594] A tribunal that is a court of record, has power to punish for contempt committed before it.[595]

4.   Use of Evidence Compelled in Other Proceedings

Transcripts of testimony given in other proceedings, if relevant, are admissible.[596] Section 13 of the *Charter*, which prohibits the use of prior testimony to incriminate a witness in a subsequent proceeding, does not apply to prevent the admission of the witness' prior testimony in administrative proceedings that may result in an order affecting that witness. This is because the word "incriminate" means to prove guilt in a criminal proceeding. Thus the transcript of testimony of a member of a profession given in their criminal trial or in a civil trial is admissible at their subsequent disciplinary hearing.[597] Likewise, if when testifying the witness claimed the protections of section 5 of the *Canada Evidence Act*, that would not prevent the admission of the witness' testimony in administrative proceedings, because the protection granted by that section only precludes use of the testimony in subsequent criminal proceedings against the witness.

The only way that a witness can prevent the subsequent use of testimony in an administrative proceeding is to claim, when testifying, protection of the section of the provincial Evidence Act that will prevent the use of the testimony in the subsequent administrative proceeding. Each provincial Evidence Act applies only to proceedings in that province. There is no way to prevent subsequent use of testimony in a proceeding before a federal tribunal.

---

[592]   *British Columbia (Securities Commission) v. Palm*, [1991] B.C.J. No. 2517 (B.C.S.C.); *Ontario Securities Commission v. Robinson*, [2009] O.J. No. 4515 (Ont. S.C.J.).

[593]   *Cornwall (Public Inquiry) v. Dunlop*, [2007] O.J. No. 4768 (Ont. S.C.J.), supplementary reasons [2008] O.J. No. 957 (Ont. Div. Ct.), [2008] O.J. No. 3673 (Ont. Div. Ct.); *Ontario (Securities Commission) v. Robinson*, [2010] O.J. No. 144 (Ont. S.C.J.); *Canada (Minister of National Revenue – M.N.R.) v. Marshall*, [2006] F.C.J. No. 1008 (F.C.).

[594]   *Wise v. Law Society of Upper Canada*, [2010] O.J. No. 2158 (Ont. Div. Ct.).

[595]   *Cotroni v. Quebec (Police Commission)*, [1977] S.C.J. No. 101; *Diamond v. Ontario (Municipal Board)*, [1962] O.J. No. 554 (Ont. C.A.).

[596]   *Darabos v. Canada (Minister of Citizenship and Immigration)*, [2008] F.C.J. No. 620 (F.C.). Except in Ontario where transcripts are not admissible except with consent of the parties: *Statutory Powers Procedure Act*, R.S.O. 1990, c. S.22, s. 15.1 [as am.]. This statutory provision is unusual and contrary to the basic principle that relevant evidence is admissible.

[597]   *Knutson v. Saskatchewan Registered Nurses Assn.*, [1990] S.J. No. 603 (Sask. C.A.); *McDonald v. Law Society of Alberta*, [1993] A.J. No. 985 (Alta. Q.B.).

T.   HEARING RELATED MATTERS TOGETHER

A tribunal has discretion whether to hear related matters together. The B.C. *ATA* and the Ontario *SPPA* grant express authority.[598]

1.   Several Incidents Involving the Same Party

Where a disciplinary proceeding is concerned with allegations of several separate incidents of misconduct, the evidence with respect to all incidents may be heard by the same panel during the same hearing.[599] The tribunal must consider each incident separately in making its decision. Proof of one incident should not lead the tribunal to conclude that all unrelated incidents are proven. Each incident must be proven separately.

"Similar fact" evidence presents an exception. Where two incidents are strikingly similar in nature, evidence tending to prove that one incident occurred may be used to support the credibility of the evidence of the other incident. However, the tribunal should carefully assess the credibility of witnesses to ensure that there is no collusion.[600]

2.   Same Evidence Relevant in More than One Matter

Matters that turn on some of the same evidence should be heard together. Separate proceedings would be repetitive and cumbersome. One proceeding permits the evidence to be adduced only once and avoids inconsistent findings of fact.[601]

Where it is alleged that a group has acted together in an improper activity, it is most efficient to initiate a single disciplinary proceeding against the group, because much of the evidence is the same for all. The holding of separate proceedings presents difficulties. If the separate proceedings are held before the same panel, there is a risk that the panel might be influenced in its consideration of the conduct of one individual by evidence it heard in a proceeding against another,[602] and this violates the right of a person to be present when evidence is heard. If the separate

---

[598] *Administrative Tribunals Act*, S.B.C. 2004, c. 45, s. 37; *Statutory Powers Procedure Act*, R.S.O. 1990, c. S.22, s. 9.1 [as am.].

[599] *College of Physicians and Surgeons v. K.*, [1987] O.J. No. 168 (Ont. C.A.).

[600] *College of Physicians and Surgeons v. K.*, [1987] O.J. No. 168 (Ont. C.A.); *College of Physicians and Surgeons (Ontario) v. Deitel*, [1997] O.J. No. 1866 (Ont. Div. Ct.), leave to appeal refused September 17, 1997 (Ont. C.A.).

[601] *McNaught v. Toronto Transit Commission*, [2005] O.J. No. 224 at paras. 61-62 (Ont. C.A.).

[602] *Law Society of Manitoba v. Crump*, [1982] M.J. No. 87 (Man. C.A.); *Threader v. Canada (Treasury Board)*, [1986] F.C.J. No. 411 (F.C.A.).

proceedings are held before separate panels there is a risk of inconsistent decisions[603] and there is the practical difficulty of the lack of a sufficient number of tribunal members to conduct numerous separate proceedings. Accordingly, a single proceeding is preferred. However, as a single proceeding against a group involves a risk that an individual may be damned by association rather than for the individual's own behaviour, it is important that a tribunal consider the evidence against each individual separately in deciding culpability.

U.   RIGHT TO MAKE SUBMISSIONS

The right to present one's case includes the right to submit argument after all the evidence has been received. By this means a party may seek to persuade a tribunal to make favourable findings of fact and assessments of credibility, and to interpret and apply law and policy in the party's favour. Parties have a right to make submissions both on substantive issues and on important procedural rulings.[604]

The tribunal may invite parties to make submissions orally or in writing or both. Written submissions are helpful if the tribunal reserves its decision. Oral argument facilitates the debate of novel and important issues. If one party is permitted to file written submissions, the same opportunity should be given to all parties and the submissions should be exchanged among the parties.[605] If there is some urgency, time limits may be imposed on the length of oral submissions.[606]

Courts do not agree on whether a tribunal may hear all submissions as to misconduct and remedy at once or should schedule a separate hearing date, after finding misconduct, for submissions on the appropriate remedy.[607] If the panel chooses to decide the merits before

---

[603] *Ontario (Minister of Transportation and Communications) v. Eat 'N Putt Ltd.*, [1985] O.J. No. 2508 (Ont. Div. Ct.).

[604] *Ladney v. Moore (Township)*, [1984] O.J. No. 3233 (Ont. Div. Ct.); *Administrative Tribunals Act*, S.B.C. 2004, c. 45, s. 32.

[605] *Communications, Energy and Paperworkers Union, Powell River Local 76 v. British Columbia (Power Engineers and Boiler and Pressure Vessel Safety Appeal Board)*, [2001] B.C.J. No. 2764 (B.C.C.A.).

[606] *Amalgamated Transit Union, Local 113 v. Ontario (Labour Relations Board)*, [2007] O.J. No. 3907 at paras. 137-142 (Ont. Div. Ct.).

[607] Separate submissions on remedy: *Brock-Berry v. Registered Nurses' Assn.*, [1995] B.C.J. No. 1876 (B.C.C.A.); *College of Physicians and Surgeons v. Petrie*, [1989] O.J. No. 187 (Ont. Div. Ct.); *Doucette v. Nova Scotia (Police Commission)*, [1980] N.S.J. No. 465 (N.S.C.A.); *Law Society of Upper Canada v. Igbinosun*, [2009] O.J. No. 2465 (Ont. C.A.); *Cymbalisty v. Chiropractors' Assn.*, [1985] S.J. No. 222 (Sask. Q.B.). Single opportunity to make submissions: *Moore v. New Brunswick Real Estate Assn.*, [2007] N.B.J. No. 311 (N.B.C.A.), leave to appeal refused [2007] S.C.C.A. No. 510; *Keess v. Saskatchewan Teachers' Federation*, [1998] S.J. No. 171 (Sask. C.A.); *Piros v. Dental Board*, [1993] N.J. No. 345 (Nfld. T.D.).

hearing submissions as to remedy, it may not revisit the decision on the merits in the remedy decision.[608] If the hearing panel's role is restricted to making a recommendation, the person being disciplined should have an opportunity to make submissions to the body who will make the final decision.[609]

V.   THE DECISION MAKERS

1.   The Person Who Hears Must Decide

The corollary of the right to present one's case is the right to have it decided by those to whom it was presented. The old legal maxim states, "the person who hears must decide".[610] The whole purpose of the right to present one's case is defeated if the decision is made or influenced by persons who have not heard the evidence and argument. Thus, a member of a tribunal who participates in a decision should not be absent from the hearing or any part of it,[611] unless the parties consent to the temporary absence.[612] A party has a right to know who decided, especially if the statutory decision maker acted on the direction of someone else.[613]

This rule does not preclude members of the panel who conducted the hearing from informally discussing the policy and legal issues with other members who were not present at the hearing and have not been assigned the case for decision. The panel members may seek the advice of their colleagues but must remain free to decide the issues as they see fit. There should be no consultation about the findings of fact because the panel members, having heard the evidence, are best able to find the facts. If a new policy or legal issue is raised, that has not been argued by the parties, it should be put to them and they should be given an opportunity to make

---

[608] *Walden v. Canada (Social Development)*, [2010] F.C.J. No. 1408 (F.C.), affd [2011] F.C.J. No. 898 (F.C.A.).

[609] *Re Munro*, [1992] S.J. No. 675 (Sask. C.A.).

[610] *Audi alterem partem*; *Moyer v. New Brunswick (Workplace Health, Safety and Compensation Commission)*, [2008] N.B.J. No. 191 (N.B.C.A.).

[611] *Doyle v. Canada (Restrictive Trade Practices Commission)*, [1985] F.C.J. No. 71 (F.C.A.), leave to appeal refused [1985] S.C.C.A. No. 46; *Bailey v. Langley Local Board of Health*, [1981] B.C.J. No. 1902 (B.C.S.C.); *O'Brien v. Canada (National Parole Board)*, [1984] F.C.J. No. 155 (F.C.T.D.); *Hayes v. Saskatchewan Housing Corp.*, [1982] S.J. No. 183 (Sask. Q.B.).

[612] *CTV Television Network Ltd. v. Canada (Canadian Radio-television and Telecommunications Commission)*, [1982] S.C.J. No. 24; *contra: Parlee v. College of Psychologists*, [2004] N.B.J. No. 191 (N.B.C.A.).

[613] *Khadr v. Canada (Attorney General)*, [2006] F.C.J. No. 888 at paras. 120-124 (F.C.).

submissions.[614] This issue is discussed further in chapter 3 under the subheading, "Independence for Tribunal Members".

A tribunal may consult a lawyer on legal issues that arise during proceedings. This lawyer must not take part in making decisions or in conducting the hearing.[615] Communications between the tribunal and its legal adviser are privileged but, if a new legal issue is raised, the parties should be told of the issue and be given an opportunity to make submissions. The decision maker may ask another tribunal member to act as a consultant subject to the same restrictions as legal advisers.[616]

The maxim that "the person who hears must decide" applies only to adjudicative decisions. It does not apply where the only requirement is for a public meeting,[617] nor to administrative decisions on whether to grant applications.[618] It also does not apply where a tribunal's governing statute clearly permits persons who were not on the hearing panel to participate in the decision. It is expected that such members would review the transcripts and other evidence to learn what happened in their absence.[619]

2.   The Need for a Quorum

A quorum prescribes the minimum number of tribunal members who are required to make a decision. Most statutes fix the number of members as well as the quorum. If not, the *Interpretation Act* may fix the quorum.[620] A vacancy in the tribunal does not affect the tribunal's power to make

---

[614] *Ellis-Don Ltd. v. Ontario (Labour Relations Board)*, [2001] S.C.J. No. 5; *Consolidated Bathurst Packaging Ltd. v. International Woodworkers of America, Local 2-69*, [1990] S.C.J. No. 20; *Tremblay v. Quebec (Commission des affaires sociales)*, [1992] S.C.J. No. 20.

[615] *Brett v. Board of Directors of Physiotherapy*, [1991] O.J. No. 44 (Ont. Div. Ct.), affd [1993] O.J. No. 1253 (Ont. C.A.); *Omineca Enterprises Ltd. v. British Columbia (Minister of Forests)*, [1993] B.C.J. No. 2337 (B.C.C.A.); *Canadian Pacific Ltd. v. Carlyle (Town)*, [1987] S.J. No. 205 at § IV (Sask. C.A.); *Ahluwalia v. College of Physicians and Surgeons*, [1999] M.J. No. 55 (Man. C.A.), leave to appeal refused [1999] S.C.C.A. No. 328; *Snider v. Manitoba Assn. of Registered Nurses*, [2000] M.J. No. 59 (Man. C.A.), leave to appeal refused [2000] S.C.C.A. No. 102.

[616] *Kranz v. Burnaby/New Westminster Assessor Area No. 10*, [1994] B.C.J. No. 1274 (B.C.S.C.), leave to appeal refused [1994] B.C.J. No. 2679 (B.C.C.A.).

[617] *Potter v. Halifax Regional School Board*, [2002] N.S.J. No. 297 (N.S.C.A.), leave to appeal refused [2002] S.C.C.A. No. 306.

[618] *Kniazeva v. Canada (Minister of Citizenship and Immigration)*, [2006] F.C.J. No. 336 (F.C.).

[619] *CTV Television Network Ltd. v. Canada (Canadian Radio-television and Telecommunications Commission)*, [1982] S.C.J. No. 24; *Lipkovits v. Canada (Canadian Radio-television and Telecommunications Commission)*, [1982] F.C.J. No. 232 (F.C.A.).

[620] *Interpretation Act, 1995*, S.S. 1995, c. I-11.2, s. 18(2); *Interpretation Act*, C.C.S.M. c. I80, ss. 19-20; *Interpretation Act*, R.S.N.L. 1990, c. I-19, s. 23.

decisions provided a quorum remains.[621] A statute may permit the Chair of the tribunal to reduce the quorum in a case.[622]

The quorum prescribed by statute applies only in respect of decisions made in the exercise of statutory powers. Fewer members than the quorum may make preliminary procedural rulings.[623] A quorum may later be assigned to preside at the hearing on the merits. Parties should be advised, at the time of the appointment of the member to hear preliminary matters, that the panel will be expanded for the hearing on the merits.[624] If the statute is amended changing the prescribed quorum, the quorum is that prescribed as at the date when the hearing commences.[625]

Where a quorum is prescribed by statute or regulation, a hearing by fewer members is invalid and a decision is void.[626] If one member is lost, leaving no quorum, the remaining members may not continue the hearing,[627] not even if the absent member is replaced, because the replacement has not heard the evidence presented before joining the panel, unless the parties consent to the change in the membership of the panel part way through the hearing.[628] Otherwise, a new panel must commence the hearing anew. Similarly, if the tribunal is constituted by a single person who is unable to complete the proceeding, the replacement must start the proceeding anew.[629] Lack of a prescribed quorum may not be waived by the parties because the purpose of a quorum is to serve the public interest through the collective wisdom of a minimum number of members.[630]

---

[621] *Unicity Taxi Ltd. v. Manitoba (Taxicab Board)*, [1992] M.J. No. 381 (Man. Q.B.), affd [1992] M.J. No. 608 (Man. C.A.).

[622] *Violi v. Quebec (Commission des affaires sociales)*, [1996] A.Q. no 3237 (Que. C.A.); The Quebec *Administrative Justice Act*, R.S.Q. c. J-3, s. 82 [as am.] permits the chair to reduce the quorum for simpler cases where expertise of another member is not needed and to increase the quorum in more complex cases.

[623] *Faghihi v. Canada (Minister of Citizenship and Immigration)*, [1999] F.C.J. No. 1300 (F.C.T.D.); *Administrative Tribunals Act*, S.B.C. 2004, c. 45, s. 26(9); *Statutory Powers Procedure Act*, R.S.O. 1990, c. S.22, s. 4.2 [as am.], 4.2.1 [as am.]; *Administrative Justice Act*, R.S.Q. c. J-3, s. 82 [as am.].

[624] *Brink's Canada Ltd. v. Canada (Human Rights Commission)*, [1996] F.C.J. No. 27 (F.C.T.D.).

[625] *Bourdon v. Québec (Comité de déontologie policière)*, [2001] J.Q. no 3491 (Que. S.C.).

[626] *Parlee v. College of Psychologists*, [2004] N.B.J. No. 191 (N.B.C.A.).

[627] *Parlee v. College of Psychologists*, [2004] N.B.J. No. 191 (N.B.C.A.). In Ontario and B.C., the remaining members may complete the hearing and give a decision: *Statutory Powers Procedure Act*, R.S.O. 1990, c. S.22, s. 4.4 [as am.]; *Administrative Tribunals Act*, S.B.C. 2004, c. 45, s. 26(7).

[628] *Moyer v. New Brunswick (Workplace Health, Safety and Compensation Commission)*, [2008] N.B.J. No. 191 (N.B.C.A.); *Grain Workers' Union, Local 333 v. Prince Rupert Grain Ltd.*, [1987] F.C.J. No. 442 (F.C.A.); *Beauregard v. Commission de la fonction publique*, [1987] J.Q. no 1602 (Que. C.A.). See *Administrative Tribunals Act*, S.B.C. 2004, c. 45, s. 26(8).

[629] *Re Manhas*, [1977] 2 F.C. 120 (F.C.T.D.).

[630] *Parlee v. College of Psychologists*, [2004] N.B.J. No. 191 (N.B.C.A.).

Most cases regarding quorum are concerned with loss of a quorum because of loss of a member. A member whose appointment to the tribunal expires ceases to be a member of each hearing panel to which the person is assigned,[631] unless the statute provides that the member's appointment continues for the purpose of completing ongoing proceedings and rendering decisions.[632] So long as the decision was signed while the person was still a member, it does not matter if the decision is released some time after the person ceased to be a member.[633] A gap in the appointment may not be critical if the person was a member at the start of the proceeding and when the decision was delivered.[634] A person ceases to be a member upon expiry of appointment, resignation from the tribunal or death. On rare occasions a quorum may be lost because a member is unable to continue to hear and decide the case. Acceptable reasons for inability include serious illness, bias and conflict of interest. Lack of time or excessive workload rarely justifies a refusal to continue.[635]

More members may be on the panel if the tribunal, in its discretion, considers the case of sufficient importance to be heard by a larger panel.[636] Tribunals that preside over lengthy proceedings routinely assign panels exceeding the quorum to reduce the risk of loss of a quorum. If more members than required commence a hearing and one member is lost, leaving a quorum that has been continuously present, the remaining members may complete the proceeding.[637]

---

[631] *Chromex Nickel Mines Ltd. v. British Columbia (Securities Commission)*, [1992] B.C.J. No. 1403 (B.C.S.C.); *Comité de surveillance de l'Association des intermédiaires en assurance de personnes du Quebec c. Murphy*, [2007] J.Q. no 3655 (Que. C.A.).

[632] See for example, *Administrative Tribunals Act*, S.B.C. 2004, c. 45, s. 7; *Statutory Powers Procedure Act*, R.S.O. 1990, c. S.22, s. 4.3 [as am.]; *Administrative Justice Act*, R.S.Q. c. J-3, s. 55; *Interpretation Act*, R.S.N.S. 1989, c. 235, s. 18A [as am.]. *Piller v. Ontario Assn. of Land Surveyors*, [2002] O.J. No. 2343 (Ont. C.A.); *Wal-Mart Canada Corp. v. United Food and Commercial Workers, Local 1400*, [2009] S.J. No. 361 (Sask. Q.B.), revd for other reasons [2010] S.J. No. 590 at para. 22 (Sask. C.A.).

[633] *Regina (City) v. Newell Smelski Ltd.*, [1996] S.J. No. 863 (Sask. C.A.).

[634] *Saisu Technologies Inc. v. Thelander*, [2004] S.J. No. 764 (Sask. Q.B.).

[635] *Conseil des écoles françaises de la communaute urbaine de Toronto v. McNeilly*, [1996] O.J. No. 1301 (Ont. Div. Ct.). The *Administrative Tribunals Act*, S.B.C. 2004, c. 45, ss. 5-6, authorizes the appointment of a replacement member for one who is incapacitated and of temporary members to help with the workload. The *Legislation Act, 2006*, S.O. 2006, c. 21, Sch. F, s. 77, authorizes the appointment of temporary replacement members.

[636] *Telus Communications Inc. v. Telecommunications Workers Union*, [2005] F.C.J. No. 1253 at paras. 62-73 (F.C.A.); *Latremouille v. Canada (Labour Relations Board)*, [1985] F.C.J. No. 22 in § 1 (F.C.A.); *Administrative Tribunals Act*, S.B.C. 2004, c. 45, s. 26; *Administrative Justice Act*, R.S.Q. c. J-3, s. 82 [as am.].

[637] *French v. Law Society of Upper Canada*, [1972] O.J. No. 1795 (Ont. H.C.J.), affd (1972), 1 O.R. (2d) 513n (Ont. C.A.), vard [1974] S.C.J. No. 125; *Re Prescott*, [1971] B.C.J. No. 678 (B.C.C.A.); *Zwirner v. University of Calgary Board of Governors*, [1977] A.J. No. 525 (Alta. C.A.); *Administrative Justice Act*, R.S.Q. c. J-3, s. 147.

3. Majority Rules

If a hearing panel consists of more than two members, a decision need not be unanimous. The majority rules.[638] Nonetheless, the panel members should consult one another and make the decision together to the extent of informing one another in a general way of the points of view of each member. They may then choose to disagree, issuing majority and dissenting decisions.[639] If on reconsideration, a majority of two (with one dissent) overrules a unanimous decision of a three-member panel, the majority decision on reconsideration prevails even though the cumulative total views of tribunal members is four to two the other way.[640]

W. DECISIONS AND ORDERS

1. Written Decisions

Unless the statute requires the decision to be in writing,[641] it may be given orally. The advantages of oral decisions include swifter justice for the parties and more efficient processing of cases by the tribunal.[642] The advantage of written decisions is that the time taken to deliberate and write encourages more careful analysis. If the statute requires that the decision be in writing, a decision given orally has no effect until a signed written decision is delivered.[643] Tribunals should endeavour to make their written decisions consistent with their oral pronouncements but, if a tribunal's written decision differs significantly from its earlier oral pronouncement, the courts are not in

---

[638] *Interpretation Act*, R.S.C. 1985, c. I-21, s. 22; *Interpretation Act*, R.S.B.C. 1996, c. 238, s. 18; *Administrative Tribunals Act*, S.B.C. 2004, c. 45, s. 26(6); *Interpretation Act*, R.S.A. 2000, c. I-8, s. 17; *Interpretation Act, 1995*, S.S. 1995, c. I-11.2, s. 18(1); *Interpretation Act*, C.C.S.M. c. I80, ss. 18-19; *Legislation Act, 2006*, S.O. 2006, c. 21, Sch. F, s. 93; *Interpretation Act*, R.S.Q. c. I-16, s. 59; *Administrative Justice Act*, R.S.Q. c. J-3, s. 145; *Interpretation Act*, R.S.N.B. 1973, c. I-13, s. 22(*d*) [as am.]; *Interpretation Act*, R.S.N.S. 1989, c. 235, s. 19(*d*) [as am.]; *Interpretation Act*, R.S.P.E.I. 1988, c. I-8, s. 17(1); *Interpretation Act*, R.S.N.L. 1990, c. I-19, s. 22(*c*) [as am.].

[639] *IBM Canada Ltd. v. Canada (Deputy Minister of National Revenue, Customs and Excise)*, [1991] F.C.J. No. 1109 (F.C.A.); *Newfoundland Assn. of Public Employees v. Memorial University (Marine Institute)*, [1998] N.J. No. 250 (N.L.C.A.).

[640] *International Union of Operating Engineers, Local 955 v. Vertex Construction Services Ltd.*, [2001] A.J. No. 1477 (Alta. Q.B.).

[641] *Administrative Tribunals Act*, S.B.C. 2004, c. 45, s. 51; *Administrative Procedures and Jurisdiction Act*, R.S.A. 2000, c. A-3, s. 7; *Statutory Powers Procedure Act*, R.S.O. 1990, c. S.22, s. 17 [as am.]; *Administrative Justice Act*, R.S.Q. c. J-3, s. 13.

[642] *Irripugge v. Canada (Minister of Citizenship and Immigration)*, [2000] F.C.J. No. 29 (F.C.T.D.).

[643] *Pryor v. Ontario Society for the Prevention of Cruelty to Animals*, [2008] O.J. No. 470 (Ont. C.A.); *Dubois v. Canada (Employment and Immigration Commission)*, [1984] F.C.J. No. 31 (F.C.A.).

agreement as to whether the written decision governs or whether significant changes are grounds to quash the decision.[644] Changes of mind after the oral pronouncement should be avoided because they may be unfair and confusing to parties who have acted in reliance on the earlier pronouncement and they may undermine confidence in the tribunal.

All members of the hearing panel should sign the decision to indicate their concurrence or dissent, though not expressly required.[645] One purpose of the signatures is to provide proof that the document is a decision of the tribunal and that each signatory participated in the decision. Another purpose is to disclose the identity of those who participated in a decision so that parties may review their involvement for bias.[646] Whether the signature of the tribunal's secretary certifying that it is a decision of the tribunal is adequate has been the subject of contrary decisions.[647] Members should not sign a draft decision containing errors, with instructions to correct the errors before release, because of the risk that tribunal staff, on checking the back page to see if it is signed, will release it without making the corrections.[648]

Decisions of federal tribunals, which determine a question of law of general public importance, must be released in both official languages.[649]

2. Notice of Decision

Notice of the decision must be given to the parties by the tribunal. Any method that is effective is acceptable. The most expeditious and inexpensive method is by email. The B.C. *ATA* and Ontario *SPPA* require that notice of the decision be sent to the parties and prescribe an alternative

---

[644] Written decision governs: *Bowen v. Edmonton (City)*, [1977] A.J. No. 560 (Alta. C.A.); *Gagnon v. College of Pharmacists*, [1997] B.C.J. No. 1362 at para. 4 (B.C.C.A.); Quashed: *Turbo Resources Ltd. v. Maison Placements Canada Inc.*, [1982] O.J. No. 1287 (Ont. Div. Ct.); *Sinnathamby v. Canada (Minister of Citizenship and Immigration)*, [2005] F.C.J. No. 242 (F.C.).

[645] *Herman Motor Sales Inc. v. Ontario (Registrar of Motor Vehicle Dealers and Salesmen)*, [1980] O.J. No. 3680 (Ont. Div. Ct.); *R.D.R. Construction Ltd. v. Nova Scotia (Rent Review Commission)*, [1982] N.S.J. No. 546 at para. 27 (N.S.C.A.); *Canadian Arsenals Ltd. v. Canada (Labour Relations Board)*, [1978] F.C.J. No. 226 (F.C.A.).

[646] *Wah Shing T.V. Ltd. v. Canada (Canadian Radio-television and Telecommunications Commission)*, [1984] F.C.J. No. 161 (F.C.T.D.).

[647] *Emerson v. Law Society of Upper Canada*, [1983] O.J. No. 3287 at para. 69 (Ont. H.C.J.); *Zwirner v. University of Calgary Board of Governors*, [1977] A.J. No. 525 at para. 22 (Alta. C.A.).

[648] *Muscillo Transport Ltd. v. Ontario (Licence Suspension Appeal Board)*, [1997] O.J. No. 3062 (Ont. Gen. Div.), affd [1998] O.J. No. 1488 (Ont. C.A.).

[649] *Official Languages Act*, R.S.C. 1985, c. 31 (4th Supp.), ss. 3, 20; *Devinat v. Canada (Immigration and Refugee Board)*, [1999] F.C.J. No. 1774 (F.C.A.), leave to appeal refused [2000] C.S.C.R. no 45.

procedure for giving notice by public advertisement.[650] Even if the parties learn of the decision some other way, the tribunal is not relieved of its obligation to notify them.[651] Notice may be given by an officer of the tribunal.[652] Notice of a decision should be sent concurrently to all parties.[653] Requirements to give public notice of decisions may be met by posting them on a website established for such notices. The onus is on members of the public to exercise due diligence to check the website.[654]

3.   Time Limits on Rendering Decisions

Some statutes specify a time limit by which the tribunal shall render a decision.[655] These time limits are not mandatory because "the right of a party should not be lost or in any way prejudiced as a result of dilatory conduct on the part of a board over which it has little or no control".[656] Their purpose is to encourage tribunals to act with dispatch. Where no time limit is stipulated, tribunals should endeavour to render decisions within a reasonable time. If they fail to do so, a party may apply to court for an order compelling the tribunal to decide[657] but may not dictate a deadline to the tribunal.[658] If circumstances change materially during the delay, parties may ask the tribunal to reopen the hearing.[659] If further information is required to make a decision, reasonable delay for this purpose may be acceptable.[660]

---

[650] *Administrative Tribunals Act*, S.B.C. 2004, c. 45, s. 52; *Statutory Powers Procedure Act*, R.S.O. 1990, c. S.22, ss. 18 [as am.] and 24. The *Administrative Justice Act*, R.S.Q. c. J-3, simply requires that the notice be sent to the parties: s. 152.

[651] *St. Peter's Evangelical Lutheran Church v. Ottawa (City)*, [1982] S.C.J. No. 90.

[652] *Orellana v. Canada (Minister of Employment and Immigration)*, [1979] F.C.J. No. 607 (F.C.A.).

[653] *Crowsnest Pass v. Board of Arbitration*, [1985] A.J. No. 982 (Alta. C.A.).

[654] *Athabasca Chipewyan First Nation v. Alberta (Minister of Energy)*, [2009] A.J. No. 1143 at paras. 73-74 (Alta. Q.B.).

[655] See *e.g.*, *Administrative Justice Act*, R.S.Q. c. J-3, s. 146. Section 12 of *Administrative Tribunals Act*, S.B.C. 2004, c. 45, requires the tribunal to issue a non-binding practice directive specifying the usual time period within which a final decision and reasons will be released after the hearing is completed.

[656] *Air-Care Ltd. v. United Steelworkers of America*, [1974] S.C.J. No. 134; *Hawrish v. Law Society (Saskatchewan)*, [1998] S.J. No. 435 (Sask. C.A.), leave to appeal refused [1998] S.C.C.A. No. 339; *Doucet v. British Columbia (Adult Forensic Psychiatric Services)*, [2000] B.C.J. No. 586 (B.C.C.A.).

[657] *Gill v. Canada (Minister of Employment and Immigration)*, [1984] 2 F.C. 1025 (F.C.A.); *Subaharan v. Canada (Minister of Citizenship and Immigration)*, [2008] F.C.J. No. 1599 (F.C.).

[658] *Jackson v. Canada (Minister of Public Safety and Emergency Preparedness)*, [2007] F.C.J. No. 94 (F.C.); *Gomez v. Canada (Minister of Public Safety and Emergency Preparedness)*, [2010] F.C.J. No. 697 (F.C.).

[659] *Tora Regina (Tower) Ltd. (c.o.b. Giant Tiger, Regina) v. Saskatchewan (Labour Relations Board)*, [2008] S.J. No. 198 (Sask. C.A.).

[660] *Alouette Amusement Canada Inc. v. Atlantic Lottery Corp.*, [1991] N.B.J. No. 465 (N.B.Q.B.); *Conille v. Canada (Minister of Citizenship and Immigration)*, [1998] F.C.J. No.

4.   Contents of Order

An order compelling a party to do or refrain from doing something must tell the party specifically what it must do. It is not sufficient to order the party to comply generally with a statute or to preserve the status quo.[661]

5.   Whether Reasons for Decision must be delivered

The delivery of reasons for decision promotes fair and transparent decision-making. The exercise of writing reasons assists the tribunal to think through the issues to reach a reasonable result and reduces the chance of an arbitrary or capricious decision. Reasons can demonstrate that the issues have been carefully considered and reinforce public confidence in the judgment and fairness of the tribunal. Without reasons, a party may have to speculate why the tribunal made an adverse decision, and may have difficulty deciding whether to appeal or otherwise challenge a decision. Similarly, a reviewing court may have difficulty understanding the rationale for a decision without reasons[662] and may choose not to give deference to the tribunal's expertise if not demonstrated in its reasons.[663]

Reasons for decision are not mandatory in all cases. Some statutes require the delivery of reasons.[664] Where there is a statutory duty to give reasons, failure to do so may render the decision void.[665] However, many statutes require tribunals to give reasons only if requested by a party.[666] A party who fails to make the request cannot later complain if reasons were

---

1553 (F.C.T.D.); *Merlis Investments Ltd. v. Canada (Minister of National Revenue)*, [2000] F.C.J. No. 1746 (F.C.T.D.); *Savage v. British Columbia (Superintendent of Motor Vehicles)*, [2006] B.C.J. No. 2947 (B.C.C.A.); *contra: Canadian National Railway Co. v. Paterson Grain*, [2010] F.C.J. No. 1231 (F.C.A.).

[661] *Aamco Automatic Transmissions Inc. v. Simpson*, [1980] O.J. No. 3695 at para. 70 (Ont. Div. Ct.); *Saskatchewan Health Care Assn. v. Service Employees International Union, Local 299*, [2007] S.J. No. 240 (Sask. Q.B.). Section 50 of the *Administrative Tribunals Act*, S.B.C. 2004, c. 45, requires specificity in orders for the payment of money.

[662] *Vancouver International Airport Authority v. Public Service Alliance of Canada*, [2010] F.C.J. No. 809 (F.C.A.); *Baker v. Canada (Minister of Citizenship and Immigration)*, [1999] S.C.J. No. 39 at paras. 37-43; *Northwestern Utilities Ltd. v. Edmonton (City)*, [1978] S.C.J. No. 107. A deficiency in reasons does not give rise to a free-standing right of appeal. The appellant must show that the deficiency prejudiced the exercise of the right of appeal: *Canadian Civil Liberties Assn. v. Ontario (Civilian Commission on Police Services)*, [2002] O.J. No. 3737 at § 4 (Ont. C.A.).

[663] *Whitehouse v. Sun Oil Co.*, [1982] A.J. No. 656 (Alta. C.A.).

[664] See for example *Administrative Tribunals Act*, S.B.C. 2004, c. 45, s. 51; *Administrative Justice Act*, R.S.Q. c. J-3, ss. 8, 13.

[665] *Comité d'Appel du Bureau Provincial de Médécine v. Chèvrefils*, [1974] C.A. 123 at 127 (Que. C.A.); *Manitoba Pool Elevators v. Assiniboine Park – Fort Garry Community Committee*, [1978] M.J. No. 1 (Man. Q.B.).

[666] See for example *Statutory Powers Procedure Act*, R.S.O. 1990, c. S.22, s. 17 [as am.].

not given.[667] Where a party has a statutory right to request reasons, a tribunal cannot impose time limits for making the request or other restrictions on that right[668] but, if a party delays too long, the tribunal may find it impossible to state reasons and may be excused from doing so.[669] The tribunal must deliver requested reasons without undue delay.[670]

In the absence of a statutory requirement, the duty of fairness may require the delivery of reasons if the decision is significant for the individual or there is a broad statutory right of appeal.[671] However, reasons may not be required if they may be discerned from a notice of allegations or an investigation report, especially if substantiated by the evidence.[672] A failure to give reasons, preceded by lack of notice of the matters to be considered, is unfair.[673] If a party fails to raise any issues that need to be resolved, reasons are not required.[674] Reasons need be given only for a final decision, not for rulings that do not finally dispose of the matter.[675]

Elected bodies that decide policy and legislative issues by way of a vote cannot give reasons for decision because each member may have different reasons for voting for or against a measure.[676]

6.   Sufficiency of Reasons

Regardless of whether there is a duty to give reasons, any reasons given must be adequate. It is not sufficient simply to outline the evidence and

---

[667] *Stoangi v. Law Society of Upper Canada (No. 2)*, [1979] O.J. No. 4296 at para. 29 (Ont. Div. Ct.).

[668] *Alvarez v. Canada (Minister of Manpower and Immigration)*, [1978] F.C.J. No. 89 (F.C.A.); *Singh v. Canada (Minister of Employment and Immigration)*, [1983] F.C.J. No. 1117 (F.C.A.).

[669] *Inter-Meridian Investing Ltd. v. Alberta (Assessment Appeal Board)*, [1997] A.J. No. 833 (Alta. C.A.); *Bau v. Canada (Minister of Employment and Immigration)*, [1987] F.C.J. No. 373 (F.C.T.D.).

[670] *Canadian Union of Public Employees, Local 1289 v. Civic Centre Corp.*, [2006] N.J. No. 299 at paras. 44-47 (N.L.T.D.).

[671] *Baker v. Canada (Minister of Citizenship and Immigration)*, [1999] S.C.J. No. 39, 174 D.L.R. (4th) 193 at para. 43; *Euston Capital Corp. v. Saskatchewan Financial Services Commission*, [2008] S.J. No. 99 (Sask. C.A.).

[672] *Syndicat des employés de production v. Canada (Human Rights Commission)*, [1989] S.C.J. No. 103 at para. 35; *Re Khaliq-Kareemi*, [1989] N.S.J. No. 98 (N.S.C.A.), leave to appeal refused [1989] S.C.C.A. No. 254.

[673] *Hutfield v. Fort Saskatchewan General Hospital District No. 98*, [1986] A.J. No. 1152 (Alta. Q.B.), affd [1988] A.J. No. 545 (Alta. C.A.).

[674] *United States of America v. Kissel*, [2008] O.J. No. 1127 at para. 33 (Ont. C.A.), leave to appeal refused [2008] S.C.C.A. No. 251.

[675] *Barnes v. Ontario (Social Benefits Tribunal)*, [2009] O.J. No. 3096 (Ont. Div. Ct.); *Canadian Imperial Bank of Commerce v. Durrer*, [2005] F.C.J. No. 1321 (F.C.).

[676] *Kirkfield Park and Arthur Oliver Residents Assn. Inc. v. Winnipeg (City)*, [1996] M.J. No. 18 (Man. C.A.), leave to appeal refused [1996] S.C.C.A. No. 155.

argument and then state the tribunal's conclusion.[677] Nor is it sufficient merely to repeat the applicable statutory provisions.[678] That does not reveal the rationale for a decision. A transcript of the tribunal's deliberations is no substitute for reasons, as it reveals only musings and observations by the panel members without coherently explaining the rationale agreed to by the panel (in addition to being inconsistent with the principle of deliberative secrecy).[679]

With respect to each important conclusion of contested fact, law and policy, the reasons should answer the question, "Why did the tribunal reach that conclusion?" Most importantly, reasons must explain why the material aspects of the position advocated by the losing party were rejected.[680] The most common fault in tribunal reasons is the failure to explain "why".

Reasons should state the findings of fact that support the conclusions and identify the evidence on which they are based. Rejection of important items of evidence and findings of credibility should be explained.[681] If an application is dismissed by reason of insufficient evidence, the material deficiencies in the evidence should be identified.[682] If a statute requires the consideration of certain factors, they should be discussed in the reasons.[683] If several incidents of misconduct were alleged in the notice of hearing, the reasons for decision should identify which incidents are proven and the reasons for the disciplinary order.[684]

---

[677] *Northwestern Utilities Ltd. v. Edmonton (City)*, [1978] S.C.J. No. 107; *Casavant v. Saskatchewan Teachers' Federation*, [2005] S.J. No. 257 (Sask. C.A.); *Boyle v. New Brunswick (Workplace Health, Safety and Compensation Commission)*, [1996] N.B.J. No. 291 (N.B.C.A.); *VIA Rail Canada Inc. v. Canada (National Transportation Agency)*, [2000] F.C.J. No. 1685 (F.C.A.).

[678] *Hannley v. Edmonton (City)*, [1978] A.J. No. 709 (Alta. C.A.); *567687 Saskatchewan Ltd. v. Prince Albert (City)*, [1987] S.J. No. 327 (Sask. Q.B.).

[679] *Attorney General of New Brunswick v. Dominion of Canada General Insurance Company*, [2010] N.B.J. No. 413 (N.B.C.A.).

[680] *Lake v. Canada (Minister of Justice)*, [2008] S.C.J. No. 23 at para. 46; *Burke v. Newfoundland and Labrador Assn. of Public and Private Employees*, [2010] N.J. No. 62 (N.L.C.A.). The website of the Saskatchewan Ombudsman contains a good manual on how to write reasons called *Practice Essentials for Administrative Tribunals* (2009), online: <http://www.ombudsman.sk.ca>.

[681] *Gerle Gold Ltd. v. Golden Rule Resources Ltd.*, [1999] F.C.J. No. 269 at para. 89 (F.C.T.D.), vard [2000] F.C.J. No. 1650 at para. 31 (F.C.A.); *Gray v. Ontario (Disability Support Program, Director)*, [2002] O.J. No. 1531 at § III (Ont. C.A.); *Law Society of Upper Canada v. Neinstein*, [2010] O.J. No. 1046 (Ont. C.A.).

[682] *Muise v. Nova Scotia (Workers' Compensation Appeal Board)*, [1991] N.S.J. No. 291 (N.S.C.A.).

[683] *Noble v. Lethbridge (City) Development Appeal Board*, [1982] A.J. No. 936 (Alta. C.A.); *Tipple's Trucking Ltd. v. Newfoundland (Public Utilities Board)*, [1983] N.J. No. 11 (Nfld. C.A.); *Attorney General of New Brunswick v. Dominion of Canada General Insurance Company*, [2010] N.B.J. No. 413 (N.B.C.A.).

[684] *Richmond v. College of Optometrists*, [1995] O.J. No. 2621 (Ont. Div. Ct.).

Reasons need not be lengthy. In most cases, a few sentences explaining the rationale for each material conclusion is sufficient.[685] Reasons need not be given on every minor point raised during the proceeding nor must reference be made to every item of evidence.[686] Tribunals that consider many applications on similar issues may use standard form reasons or follow precedents, provided each decision is based on the facts of the case.[687]

7. Who May Draft the Reasons for Decision?

The hearing panel should designate one of its members to draft the tribunal's reasons for decision. The reasons should not be drafted by a person who is not on the panel,[688] most certainly not by one of the parties. Reasons written by someone else are presumed to reflect the decision of that person rather than the decision of the tribunal. However, a tribunal that makes the decision itself and composes its own reasons may obtain typing, editorial and legal assistance from persons who are independent of the parties.[689] A tribunal may ask its staff to prepare summaries of the testimony but staff must not make findings or express opinions on the evidence.[690] If a hearing is not required, staff may review the materials that have been filed and prepare a report for the decision maker.[691] A staff summary must fairly describe all of the relevant evidence.[692]

---

[685] *Vancouver International Airport Authority v. Public Service Alliance of Canada*, [2010] F.C.J. No. 809 (F.C.A.).

[686] *Clifford v. Ontario Municipal Employees Retirement System*, [2009] O.J. No. 3900 (Ont. C.A.), leave to appeal refused [2009] S.C.C.A. No. 461; *Stelco Inc. v. British Steel Canada Inc.*, [2000] F.C.J. No. 286 (F.C.A.); *Cepeda-Gutierrez v. Canada (Minister of Citizenship and Immigration)*, [1998] F.C.J. No. 1425 (F.C.T.D.); *Gourenko v. Canada (Solicitor General)*, [1995] F.C.J. No. 682 (F.C.T.D.).

[687] *Samkov v. Canada (Minister of Citizenship and Immigration)*, [1994] F.C.J. No. 1936 (F.C.T.D.).

[688] *Adair v. Ontario (Health Disciplines Board)*, [1993] O.J. No. 2752 (Ont. Div. Ct.); *Sawyer v. Ontario (Racing Commission)*, [1979] O.J. No. 4236 (Ont. C.A.); *Wolfrom v. Assn. of Professional Engineers and Geoscientists*, [2001] M.J. No. 437 (Man. C.A.). See further discussion in chapter 3 on Bias "B.3. Independence from the Parties".

[689] *Bovbel v. Canada (Minister of Employment and Immigration)*, [1994] F.C.J. No. 190 (F.C.A.), leave to appeal refused [1994] S.C.C.A. No. 186; *Khan v. College of Physicians and Surgeons*, [1992] O.J. No. 1725 at § E (Ont. C.A.); *Wolfrom v. Assn. of Professional Engineers and Geoscientists*, [2001] M.J. No. 437 (Man. C.A.).

[690] *Armstrong v. Royal Canadian Mounted Police (Commissioner)*, [1998] F.C.J. No. 42 (F.C.A.).

[691] *Silion v. Canada (Minister of Citizenship and Immigration)*, [1999] F.C.J. No. 1390 (F.C.T.D.).

[692] *Tameh v. Canada (Minister of Public Safety and Emergency Preparedness)*, [2008] F.C.J. No. 1111 (F.C.).

X.   SETTLEMENT

Administrative proceedings may be settled by agreement,[693] provided the tribunal's approval is obtained. A tribunal should not approve an agreement that is contrary to the statute. These settlement agreements are different from contracts between private parties in that their terms must be consistent with the purposes and requirements of the statute.[694]

A tribunal may not lawfully exercise its statutory mandate to make an order implementing a settlement, unless sufficient facts are admitted to justify the agreed-upon order. The American "neither admit nor deny" compromise is not available in Canada because, absent an adequate factual foundation, a tribunal has no statutory authority to make an order. As the purpose of discretionary statutory authority is to enable the tribunal to remedy certain types of fact situations, the tribunal must be satisfied that the order is justified by the facts. Also, the public show of remorse that is inherent in an admission of wrongdoing serves the public interest mandate of regulatory discipline. Facts admitted for the purpose of settlement may not be kept confidential and are binding on the admitting party for all purposes.[695] A party who is unwilling to admit facts may choose instead not to contest the evidence presented to the tribunal.

If the tribunal is of the opinion that the agreed facts justify an order different from that to which the parties have agreed, the tribunal may, after giving the parties an opportunity to make submissions, make a different order. The nature of the order is in the discretion of the tribunal, regardless of the agreement of the parties.[696]

Given that a settlement is a compromise, one party's agreement does not set a precedent for other parties who choose not to compromise.[697]

Where settlement is not achieved, all admissions made by a party for the purpose of negotiating settlement must be kept confidential and may not be disclosed or used against that party in any proceeding.[698]

---

[693] This is explicitly encouraged in B.C., Ontario and Quebec: *Administrative Tribunals Act*, S.B.C. 2004, c. 45, ss. 16, 17, 29; *Statutory Powers Procedure Act*, R.S.O. 1990, c. S.22, ss. 4.1 [as am.], 4.8 [as am.]; *Administrative Justice Act*, R.S.Q. c. J-3, ss. 119.1-124 [as am.], 134.

[694] *Salway v. Association of Professional Engineers and Geoscientists of British Columbia*, [2009] B.C.J. No. 1570 (B.C.C.A.); *Amerato v. Ontario (Motor Vehicle Dealers Act, Registrar)*, [2005] O.J. No. 3713 (Ont. C.A.); *Consumers' Distributing Co. v. Ontario (Human Rights Commission)*, [1987] O.J. No. 103 (Ont. Div. Ct.).

[695] *Buckingham Securities Corp. (Receiver of) v. Miller Bernstein LLP*, [2008] O.J. No. 1859 (Ont. S.C.J.).

[696] *Grafton Street Restaurant Ltd. v. Nova Scotia (Utility and Review Board)*, [2002] N.S.J. No. 423 (N.S.C.A.); *Robinson v. Ontario (Racing Commission)*, [2004] O.J. No. 1591 (Ont. Div. Ct.); *Sclater v. College of Teachers*, [2000] O.J. No. 1428 (Ont. Div. Ct.).

[697] *Re Cartaway Resources Corp.*, [2004] S.C.J. No. 22 at para. 68.

Failure of the parties to make efforts to settle a matter does not preclude the tribunal from proceeding,[699] except in human rights cases. Human rights commissions are required by statute to attempt to effect a settlement and may proceed to a hearing only if they are unable to do so.[700] Settlement is regarded as a better way, than adjudication, of promoting understanding of the objectives of human rights laws.[701] For this reason, the jurisdiction of a human rights commission is ousted if the complainant executes a release of all claims. Before accepting the release as valid and binding, the commission may make inquiries to determine whether the release is valid and enforceable and consistent with the purposes of human rights law.[702] The commission may review an agreement entered into by a complainant before the complaint was filed to determine whether it is a valid settlement or an invalid contract to opt out of human rights law.[703] If the complainant refuses to accept a reasonable offer of settlement, the complaint may be dismissed without a hearing.[704]

[698]   *Canadian Broadcasting Corp. v. Paul*, [2001] F.C.J. No. 542 (F.C.A.); *Administrative Tribunals Act*, S.B.C. 2004, c. 45, s. 29.

[699]   *Laplante v. Canada (Attorney General)*, [2003] F.C.J. No. 896 (F.C.A.).

[700]   *Alberta (Human Rights Commission) v. Pro Western Plastics Ltd.*, [1983] A.J. No. 878 (Alta. C.A.).

[701]   *Woolworth Canada Inc. v. Newfoundland (Human Rights Commission)*, [1994] N.J. No. 25 (Nfld. T.D.).

[702]   *Consumers' Distributing Co. v. Ontario (Human Rights Commission)*, [1987] O.J. No. 103 (Ont. Div. Ct.); *Chow v. Mobil Oil Canada Ltd.*, [1999] A.J. No. 949 (Alta. Q.B.).

[703]   *Gee v. Canada (Minister of National Revenue)*, [2002] F.C.J. No. 12 (F.C.A.); *Bucyrus Blades of Canada Ltd. v. McKinley*, [2005] O.J. No. 231 (Ont. Div. Ct.), leave to appeal refused July 18, 2005 (Ont. C.A.).

[704]   *Carter v. Travelex Canada Ltd.*, [2009] B.C.J. No. 828 (B.C.C.A.); *Losenno v. Ontario (Human Rights Commission)*, [2005] O.J. No. 4315 (Ont. C.A.), leave to appeal refused [2005] S.C.C.A. No. 531.

Chapter 3

DISCRETION AND BIAS

A. DISCRETION

Most statutory authority is discretionary. Legislators cannot contemplate all of the circumstances and conduct to be regulated within a field of activity. Someone must be given the responsibility of applying the legislation to each situation as it arises. Also, legislation may be ineffective if no one is appointed to ensure compliance. Such a person is granted discretion to determine whether a specific situation is covered by the legislation and whether a compliance order or other remedy is warranted. Discretion may be conferred so that considerations of policy and the public interest may be taken into account when applying the statute to specific circumstances.

The exercise of discretion involves choice from among options. Some tribunals are empowered to choose whether to grant or deny an application. Others may choose whether to exclude from a regulated activity someone who has behaved improperly. Tribunals that have broad discretion to regulate a particular sphere of activity may choose how best to go about that task. This chapter discusses how discretion may properly be exercised and the criteria that may be taken into account.

The word "may" in the grant of authority typically indicates some discretion but not the scope of the discretion. That is determined by prescribed factors and restrictions and by the policy and objects of the statute. Sometimes the restrictions are so confining that the word "may" simply indicates a power to act without discretion if prescribed circumstances are present.[1]

1. Promote the Objects of the Statute

Discretion is not absolute or unfettered.[2] Decision makers cannot simply do as they please. All discretionary powers must be exercised within certain basic parameters. The primary rule is that discretion should be

---

[1] *Cha v. Canada (Minister of Citizenship and Immigration)*, [2006] F.C.J. No. 491 (F.C.A.); *Khadr v. Canada (Attorney General)*, [2006] F.C.J. No. 888 at paras. 102-112 (F.C.); *Georgia Strait Alliance v. Canada (Minister of Fisheries and Oceans)*, [2010] F.C.J. No. 1471 (F.C.).

[2] *Multi-Malls Inc. v. Ontario (Minister of Transportation and Communications)*, [1976] O.J. No. 2288 at para. 30 (Ont. C.A.); *Bellemare c. Lisio*, [2010] J.Q. no 3927 at para. 30 (Que. C.A.), leave to appeal refused [2010] S.C.C.A. No. 254.

used to promote the policies and objects of the governing Act.[3] These are gleaned from a reading of the statute as a whole using ordinary methods of interpretation. Conversely, discretion may not be used to frustrate or thwart the intent of the statute. A discretionary power should not be used to achieve a purpose not contemplated by the Act.[4] This use is labelled as an "improper purpose".

Discretionary decisions should be based primarily upon consideration of factors pertinent to the policy and objects of the statute.[5] "A public authority in the exercise of its statutory powers may not act on extraneous, irrelevant and collateral considerations."[6] Nor may the public authority ignore relevant considerations. It should consider all factors relevant to the proper fulfilment of its statutory decision-making duties.[7]

Some tribunals have power to make an order where in its opinion to do so would be in the "public interest". This is not an unfettered power. The decision must be based on the facts of the case and must serve the purposes of the statute granting the power.[8] The consideration of the "public interest" cannot be restricted to a segment of society but must also take into account the concerns of society generally.[9] Some statutes grant broad authority to manage all aspects of a particular field of activity, conferring wide authority to manoeuvre. The confines of the statutory authority and the purposes of the statutory mandate must still be respected.[10]

---

[3]   *Oakwood Development Ltd. v. St. François Xavier (Rural Municipality)*, [1985] S.C.J. No. 49 at para. 15; *Doctors Hospital v. Ontario (Minister of Health)*, [1976] O.J. No. 2098 at para.45 (Ont. Div. Ct.).

[4]   *Multi-Malls Inc. v. Ontario (Minister of Transportation and Communications)*, [1976] O.J. No. 2288 at para. 30 (Ont. C.A.); *Fisheries Assn. of Newfoundland and Labrador Ltd. v. Newfoundland (Minister of Fisheries, Food and Agriculture)*, [1996] N.J. No. 286 (Nfld. C.A.).

[5]   *Roncarelli v. Duplessis*, [1959] S.C.J. No. 1; *Canadian Assn. of Regulated Importers v. Canada (Attorney General)*, [1994] F.C.J. No. 1 (F.C.A.), leave to appeal refused [1994] S.C.C.A. No. 99; *Carpenter Fishing Corp. v. Canada*, [1997] F.C.J. No. 1811 (F.C.A.), leave to appeal refused [1999] S.C.C.A. No. 349.

[6]   *Bareham v. London (Board of Education)*, [1984] O.J. No. 3252 at para. 22 (Ont. C.A.).

[7]   *Canadian Union of Public Employees v. Ontario (Minister of Labour)*, [2003] S.C.J. No. 28 at para. 172; *Oakwood Development Ltd. v. St. François Xavier (Rural Municipality)*, [1985] S.C.J. No. 49 at para. 15; *Almon Equipment Ltd. v. Canada (Attorney General)*, [2010] F.C.J. No. 948 (F.C.A.).

[8]   *Committee for Equal Treatment of Asbestos Minority Shareholders v. Ontario (Securities Commission)*, [2001] S.C.J. No. 38; *Lindsay v. Manitoba (Motor Transport Board)*, [1989] M.J. No. 432 (Man. C.A.), leave to appeal refused [1989] S.C.C.A. No. 396; *Vallières v. Courtiers J.D. and Associés Ltée*, [1998] A.Q. no 3072, 9 Admin. L.R. (3d) 26 (Que. C.A.).

[9]   *Waycobah First Nation v. Canada (Attorney General)*, [2010] F.C.J. No. 1486 (F.C.), affd [2011] F.C.J. No. 847 (F.C.A.).

[10] *ATCO Gas and Pipelines Ltd. v. Alberta (Energy and Utilities Board)*, [2006] S.C.J. No. 4.

2. Bad Faith

All decision makers are expected to act in good faith. Powers must not be abused and should not be exercised arbitrarily or dishonestly.[11] The leading case on abuse of power is *Roncarelli v. Duplessis.*[12] In that case, a restaurant owner's liquor licence was revoked because he had posted bail for many Jehovah's Witnesses who were being prosecuted under municipal by-laws for distributing their publications without a peddlar's licence. These reasons had nothing to do with liquor licensing. Discrimination contrary to s. 15 of the *Charter* is evidence of bad faith. A decision should not be influenced by a party's race, religion, gender, or other similarly irrelevant criteria,[13] except to ameliorate the condition of a historically disadvantaged group.[14]

Since it is a serious accusation to allege bad faith, the onus is on the accuser to establish that the decision maker acted in bad faith. It is insufficient to allege only that the decision is adverse, that reasons were not given or that there exists a different opinion as to what constitutes the public interest. Innuendo is not evidence. Bad faith must be proven expressly and unequivocally.[15]

Bad faith is difficult to prove. The accuser must present direct evidence of the public official's words or conduct or indirect evidence to show that all the circumstances lead to only one conclusion, that of a bad faith motive. Because this is a very serious allegation requiring proof that the decision maker knew that what he or she was doing was unlawful and did it deliberately, proof of negligence is not sufficient, though gross negligence may, together with other circumstances, provide circumstantial evidence of bad faith.[16] A decision maker who acts surreptitiously and without candour may be suspected of lacking good faith. A hasty decision pushed through without following the decision maker's usual processes may also be suspect. A decision made for an improper purpose or on the basis of extraneous considerations may suggest bad faith. However, one

---

[11] A tribunal member who pled guilty to accepting bribes was sentenced to six years imprisonment: *R. v. Bourbonnais*, [2006] J.Q. no 14147 (Que. S.C.).

[12] [1959] S.C.J. No. 1, [1959] S.C.R. 121.

[13] *Roncarelli v. Duplessis*, [1959] S.C.J. No. 1, [1959] S.C.R. 121; *H.G. Winton Ltd. v. North York (Borough)*, [1978] O.J. No. 3488 (Ont. Div. Ct.); *Bachmann v. St. James-Assiniboia School Division No. 2*, [1984] M.J. No. 181 (Man. C.A.).

[14] *Moresby Explorers Ltd. v. Canada (Attorney General)*, [2007] F.C.J. No. 1116 at para. 31 (F.C.A.), leave to appeal refused [2007] S.C.C.A. No. 536.

[15] *Carpenter Fishing Corp. v. Canada*, [1997] F.C.J. No. 1811 at para. 30 (F.C.A.), leave to appeal refused [1999] S.C.C.A. No. 349; *K & B Ambulance Ltd. v. Prince Albert (City)*, [1977] S.J. No. 414 (Sask. C.A.).

[16] *Odhavji Estate v. Woodhouse*, [2003] S.C.J. No. 74; *McCullock-Finney v. Québec (Barreau)*, [2004] S.C.J. No. 31; *Entreprises Sibeca Inc. v. Frelighsburg (Municipality)*, [2004] S.C.J. No. 57 at paras. 26-27.

of these factors alone is insufficient but several factors together may indicate bad faith.[17] Tribunal members, who have previously been admonished by a Superior Court for conducting hearings unfairly, may be acting in bad faith if they continue to follow similar unfair procedure.[18]

3.   Fettering Discretion

Many tribunals issue guidelines indicating the considerations by which they will be guided in the exercise of their discretion or explaining how they interpret a particular statutory provision. The publication of policies and guidelines is a helpful practice. It gives regulated persons advance knowledge of the tribunal's opinion on various subjects so that they may govern their affairs accordingly. It assists applicants by listing the criteria that will be considered when deciding whether to grant the application. Also, in tribunals that have many members presiding over a large number of proceedings, guidelines ensure a certain level of consistency and avoid a patchwork of arbitrary and haphazard decisions.[19] Some tribunals publish proposed policies and invite comment from members of the public before the policies are adopted. This practice also is to be encouraged. Specific statutory authority to issue policy statements is not required.[20]

However, care must be taken so that guidelines formulated to structure the use of discretion do not crystallize into binding and conclusive rules. Discretion, once conferred, may not be restricted or fettered in scope. If discretion is too tightly circumscribed by guidelines, the flexibility and judgment that are an integral part of discretion may be lost.[21] A balance must be struck between ensuring uniformity and allowing flexibility in the exercise of discretion. The tribunal may not fetter its discretion by treating the guidelines as binding rules and refusing to consider other valid and relevant criteria.[22] In the circumstances of each individual case, the tribunal

---

[17]   *Libbey Canada Inc. v. Ontario (Ministry of Labour)*, [1999] O.J. No. 246 (Ont. C.A.).

[18]   *Koehler v. Warkworth Institution*, [1991] F.C.J. No. 246 (F.C.T.D.).

[19]   *Thamotharem v. Canada (Minister of Citizenship and Immigration)*, [2007] F.C.J. No. 734 (F.C.A.); *Nu-Pharm Inc. v. Québec (Ministre de la Santé et des Services sociaux)*, [2000] J.Q. no 5116, 36 Admin. L.R. (3d) 256 (Que. C.A.), leave to appeal refused July 13, 2001.

[20]   *Ainsley Financial Corp. v. Ontario (Securities Commission)*, [1994] O.J. No. 2966 (Ont. C.A.).

[21]   *Dawkins v. Canada (Minister of Employment and Immigration)*, [1991] F.C.J. No. 505 (F.C.T.D.).

[22]   *Maple Lodge Farms Ltd. v. Canada*, [1980] F.C.J. No. 171 at para. 29 (F.C.A.), affd [1982] S.C.J. No. 57; *Testa v. British Columbia (Workers' Compensation Board)*, [1989] B.C.J. No. 665 (B.C.C.A.); *Lewis v. British Columbia (Superintendent of Motor Vehicles)*, [1980] B.C.J. No. 1433 (B.C.S.C.); *Brown v. Alberta*, [1991] A.J. No. 605 (Alta. Q.B.).

should consider whether it is appropriate to apply the policy.[23] A policy may not contain mandatory rules that must be followed in all cases[24] nor may it contradict the statute or regulation.[25] Conversely, recognizing that people arrange their affairs in reliance on published policy, departures from policy in specific cases should be explained.[26] Applicable guidelines, policies and directives should be disclosed to parties so that they may make representations regarding their application in their case.[27]

If a statute requires the application of policies or directives, then they must be applied because they have the status of law[28] though the decision maker retains discretion to consider whether the policy applies in the circumstances of the case before it.[29] These policies may not be applied retroactively without statutory authority.[30]

Tribunals may take into account their previous decisions but should not regard those decisions as binding precedent.[31] The doctrine of *stare decisis* should not be applied because tribunals should be flexible to adapt to new situations and changing times.[32]

---

[23] *Carpenter Fishing Corp. v. Canada*, [1997] F.C.J. No. 1811 at para. 29 (F.C.A.), leave to appeal refused [1999] S.C.C.A. No. 349; *Waycobah First Nation v. Canada (Attorney General)*, [2010] F.C.J. No. 1486 (F.C.), affd [2011] F.C.J. No. 847 (F.C.A.).

[24] *Ainsley Financial Corp. v. Ontario (Securities Commission)*, [1994] O.J. No. 2966 (Ont. C.A.); *Ha v. Canada (Minister of Citizenship and Immigration)*, [2004] F.C.J. No. 174 in § 2 (F.C.A.).

[25] *Ainsley Financial Corp. v. Ontario (Securities Commission)*, [1994] O.J. No. 2966 (Ont. C.A.); *Ha v. Canada (Minister of Citizenship and Immigration)*, [2004] F.C.J. No. 174 in § 2 (F.C.A.); *Fairhaven Billiards Inc. v. Saskatchewan (Liquor and Gaming Authority)*, [1999] S.J. No. 307 (Sask. C.A.).

[26] *C.E. Jamieson & Co. (Dominion) Ltd. v. Canada (Attorney General)*, [1987] F.C.J. No. 826 (F.C.T.D.).

[27] *Innisfil (Township) v. Barrie (City)*, [1977] O.J. No. 2394 (Ont. Div. Ct.), leave to appeal refused (1977), 17 O.R. (2d) 277*n* (Ont. C.A.); *Innisfil (Township) v. Vespra (Township)*, [1981] S.C.J. No. 73; *Sebastian v. Saskatchewan (Workers' Compensation Board)*, [1994] S.J. No. 523 (Sask. C.A.), leave to appeal refused [1994] S.C.C.A. No. 533; *Island Timberlands LP v. Canada (Minister of Foreign Affairs)*, [2008] F.C.J. No. 1829 (F.C.).

[28] *Bell Canada v. Canadian Telephone Employees Assn.*, [2003] S.C.J. No. 36; *Newfoundland (Workers' Compensation Commission) v. Jesso*, [2001] N.J. No. 260 (Nfld. C.A.); *Dot Motor Inns Ltd. v. Alberta (Workers' Compensation Board Appeals Commission)*, [2003] A.J. No. 561 (Alta. C.A.); *Guy v. Nova Scotia (Workers' Compensation Appeals Tribunal)*, [2008] N.S.J. No. 1 (N.S.C.A.); *Toronto (City) v. R & G Realty Management Inc.*, [2009] O.J. No. 3358 (Ont. Div. Ct.).

[29] *Braden-Burry Expediting Services Ltd. v. Northwest Territories (Workers' Compensation Board)*, [1999] N.W.T.J. No. 84 (N.W.T.C.A.); *Gavin v. Canada (Attorney General)*, [1999] F.C.J. No. 676 (F.C.T.D.).

[30] *Skyline Roofing Ltd. v. Alberta (Workers' Compensation Board)*, [2001] A.J. No. 985 at para. 62 (Alta. Q.B.).

[31] *Danakas v. Canada (War Veterans Allowance Board)*, [1985] F.C.J. No. 32 (F.C.A.).

[32] *Medicine Hat College v. Alberta (Public Service Employee Relations Board)*, [1987] A.J. No. 529 (Alta. Q.B.).

A tribunal may not make promises as to the future exercise of its powers because to do so improperly fetters the tribunal's future discretion. A tribunal may not, by contract, bind itself to exercise its discretion in a particular way. A tribunal may not give an undertaking that prevents it in the future from exercising its discretion in the public interest or requires it to make a decision without following its usual processes.[33] A party may not by contract be released from its statutory duties because the statute must be given effect.[34] A disciplinary tribunal may not promise that it will not investigate or discipline a member for misconduct.[35] A party may not claim that it has a legitimate expectation that the tribunal will decide in accordance with a promise previously given. The doctrine of legitimate expectations, which may give rise to procedural rights, is not a source of substantive rights. Similarly, a representation made by or on behalf of the tribunal does not create an estoppel requiring that a discretionary power be exercised in accordance with the representation. The tribunal retains its discretion on whether and how to exercise the power right up until the power is exercised and the final decision is made.[36] Similarly, a recommendation made pursuant to statutory authority does not fetter the decision maker.[37] It may be difficult to distinguish between an unenforceable promise to decide a particular way and an enforceable decision that will be implemented once certain conditions are satisfied. The latter may have to be implemented if all the conditions are met, unless there are policy reasons for reversing the decision.[38]

4.   Refusal to Exercise Discretion

A tribunal may not refuse to exercise its statutory discretion. It may not refuse to deal with the matters over which it has a power of decision. It may not thwart the intention of the statute by failing to carry out the

---

[33]   *Pacific National Investments Ltd. v. Victoria (City)*, [2000] S.C.J. No. 64; *Happy Adventure Sea Products (1991) Ltd. v. Newfoundland and Labrador (Minister of Fisheries and Aquaculture)*, [2006] N.J. No. 300 (N.L.C.A.); *Amerato v. Ontario (Motor Vehicle Dealers Act, Registrar)*, [2005] O.J. No. 3713 (Ont. C.A.).

[34]   *Maritime Electric Co. v. General Dairies Ltd.*, [1937] J.C.J. No. 3 (P.C.); *Hoffman-La Roche (F.) AG v. Canada (Commissioner of Patents)*, [2003] F.C.J. No. 1760 (F.C.).

[35]   *Mohan v. College of Physicians and Surgeons*, [1991] O.J. No. 1010 (Ont. Gen. Div.).

[36]   *Ref. re Canada Assistance Plan (B.C.)*, [1991] S.C.J. No. 60 at para. 59; *Comeau's Sea Foods Ltd. v. Canada (Minister of Fisheries and Oceans)*, [1997] S.C.J. No. 5; *Baker v. Canada (Minister of Citizenship and Immigration)*, [1999] S.C.J. No. 39 at para. 26; *Libbey Canada Inc. v. Ontario (Ministry of Labour)*, [1999] O.J. No. 246 at para. 57 (Ont. C.A.); *Lachine General Hospital Corp. v. Quebec (Attorney General)*, [1996] A.Q. no 3406, 142 D.L.R. (4th) 659 at 712-24 (Que. C.A.); *Sturdy Truck Body (1972) Ltd. v. Canada*, [1995] F.C.J. No. 720 (F.C.T.D.).

[37]   *Thomson v. Canada (Deputy Minister of Agriculture)*, [1992] S.C.J. No. 13.

[38]   *Mount Sinai Hospital Center v. Quebec (Minister of Health and Social Services)*, [2001] S.C.J. No. 43; *Comeau's Sea Foods v. Canada (Minister of Fisheries and Oceans)*, [1997] S.C.J. No. 5.

statutory mandate.[39] It may not screen out an application within its jurisdiction just because it doubts the strength of the applicant's proof.[40] A tribunal has a duty to exercise the power conferred upon it, and does not have a discretion as to whether it will perform that duty. It must perform it; otherwise the statutory scheme is rendered useless.

B. INDEPENDENCE AND IMPARTIALITY

Independence and impartiality are two distinct concepts.[41] Independence of a tribunal refers to the extent that the tribunal's statutory structure frees it from interference by its political masters and others. Independence of a tribunal member refers to the extent to which a member is free to make decisions without interference or influence from others in the tribunal or the persons who appointed them. Member independence also refers to that individual's personal connections with a party or some other person who may influence their decision. This latter form of independence is case-specific. Impartiality is personal to an individual decision maker and specific to the circumstances of the case to be decided. It refers to personal interests and opinions which reflect the state of mind that the tribunal member brings to bear on the decision. Bias is an attitude of mind unique to an individual.[42] All of these concepts tend to be discussed under the general heading of "bias".

The test is the same for independence and impartiality. Would a reasonable person, knowing the facts, believe that the member may be influenced by improper considerations to favour one side? A reasonable apprehension is one held by a well-informed member of the public who is familiar with the decision-making process that governs the tribunal and with the facts relevant to the alleged bias.[43] The test is not actual bias because it is difficult to prove the actual state of mind of an individual. Proof of a reasonable apprehension of bias is sufficient.[44] It need not be

---

[39] *Padfield v. Minister of Agriculture, Fisheries and Food*, [1968] A.C. 997 at 1053 (H.L.); *Greenisle Environmental Inc. v. Prince Edward Island*, [2005] P.E.I.J. No. 41 (P.E.I.S.C.).

[40] *Ahmed v. Ontario (Criminal Injuries Compensation Board)*, [2008] O.J. No. 2478 (Ont. Div. Ct.).

[41] *Bell Canada v. Canadian Telephone Employees Assn.*, [2003] S.C.J. No. 36; *Canadian Pacific Ltd. v. Matsqui Indian Band*, [1995] S.C.J. No. 1 at para. 62.

[42] *Bennett v. British Columbia (Securities Commission)*, [1992] B.C.J. No. 1655 (B.C.C.A.), leave to appeal refused [1992] 6 W.W.R. lvii; *Zündel v. Toronto Mayor's Committee on Community and Race Relations*, [2000] F.C.J. No. 679 (F.C.A.), leave to appeal refused [2000] S.C.C.A. No. 322.

[43] *Committee for Justice and Liberty v. Canada (National Energy Board)*, [1976] S.C.J. No. 118; *Bell Canada v. Canadian Telephone Employees Assn.*, [2003] S.C.J. No. 36.

[44] *Wewaykum Indian Band v. Canada*, [2003] S.C.J. No. 50; *Spence v. Spencer*, [1987] S.J. No. 5 (Sask. C.A.), leave to appeal refused [1987] S.C.C.A. No. 115; *Setlur v. Canada (Attorney General)*, [2000] F.C.J. No. 1945 (F.C.A.).

shown that the apprehended bias actually prejudiced a party or affected the result. It is sufficient that the apprehended bias may have done so. Even decision makers who are confident that they can act impartially, despite the appearance of bias, may be disqualified.[45]

The standards of bias range from the simple expectation that, despite all influences, the decision maker will remain open to persuasion (keep an open mind), to an expectation that the tribunal will maintain the high level of independence and impartiality expected of courts. In every case it is necessary to begin the analysis with an examination of the statutory framework to determine what standard applies. This turns on the tribunal's nature and role, as established by its statutory mandate and structure, on whether its role is more in the nature of policy development, the management of a regulatory field or the adjudication of disputes, and on whether the procedure prescribed by statute was followed.[46]

Some tribunals in Ontario and Quebec are required to have a code of conduct or code of ethics which address issues such as conflict of interest.[47]

1. Independence for the Tribunal

Bias at an institutional or structural level can be shown only if a fully-informed person would have a reasonable apprehension of bias in a substantial number of cases decided by that tribunal.[48] If not, allegations of bias must be decided on a case-by-case basis. Institutional bias is rarely found because it is usually authorized by statute. For example, where a statute empowers the same body to act as investigator, prosecutor, and judge, this bias is authorized.[49] This exception does not extend to bias authorized by rules issued by the tribunal.[50]

Many tribunals comprise members appointed from within the community that the tribunal regulates because they are the most knowledgeable and experienced in the regulated subject. This involvement in the field does

---

[45] *Spence v. Spencer*, [1987] S.J. No. 5 (Sask. C.A.), leave to appeal refused [1987] S.C.C.A. No. 115.

[46] *Imperial Oil Ltd. v. Quebec (Minister of the Environment)*, [2003] S.C.J. No. 59; *Bell Canada v. Canadian Telephone Employees Assn.*, [2003] S.C.J. No. 36; *Ocean Port Hotel Ltd. v. British Columbia (General Manager, Liquor Control and Licensing Branch)*, [2001] S.C.J. No. 17.

[47] *Adjudicative Tribunals Accountability, Governance and Appointments Act, 2009*, S.O. 2009, c. 33, Sch. 5; *Administrative Justice Act*, R.S.Q. c. J-3, Title III.

[48] *Canadian Pacific Ltd. v. Matsqui Indian Band*, [1995] S.C.J. No. 1 at para. 62.

[49] *Brosseau v. Alberta (Securities Commission)*, [1989] S.C.J. No. 15, 57 D.L.R. (4th) 458 at 464; *Bell Canada v. Canadian Telephone Employees Assn.*, [2003] S.C.J. No. 36, at para. 40.

[50] *Griffin v. Summerside (City) Director of Police Services*, [1998] P.E.I.J. No. 30 (P.E.I.S.C.).

not evidence partiality.[51] Some tribunals have the power to order the payment of costs, or some other financial assessment, to the tribunal or the community. This financial benefit does not create an apprehension in a reasonably well-informed person that the tribunal might not decide fairly. The pecuniary interest is too remote, because it accrues to the community as a whole and not to the tribunal members individually.[52]

A court may not substitute a different tribunal for the one designed by the legislature.[53] The rule against bias is a rule of common law which must give way to statute. Bias created by statute is not disqualifying because a court cannot strike down a statutory provision unless it violates the Constitution.[54] There is no constitutional right to a hearing before an independent and impartial tribunal. Accordingly, the test for independence of judges, which has a constitutional basis, cannot apply to administrative tribunals, which are creatures of statute and operate as part of government. Tribunals cannot be as independent as judges because tribunals are established to implement and, often, to make government policy. The requirement for independence was developed in the adjudicative context of the courts. It cannot be strictly applied to a policy-making context because democracy requires accountability to the electorate for policy choices. For their policy decisions, tribunals are accountable to the electorate through their Minister. The Minister's accountability for their policy decisions entitles the Minister to have some influence over their policy choices, which may be exercised through the power to appoint members or through a statutory power to issue directives, and through less formal methods of persuasion, except to the extent that the statute grants the tribunal independence from Ministerial influence.[55]

---

[51] *Ontario v. Gratton-Masuy Environmental Technologies Inc.*, [2010] O.J. No. 2935 at para. 108 (Ont. C.A.); *Merchant v. Law Society of Alberta*, [2008] A.J. No. 1211 (Alta. C.A.), leave to appeal refused [2009] S.C.C.A. No. 4; *Denby v. Agriculture, Food and Rural Affairs Appeal Tribunal*, [2006] O.J. No. 1968 at para. 46 (Ont. Div. Ct.).

[52] *Pearlman v. Manitoba Law Society Judicial Committee*, [1991] S.C.J. No. 66; *Canadian Pacific Ltd. v. Matsqui Indian Band*, [1995] S.C.J. No. 1 at para. 62.

[53] *Canadian Union of Public Employees v. Ontario (Minister of Labour)*, [2003] S.C.J. No. 28 at para. 190.

[54] *Ocean Port Hotel Ltd. v. British Columbia (General Manager, Liquor Control and Licensing Branch)*, [2001] S.C.J. No. 17; *Brosseau v. Alberta (Securities Commission)*, [1989] S.C.J. No. 15 at para. 20; *Zündel v. Canada (Minister of Citizenship and Immigration)*, [1997] F.C.J. No. 1638 (F.C.A.), leave to appeal refused [1997] S.C.C.A. No. 670.

[55] *Ocean Port Hotel Ltd. v. British Columbia (General Manager, Liquor Control and Licensing Branch)*, [2001] S.C.J. No. 17; *Canada (Canadian Wheat Board) v. Canada (Attorney General)*, [2009] F.C.J. No. 695 (F.C.A), leave to appeal refused [2009] S.C.C.A. No. 366.

2.   Independence for Tribunal Members

Except to the extent authorized by statute,[56] members of adjudicative tribunals should be independent from those who appoint them and pay their salaries so that they can adjudicate each case free from interference. The factors to be considered include security of tenure, security of remuneration and administrative control. These factors must be considered within the context of the functions being performed by the particular tribunal at issue, the nature of the tribunal, the interests at stake and other indices of independence such as oaths of office. Both the statutory framework and the actual practices of the tribunal are relevant. Actual practices include the chain of command, legal direction, methods of selection of panel members, monitoring and scheduling of cases.[57]

Whether a tribunal member can be dismissed from office prior to the expiry of the term of appointment depends on whether security of tenure is granted by statute.[58] Regardless, a member's appointment may be terminated for cause, including for failure to comply with Minister's directives or a code of conduct.[59] If a member's position is abolished by statute, compensation may be payable.[60]

The appointment to a tribunal of persons connected with the elected political party is not improper because it is an accepted way of ensuring that tribunal policy choices are consistent with those of the elected government.[61] An elected member of the ruling party should not advocate before a tribunal on behalf of a constituent.[62] The ruling party may influence matters of policy but not the adjudication of individual cases.

Internal working relationships do not alone give rise to a reasonable apprehension of bias. The bureaucratic model of decision making expects staff who investigate or process a matter to work with the decision maker

---

[56]   *Ocean Port Hotel Ltd. v. British Columbia (General Manager, Liquor Control and Licensing Branch)*, [2001] S.C.J. No. 17.

[57]   *Canadian Pacific Ltd. v. Matsqui Indian Band*, [1995] S.C.J. No. 1; *Katz v. Vancouver Stock Exchange*, [1995] B.C.J. No. 2018 (B.C.C.A.), affd [1996] S.C.J. No. 95; *2747-3174 Québec Inc. v. Québec (Régie des permis d'alcool)*, [1996] S.C.J. No. 112.

[58]   *Hewat v. Ontario*, [1998] O.J. No. 802 (Ont. C.A.) (But see *Legislation Act, 2006*, S.O. 2006, c. 21, Sch. F, s. 76); *Saskatchewan Federation of Labour v. Saskatchewan (Attorney General)*, [2010] S.J. No. 124 (Sask. C.A.); *Keen v. Canada (Attorney General)*, [2009] F.C.J. No. 402 (F.C.); *Martin v. Vancouver (City)*, [2008] B.C.J. No. 823 (B.C.C.A.), leave to appeal refused [2008] S.C.C.A. No. 321.

[59]   *Nova Scotia v. Nova Scotia (Minister of Education)*, [2008] N.S.J. No. 285 (N.S.C.A.); *Wedge v. Canada (Attorney General)*, [1997] F.C.J. No. 872 (F.C.).

[60]   *Wells v. Newfoundland*, [1999] S.C.J. No. 50.

[61]   *Fletcher v. Manitoba Public Insurance Corp.*, [2004] M.J. No. 443 (Man. C.A.).

[62]   *Fundy Linen Service Inc. v. New Brunswick (Workplace Health, Safety and Compensation Commission)*, [2009] N.B.J. No. 41 (N.B.C.A.).

or be on the hearing panel.[63] Many tribunals are part of a government department. Bias in one branch of the department cannot be imputed to another branch that has carriage of the matter.[64] Even bias on the part of the Minister in charge of the department does not make the adjudicator employed by the Ministry biased.[65] Nor may bias on the part of an employee of the tribunal or a member who is not on the hearing panel be imputed to the hearing panel.[66] The fact that hearing panel members have sat on other panels with disqualified members is not sufficient.[67] Only bias on the part of a person who has a central role in advising or assisting the adjudicator in the case to be decided may raise a reasonable apprehension that the adjudicator is biased in that case.[68]

Many tribunals have internal consultation processes to ensure consistency in decision-making and to involve all tribunal members in the debate of policy and legal issues that arise in specific cases. This consultation is especially appropriate where public interest and policy considerations play an important part in ensuring effective regulation. Most tribunals are not engaged in simply deciding disputes between private parties. Their decisions may have ramifications for all participants in the field regulated by the tribunal. Consultation and debate among tribunal members enhances effective regulation. It enables decision makers to take advantage of the expertise of other tribunal members not assigned to the case in order to be able to render a more thoughtful decision.

This consultation typically takes place in the absence of the parties who may raise concerns about improper influence. Provided the process chosen by the tribunal for consultation does not impede the ability of the presiding members to decide the case as they see fit according to their

---

[63] *Egerton v. Appraisal Institute of Canada*, [2009] O.J. No. 1880 (Ont. C.A.); *Domke v. Alberta (Energy Resources Conservation Board)*, [2008] A.J. No. 650 (Alta. C.A.); *Waterman v. Canada (Attorney General)*, [2009] F.C.J. No. 991 (F.C.); *Searles v. Alberta (Health and Wellness)*, [2010] A.J. No. 602 (Alta. Q.B.), affd [2011] A.J. No. 521 (Alta. C.A.). But see: *Kozak v. Canada (Minister of Citizenship and Immigration)*, [2006] F.C.J. No. 477 (F.C.A.).

[64] *Mondesir v. Manitoba Assn. of Optometrists*, [1998] M.J. No. 336 (Man. C.A.), leave to appeal refused [1998] S.C.C.A. No. 405.

[65] *Mohammad v. Canada (Minister of Employment and Immigration)*, [1988] F.C.J. No. 1141 (F.C.A.), leave to appeal refused [1989] S.C.C.A. No. 86; *Cervenakova v. Canada (Minister of Citizenship and Immigration)*, [2010] F.C.J. No. 1591 (F.C.).

[66] *Histed v. Law Society (Manitoba)*, [2006] M.J. No. 290 (Man. C.A.), leave to appeal refused [2006] S.C.C.A. No. 436; *Telus Communications Inc. v. Telecommunications Workers Union*, [2005] F.C.J. No. 1253 (F.C.A.); *Eastern Provincial Airways Ltd. v. Canada (Labour Relations Board)*, [1983] F.C.J. No. 907 at § 6 (F.C.A.); *Duguay v. New Brunswick (Industrial Relations Board)*, [1982] N.B.J. No. 254 at para. 21 (N.B.Q.B.); *Re United Food and Commercial Workers, Local 1252*, [1987] N.J. No. 494 (Nfld. T.D.).

[67] *College of Physicians and Surgeons (Ontario) v. Au*, [2006] O.J. No. 1994 (Ont. Div. Ct.); *Lavesta Area Group v. Alberta (Energy and Utilities Board)*, [2009] A.J. No. 415 (Alta. C.A.).

[68] *Baker v. Canada (Minister of Citizenship and Immigration)*, [1999] S.C.J. No. 39 at para. 45.

consciences and opinions, such consultation does not create an appearance of bias or lack of independence. A process for voluntary consultation with freedom to accept or reject the group view is acceptable. A process for compulsory consultation or a requirement to decide in accordance with the majority view is not acceptable. The decision to consult must be up to the decision makers. It should not be imposed on them. If they do not wish to consult, they must be truly free to choose not to do so. Compulsory consultation creates an appearance of a lack of independence, if not actual constraint. Mere influence is to be distinguished from constraint. The criteria for independence is not absence of influence but rather freedom to decide according to one's own conscience and opinions. The possibility that moral suasion may be felt by the panel, if their opinions are not shared by other tribunal members, is of no consequence because decision makers are entitled to change their minds during deliberations whether this change of mind is the result of discussions with colleagues or the result of their own reflection on the matter.

While legal and policy issues may be discussed, factual issues may not. The evaluation of evidence must be done by those who heard it. All discussions with tribunal colleagues should be based on the findings of fact as determined by the panel who heard the evidence.[69]

3.   Independence from the Parties

It is assumed that a decision maker may favour persons with whom there is an emotional attachment. A tribunal member may be perceived as biased if a party or witness is a relative, friend or business associate.[70] If the tribunal member previously acted in an adversarial role against the party in a related proceeding, there may be a reasonable apprehension of bias.[71] Likewise, a member may be perceived as biased if associated with a competitor of a party where the competitor may gain an advantage if the decision goes

---

[69]   *Consolidated Bathurst Packaging Ltd. v. International Woodworkers of America, Local 2-69*, [1990] S.C.J. No. 20; *Tremblay v. Québec (Commission des affaires sociales)*, [1992] S.C.J. No. 20; *Ellis-Don Ltd. v. Ontario (Labour Relations Board)*, [2001] S.C.J. No. 5.

[70]   *Rothesay Residents Assn. Inc. v. Rothesay Heritage Preservation and Review Board*, [2006] N.B.J. No. 227 (N.B.C.A.); *Transport and Allied Workers Union, Local 855 v. Newfoundland Construction Labour Relations Assn.*, [2000] N.J. No. 24 (Nfld. T.D.).

[71]   *Kankam v. Canada (Minister of Employment and Immigration)*, [1993] F.C.J. No. 1162 (F.C.T.D.); *Graham Construction and Engineering Ltd. v. BFI Constructors Ltd.*, [2001] S.J. No. 526 (Sask. Q.B.).

against the party.[72] However, a business relationship involving a spouse of a member may not give rise to a reasonable apprehension of bias.[73]

A past connection with a party, before the party had any interest in the matter at hand, does not give rise to a reasonable apprehension of bias. Members of tribunals are often drawn from among the experts in the field who, before their appointment, appeared before the tribunal on behalf of parties. The prior professional association does not give rise to a reasonable apprehension of bias unless the member, before being appointed to the tribunal, had some involvement in the matter now before the tribunal.[74] In the smaller provinces, the number of suitable and qualified candidates for appointment is so small that part-time members, who continue to practice in the field, occasionally appear as representatives or witnesses at hearings before panels of their tribunal colleagues. This does not give rise to a reasonable apprehension of bias provided that, if the decision is reserved, the part-time member does not sit on any panels with those colleagues until after the decision is rendered.[75]

The government is frequently a party before tribunals. The fact that this party created the tribunal, appointed the tribunal members, and made the law applied by the tribunal, does not give rise to a reasonable apprehension of bias,[76] nor does a political connection between a tribunal member and the governing political party.[77] A contemporaneous employment connection between a tribunal member and the government may give rise to a reasonable apprehension of bias if the employment is with a department represented before the tribunal in the case.[78]

In appeals the lower decision maker may participate as a party and testify as a witness. This does not give rise to bias on the part of the appeal panel

---

[72] *Bennett v. British Columbia (Superintendent of Brokers)*, [1993] B.C.J. No. 2519 (B.C.C.A.), leave to appeal refused [1994] S.C.C.A. No. 52.

[73] *Newfoundland (Treasury Board) v. Newfoundland Assn. of Public Employees*, [1999] N.J. No. 356 (Nfld. T.D.).

[74] *Wewaykum Indian Band v. Canada*, [2003] S.C.J. No. 50; *Committee for Justice and Liberty v. Canada (National Energy Board)*, [1976] S.C.J. No. 118; *British Columbia Assn. of Optometrists v. British Columbia (Minister of Health)*, [1998] B.C.J. No. 186 (B.C.S.C.); *Ackroyd Food Services Ltd. v. Canway Inns Ltd.*, [1998] M.J. No. 609 (Man. Q.B.); *Li v. College of Physicians and Surgeons*, [2004] O.J. No. 4032 (Ont. Div. Ct.).

[75] *Bussiere v. Grain Services Union*, [1998] S.J. No. 590 (Sask. Q.B.).

[76] *Bell Canada v. Canadian Telephone Employees Assn.*, [2003] S.C.J. No. 36 at para. 39.

[77] *Fletcher v. Manitoba Public Insurance Corp.*, [2004] M.J. No. 443 (Man. C.A.), leave to appeal refused [2005] S.C.C.A. No. 80.

[78] *Eckervogt v. British Columbia (Minister of Employment and Investment)*, [2004] B.C.J. No. 1492 (B.C.C.A.); *Ahumada v. Canada (Minister of Citizenship and Immigration)*, [2001] F.C.J. No. 522 (F.C.A.).

because it is expected that the lower decision maker will stand behind and seek to justify the decision.[79]

Many labour arbitrations are before tripartite panels. Each party nominates a member and then an independent chair is appointed by those nominees, by the Ministry, or by a judge. The parties' nominees are expected to be sympathetic to the interests of the party that nominated them. Statutes governing labour arbitrations often provide that a nominee may not be a member of the union or an employee of the employer. Also, a party may not appoint as its nominee its counsel who represents it in the case to be heard by the tribunal or any other person who is closely connected with the case.[80] Other partisanship is usually not disqualifying.[81] The independent chair must, however, be impartial. Greater independence is expected of labour boards. Though labour boards include among their members representatives of employees and employers, these members may not act as advocates of the groups from whose ranks they were appointed. All members of a labour board are expected to approach hearings impartially.[82]

A tribunal that has decided a previous dispute between the same parties is not considered biased in favour of the winning party.[83] Some tribunals have repeated dealings with the same parties. They are not biased merely because they have previously dealt with the same parties on similar matters.[84] However, the courts are divided as to whether there is bias if the previous adverse decision turned on the party's credibility.[85]

A tribunal should not meet privately with one party in the absence of other parties or hold private interviews with witnesses,[86] except on

---

[79]   *Austin v. Ontario (Racing Commission)*, [2007] O.J. No. 3249 (Ont. C.A.); *Denby v. Agriculture, Food and Rural Affairs Appeal Tribunal*, [2006] O.J. No. 1968 at para. 46 (Ont. Div. Ct.).

[80]   *Prince Edward Island (Private Training Schools Act, Administrator) v. Prince Edward Island (Private Training Schools Act, Appeals Board)*, [1998] P.E.I.J. No. 58 (P.E.I.S.C.).

[81]   *Yorkton (City) v. Yorkton Professional Fire Fighters Assn., Local 1527*, [2001] S.J. No. 711 (Sask. C.A.).

[82]   *Refrigeration Workers Union v. British Columbia (Labour Relations Board)*, [1986] B.C.J. No. 286 (B.C.C.A.).

[83]   *Kinaschuk v. Weiser*, [1983] B.C.J. No. 1854 (B.C.S.C.); *Acharya v. Newfoundland (Medical Board)*, [1986] N.J. No. 163 (Nfld. T.D.).

[84]   *Brosseau v. Alberta (Securities Commission)*, [1989] S.C.J. No. 15 at paras. 30-31.

[85]   Bias: *Batorski v. Moody*, [1983] O.J. No. 3129 (Ont. Div. Ct.); *Huerto v. College of Physicians and Surgeons*, [1994] S.J. No. 390 (Sask. Q.B.), affd [1996] S.J. No. 56 (Sask. C.A.); *McCormack v. Toronto (City) Police Service*, [2005] O.J. No. 5149 (Ont. Div. Ct.). No bias: *Forget v. Law Society of Upper Canada*, [2002] O.J. No. 422 (Ont. Div. Ct.); *Gonzales v. Canada (Secretary of State)*, [1993] F.C.J. No. 1305 (F.C.T.D.).

[86]   *Kane v. University of British Columbia*, [1980] S.C.J. No. 32; *Spence v. Spencer*, [1987] S.J. No. 5 (Sask. C.A.), leave to appeal refused [1987] S.C.C.A. No. 115; *Gal Cab Investments Ltd. v. Northwest Territories (Liquor Licensing Board)*, [1986] N.W.T.J. No. 118 (N.W.T.C.A.).

consent.[87] If it is necessary to discuss procedural matters with the parties, it should be done by meeting or teleconference with all parties, or the contact should be made by the tribunal's registrar and not by any panel member.[88] A tribunal staff member, who has presented the case against the other parties, should not be present while the tribunal deliberates.[89] Similarly, tribunal counsel may not perform the overlapping functions of prosecutor and advisor to the tribunal.[90]

The rule against meeting privately with parties and witnesses does not apply to those who make policy decisions. They may consult whomever they choose to gather information and advice as to how the public interest may best be served.[91]

After a hearing has concluded and the decision reserved, parties who are tempted to write letters to the tribunal providing additional information or clarification should refrain from doing so. A tribunal ought not to consider such letters.[92] If it is necessary to put additional evidence or argument to the tribunal, a request should be made to reopen the hearing.

A tribunal should not ask a party to write its reasons for decision. This gives the appearance that the decision is not the tribunal's and that the tribunal was predisposed toward that party. A party is entitled to the reasons of the tribunal, not those of the opposing party.[93]

Tribunal members should resist the temptation when on circuit to socialize during the evenings with witnesses and lawyers who are also from out of town.[94] Such social camaraderie may give rise to a reasonable apprehension of bias in favour of those whose company was enjoyed as it may be assumed that the tribunal member heard evidence or submissions in the absence of other parties. Hearings are often conducted in buildings

---

[87] *Air Canada Pilots Assn. v. Air Line Pilots Assn.*, [2005] F.C.J. No. 906 (F.C.), affd [2006] F.C.J. No. 255 (F.C.A.), leave to appeal refused [2006] S.C.C.A. No. 137; *Quintette Coal Ltd. v. British Columbia (Assessment Appeal Board)*, [1984] B.C.J. No. 2911 at § IV (B.C.S.C.); *Re Cardinal Insurance Co.*, [1982] F.C.J. No. 516 at § (2) (F.C.A.), leave to appeal refused [1982] S.C.C.A. No. 104.

[88] *Setlur v. Canada (Attorney General)*, [2000] F.C.J. No. 1945 (F.C.A.).

[89] *Setlur v. Canada (Attorney General)*, [2000] F.C.J. No. 1945 (F.C.A.). See also *2747-3174 Québec Inc. v. Québec (Régie des permis d'alcool)*, [1996] S.C.J. No. 112; *Haight-Smith v. Kamloops School District No. 34*, [1988] B.C.J. No. 918 (B.C.C.A.); *United Enterprises Ltd. v. Saskatchewan (Liquor and Gaming Licensing Commission)*, [1996] S.J. No. 798 (Sask. Q.B.).

[90] *Violette v. Dental Society*, [2004] N.B.J. No. 5 at § C1 (N.B.C.A.).

[91] *Pembroke Civic Hospital v. Ontario (Health Services Restructuring Commission)*, [1997] O.J. No. 3142 at paras. 29-33 (Ont. Div. Ct.), leave to appeal refused September 10, 1997 (Ont. C.A.).

[92] *Banca Nazionale del Lavoro of Canada Ltd. v. Lee-Shanok*, [1988] F.C.J. No. 594 (F.C.A.).

[93] *Sawyer v. Ontario (Racing Commission)*, [1979] O.J. No. 4236 (Ont. C.A.).

[94] *Reid v. Wigle*, [1980] O.J. No. 3701 (Ont. Div. Ct.); *United Enterprises Ltd. v. Saskatchewan (Liquor and Gaming Licensing Commission)*, [1996] S.J. No. 798 (Sask. Q.B.).

in which tribunal members encounter parties and witnesses outside the hearing room. Discussion of the case should be avoided.[95]

In municipal affairs, it is not unusual for individual councillors to be lobbied before and after a public hearing by proponents and opponents of a proposed development. The councillors do not thereby become biased.[96] However, the council or a committee of council may become biased if it hears one party in the absence of others.[97]

4.   Personal Interests

Decision makers must not allow their personal interests to influence their exercise of statutory powers. A tribunal member who has a pecuniary interest in the case that the member is called upon to decide is biased. This exists where the tribunal member, or a person connected to that member, may benefit or suffer financially from the decision. A statutory power may not be exercised for personal profit.[98] The fact that a tribunal member has had a personal experience similar to the factual subject of the hearing does not give rise to a reasonable apprehension of bias.[99]

A tribunal should not judge its own case. It should not be in the position of having to consider its own application, which a reasonable observer may assume would be granted. However, a municipal council is permitted to judge its own application to develop its land.[100] Tribunal members should not judge their own complaints.[101] Tribunal members should not testify as witnesses in the proceeding over which they preside.[102] Reasonable parties may assume that, when assessing credibility, members will prefer their own testimony over that of other witnesses. Tribunal members who had some involvement in the matter which is the

---

95   *Weyer v. Canada*, [1988] F.C.J. No. 137 at § 2 (F.C.A.), leave to appeal refused [1988] S.C.C.A. No. 173.

96   *Eighth Street Business Assn. v. Saskatoon (City)*, [2001] S.J. No. 650 (Sask. Q.B.); *Nova Scotia (Heritage Trust) v. Nova Scotia (Provincial Planning Appeal Board)*, [1981] N.S.J. No. 586 at para. 197 (N.S.T.D.).

97   *Bourque v. Richmond (Township)*, [1978] B.C.J. No. 1224 (B.C.C.A.).

98   *Obichon v. Heart Lake First Nation No. 176*, [1988] F.C.J. No. 307 (F.C.T.D.); *Sacks v. Campbell*, [1991] O.J. No. 2213 (Ont. Div. Ct.); *Gowman v. British Columbia (Provincial Agricultural Land Commission)*, [2009] B.C.J. No. 364 (B.C.S.C.).

99   *Law Society of Upper Canada v. Neinstein*, [2010] O.J. No. 1046 (Ont. C.A.).

100   *St. Clements Ratepayers Assn. Inc. v. St. Clements (Rural Municipality)*, [2001] M.J. No. 380 (Man. Q.B.), affd [2002] M.J. No. 208 (Man. C.A.).

101   *Great Atlantic and Pacific Co. of Canada Ltd. v. Ontario (Human Rights Commission)*, [1993] O.J. No. 1278 (Ont. Div. Ct.); *Griffin v. Summerside (City) Director of Police Services*, [1998] P.E.I.J. No. 30 (P.E.I.S.C.).

102   *Kalina v. Directors of Chiropractic*, [1981] O.J. No. 3219 (Ont. Div. Ct.), leave to appeal refused (1982), 35 O.R. (2d) 626n (Ont. C.A.).

subject of the hearing should not preside because they may view their own actions in a better light than might an impartial observer.[103] However, the fact that a party has commenced a lawsuit against a decision maker does not give rise to a reasonable apprehension of bias.[104]

Statutes governing elected municipal councils and school boards set out strict rules concerning conflict of interest and prescribe the rules to be followed when members have an interest in the matter to be decided.[105] Usually these members must declare their interest in advance, absent themselves from the hearing room during deliberations, and abstain from voting on the decision.

5.   Prejudgment

Tribunal members should not prejudge a case. They should not make up their minds so strongly in advance that they cannot be influenced at the hearing to decide another way. They should not hold predetermined views, regardless of the merits of the case.[106] They should not make their decision before the hearing is concluded.[107] Otherwise, the extent to which a member may hold opinions before deciding a case depends on the circumstances. Greater leeway is enjoyed by investigators, by those who decide policy issues and by elected officials than by adjudicators.

Elected tribunal members on municipal councils and school boards often let their views be known. They may have been elected because they were for or against a proposal. This does not taint them. If they are required to hold a hearing, all that can be expected of them is that they hear and consider alternative views with an open mind.[108] To disqualify an

---

[103] *Brown v. Waterloo (Region) Commissioners of Police*, [1980] O.J. No. 3871 (Ont. C.A.); *Weimer v. Symons*, [1987] S.J. No. 276 (Sask. Q.B.).

[104] *Grabowski v. Joint Chiropractic Professional Review Committee*, [2000] S.J. No. 331 (Sask. C.A.), leave to appeal refused [2000] S.C.C.A. No. 388; *Imperial Oil Ltd. v. Quebec (Minister of the Environment)*, [2003] S.C.J. No. 59.

[105] See for example, *Gillespie v. Wheeler*, [1979] S.C.J. No. 61; *Arbez v. Johnson*, [1998] M.J. No. 257 (Man. C.A.), leave to appeal refused [1998] S.C.C.A. No. 375; *Greene v. Borins*, [1985] O.J. No. 2510 (Ont. Div. Ct.); *Calgary Roman Catholic Separate School District No. 1 v. O'Malley*, [2007] A.J. No. 1065 (Alta. Q.B.).

[106] *Committee for Justice and Liberty v. Canada (National Energy Board)*, [1976] S.C.J. No. 118; *Concordia Hospital v. Manitoba Nurses' Union, Local 27*, [2004] M.J. No. 445 (Man. Q.B.).

[107] *Sternberg v. Ontario (Racing Commission)*, [2008] O.J. No. 3864 (Ont. Div. Ct.); *Xu v. Canada (Minister of Citizenship and Immigration)*, [1999] F.C.J. No. 1184 (F.C.T.D.); *Tolosa v. Canada (Minister of Citizenship and Immigration)*, [2008] F.C.J. No. 1000 (F.C.).

[108] *Save Richmond Farmland Society v. Richmond (Township)*, [1990] S.C.J. No. 79; *Old St. Boniface Residents Assn. Inc. v. Winnipeg (City)*, [1990] S.C.J. No. 137.

elected member, it must be shown that the member prejudged the matter to such an extent that representations to the contrary would be futile.[109]

The same test applies to all decisions that are based on policy considerations regardless whether the decision maker is elected or appointed.[110] Persons who decide such questions must keep an open mind. Their expression of strong opinions prior to a hearing does not, alone, disqualify them.[111]

Tribunal members may be chosen for appointment because of their public advocacy in the field. It is often those people who are the most knowledgeable and engaged in the subject governed by the tribunal. Appointment to tribunals is not restricted to bureaucrats and experts. Statements made prior to appointment in support of interests then represented do not disqualify these persons.[112] However, these members should not be predisposed to decide every case in favour of the interests previously advocated but, instead, should be careful to base all decisions on the evidence and arguments presented in each case.[113]

An investigator has a wide licence to make public comments, so long as the statements do not indicate a mind so closed that any submissions would be futile.[114] An investigator is expected to be suspicious.[115] The test at the investigation stage is open-mindedness.[116] The same test applies to human rights commissions because their role is that of a protagonist.[117]

Regulators who decide applications often develop the case through investigation, discussions and correspondence before coming to a final decision. The expression of preliminary views by the regulator does not

---

[109] *Newfoundland Telephone Co. v. Newfoundland (Board of Commissioners of Public Utilities)*, [1992] S.C.J. No. 21.

[110] *Idziak v. Canada (Minister of Justice)*, [1992] S.C.J. No. 97 at para. 60; *TransCanada Pipelines Ltd. v. Beardmore (Township)*, [2000] O.J. No. 1066 at para. 147 (Ont. C.A.), leave to appeal refused [2000] S.C.C.A. No. 264; *Atkins v. Calgary (City)*, [1994] A.J. No. 950 (Alta. C.A.).

[111] *Newfoundland Telephone Co. v. Newfoundland (Board of Commissioners of Public Utilities)*, [1992] S.C.J. No. 21.

[112] *Newfoundland Light and Power Co. v. Newfoundland (Public Utilities Board)*, [1987] N.J. No. 56 (C.A.), leave to appeal refused [1987] S.C.C.A. No. 230.

[113] *Newfoundland Telephone Co. v. Newfoundland (Board of Commissioners of Public Utilities)*, [1992] S.C.J. No. 21.

[114] *Newfoundland Telephone Co. v. Newfoundland (Board of Commissioners of Public Utilities)*, [1992] S.C.J. No. 21.

[115] *College of Physicians and Surgeons (Alberta) v. J.H.*, [2008] A.J. No. 463 (Alta. Q.B.).

[116] *Regina (City) Police v. Saskatchewan (Human Rights Commission)*, [1992] S.J. No. 547 (Sask. C.A.).

[117] *Zündel v. Canada (Attorney General)*, [1999] F.C.J. No. 964 (F.C.T.D.), affd [2000] F.C.J. No. 2057 (F.C.A.); *Crown Packaging Ltd. v. British Columbia (Human Rights Commission)*, [2002] B.C.J. No. 489 (B.C.C.A.).

give rise to a reasonable apprehension of bias so long as the regulator kept an open mind before making a final decision.[118]

Decision makers who are expected to decide on the basis of their personal knowledge of the subject, rather than on the basis of evidence, may have formed general opinions before their appointment.[119]

Even for adjudicators, unbiased does not mean uninformed. It means only that the decision maker should be open to persuasion. An adjudicator may review the files and hold tentative views on the matters at issue.[120] Provided they are open to hearing and considering the information and submissions of the parties, a statement of preliminary findings is not objectionable.[121] Likewise, the fact that they have reviewed prejudicial evidence, which they have ruled inadmissible, does not raise a reasonable apprehension of bias.[122] However, if an adjudicator has met with the parties for the purpose of assisting them, unsuccessfully, to settle the case, there may be a reasonable apprehension of bias if the adjudicator proceeds to hear and decide the case,[123] but not if the adjudicator has simply rejected a settlement that was presented for approval[124] or accepted a settlement on agreed facts.[125]

The precise state of mind of an adjudicator is unknown. Evidence of prejudgment is based on their words and conduct. A single inappropriate comment may not give rise to a reasonable apprehension of bias, but a series of them might do so. It is unwise for adjudicators to express opinions on the merits or strength of the case until after all evidence and submissions have been heard.[126] They should not speak to the media about the merits of the case.[127] Adjudicators should not make flippant or pejorative remarks about parties or anyone else.[128] Use of intemperate language or the display

---

[118] *Halfway River First Nation v. British Columbia (Ministry of Forests)*, [1999] B.C.J. No. 1880 at paras. 67-75 (B.C.C.A.).

[119] *Paine v. University of Toronto*, [1981] O.J. No. 3187 (Ont. C.A.), leave to appeal refused [1982] 1 S.C.R. x; *Alberta Civil Service Assn. v. Farran*, [1979] A.J. No. 830 (Alta. C.A.).

[120] *Aitken v. Frontier School Division 48*, [1985] M.J. No. 121 at para. 32 (Man. C.A.).

[121] *550551 Ontario Ltd. v. Framingham*, [1991] O.J. No. 1035 (Ont. Div. Ct.).

[122] *Ponce de Leon v. Canada (Minister of Citizenship and Immigration)*, [1998] F.C.J. No. 1532 (F.C.T.D.).

[123] *Todd Ranch Ltd. v. Alberta (Surface Rights Board)*, [1995] A.J. No. 279 (Alta. Q.B.); *Beznec v. Apocan Inc.*, [1996] N.B.J. No. 276 (N.B.C.A.).

[124] *Robinson v. Ontario (Racing Commission)*, [2004] O.J. No. 1591 (Ont. Div. Ct.).

[125] *Ochnik v. Ontario Securities Commission*, [2007] O.J. No. 1730 at para. 42 (Ont. Div. Ct.).

[126] *Halifax Infirmary Hospital v. Nova Scotia Nurses' Union*, [1981] N.S.J. No. 558 (N.S.C.A.); *Re Rodrigues*, [1987] N.J. No. 309 (Nfld. T.D.); *Lim v. Manitoba (Health Services Commission)*, [1983] M.J. No. 362 at para. 22 (Man. Q.B.).

[127] *Pelletier v. Canada (Attorney General)*, [2008] F.C.J. No. 1006 (F.C.).

[128] *Chrétien v. Canada (Commission of Inquiry into the Sponsorship Program and Advertising Activities, Gomery Commission)*, [2008] F.C.J. No. 973 (F.C.), affd [2010] F.C.J. No. 1274

of feelings of antagonism and hostility toward a party are unacceptable,[129] as are discriminatory or sexist comments.[130] An adjudicator who repeatedly interferes in cross-examination or questions witnesses to such an extent as to appear to descend into the arena may be suspected of bias.[131]

The improper conduct must relate to the case being decided by the tribunal member. Unrelated misconduct is irrelevant.[132] How an adjudicator has decided similar cases cannot be evidence of bias.[133]

Protests by the tribunal against derogatory comments made by a party do not give rise to a reasonable apprehension of bias. The tribunal may control abuse of its processes.[134]

To be disqualifying, the improper comments must have been made by the person presiding at the hearing. Inappropriate statements made by others are not evidence that the adjudicator is biased,[135] except those made by a person who is in a position to influence the adjudicator's decision.[136] Inappropriate comments made by a spouse of a tribunal member are not disqualifying.[137] Where a case is to be re-heard before a different panel,

---

(F.C.A.); *Re Rodrigues*, [1987] N.J. No. 309 (Nfld. T.D.); *Service Employees International Union, Local 246 v. Heritage Nursing Homes Ltd.*, [1977] O.J. No. 2468 (Ont. Div. Ct.).

[129] *Milstein v. College of Pharmacy*, [1978] O.J. No. 3434 (Ont. C.A.); *Chung v. Canada (Minister of Citizenship and Immigration)*, [1998] F.C.J. No. 1891 (F.C.T.D.); *McKeon v. Canada (Attorney General)*, [1996] F.C.J. No. 805 (F.C.T.D.).

[130] *Baker v. Canada (Minister of Citizenship and Immigration)*, [1999] S.C.J. No. 39 at para. 48; *Yusuf v. Canada (Minister of Employment and Immigration)*, [1991] F.C.J. No. 1049 (F.C.A.); *Begum v. Canada (Minister of Citizenship and Immigration)*, [1995] F.C.J. No. 382 (F.C.T.D.); *Chiebuka v. Canada (Ministre de la Citoyenneté et de l'Immigration)*, [2000] F.C.J. No. 1745 (F.C.T.D.).

[131] *Solicitor "X" v. Nova Scotia Barristers' Society*, [1998] N.S.J. No. 428 (N.S.C.A.); *Kumar v. Canada (Minister of Employment and Immigration)*, [1987] F.C.J. No. 1015 (F.C.A.); *Guermache v. Canada (Minister of Citizenship and Immigration)*, [2004] F.C.J. No. 1058 (F.C.); *Olvera-Paoletti v. Canada (Minister of Citizenship and Immigration)*, [2008] F.C.J. No. 569 (F.C.).

[132] *Laplante v. Canada (Treasury Board)*, [1991] F.C.J. No. 1051 (F.C.A.).

[133] *Victoria v. Canada (Minister of Citizenship and Immigration)*, [2009] F.C.J. No. 532 (F.C.).

[134] *Chromex Nickel Mines Ltd. v. British Columbia (Securities Commission)*, [1992] B.C.J. No. 1403 at § III (B.C.S.C.).

[135] *Ross v. New Brunswick (Board of School Trustees, District No. 15)*, [1990] N.B.J. No. 847 (N.B.C.A.); *Mohammad v. Canada (Minister of Employment and Immigration)*, [1988] F.C.J. No. 1141 (F.C.A.), leave to appeal refused [1989] S.C.C.A. No. 86; *Zündel v. Toronto Mayor's Committee on Community and Race Relations*, [2000] F.C.J. No. 679 (F.C.A.), leave to appeal refused [2000] S.C.C.A. No. 322; *Muscillo Transport Ltd. v. Ontario (Licence Suspension Appeal Board)*, [1997] O.J. No. 3062 (Ont. Gen. Div.), affd [1998] O.J. No. 1488 (Ont. C.A.).

[136] *Baker v. Canada (Minister of Citizenship and Immigration)*, [1999] S.C.J. No. 39 at para. 45; *Adair v. Ontario (Health Disciplines Board)*, [1993] O.J. No. 2752 (Ont. Div. Ct.).

[137] *Cameron v. East Prince Health Authority*, [1999] P.E.I.J. No. 44 at paras. 76-84 (P.E.I.S.C.).

publicity surrounding the first hearing, even if generated by the tribunal, does not give rise to a reasonable apprehension of bias.[138]

6.   Procedure

It is presumed that a tribunal member will act fairly and impartially, in the absence of evidence to the contrary. The onus of proving bias lies on the person who alleges it.[139] A real likelihood or probability of bias must be demonstrated. Mere suspicion is not enough.[140] Bias must be proven with evidence under oath unless the facts are on the record or volunteered by the tribunal member. An allegation that turns on comments made by the member outside the hearing room must be proven by direct evidence from a person who heard the comments. It is not sufficient to file a newspaper clipping without an affidavit from the journalist who heard the reported comments[141] or an admission by the member that the comments were made.

An allegation of bias should be made first to the tribunal member.[142] This shows respect for the tribunal by giving it an opportunity to correct the problem when it first arises. It is faster and cheaper than an application for judicial review. The need to confront the member directly should cause a party to take greater care in making allegations of bias. Also, it allows the member to state the facts on the record, creating a record for subsequent review by a court.[143] This type of unsworn evidence is accepted by reviewing courts because it would be unseemly to permit a party to cross-examine a tribunal member and because tribunals have sufficient institutional controls to ensure reliability of the information.

If known, allegations of bias should be raised at the outset of the hearing because a biased tribunal member can influence the other members and taint the whole decision, even though a majority of members were not biased. If a biased member is removed from the panel at the outset, the remaining members of the panel are not tainted with

---

[138] *Finch v. Assn. of Professional Engineers and Geoscientists*, [1996] B.C.J. No. 743 (B.C.C.A.), leave to appeal refused [1996] S.C.C.A. No. 272.

[139] *Mugesera v. Canada (Minister of Citizenship and Immigration)*, [2005] S.C.J. No. 40.

[140] *Zündel v. Toronto Mayor's Committee on Community and Race Relations*, [2000] F.C.J. No. 679 at para. 36 (F.C.A.), leave to appeal refused [2000] S.C.C.A. No. 322; *Ellis-Don Ltd. v. Ontario (Labour Relations Board)*, [2001] S.C.J. No. 5.

[141] *Cameron v. East Prince Health Authority*, [1999] P.E.I.J. No. 44 at para. 64 (P.E.I.T.D.).

[142] *Communications, Energy and Paperworkers Union of Canada, Local 60N v. Abitibi Consolidated Co. of Canada*, [2008] N.J. No. 11 at paras. 35-39 (N.L.C.A.); *Jogendra v. Ontario (Human Rights Tribunal)*, [2011] O.J. No. 2518 (Ont. S.C.J.).

[143] *TELUS Communications Inc. v. Telecommunications Workers Union*, [2005] F.C.J. No. 1253 at paras. 25-34 (F.C.A.).

bias.[144] The removed member should have nothing further to do with the proceeding and should avoid communication with the panel until after the final decision is made.[145]

When an allegation of bias is made, the tribunal should rule on the allegation. If it rules that it is not biased, it may continue with the hearing. It is not obliged to halt the proceeding. A tribunal is not to be paralysed every time someone alleges bias.[146]

The parties may be unaware that there is a circumstance that may give rise to a reasonable apprehension of bias. A tribunal member who is aware of a problem may recuse him or herself from the hearing without consulting the parties.[147] If uncertain whether the parties would be concerned about the situation, the member should state the facts at the outset of the hearing and invite the parties to make submissions as to whether there is a reasonable apprehension of bias.

7.   Objection and Waiver

Bias may be waived. A party who was aware of bias during the proceeding, but failed to object, may not complain later when the decision is adverse. The genuineness of the apprehension becomes suspect when it is not stated promptly. A party should raise a concern about bias when first aware of it but, given the onus of proof that must be met to allege bias, waiver should be found only if the party had sufficient knowledge of the facts. The onus is on the party alleging waiver to prove it.[148]

It is unwise and unnecessary for a party to leave the hearing after the tribunal has ruled against an objection. If the objection was clearly raised, continued participation will not be seen as acquiescence.[149]

---

[144] *Lavesta Area Group v. Alberta (Energy and Utilities Board)*, [2009] A.J. No. 415 (Alta. C.A.).

[145] *Roberts v. College of Nurses*, [1999] O.J. No. 2281 (Ont. S.C.J.).

[146] *Flamborough (Town) v. Canada (National Energy Board)*, [1984] F.C.J. No. 526 (F.C.A.), leave to appeal refused [1984] 2 S.C.R. vii.

[147] *Kentville (Town) v. Nova Scotia (Human Rights Commission)*, [2004] N.S.J. No. 117 (N.S.C.A.).

[148] *Canada (Human Rights Commission) v. Taylor*, [1990] S.C.J. No. 129; *Stetler v. Ontario (Agriculture, Food and Rural Affairs Appeal Tribunal)*, [2005] O.J. No. 2817 at paras. 96-100 (Ont. C.A.); *Eckervogt v. British Columbia (Minister of Employment and Investment)*, [2004] B.C.J. No. 1492 at paras. 46-49 (B.C.C.A.); *Rothesay Residents Assn. Inc. v. Rothesay Heritage Preservation and Review Board*, [2006] N.B.J. No. 227 (N.B.C.A.).

[149] *Chaudhry v. Canada (Minister of Citizenship and Immigration)*, [2006] F.C.J. No. 1280 (F.C.); *McGill v. Brantford (City)*, [1980] O.J. No. 3608 at paras. 50-53 (Ont. Div. Ct.).

8.   Necessity

As bias is a rule of common law, it may not be applied to disqualify an entire tribunal because the statutory mandate must be carried out.[150] If the disqualification of a tribunal member for bias leaves the tribunal unable to provide a quorum, the biased member may serve.[151]

A tribunal that has statutory authority to delegate its powers may do so to avert a problem of bias.[152] A court may have statutory authority to appoint a disinterested person in place of a public officer who is disqualified.[153] A court may not require a Minister to delegate Ministerial powers to an official because power is conferred on a Minister for reasons of political accountability.[154]

---

[150] *Telus Communications Inc. v. Telecommunications Workers Union*, [2005] F.C.J. No. 1253 at para. 42 (F.C.A.); *Caccamo v. Canada (Minister of Manpower and Immigration)*, [1977] F.C.J. No. 152 (F.C.A.).

[151] *Kalina v. Directors of Chiropractic*, [1981] O.J. No. 3219 (Ont. Div. Ct.), leave to appeal refused (1982), 35 O.R. (2d) 626*n* (Ont. C.A.).

[152] *Dalhousie University v. Aylward*, [2002] N.S.J. No. 267 (N.S.C.A.).

[153] *Public Officers Act*, R.S.O. 1990, c. P.45, s. 16; *Service Employees International Union, Local 204 v. Johnson*, [1997] O.J. No. 3569 (Ont. Gen. Div.); *Jogendra v. Ontario (Human Rights Tribunal)*, [2011] O.J. No. 2518 (Ont. S.C.J.).

[154] *Canadian Union of Public Employees v. Ontario (Minister of Labour)*, [2003] S.C.J. No. 28 at para. 122.

Chapter 4

DECISION-MAKING POWERS

A. INTRODUCTION

Being created by statute, an administrative tribunal has only those powers conferred on it by statute[1] or, in the case of a non-statutory tribunal, by its constating documents. It has no inherent power to make orders or to take proceedings that may affect interests of members of the public. A tribunal may not make any order that affects a person's substantive rights or obligations without express authority. Most Interpretation Acts confer on tribunals all powers that are necessary to enable them to make the decisions and to do the things they are expressly empowered to do.[2] These powers exist by necessary implication from the wording of the Act, its structure, and its purpose. Thus, a tribunal's powers should not be sterilized by overly technical interpretation, but rather should be interpreted so as to enable the tribunal to fulfil the purposes of the statute.[3] If a tribunal has broad authority to make any order to remedy a violation of the Act, the remedy must be related to the violation, its consequences and the purposes of the Act.[4]

An exception to this requirement is the power of the government to spend public money. Canadian governments establish and administer many programs without express statutory authority. Most of these programs are in health and welfare. Like any private philanthropist, the Crown has the capacity to establish programs for public benefit and to define or restrict the distribution of benefits. Provided no statute governs the field and the programs do not affect any person's liberties, legal rights

---

[1] *Inuit Tapirisat of Canada v. Canada (Attorney General)*, [1980] S.C.J. No. 99; *ATCO Gas and Pipelines Ltd. v. Alberta (Energy and Utilities Board)*, [2006] S.C.J. No. 4 at para. 35; *Dunsmuir v. New Brunswick*, [2008] S.C.J. No. 9 at para. 29.

[2] *Interpretation Act*, R.S.C. 1985, c. I-21, s. 31(2) [as am.]; *Interpretation Act*, R.S.B.C. 1996, c. 238, s. 27(2); *Interpretation Act*, R.S.A. 2000, c. I-8, s. 25(2); *Interpretation Act, 1995*, S.S. 1995, c. I-11.2, s. 25(*b*); *Interpretation Act*, C.C.S.M. c. I80, s. 32; *Legislation Act, 2006*, S.O. 2006, c. 21, Sch. F, s. 78; *Interpretation Act*, R.S.Q. c. I-16, s. 57; *Interpretation Act*, R.S.N.B. 1973, c. I-13, s. 22(*b*) [as am.]; *Interpretation Act*, R.S.N.S. 1989, c. 235, s. 19(*b*) [as am.]; *Interpretation Act*, R.S.P.E.I. 1988, c. I-8, s. 24(2); *Interpretation Act*, R.S.N.L. 1990, c. I-19, s. 22(*b*) [as am.].

[3] *ATCO Gas and Pipelines Ltd. v. Alberta (Energy and Utilities Board)*, [2006] S.C.J. No. 4 at § 2.3.3; *R. v. 974649 Ontario Inc.*, [2001] S.C.J. No. 79 at para. 38.

[4] *Royal Oak Mines Inc. v. Canada (Labour Relations Board)*, [1996] S.C.J. No. 14 at para. 56; *Murdoch v. Canada (Royal Canadian Mounted Police)*, [2005] F.C.J. No. 522 (F.C.).

or duties, they are legal.[5] Similarly, the royal prerogative is a source of authority to regulate in subject areas not governed by statute, most often, national security and the conferral of honours.[6]

A tribunal may determine the scope of its own powers and must do so when its authority is questioned. If uncertain as to whether it has authority, it should invite submissions and make a decision on this question. It need not defer the question to a court.[7] Likewise, an arbitrator appointed pursuant to a collective agreement may interpret the agreement to determine the scope of its powers.[8] Questions as to the scope of a tribunal's powers should be resolved before the powers are exercised. Where this issue depends on the facts, a tribunal may reserve its decision as to the scope of its authority until after hearing the evidence.[9] If a tribunal makes a preliminary ruling that it has jurisdiction, it may reconsider this issue after hearing the evidence.[10]

When making a decision, a tribunal need not state the source of its power. A tribunal may exercise a combination of its powers from different sources without identifying them. All that matters is that the tribunal have authority to act, not that it identify its authority.[11]

If a tribunal does not have the power to do what is requested of it, the parties cannot by consent confer the power upon it. Lack of power may not be waived, nor may parties by their acquiescence confer on a tribunal a power that it does not have.[12] Powers cannot be expanded by

---

[5] *Pharmaceutical Manufacturers Assn. v. British Columbia (Attorney General)*, [1997] B.C.J. No. 1902 (B.C.C.A.), leave to appeal refused [1997] S.C.C.A. No. 529; *Simon v. Metropolitan Toronto (Municipality)*, [1993] O.J. No. 101 (Ont. Div. Ct.).

[6] *Operation Dismantle Inc. v. Canada*, [1985] S.C.J. No. 22; *Black v. Canada (Prime Minister)*, [2001] O.J. No. 1853 (Ont. C.A.).

[7] *McLeod v. Egan*, [1974] S.C.J. No. 62; *Toronto (City) v. Goldlist Properties Inc.*, [2003] O.J. No. 3931 (Ont. C.A.); *Nova Scotia (Director of Assessment) v. Homburg L.P. Management Inc.*, [2006] N.S.J. No. 394 (N.S.C.A.).

[8] *Retail, Wholesale and Department Store Union, Local 540 v. Saskatchewan (Minister of Labour)*, [1984] S.J. No. 563 (Sask. Q.B.).

[9] *Jacmain v. Canada (Attorney General)*, [1977] S.C.J. No. 111; *Gloin v. Canada (Attorney General)*, [1977] F.C.J. No. 248 (F.C.A.), leave to appeal refused (1979), 25 N.R. 610n; *Union des Employées d'Hotel, Motel et Club v. Québec (Tribunal du Travail)*, [1977] C.A. 337 (Que. C.A.); *New Brunswick Council of Hospital Unions v. New Brunswick (Board of Management)*, [1986] N.B.J. No. 151 (N.B.C.A.); *Newfoundland (Human Rights Commission) v. Newfoundland (Dept. of Health)*, [1998] N.J. No. 129 (Nfld. C.A.).

[10] *International Brotherhood of Electrical Workers, Local 1733 v. New Brunswick Power Corp.*, [1994] N.B.J. No. 551 (N.B.Q.B.).

[11] *British Columbia (Milk Board) v. Grisnich*, [1995] S.C.J. No. 35.

[12] *Pagee v. Director (Winnipeg Central)*, [2000] M.J. No. 180 at para. 10 (Man. C.A.); *Gough v. Peel Regional Police Service*, [2009] O.J. No. 1155 (Ont. Div. Ct.); *Scivitarro v. British Columbia (Minister of Human Resources)*, [1982] B.C.J. No. 1621 (B.C.S.C.).

contract between the tribunal and the parties it regulates.[13] Arbitration boards, however, are an exception. Parties can confer powers on an arbitration board with express consent or by acquiescence.[14]

If decision-making powers are conferred by statute on a tribunal that does not exist, the Minister responsible for the statute may exercise the powers, provided the procedures prescribed by statute are followed.[15]

B.   CHANGES TO A STATUTE OR REGULATION

A tribunal may not apply a statute or regulation retrospectively to an event that occurred before the legislation was enacted, unless the statute provides that it is to apply retrospectively.[16] Thus a tribunal may not make disciplinary orders for conduct committed before it had the power to make such orders[17] but, if the purpose of the order is to protect the public, it may be made to prevent a repeat of the conduct. An order that speaks to the future is not retroactive even if based on past conduct.[18]

Amendment or repeal of legislation does not affect accrued substantive rights granted pursuant to tribunal orders made under the repealed provisions, unless the statute expressly repeals or declares those orders void.[19] Interpretation Acts provide that repeal and amendment do not affect any investigation, proceeding, or remedy in respect of rights or obligations that have accrued beforehand.[20] There is no duty to warn

---

[13] *Ontario (Chicken Producers' Marketing Board) v. Canada (Chicken Marketing Agency)*, [1992] F.C.J. No. 929 (F.C.T.D.); *Salway v. Assn. of Professional Engineers and Geoscientists of British Columbia*, [2009] B.C.J. No. 1570 (B.C.C.A.).

[14] *Hunter Rose Co. v. Graphic Arts International Union, Local 28B*, [1979] O.J. No. 4226 (Ont. C.A.).

[15] *Kennibar Resources Ltd. v. Saskatchewan (Minister of Energy and Mines)*, [1991] S.J. No. 164 (Sask. C.A.).

[16] *Latif v. Canada (Canadian Human Rights Commission)*, [1979] F.C.J. No. 216 (F.C.A.).

[17] *Thow v. British Columbia (Securities Commission)*, [2009] B.C.J. No. 211 (B.C.C.A.), but see: *Alberta (Securities Commission) v. Brost*, [2008] A.J. No. 1071 at paras. 56-57 (Alta. C.A.); *Cressman v. Ontario College of Teachers*, [2005] O.J. No. 565 (Ont. Div. Ct.); *Jellis v. Appraisal Institute*, [1986] A.J. No. 637 (Alta. Q.B.).

[18] *Brosseau v. Alberta (Securities Commission)*, [1989] S.C.J. No. 15.

[19] *A & L Investments Ltd. v. Ontario (Minister of Housing)*, [1997] O.J. No. 4199 (Ont. C.A.), leave to appeal refused [1997] S.C.C.A. Nos. 657, 658.

[20] *Interpretation Act*, R.S.C. 1985, c. I-21, s. 43(e); *Interpretation Act*, R.S.B.C. 1996, c. 238, s. 35(1)(e); *Interpretation Act*, R.S.A. 2000, c. I-8, s. 35(1)(e); *Interpretation Act, 1995*, S.S. 1995, c. I-11.2, s. 34(1); *Interpretation Act*, C.C.S.M. c. I80, s. 46; *Legislation Act, 2006*, S.O. 2006, c. 21, Sch. F, s. 51; *Interpretation Act*, R.S.Q. c. I-16, s. 12; *Interpretation Act*, R.S.N.B. 1973, c. I-13, s. 8(1)(e) [as am.]; *Interpretation Act*, R.S.N.S. 1989, c. 235, s. 23(1)(e); *Interpretation Act*, R.S.P.E.I. 1988, c. I-8, s. 32(e); *Interpretation Act*, R.S.N.L. 1990, c. I-19, s. 29(1)(e). See also *McDoom v. Canada (Minister of Manpower and Immigration)*, [1977] F.C.J. No. 148 (F.C.T.D.).

applicants of pending statutory changes that may affect their application.[21] Procedural changes may be applied to pending proceedings provided they do not affect substantive rights.[22] Interpretation Acts provide that every proceeding commenced before the amendment of the Act under which it is conducted shall be continued in conformity with substituted procedural provisions as far as may consistently be done.[23] When significant amendments are made to a regulatory regime, transitional provisions are often included.[24] Where the transitional provision provides that the old Act continues to apply to hearings commenced before the new Act comes into force, the hearing is commenced when the tribunal begins to hear evidence on the merits, not when the notice of hearing is issued.[25]

C.　POWER TO ISSUE SPECIFIC TYPES OF ORDERS

1.　Power to Order Payment of Money

Compensation or damages may not be awarded without express statutory authority.[26] A power to award compensation is not a power to penalize a bad actor by awarding punitive damages.[27] It may be exercised only to compensate a person for losses caused by wrongful acts of another which are within the tribunal's jurisdiction to award compensation. There must be a causal link in that the loss must have been caused by the wrongful conduct. The goal is to make the victim whole for the damage caused by the misconduct. Evidence

---

[21]　*dela Fuente v. Canada (Minister of Citizenship and Immigration)*, [2006] F.C.J. No. 774 at para. 20 (F.C.A.), leave to appeal refused, [2006] S.C.C.A. No. 291.

[22]　*University of Saskatchewan v. Women 2000*, [2006] S.J. No. 231 (Sask. C.A.); *Coyle v. British Columbia (Minister of Education)*, [1978] B.C.J. No. 1258 (B.C.S.C.); *Flores v. Canada (Minister of Employment and Immigration)*, [1979] F.C.J. No. 90 (F.C.A.); *Ford v. Canada (National Parole Board)*, [1976] F.C.J. No. 150 (F.C.T.D.).

[23]　*Interpretation Act*, R.S.C. 1985, c. I-21, s. 44(*d*); *Interpretation Act*, R.S.B.C. 1996, c. 238, s. 36(1)(*c*); *Interpretation Act*, R.S.A. 2000, c. I-8, s. 36(1)(*c*); *Interpretation Act, 1995*, S.S. 1995, c. I-11.2, s. 35(1) [as am.]; *Interpretation Act*, C.C.S.M. c. I80, s. 47; *Legislation Act, 2006*, S.O. 2006, c. 21, Sch. F, s. 52; *Interpretation Act*, R.S.Q. c. I-16, s. 13 [as am.]; *Interpretation Act*, R.S.N.B. 1973, c. I-13, s. 8(2)(*d*) [as am.]; *Interpretation Act*, R.S.N.S. 1989, c. 235, s. 23(3)(*d*); *Interpretation Act*, R.S.P.E.I. 1988, c. I-8, s. 31(*c*); *Interpretation Act*, R.S.N.L. 1990, c. I-19, s. 29(2)(*d*).

[24]　*Medovarski v. Canada (Minister of Citizenship and Immigration)*, [2005] S.C.J. No. 31 at para. 17; *Finlay v. Alberta Pharmaceutical Assn.*, [2000] A.J. No. 418 (Alta. C.A.).

[25]　*Baker v. Law Society of Upper Canada*, [2004] O.J. No. 131 (Ont. Div. Ct.); *Bourdon v. Québec (Comité de déontologie policière)*, [2001] J.Q. no 3491 (Que. S.C.).

[26]　*Ontario (Board of Funeral Services, Registrar) v. Schmolinski*, [2007] O.J. No. 4355 (Ont. Div. Ct.); *Westfair Foods Ltd. v. Retail, Wholesale and Department Store Union, Local 454*, [1993] S.J. No. 209 (Sask. Q.B.); *Bougoin c. Fédération des producteurs acéricoles du Québec*, [2010] J.Q. no 8699 (Que. C.A.), leave to appeal refused [2010] S.C.C.A. No. 375.

[27]　*Nova Scotia Construction Safety Assn. v. Nova Scotia (Human Rights Commission)*, [2006] N.S.J. No. 210 at para. 143 (N.S.C.A.).

of financial loss and attempts to mitigate that loss may be considered.[28] In employment cases, compensation may include amounts for loss of earnings, loss of continued employment and emotional pain and suffering.[29] A power to award compensation or expenses does not include power to award costs.[30]

A tribunal may not order a party to pay costs without express statutory authority,[31] though statutory power to prevent abuse of process may authorize an order to pay expenses in an egregious case.[32] Only a party may be ordered to pay costs.[33] Statutory authority to order a party to pay the tribunal's costs does not violate s. 7 of the *Charter*, nor give rise to a reasonable apprehension of bias.[34] Costs are not a penalty as their purpose is to reimburse the tribunal its expenses.[35] A power to order the payment of "costs of the investigation" includes the costs of the hearing that results from the investigation,[36] but a power to order payment of the "costs of the hearing" does not include the costs of the investigation.[37] The costs should be for the parts of the investigation and hearing that related to misconduct that was proven.[38] A person, against whom allegations of misconduct are not proven, may be awarded costs only pursuant to express statutory authority.[39]

---

[28] *Chopra v. Canada (Attorney General)*, [2007] F.C.J. No. 1134 (F.C.A.); *Ayangma v. Prince Edward Island Eastern School Board*, [2008] P.E.I.J. No. 31 (P.E.I.C.A.), leave to appeal refused [2009] S.C.C.A. No. 19; *Pitawanakwat v. Canada (Attorney General)*, [1994] F.C.J. No. 552 (F.C.T.D.); *Ontario v. Ontario Public Service Employees Union*, [1990] O.J. No. 635 (Ont. Div. Ct.).

[29] *169809 Canada Ltd. v. Alter*, [1995] O.J. No. 4902 (Ont. Gen. Div.); *Walden v. Canada (Social Development)*, [2010] F.C.J. No. 1408 (F.C.), affd [2011] F.C.J. No. 898 (F.C.A.).

[30] *Canada (Attorney General) v. Mowat*, [2009] F.C.J. No. 1359 (F.C.A.), leave to appeal granted [2009] S.C.C.A. No. 545; *Halifax (Regional Municipality) v. Nova Scotia (Human Rights Commission)*, [2005] N.S.J. No. 156 (N.S.C.A.); *Quereshi v. Ontario (Human Rights Commission)*, [2006] O.J. No. 1782 (Ont. Div. Ct.).

[31] *Moncton (City) v. Buggie*, [1985] N.B.J. No. 276 at para. 35 (N.B.C.A.), leave to appeal refused [1986] S.C.C.A. No. 2; *Ontario (Attorney General) v. Ontario (Review Board)*, [2010] O.J. No. 207 (Ont. C.A.); *Ontario (Environmental Protection Act, Director) v. Becker Milk Co.*, [2005] O.J. No. 4514 (Ont. Div. Ct.); *Franklin v. College of Physicians and Surgeons of Ontario*, [2007] O.J. No. 3906 (Ont. Div. Ct.); *Brooks v. Board of Examiners in Psychology*, [1995] N.S.J. No. 415 (N.S.S.C.); *Ontario Human Rights Commission v. Jeffrey*, [2007] O.J. No. 3767 (Ont. Div. Ct.). See for example, *Administrative Tribunals Act*, S.B.C. 2004, c. 45, s. 15; *Statutory Powers Procedure Act*, R.S.O. 1990, c. S.22, s. 17.1 [as am.].

[32] *Royal & SunAlliance Insurance Co. of Canada v. Volfson*, [2005] O.J. No. 4523 (Ont. Div. Ct.).

[33] *Nolan v. Kerry (Canada) Inc.*, [2009] S.C.J. No. 39 at paras. 116-117.

[34] *Pearlman v. Manitoba Law Society Judicial Committee*, [1991] S.C.J. No. 66.

[35] *Brand v. College of Physicians and Surgeons*, [1990] S.J. No. 360 (Sask. C.A.).

[36] *Barik v. College of Physicians and Surgeons*, [1992] S.J. No. 50 (Sask. C.A.).

[37] *Logan v. Denturist Licensing Board*, [1994] N.S.J. No. 91 (N.S.S.C.).

[38] *Pezim v. British Columbia (Superintendent of Brokers)*, [1994] S.C.J. No. 58 at para. 109; *Logan v. Denturist Licensing Board*, [1994] N.S.J. No. 91 (N.S.S.C.).

[39] *Logan v. Denturist Licensing Board*, [1994] N.S.J. No. 91 (N.S.S.C.); *Regular v. Law Society (Nfld.)*, [1995] N.J. No. 241 (Nfld. T.D.).

The amount of the costs should be reasonable and should be on a partial-indemnity scale.[40] A costs premium may not be awarded.[41] Procedural fairness requires that parties be given an opportunity to make submissions as to costs. When fixing costs, a tribunal should explain how it arrived at each amount awarded.[42]

A power to award costs does not permit a tribunal to order that anticipated costs be paid before the hearing commences, in the absence of express provision for intervenor funding,[43] nor does it include a power to order a party to post security for costs in advance of the hearing.[44] A tribunal may award costs only after the completion of the proceeding or the part of the proceeding to which they relate.[45]

A tribunal that has authority to award costs to the successful party may not arbitrarily refuse to award costs. It must exercise its discretion in each case on the basis of relevant factors. Normally costs should follow the event except in exceptional circumstances.[46] However, a tribunal may refuse to order the payment of costs by a losing government party that acted in good faith in the pursuit of its statutory mandate.[47]

Public interest intervenors may have special financial arrangements that would result in reduced costs awards if only out-of-pocket expenses were reimbursed. A tribunal may fix the costs that may be reasonably attributed to their participation as if they had been incurred, whether or not they correspond to actual out-of-pocket expenses.[48]

---

[40]   *Roberts v. College of Dental Surgeons*, [1999] B.C.J. No. 357 (B.C.C.A.); *Huerto v. College of Physicians and Surgeons*, [1994] S.J. No. 390 at paras. 94-98 (Sask. Q.B.), affd [1996] S.J. No. 56 (Sask. C.A.).

[41]   *Ontario (Ministry of Natural Resources) v. 555816 Ontario Inc.*, [2009] O.J. No. 238 (Ont. Div. Ct.).

[42]   *Donnini v. Ontario (Securities Commission)*, [2005] O.J. No. 240 (Ont. C.A.); *Green, Michaels and Associates Ltd. v. Alberta (Public Utilities Board)*, [1979] A.J. No. 826 (Alta. C.A.); *Hatfield v. Nova Scotia Barristers' Society*, [1978] N.S.J. No. 677 at para. 59 (N.S.C.A.).

[43]   *Pétrolière Impériale v. Fédération nationale des assoc. de consommateurs*, [1999] J.Q. no 1040 (Que. S.C.).

[44]   *Ramot Gil Development Corp. v. Precision Homes Corp.*, [1979] O.J. No. 4485 (Ont. Div. Ct.).

[45]   *Manitoba Society of Seniors Inc. v. Greater Winnipeg Gas Co.*, [1982] M.J. No. 127 (Man. C.A.); *Hamilton-Wentworth (Regional Municipality) v. Hamilton-Wentworth Save the Valley Committee Inc.*, [1985] O.J. No. 1881 (Ont. Div. Ct.), leave to appeal refused (1985), 17 O.M.B.R. 511 (Ont. C.A.); *Re Ontario Energy Board*, [1985] O.J. No. 2582 (Ont. Div. Ct.).

[46]   *Canada (Attorney General) v. EDS Canada Ltd.*, [2004] F.C.J. No. 535 (F.C.A.); *Canada (Attorney General) v. Georgian College of Applied Arts and Technology*, [2003] F.C.J. No. 801, [2004] F.C.J. No. 1454 (F.C.A.); *Alkali Lake Indian Band v. Westcoast Transmission Co.*, [1984] B.C.J. No. 1642 (B.C.C.A.); *Regular v. Law Society of Newfoundland*, [1995] N.J. No. 241 (Nfld. T.D.).

[47]   *Cabre Exploration Ltd. v. Alberta (Environmental Appeal Board)*, [2001] A.J. No. 463 (Alta. Q.B.).

[48]   *Bell Canada v. Consumers' Assn.*, [1986] S.C.J. No. 8.

A tribunal, with express statutory authority, may impose a financial penalty in the nature of a fine. The amount of the penalty may be determined by the application of principles of specific and general deterrence and should be proportionate to furthering the remedial purposes of the Act.[49] Authority to order the payment of a financial penalty is not authority to order restitution.[50] A regulatory fine is extinguished by bankruptcy but an order suspending a licence for failure to pay the fine survives and may be enforced after bankruptcy.[51]

A fee may be charged only with statutory authority.[52] As the purpose is to cover the costs of regulation, the amount levied should correlate to the cost of the regulatory service provided.[53] The fee may be collected prior to providing the service.[54] An offer to pay additional money in exchange for the issuance of a licence may not be accepted even if the funds are to be used to advance public interest goals.[55]

2. Licensing Powers

Protection of the public is an important purpose of licensing. Each applicant for a licence, or for renewal of a licence, must show that it is competent, trustworthy and in compliance with regulatory requirements. An applicant must honestly provide information respecting qualifications, experience and past conduct.[56] A licence may be refused to a corporate applicant whose shareholders and associates would be refused a licence. The concept of the "corporate veil", which shields shareholders from financial liability for corporate acts, does not apply in the licensing context.[57]

Licensing is also used as a tool to manage natural resources so that they are not depleted and to manage markets for farm products and services

---

[49] *Re Cartaway Resources Corp.*, [2004] S.C.J. No. 22; *Biller v. British Columbia (Securities Commission)*, [2001] B.C.J. No. 515 (B.C.C.A.).

[50] *Crundwell (A.E.) and Assoc. Ltd. v. Manitoba (Taxicab Board)*, [2001] M.J. No. 359 (Man. C.A.).

[51] *Hover (Trustee of) v. Alberta Dental Assn.*, [2005] A.J. No. 220 (Alta. C.A.).

[52] *Oulton v. Nova Scotia (Chicken Farmers)*, [2002] N.S.J. No. 127 (N.S.S.C.), affd [2002] N.S.J. No. 513 (N.S.C.A.). See general authority to charge fee: *Legislation Act, 2006*, S.O. 2006, c. 21, Sch. F, s. 83.

[53] *Re Eurig Estate*, [1998] S.C.J. No. 72; *620 Connaught Ltd. v. Canada (Attorney General)*, [2008] S.C.J. No. 7.

[54] *Li v. Canada (Minister of Citizenship and Immigration)*, [2011] F.C.J. No. 471 (F.C.A.).

[55] *Assoc. des crabiers acadiens v. Canada (Attorney General)*, [2006] F.C.J. No. 1566 (F.C.).

[56] *Ontario (Motor Vehicle Dealers Act, Registrar) v. Unity-A-Automotive Inc.*, [2009] O.J. No. 5198 (Ont. Div. Ct.); *Alves v. Ontario (Superintendent of Financial Services)*, [2009] O.J. No. 2950 (Ont. Div. Ct.).

[57] *Villetard's Eggs Ltd. v. Canada (Egg Marketing Agency)*, [1995] F.C.J. No. 598 (F.C.A.); *Davies v. Ontario College of Pharmacists*, [2003] O.J. No. 91 (Ont. Div. Ct.).

such as taxis and carriers, so that over-supply does not result in the type of cut-throat competition that puts providers out of business. Policy concerns relating to the management of the resource or supply are relevant in deciding whether to issue an individual licence.[58] General authority to regulate, by licensing and other powers, includes the power to limit the number of licences issued.[59]

If a licence is authorized but not issued until certain conditions are met, the authorization may be rescinded at any time up until the licence is actually issued, without following the requirements for revoking a licence.[60] A power to impose conditions may be exercised to impose conditions unique to each licence as well as identical conditions on all licences without the need to pass a regulation prescribing the rules applicable to all licences.[61] Conditions must be consistent with the statutory purpose of licensing.[62] A power to grant a licence includes a power to amend or revoke any licence previously granted.[63] A licence is issued for a fixed time period, typically one year, so that suitability may be periodically reassessed in accordance with licensing purposes, including the licensee's compliance with regulatory requirements. There is no right to a renewal of a licence.[64] Though licences are sometimes bought and sold, a licence does not vest any interest or property right in the licensee beyond the profits earned or a property right in natural resources acquired pursuant to a licence.[65] It is merely a privilege to engage in the licensed business until the licence expires, which may not be transferred without approval.

[58]   *Comeau's Sea Foods Ltd. v. Canada (Minister of Fisheries and Oceans)*, [1997] S.C.J. No. 5; *St. Anthony Seafoods Ltd. Partnership v. Newfoundland and Labrador (Minister of Fisheries and Aquaculture)*, [2004] N.J. No. 336 (N.L.C.A.), leave to appeal refused [2004] S.C.C.A. No. 548; *R. v. Huovinen*, [2000] B.C.J. No. 1365 (B.C.C.A), leave to appeal refused [2000] S.C.C.A. No. 478; *Unicity Taxi Ltd. v. Manitoba (Taxicab Board)*, [1992] M.J. No. 381 (Man. Q.B.), affd [1992] M.J. No. 608 (Man. C.A.).

[59]   *United Taxi Drivers' Fellowship of Southern Alberta v. Calgary (City)*, [2004] S.C.J. No. 19.

[60]   *Comeau's Sea Foods Ltd. v. Canada (Minister of Fisheries and Oceans)*, [1997] S.C.J. No. 5; *Wagowsky v. Metropolitan Toronto (Municipality)*, [1997] O.J. No. 3566 (Ont. Div. Ct.).

[61]   *R. v. Cox*, [2003] N.J. No. 98 (N.L.T.D.), affd [2004] N.J. No. 316 (N.L.C.A.).

[62]   *ATCO Gas and Pipelines Ltd. v. Alberta (Energy and Utilities Board)*, [2006] S.C.J. No. 4; *Zenner v. Prince Edward Island College of Optometrists*, [2005] S.C.J. No. 80.

[63]   *Manitoba (Motor Transport Board) v. Purolator Courier Ltd.*, [1981] S.C.J. No. 88.

[64]   *Genex Communications Inc. v. Canada (Attorney General)*, [2005] F.C.J. No. 1440 (F.C.A.), leave to appeal refused [2005] C.S.C.R. no 485; *Tucker v. Canada (Minister of Fisheries and Oceans)*, [2000] F.C.J. No. 1868 (F.C.T.D.), affd [2001] F.C.J. No. 1862 (F.C.A.).

[65]   *Saulnier v. Royal Bank of Canada*, [2008] S.C.J. No. 60.

3. Discipline

A licence may be revoked or suspended for misconduct. The primary purpose of these orders is to protect the public.[66] Professional misconduct is typically undefined. It includes a violation of express regulatory requirements,[67] dishonourable conduct and failure to meet the standards of the profession. The discipline committee comprises members of the profession who base their decision on objective standards of the profession. If the conduct may reasonably be regarded by members of the profession as dishonourable or unprofessional, it constitutes professional misconduct.[68] A technique or exercise of judgment may be found not to be professional misconduct if it is approved by a responsible and competent body of professional opinion, even though the majority of the profession do not approve.[69] To be "professional misconduct", the impugned conduct must reasonably relate to the practice of the profession.[70] "Conduct unbecoming" includes misconduct unrelated to the practice of the profession that reflects upon the profession as a whole and upon the person's suitability to be a member of it.[71]

It is not necessary to make a finding of criminal intent or knowledge because the purpose of professional discipline is to protect the public from harm whether intentionally caused or not. However, whether a defence of due diligence is available is not settled.[72] That defence was developed in the criminal context: A person who took reasonable care to avoid committing the crime should not be convicted. Regardless, the issue of diligence is relevant to the nature of the remedy necessary to protect the public.

---

[66] *Brosseau v. Alberta (Securities Commission)*, [1989] S.C.J. No. 15.

[67] *Manitoba Chiropractors Assn. v. Alevizos*, [2003] M.J. No. 206 (Man. C.A.).

[68] *Pearlman v. Law Society (Man.)*, [1989] M.J. No. 430 (Man. C.A.); *Young v. College of Physicians and Surgeons (Sask.)*, [2005] S.J. No. 614 (Sask. C.A.); *Matthews v. Board of Directors of Physiotherapy*, [1987] O.J. No. 838 (Ont. C.A.).

[69] *Brett v. Board of Directors of Physiotherapy*, [1991] O.J. No. 44 (Ont. Div. Ct.), affd [1993] O.J. No. 1253 (Ont. C.A.).

[70] *Li v. College of Pharmacists*, [1994] B.C.J. No. 1830 (B.C.C.A.); *Davies v. Ontario College of Pharmacists*, [2003] O.J. No. 91 (Ont. Div. Ct.).

[71] *College of Dental Surgeons v. Walker*, [1993] B.C.J. No. 2305 (B.C.S.C.); *Coady v. Royal Newfoundland Constabulary Public Complaints Commission*, [2007] N.J. No. 139 (N.L.T.D.).

[72] *New Brunswick (Minister of Public Safety) v. 504174 N.B. Ltd.*, [2005] N.B.J. No. 55 (N.B.C.A.); *Erikson v. Ontario (Securities Commission)*, [2003] O.J. No. 593 (Ont. Div. Ct.); *Gordon Capital Corp. v. Ontario (Securities Commission)*, [1991] O.J. No. 934 (Ont. Div. Ct.).

Disciplinary proceedings may be taken against a member facing criminal or regulatory charges with respect to the same conduct.[73] The primary purposes of disciplinary proceedings are to protect the public from similar misconduct in the future and to maintain professional standards, while the purposes of criminal and quasi-criminal proceedings are to punish for past misconduct and to make the miscreant account to society for his or her wrong. (See further discussion below regarding two tribunals with jurisdiction.)

Members who have resigned their membership may not be disciplined, without express authority. Most professional regulators have express authority to require a member to obtain permission to resign or to discipline former members for acts committed prior to resignation, which precludes members from resigning to escape discipline.[74]

In determining the nature of the disciplinary order, the emphasis must be on protection of the public. This entails an assessment of the degree of risk to the public if the practitioner is permitted to continue to practise the profession. Criminal law sentencing principles do not apply to the issue of whether to suspend or revoke a licence,[75] but may be applied when deciding whether to impose a deterrent penalty in the nature of a fine.[76] The nature and severity of the disciplinary order should relate to the nature and seriousness of the misconduct.[77] The likelihood that the member can be rehabilitated may be taken into account.[78] If there is statutory authority to attach conditions to reinstatement of membership, a psychiatric assessment may be required where there are findings of dysfunctional or abnormal behaviour. The conditions must specify the requirements of the assessment sufficiently for the member to know what conditions must be met in order to be re-admitted to the profession.[79] Likewise, a requirement for specified educational upgrading may be imposed.[80]

---

[73] *R. v. Shubley*, [1990] S.C.J. No. 1; *Barry v. Alberta (Securities Commission)*, [1986] A.J. No. 110 (Alta. C.A.), affd [1989] S.C.J. No. 15; *R. v. Wigglesworth*, [1987] S.C.J. No. 71; *1022049 Alberta Ltd. v. Medicine Hat (City)*, [2007] A.J. No. 348 (Alta. C.A.).

[74] *Chalmers v. Toronto Stock Exchange*, [1989] O.J. No. 1839 (Ont. C.A.), leave to appeal refused [1989] S.C.C.A. No. 446; *Pelletier v. Law Society*, [1989] N.B.J. No. 34 (N.B.C.A.); *Taub v. Investment Dealers Assn. of Canada*, [2009] O.J. No. 3552 (Ont. C.A.).

[75] *McKee v. College of Psychologists*, [1994] B.C.J. No. 1778 (B.C.C.A.).

[76] *Re Cartaway Resources Corp.*, [2004] S.C.J. No. 22.

[77] *Stetler v. Ontario Flue-Cured Tobacco Growers' Marketing Board*, [2009] O.J. No. 1050 (Ont. C.A.); *Stevens v. Law Society of Upper Canada*, [1979] O.J. No. 4546 (Ont. Div. Ct.); *Adamo v. College of Physicians and Surgeons of Ontario*, [2007] O.J. No. 1168 (Ont. Div. Ct.).

[78] *Brock-Berry v. Registered Nurses' Assn.*, [1995] B.C.J. No. 1876 at para. 29 (B.C.C.A.).

[79] *Brand v. College of Physicians and Surgeons*, [1991] S.J. No. 417 (Sask. Q.B.).

[80] *Zenner v. Prince Edward Island College of Optometrists*, [2005] S.C.J. No. 80; *Modi v. Ontario (Health Professions Board)*, [1996] O.J. No. 539 (Ont. Div. Ct.). (Note: These cases discuss the imposition of educational upgrading absent discipline.)

4.   Interim Remedies

To protect the public, some tribunals have statutory authority to issue interim orders before holding a hearing.[81] If there is a risk to the public from the continuing practice of a licensee, the licence may be suspended pending a hearing. To protect the environment, emergency orders may be made. Usually a hearing need not be held before making an interim order.[82] These powers are in the nature of injunctions and should be used sparingly, especially where the suspension deprives a person of a source of income.[83] If the suspension order is not made promptly upon learning of the risk to the public, a court may question the need to act without a hearing.[84] Most statutes that authorize interim suspension orders specify a short time limit within which a hearing must be held. If no time limit is specified, the hearing should be held as soon as possible.[85]

Tribunals that regulate rates charged to consumers may grant interim rate increases to relieve applicants from financial difficulties caused by the duration of rate-application proceedings. Interim rate increases may be varied or rescinded by the final order.[86]

An interim remedy granted to maintain the status quo pending a hearing should be precise as to the acts that must or must not be done.[87]

5.   Retroactive Orders

No order may take effect prior to the date it is made without express authority. Orders must be prospective in effect.[88] However, benefits may be reinstated on appeal effective the date they were revoked.[89] Rates may

---

[81]   See for example, *Administrative Tribunals Act*, S.B.C. 2004, c. 45, s. 15; *Statutory Powers Procedure Act*, R.S.O. 1990, c. S.22, s. 16.1 [as am.].

[82]   *Bunn v. Law Society of Manitoba*, [1990] M.J. No. 76 (Man. Q.B.), vard [1990] M.J. No. 87 (Man. C.A.); *Walpole Island First Nation v. Ontario*, [1996] O.J. No. 4682 (Ont. Div. Ct.).

[83]   *Re James*, [1982] B.C.J. No. 1555 (B.C.S.C.); *Farbeh v. College of Pharmacists of British Columbia*, [2009] B.C.J. No. 1640 (B.C.S.C.).

[84]   *Marston c. Autorité des marches financiers*, [2009] J.Q. no 13816 at para. 64 (Que. C.A.).

[85]   *Menon v. College of Physicians and Surgeons (N.B.)*, [2007] N.B.J. No. 270 (N.B.Q.B.).

[86]   *Bell Canada v. Canada (Canadian Radio-television and Telecommunications Commission)*, [1989] S.C.J. No. 68.

[87]   *Saskatchewan Health Care Assn. v. Service Employees International Union, Local 299*, [2007] S.J. No. 240 (Sask. Q.B.).

[88]   *Day and Ross Ltd. v. Jumbo Motor Express*, [1972] N.B.J. No. 74 (N.B.C.A.); *Western Decalta Petroleum Ltd. v. Alberta (Public Utilities Board)*, [1978] A.J. No. 597 (Alta. C.A.).

[89]   *Kelley v. New Brunswick (Workplace Health, Safety and Compensation Commission)*, [2009] N.B.J. No. 165 (N.B.C.A.).

be fixed as at the date of the interim rate order or application[90] but may not compensate for a windfall or loss resulting from a prior final rate order.[91] Authority to review a decision fixing rates may be exercised to adjust the rates effective the date of the earlier order.[92] An order, directing the use of funds that were ordered put aside in case of a difference between forecast and actual revenues and costs, is not regarded as retroactive.[93] If a statutory requirement for prior approval cannot be met due to urgency, necessity may permit retroactive approval.[94]

6.   Contempt Powers

Every tribunal has an inherent power to control its own processes but may not punish a person for contempt unless it is granted, by statute, the powers of a superior court to enforce its own orders.[95]

D.   POST-DECISION POWERS

After a decision has been made, may a tribunal reconsider it? May it vary, amend, or rescind its order? May it reopen a hearing that it has completed? To a limited extent, every tribunal has some post-decision powers, even if they are not expressly conferred by statute. Clerical and arithmetic errors may be corrected.[96] If the decision turned on a finding of fact that was incorrect due to mistake or a party's dishonesty, the factual error may be corrected and the decision reconsidered,[97] but new evidence is not a ground to reconsider.[98] If the tribunal forgot to deal with an issue or issued an

---

[90]   *Nova Corp. v. Amoco Canada Petroleum Co.*, [1981] S.C.J. No. 92; *Eurocan Pulp and Paper Co. v. British Columbia (Energy Commission)*, [1978] B.C.J. No. 1228 (B.C.C.A.).

[91]   *Northland Utilities (Yellowknife) Ltd. v. Northwest Territories (Public Utilities Board)*, [2010] N.W.T.J. No. 91 (N.W.T.S.C.).

[92]   *Scott v. Nova Scotia (Rent Review Commission)*, [1977] N.S.J. No. 571 (N.S.C.A.).

[93]   *Bell Canada v. Bell Aliant Regional Communications*, [2009] S.C.J. No. 40.

[94]   *C.-W. (C.) (Litigation guardian of) v. Ontario (Health Insurance Plan, General Manager)*, [2009] O.J. No. 140 (Ont. Div. Ct.).

[95]   *Chrysler Canada Ltd. v. Canada (Competition Tribunal)*, [1992] S.C.J. No. 64; *Sternberg v. Ontario (Racing Commission)*, [2008] O.J. No. 3864 (Ont. Div. Ct.).

[96]   *Muscillo Transport Ltd. v. Ontario (Licence Suspension Appeal Board)*, [1997] O.J. No. 3062 (Ont. Gen. Div.), affd [1998] O.J. No. 1488 (Ont. C.A.); *New Brunswick Publishing Co. v. New Brunswick (Executive Director of Assessment)*, [2002] N.B.J. No. 163 (N.B.Q.B.).

[97]   *Grier v. Metro International Trucks Ltd.*, [1996] O.J. No. 538 (Ont. Div. Ct.); *Chan v. Canada (Minister of Citizenship and Immigration)*, [1996] F.C.J. No. 838 at para. 28 (F.C.T.D.); *Park v. Canada (Minister of Citizenship and Immigration)*, [1998] F.C.J. No. 133 (F.C.T.D.).

[98]   *Nazifpour v. Canada (Minister of Citizenship and Immigration)*, [2007] F.C.J. No. 179 (F.C.A.), leave to appeal refused [2007] S.C.C.A. No. 196; *contra: Kurukkal v. Canada (Minister of Citizenship and Immigration)*, [2010] F.C.J. No. 1159 (F.C.A.).

ambiguous decision, it may deliver supplementary reasons to address the issue or clarify the ambiguity,[99] but this may not be done to strengthen a decision in anticipation of appeal.[100] If the decision is a nullity because required procedure was not followed, or if a court has quashed the decision, the tribunal may start again.[101] If the decision was made in the absence of a person affected by the order, who should have been notified but was not, the tribunal may reopen the matter.[102] If a party was unable, through no personal fault, to exercise the right to be heard, the hearing may be reopened.[103] The investigation of a closed complaint may be reopened even if the subject of the investigation has been told that no further action will be taken.[104] It is not accurate to characterize any of these circumstances as a "re-hearing" or a new proceeding. They are a continuation of the original proceeding that was not properly completed.[105]

There is no inherent power to reconsider a decision after it has been made. After a final decision has been rendered, a tribunal is *functus officio*. The issue, then, is whether a final decision has been rendered. A tribunal has a continuing power to change its mind until the final decision is released. If the statute requires that the final decision be in writing or embodied in a formal order, there may be no final decision until these requirements are fulfilled.[106] Preliminary rulings on any issue may be revisited and changed in the final decision.[107] If the statute prescribes two steps to issue a licence, its authorization then its actual issuance, an authorization may be revoked until the licence is issued.[108] A decision

---

[99] *Nova Scotia Government and General Employees Union v. Capital District Health Authority*, [2006] N.S.J. No. 281 (N.S.C.A.); *Severud v. Canada (Employment and Immigration Commission)*, [1991] F.C.J. No. 68 (F.C.A.).

[100] *Sea-Scape Landscaping v. New Brunswick (Workplace Health, Safety and Compensation Commission)*, [2004] N.B.J. No. 348 (N.B.C.A.); *Jacobs Catalytic Ltd. v. International Brotherhood of Electrical Workers, Local 353*, [2009] O.J. No. 4501 (Ont. C.A.).

[101] *Chandler v. Alberta Assn. of Architects*, [1989] S.C.J. No. 102.

[102] *Di Leo v. Hétu*, [1982] C.S. 442 (Que. S.C.).

[103] *Kaur v. Canada (Minister of Employment and Immigration)*, [1989] F.C.J. No. 1100 (F.C.A.); *Zutter v. British Columbia (Council of Human Rights)*, [1995] B.C.J. No. 626 (B.C.C.A.), leave to appeal refused [1995] S.C.C.A. No. 243.

[104] *Holder v. College of Physicians and Surgeons*, [2002] M.J. No. 405 (Man. C.A.), leave to appeal refused [2002] S.C.C.A. No. 519.

[105] *Nicholson v. Haldimand-Norfolk (Regional Municipality) Commissioners of Police*, [1980] O.J. No. 3845 (Ont. C.A.), leave to appeal refused [1981] 1 S.C.C.A. No. 254; *Webb v. Ontario (Securities Commission)*, [1987] O.J. No. 161 (Ont. Div. Ct.).

[106] *Bowen v. Edmonton (City)*, [1977] A.J. No. 560 (Alta. C.A.); *Brigham v. Ontario (Residential Premises Rent Review Board)*, [1979] O.J. No. 4360 (Ont. Div. Ct.).

[107] *Vatanabadi v. Canada (Minister of Employment and Immigration)*, [1993] F.C.J. No. 323 (F.C.A.); *International Brotherhood of Electrical Workers, Local 1733 v. New Brunswick Power Corp.*, [1994] N.B.J. No. 551 (N.B.Q.B.); *Brysenko v. Canada (Minister of Citizenship and Immigration)*, [2000] F.C.J. No. 1443 (F.C.T.D.).

[108] *Comeau's Sea Foods Ltd. v. Canada (Minister of Fisheries and Oceans)*, [1997] S.C.J. No. 5; *Wagowsky v. Metropolitan Toronto (Municipality)*, [1997] O.J. No. 3566 (Ont. Div. Ct.).

made in the public interest may be reversed before it is implemented if there are good policy reasons for the reversal.[109]

An arbitrator may retain jurisdiction to deal with outstanding matters but not with respect to matters that have been finally decided.[110] If the award leaves unresolved matters that had been remitted to the arbitrator, the arbitrator may reconvene to complete the assigned duty.[111]

When should an express power[112] to re-hear a matter be exercised? Typically these powers are broadly drafted and may be exercised whenever appropriate,[113] unless expressly restricted to certain circumstances (as in B.C.). Many tribunals issue policy statements indicating the types of circumstances when a matter may be re-heard. The tribunal should not refuse to re-hear in other circumstances and should be willing to reconsider whenever appropriate.[114] An express power to re-hear may be exercised even after the decision has been approved by a Minister or filed and made an order of the court.[115]

Express powers to re-hear have been exercised in a variety of situations. Orders may be amended to give effect to what was intended and to correct inadvertent errors.[116] If parties misapprehended the purpose of the hearing or the issues, a re-hearing may be granted.[117] New hearings may be held to cure the prejudice caused to a party by procedural deficiencies.[118]

---

[109] *Mount Sinai Hospital Center v. Québec (Minister of Health and Social Services)*, [2001] S.C.J. No. 43; *Comeau's Sea Foods Ltd. v. Canada (Minister of Fisheries and Oceans)*, [1997] S.C.J. No. 5; *St. Anthony Seafoods Ltd. Partnership v. Newfoundland and Labrador (Minister of Fisheries and Aquaculture)*, [2004] N.J. No. 336 (N.L.C.A.), leave to appeal refused [2004] S.C.C.A. No. 548.

[110] *Sydney (City) v. Canadian Union of Public Employees, Local 933*, [1985] N.S.J. No. 465 (N.S.C.A.); *Canada v. Exley*, [1985] F.C.J. No. 331 (F.C.A.); *Jacobs Catalytic Ltd. v. International Brotherhood of Electrical Workers, Local 353*, [2009] O.J. No. 4501 (Ont. C.A.); *contra*: *Nova Scotia Government and General Employees Union v. Capital District Health Authority*, [2006] N.S.J. No. 281 (N.S.C.A.).

[111] *Wall v. Nipawin Union Hospital*, [1981] S.J. No. 991 (Sask. Q.B.); *Canadian National Railways v. McIntyre Mines*, [1978] A.J. No. 929 (Alta. T.D.).

[112] See for example, B.C. *Administrative Tribunals Act*, S.B.C. 2004, c. 45, s. 53; *Statutory Powers Procedure Act*, R.S.O. 1990, c. S.22, s. 21.2 [as am.]; *Administrative Justice Act*, R.S.Q. c. J-3, s. 154.

[113] *Russell v. Toronto (City)*, [2000] O.J. No. 4762 (Ont. C.A.), leave to appeal refused [2001] S.C.C.A. No. 79.

[114] *Hall v. Ontario (Ministry of Community and Social Services)*, [1997] O.J. No. 5212 (Ont. Div. Ct.).

[115] *Nurani v. Alberta (Environmental Appeal Board)*, [1997] A.J. No. 1163 (Alta. Q.B.).

[116] *Telus Communications Inc. v. Canada (Canadian Radio-television and Telecommunications Commission)*, [2004] F.C.J. No. 1808 (F.C.A.), leave to appeal refused [2004] S.C.C.A. No. 573; *Parent Cartage Ltd. v. Ontario (Highway Transport Board)*, [1979] O.J. No. 4369 (Ont. C.A.).

[117] *Canada (Minister of Employment and Immigration) v. Chung*, [1992] F.C.J. No. 1150 (F.C.A.); *Steinman Transportation Ltd. v. Ontario (Highway Transport Board)*, [1980] O.J. No. 3683 (Ont. Div. Ct.).

[118] *Gill v. Canada (Minister of Employment and Immigration)*, [1987] F.C.J. No. 53 (F.C.A.).

Where a court decision changed the interpretation of a statutory provision, previous decisions that were based on an erroneous interpretation may be reopened.[119] The power to re-hear may be exercised when a fraud has been practiced upon the tribunal,[120] and where the previous decision may have been tainted by conflict of interest, bias, bribery, or corruption of a member of the panel.[121]

A review panel exercising a general power to re-hear may substitute its opinion on a question of policy for that of the original decision.[122] Its authority is not restricted to the correction of errors of fact, law and procedure. However, where statutory authority is granted only to correct errors, the decision should not be changed simply because the review panel holds a different opinion. It must find a fatal error.[123] In either case, a tribunal may not make an order that it could not have made initially.[124]

If the power to re-hear may be exercised only on new evidence, a matter may be re-heard if the new evidence could not have been obtained by reasonable diligence before the first hearing and it is material, that is, there is a reasonable possibility that it could persuade the tribunal to change its original decision.[125] The new evidence must be of a circumstance or event that existed (though unknown) at the time of the first decision, not of something that occurred after the decision was rendered.[126] On re-hearing, all of the evidence should be considered, not just the new evidence.[127]

A power to re-hear may not be exercised to inquire into an issue that does not bear on the original decision. A power to reconsider a licence application after the licence has been granted may not be used to inquire

---

[119] *Campbell v. Prince Edward Island (Workers' Compensation Board)*, [1997] P.E.I.J. No. 56 (P.E.I.C.A.); *contra: Kelly Western Services Ltd. v. Manitoba (Municipal Board)*, [2000] M.J. No. 323 (Man. Q.B.).

[120] *Parent Cartage Ltd. v. Ontario (Highway Transport Board)*, [1979] O.J. No. 4369 (Ont. C.A.).

[121] *CP Express Ltd. v. Ontario (Highway Transport Board)*, [1979] O.J. No. 4380 (Ont. Div. Ct.).

[122] *Russell v. Toronto (City)*, [2000] O.J. No. 4762 (Ont. C.A.), leave to appeal refused [2001] S.C.C.A. No. 79.

[123] *Godin c. Québec (Société de l'assurance automobile)*, [2003] J.Q. no 9567, 6 Admin. L.R. (4th) 284 (Que. C.A.); *M.L. c. Québec (Procureur general)*, [2007] J.Q. no 10129 (Que. C.A.); *Bourassa v. Commissions des lesions professionnelles*, [2003] J.Q. no 10630 (Que. C.A.), leave to appeal refused [2003] C.S.C.R. no 461.

[124] *Canadian Union of Public Employees, Local 41 v. Alberta (Board of Industrial Relations)*, [1978] A.J. No. 632 (Alta. C.A.).

[125] *Kent v. Canada (Attorney General)*, [2004] F.C.J. No. 2083 (F.C.A.); *Page v. New Brunswick (Workplace Health, Safety and Compensation Commission)*, [2006] N.B.J. No. 394 (N.B.C.A.).

[126] *Épiciers Unis Métro-Richelieu Inc. v. Québec (Régie des alcools, des courses et des jeux)*, [1996] A.Q. no 330 (Que. C.A.), leave to appeal refused [1996] C.S.C.R. no 210.

[127] *Kent v. Canada (Attorney General)*, [2004] F.C.J. No. 2083 (F.C.A.).

into new complaints against the licensee.[128] The statutory powers respecting complaints should be used. However, when reconsidering a disciplinary remedy, the reconsideration should be based on current circumstances[129] to achieve the remedy's public protection purpose.

A party has no right and a tribunal is not obliged to re-hear a matter.[130] A tribunal has discretion.[131] A tribunal may refuse a request to re-hear a matter if a considerable period of time has passed since the original decision,[132] or if the request is a tactic to delay implementation of the order or to extend a limitation period.[133] A matter should not be re-heard if a party has acted to its prejudice on the strength of the previous decision. For example, if a person entered into a binding contract upon being granted a licence, the decision to grant the licence should not be reviewed,[134] but a decision may be reversed, despite a contract, if laboratory test results indicate that the certificate should not have been granted.[135] A decision that implemented a settlement agreement should not be reopened if the parties have performed their obligations under the agreement.[136]

A person whose application was denied may file a new application but a repeat applicant who does not provide more information, which would warrant fresh consideration, may be precluded from filing repetitive applications that attempt to re-litigate an application that has been decided.[137] A tribunal deciding a repeat application, by an applicant who did not accept conditions attached to a previous grant of the application, is not bound by its first decision and may decide all issues

---

[128] *Parent Cartage Ltd. v. Ontario (Highway Transport Board)*, [1979] O.J. No. 4369 (Ont. C.A.).

[129] *Stetler v. Ontario Flue-Cured Tobacco Growers' Marketing Board*, [2009] O.J. No. 1050 (Ont. C.A.).

[130] *Union Canadienne de l'Industrie des Pêches v. des Travailleurs, Local 140*, [1981] N.B.J. No. 83 (N.B.C.A.); *Sparrow v. Canada (Minister of Manpower and Immigration)*, [1977] F.C.J. No. 50 (F.C.T.D.); *Jordan v. York University Faculty Assn.*, [1977] O.J. No. 2526 (Ont. Div. Ct.); *Garba v. Lajeunesse*, [1978] F.C.J. No. 179 (F.C.A.).

[131] *Hospital Employees Union v. Peace Arch District Hospital*, [1989] B.C.J. No. 286 (B.C.C.A.).

[132] *Roeder v. British Columbia (Securities Commission)*, [2005] B.C.J. No. 693 (B.C.C.A.); *Webber v. Neil*, [1996] N.J. No. 268 (Nfld. T.D.); *Commercial Union Assurance v. Ontario (Human Rights Commission)*, [1987] O.J. No. 438 (Ont. Div. Ct.), affd [1988] O.J. No. 405 (Ont. C.A.).

[133] *Lodger's International Ltd. v. O'Brien*, [1983] N.B.J. No. 128 (N.B.C.A.).

[134] *Laidlaw Transport Ltd. v. Bulk Carriers Ltd.*, [1979] O.J. No. 4135 (Ont. Div. Ct.).

[135] *Saskatchewan Wheat Pool v. Canadian Grain Commission*, [2004] F.C.J. No. 1568 (F.C.).

[136] *Manitoba v. Happy Penny Donut Palace*, [1985] M.J. No. 114 (Man. C.A.).

[137] *Kaloti v. Canada (Minister of Citizenship and Immigration)*, [2000] F.C.J. No. 365 (F.C.A.); *Kurukkal v. Canada (Minister of Citizenship and Immigration)*, [2009] F.C.J. No. 866 (F.C.), vard [2010] F.C.J. No. 1159 (F.C.A.); *Regional Assessment Commissioner, Region No. 9 v. 674951 Ontario Ltd.*, [1999] O.J. No. 3774 (Ont. Div. Ct.); *Sawatsky v. Norris*, [1992] O.J. No. 1253 (Ont. Gen. Div.); *Baron v. Nova Scotia (Community Services)*, [2009] N.S.J. No. 239 (N.S.S.C.).

afresh.[138] A power to reconsider an application may not be used to compel an applicant to revise its application. The tribunal may review only the application originally filed and further particulars it requires.[139]

On whose initiative may a tribunal exercise its power to re-hear? If the statute empowers the tribunal to re-hear a matter, but is silent as to who may cause the re-hearing, the matter may be re-heard at the request of any person affected by the order or on the tribunal's own initiative.[140] If the statute grants a power to re-hear only at the request of a party, the tribunal may not re-hear on its own initiative.[141]

May the matter be re-heard by the original panel? There is no need to constitute a new panel unless the original panel is no longer impartial[142] or is unavailable. If a statute permits the matter to be re-heard by a different panel only where the original panel is unable to re-hear it, mere unwillingness on the part of the original panel is not sufficient.[143]

The duty of procedural fairness must be observed when reconsidering the merits of a decision if new evidence or submissions will be heard,[144] but not when deciding whether to reconsider a decision.[145] Implementation of the decision may be stayed pending reconsideration.[146]

E. PREVIOUS DECISIONS ARE NOT BINDING

When a tribunal is faced with a new case raising legal or policy issues similar to those decided in a previous case between the same parties, the tribunal is not bound by the concept of *res judicata*. This flexibility enables a tribunal to apply the public interest in a way that reflects the evolution of policy and effectively regulates dynamic and ongoing relationships between parties. A tribunal may permit re-litigation and may come to a

---

[138] *Davidson v. Calgary (City)*, [2007] A.J. No. 1317 (Alta. C.A.).

[139] *Canadian Pacific Ltd. v. Canada (Transport Commission)*, [1980] F.C.J. No. 99 (F.C.A.).

[140] *Canadian Pacific Ltd. v. Canada (Transport Commission)*, [1980] F.C.J. No. 99 (F.C.A.).

[141] *Canada (Employment and Immigration Commission) v. Macdonald Tobacco Inc.*, [1981] S.C.J. No. 35.

[142] *Equipements Mailloux Inc. v. Commission de la Protection du territoire Agricole*, [1983] C.S. 26 (Que. S.C.).

[143] *Scivitarro v. British Columbia (Minister of Human Resources)*, [1982] B.C.J. No. 1621 (B.C.S.C.).

[144] *Stocker v. Fredericton (City)*, [1978] N.B.J. No. 99 (N.B.Q.B.); *Re Holwell*, [1982] N.J. No. 184 (Nfld. T.D.).

[145] *Barnes v. Ontario (Social Benefits Tribunal)*, [2009] O.J. No. 3096 (Ont. Div. Ct.).

[146] *United Food and Commercial Workers, Local 1400 v. Wal-Mart Canada Corp.*, [2009] S.J. No. 409 (Sask. C.A.).

different conclusion without risk of court interference.[147] However, the importance of stability in an industry requires that a tribunal have good reason for reversing its decisions.[148]

A tribunal may refuse to permit parties to re-litigate factual questions. It may rely on findings of fact made in previous proceedings between the same parties, if these findings are relevant to the present proceeding and there is no new evidence that would support a different finding.[149]

Immigration and mental health statutes require periodic reviews of the detention of individuals. Though, the issue on review is whether, in the current circumstances, continued detention is warranted, the tribunal should have regard to and should not depart from its previous detention decisions without compelling reasons.[150]

The principle of *stare decisis* does not apply to tribunals.[151] A tribunal is not bound to follow its own previous decisions on similar issues.[152] Its decisions may reflect changing circumstances and evolving policy in the field it governs. A departure from a previous ruling should be explained.[153] The analytical framework of previous decisions should be reviewed to reduce the risk of arbitrariness[154] and the tribunal should be open to argument as to why a previous decision ought not to be followed.[155] Otherwise the different decision may be regarded as an aberration.[156] If, in another case, a court determined the correct interpretation of a statutory

---

[147] *Sackville (Town) v. Canadian Union of Public Employees, Local 1188*, [2007] N.B.J. No. 97 (N.B.C.A.); *Al Yamani v. Canada (Minister of Citizenship and Immigration)*, [2003] F.C.J. No. 1931 (F.C.A.), leave to appeal refused [2004] S.C.C.A. No. 62; *New Brunswick (Executive Director of Assessment) v. Ganong Bros. Ltd.*, [2004] N.B.J. No. 219 (N.B.C.A.); *Manitoba Food and Commercial Workers Union v. Canada Safeway Ltd.*, [1981] S.C.J. No. 75, adopting dissenting reasons of Monnin J.A. [1981] M.J. No. 89 (Man. C.A.).

[148] *Canadian Red Cross Society v. United Steelworkers*, [1991] N.B.J. No. 314 (N.B.C.A.).

[149] *New Brunswick (Executive Director of Assessment) v. Ganong Bros. Ltd.*, [2004] N.B.J. No. 219 (N.B.C.A.); *Tandy Electronics Ltd. (Radio Shack) v. United Steelworkers of America*, [1980] O.J. No. 3727 (Ont. Div. Ct.), leave to appeal to C.A. refused (1980), 30 O.R. (2d) 29n (Ont. C.A.).

[150] *Canada (Minister of Citizenship and Immigration) v. Thanabalasingham*, [2004] F.C.J. No. 15 (F.C.A.).

[151] *Domtar Inc. v. Québec (Commission d'appel en matière de lésions professionnelles)*, [1993] S.C.J. No. 75; *Halifax Employers Assn. v. International Longshoremen's Assn., Local 269*, [2004] N.S.J. No. 316 at para. 82 (N.S.C.A.), leave to appeal refused [2004] S.C.C.A. No. 464.

[152] *Maitland Capital Ltd. v. Alberta (Securities Commission)*, [2009] A.J. No. 523 (Alta. C.A.).

[153] *J.D. Irving, Ltd. v. International Longshoremen's Assn., Local 273*, [2003] F.C.J. No. 951 (F.C.A.), leave to appeal refused [2003] S.C.C.A. No. 393.

[154] *Canadian Union of Public Employees, Local 2745 v. New Brunswick (Board of Management)*, [2004] N.B.J. No. 110 (N.B.C.A.), leave to appeal refused [2004] S.C.C.A. No. 215.

[155] *Dominion Stores Ltd. v. Retail, Wholesale and Department Store Union, Local 414*, [1981] O.J. No. 1013 (Ont. Div. Ct.).

[156] *United Brotherhood of Carpenters and Joiners of America, Local 1985 v. Graham Construction and Engineering Ltd.*, [2008] S.J. No. 319 (Sask. C.A.), leave to appeal refused [2008] S.C.C.A. No. 343.

provision, the tribunal must apply the court's interpretation.[157] However, if a court has merely upheld an earlier tribunal interpretation of the provision as reasonable, the tribunal need not follow that interpretation if it prefers another interpretation that is also reasonable.[158]

F. TWO TRIBUNALS WITH JURISDICTION AND ATTEMPTS TO RE-LITIGATE

Sometimes two tribunals have jurisdiction under different statutes over the same subject matter. For example, both a human rights commission and a labour arbitrator may have jurisdiction over a complaint of discrimination filed by a unionized employee. Both a municipal board and a Superior Court may have jurisdiction to review a municipal by-law.

If one tribunal has exclusive jurisdiction over the subject matter of the dispute, it should be litigated before that tribunal. The subject matter of the dispute is determined, not by the party's legal characterization of the claim, but rather by the factual context.[159] This issue is not determined according to which procedure provides adequate redress but rather in accordance with legislative intent as to the forum in which the matter should be decided.[160]

Where neither tribunal has exclusive jurisdiction, the parties may choose their forum but, if the issue is more central to the mandate of another tribunal who has expertise in the subject, the chosen tribunal may decline to hear the case leaving the parties to take it to the other tribunal.[161] If the proceeding is initiated by the tribunal, a court will not preclude that tribunal from considering an issue which, though within its jurisdiction, is more centrally within the mandate of another tribunal,[162] unless that other tribunal has exclusive jurisdiction.[163]

---

[157] *Canada (Minister of Citizenship and Immigration) v. Stephenson*, [2008] F.C.J. No. 97 (F.C.).

[158] *Essex County Roman Catholic School Board v. Ontario English Catholic Teachers' Assn.*, [2001] O.J. No. 3602 (Ont. C.A.); *Nova Scotia Nurses' Union v. Camp Hill Hospital*, [1989] N.S.J. No. 409 (N.S.C.A.), leave to appeal refused (1990), 110 N.R. 80*n*.

[159] *Weber v. Ontario Hydro*, [1995] S.C.J. No. 59; *Quebec (Attorney General) v. Quebec (Human Rights Tribunal)*, [2004] S.C.J. No. 35; *Quebec (Commission des droits de la personne et des droits de la jeunesse) v. Quebec (Attorney General)*, [2004] S.C.J. No. 34; *Regina Police Assn. Inc. v. Regina (City) Board of Police Commissioners*, [2000] S.C.J. No. 15; *Bisaillon v. Concordia University*, [2006] S.C.J. No. 19; *Snopko v. Union Gas Ltd.*, [2010] O.J. No. 1335 (Ont. C.A.).

[160] *Vaughan v. Canada*, [2005] S.C.J. No. 12.

[161] *Country Pork Ltd. v. Ashfield (Township)*, [2002] O.J. No. 2975 (Ont. C.A.); *Ontario Hydro v. Kelly*, [1998] O.J. No. 1877 (Ont. Gen. Div.); *Sparrow v. Manufacturers Life Insurance Co.*, [2004] M.J. No. 461 (Man. Q.B.).

[162] *Wilder v. Ontario (Securities Commission)*, [2001] O.J. No. 1017 (Ont. C.A.).

[163] *Canada (Canadian Transportation Agency) v. Morten*, [2010] F.C.J. No. 1249 (F.C.).

A party, who is dissatisfied with a decision made by one tribunal, may be precluded by issue estoppel from re-litigating the matter before another tribunal or court. Issue estoppel applies when the same question has been decided, that decision was final, and the same parties participated in the earlier decision.[164] The second tribunal may refuse to apply issue estoppel where its application would work an injustice.[165] In addition, a party may be precluded from re-litigating issues where to do so amounts to a collateral attack on the decision of the first tribunal. Tribunal decisions may be challenged only by way of appeal or judicial review. An attempt to challenge them in any other proceeding is an impermissible collateral attack.[166] However, where the remedy sought from the second tribunal was not available from the first tribunal, re-litigation may be permitted,[167] unless re-litigation of factual issues would amount to an abuse of process.[168]

Both disciplinary proceedings and criminal or quasi-criminal proceedings may be taken against the same person for the same acts because they have different purposes. The primary purpose of disciplinary proceedings is to protect the public and to maintain professional standards, while the purpose of criminal proceedings is to punish for past misconduct.[169] Moreover, contemporaneous criminal and administrative proceedings do not violate an accused's right to a fair trial under s. 11(*d*) of the *Charter*, even where the police have received assistance in their investigation from agency investigators. Co-operation between agency and police investigators is sensible and efficient provided it does not enable police to obtain evidence that would be otherwise unavailable to them. Even then, the impact of the assistance on an accused's right to a fair trial is relevant only to the conduct of the criminal trial and not to the conduct of the administrative proceeding.[170]

---

[164] *Danyluk v. Ainsworth Technologies Inc.*, [2001] S.C.J. No. 46; *Penner v. Niagara (Police Services Board)*, [2010] O.J. No. 4046 (Ont. C.A.), leave to appeal pending [2010] S.C.C.A. No. 441; *New Brunswick (Executive Director of Assessment) v. Ganong Bros. Ltd.*, [2004] N.B.J. No. 219 (N.B.C.A.); *Nova Scotia (Human Rights Commission) v. Dural*, [2003] N.S.J. No. 418 (N.S.C.A.).

[165] *Danyluk v. Ainsworth Technologies Inc.*, [2001] S.C.J. No. 46.

[166] *R. v. Consolidated Maybrun Mines Ltd.*, [1998] S.C.J. No. 32; *Sprint Canada Inc. v. Bell Canada*, [1999] O.J. No. 63 (Ont. C.A.).

[167] *International Alliance of Theatrical Stage Employees Moving Picture Technicians, Artists and Allied Crafts of the United States, its Territories and Canada, Stage Local 56 v. Société de la Place des Arts de Montréal*, [2004] S.C.J. No. 4; *Evans v. Canada (Public Service Commission)*, [1983] S.C.J. No. 40; *Domtar Inc. v. Québec (Commission d'appel en matière de lésions professionnelles)*, [1993] S.C.J. No. 75.

[168] *Toronto (City) v. Canadian Union of Public Employees, Local 79*, [2003] S.C.J. No. 64.

[169] *R. v. Shubley*, [1990] S.C.J. No. 1; *Barry v. Alberta (Securities Commission)*, [1986] A.J. No. 110 (Alta. C.A.), affd (*sub nom. Brosseau v. Alberta (Securities Commission)*) [1989] S.C.J. No. 15; *R. v. Wigglesworth*, [1987] S.C.J. No. 71.

[170] *Phillips v. Nova Scotia (Commission of Inquiry into the Westray Mine Tragedy)*, [1995] S.C.J. No. 36.

Facts that resulted in a criminal conviction may not be re-litigated in a discipline hearing. The criminal conviction is binding.[171] However, conduct for which an acquittal was entered may be re-litigated, because rules of evidence and the standard of proof are different. The tribunal may hear the evidence and reach its own decision.[172]

What if two tribunals both render valid decisions which have the effect of imposing conflicting obligations on a party, so that compliance with one decision results in violation of the other decision? Only conflicting obligations provide grounds for court interference. Conflicting interpretations of a legislative provision do not.[173] A party subject to conflicting obligations may apply to court for an order as to which decision prevails. The considerations include the relative importance of each tribunal's mandate, the extent to which the decision is central to that mandate, and the extent to which each tribunal, in reaching its decision, was fulfilling a policy-making or policy implementation role.[174] If compliance with an order of a provincial tribunal, authorized by a provincial statute, causes a party to violate a federal statute, the order is inoperative.[175]

G. DELEGATION

There is a general rule that, unless expressly authorized, a tribunal may not delegate its powers to another. The Latin maxim states, "*delegatus non potest delegare*". A tribunal must itself make all decisions it is empowered by statute to make. It cannot allow its decision to be made by anyone else. A tribunal may not delegate its decision-making powers to a member or employee.[176] A tribunal may not delegate to another tribunal[177] nor defer to the opinions or approval granted by other public authorities.[178]

---

[171] *Toronto (City) v. Canadian Union of Public Employees, Local 79*, [2003] S.C.J. No. 64.

[172] *Bennett v. British Columbia (Securities Commission)*, [1992] B.C.J. No. 1655 (B.C.C.A.), leave to appeal refused [1992] 6 W.W.R. lvii; *Haché v. Lunenburg County District School Board*, [2004] N.S.J. No. 120 (N.S.C.A.).

[173] *Domtar Inc. v. Québec (Commission d'appel en matière de lésions professionnelles)*, [1993] S.C.J. No. 75.

[174] *British Columbia Telephone Co. v. Shaw Cable Systems (B.C.) Ltd.*, [1995] S.C.J. No. 54.

[175] *Garland v. Consumers' Gas Co.*, [2004] S.C.J. No. 21.

[176] *Phillips v. New Brunswick (Workplace Health, Safety and Compensation Commission)*, [1997] N.B.J. No. 21 (N.B.C.A.); *Amerato v. Ontario (Motor Vehicle Dealers Act, Registrar)*, [2005] O.J. No. 3713 (Ont. C.A.); *Salway v. Association of Professional Engineers and Geoscientists of British Columbia*, [2009] B.C.J. No. 1570 (B.C.C.A.).

[177] *Dalhousie University v. Aylward*, [2002] N.S.J. No. 267 (N.S.C.A.).

[178] *Giordani v. Brandon (City)*, [1997] M.J. No. 179 (Man. Q.B.), affd [1997] M.J. No. 634 (Man. C.A.); *Bimini Neighbourhood Pub Ltd. v. Gould*, [1984] B.C.J. No. 2859 (B.C.S.C.); *contra: Prairie Acid Rain Coalition v. Canada (Minister of Fisheries and Oceans)*, [2006] F.C.J. No. 129 (F.C.A.), leave to appeal refused [2006] S.C.C.A. No. 197.

Provided the tribunal retains decision-making authority and complies with requirements of procedural fairness, it may obtain information and opinions from others,[179] accept findings of another agency,[180] or impose standards developed by other authorities.[181] The task of fact-finding may be delegated to subordinates.[182] An employee may be asked to investigate and report.[183] In addition, the decisions of several authorities relating to the same matter may be channelled through one agency.[184]

Interpretation Acts provide that a power conferred on a public officer may be exercised by that officer's "lawful deputy".[185] These words have been narrowly interpreted to permit only the officer's immediate subordinate to act. It does not allow the officer to delegate to anyone.[186]

Cabinet has an implied power to delegate its decision-making powers. Because of the nature of Cabinet, it is assumed that the legislature or Parliament did not intend that the full Cabinet exercise all decision-making powers. These powers may be delegated to one or more members of the Executive Council.[187] If a hearing must be held before a decision may be made by Cabinet, the hearing function may be delegated.[188] Authority to make regulations respecting a subject may be exercised by making a regulation that establishes the general policy and delegates to public officials authority to fill in the regulatory details.[189]

---

[179] *Can-Du Air Ltd. v. Canada (Minister of Transport)*, [1994] F.C.J. No. 429 (F.C.T.D.); *Abitibi-Consolidated Inc. v. Canada (Minister of Foreign Affairs)*, [2008] F.C.J. No. 1419 (F.C.); *Grant v. Metro. Toronto (Municipality)*, [1978] O.J. No. 3537 (Ont. Div. Ct.).

[180] *Prairie Acid Rain Coalition v. Canada (Minister of Fisheries and Oceans)*, [2006] F.C.J. No. 129 (F.C.A.), leave to appeal refused [2006] S.C.C.A. No. 197.

[181] *Goodrich v. Flagstaff (County) (Subdivision and Development Appeal Board)*, [2002] A.J. No. 1517 (Alta. C.A.).

[182] *Patchett v. Law Society*, [1978] B.C.J. No. 1387 (B.C.S.C.).

[183] *Saskatchewan Indian Gaming Authority Inc. v. National Automobile, Aerospace, Transportation and General Workers Union of Canada*, [2002] S.J. No. 414 (Sask. Q.B.).

[184] *R. v. NDT Ventures Ltd.*, [2001] N.J. No. 363 (Nfld. C.A.).

[185] *Interpretation Act*, R.S.C. 1985, c. I-21, s. 24 [as am.]; *Interpretation Act*, R.S.B.C. 1996, c. 238, s. 23; *Interpretation Act*, R.S.A. 2000, c. I.8, s. 21 [as am.]; *Interpretation Act, 1995*, S.S. 1995, c. I-11.2, ss. 23, 23.1, 23.2 [as am.]; *Interpretation Act*, C.C.S.M. c. I80, ss. 29(3), 31, 32(4); *Legislation Act, 2006*, S.O. 2006, c. 21, Sch. F, s. 77(b); *Interpretation Act*, R.S.Q. c. I-16, ls. 56(2); *Interpretation Act*, R.S.N.S. 1989, c. 235, s. 18(2); *Interpretation Act*, R.S.N.L. 1990, c. I-19, s. 21.

[186] *Canadian Bronze Co. v. Canada (Deputy Minister of National Revenue, Customs and Excise)*, [1985] F.C.J. No. 75 (F.C.A.). For a broader interpretation, see: *R. v. Corcoran*, [1999] N.J. No. 311 (Nfld. T.D.).

[187] *Gray Line of Victoria Ltd. v. Chabot*, [1980] B.C.J. No. 2028 (B.C.S.C.).

[188] *Desjardins v. Bouchard*, [1982] F.C.J. No. 238 (F.C.A.).

[189] *Peralta v. Ontario*, [1985] O.J. No. 2304 (Ont. C.A.), affd [1988] S.C.J. No. 92; *R. v. Cox*, [2003] N.J. No. 98 (N.L.T.D.), affd [2004] N.J. No. 316 (N.L.C.A.); *Association of Professional Engineers of Ontario v. Ontario (Minister of Municipal Affairs and Housing)*, [2007] O.J. No. 1971 at paras. 40-45 (Ont. Div. Ct.).

Powers conferred on a Minister are typically exercised by officials in the department. "The tasks of a Minister of the Crown in modern times are so many and varied that it is unreasonable to expect them to be performed personally."[190] This is not really delegation. A decision of an official is the decision of the Minister in the sense that the Minister is responsible to Parliament for the decision.[191] Thus the Minister's delegate need not be independent of the Minister.[192] The Minister need not give guidance to subordinates as to the appropriate exercise of the Minister's authority.[193] However, if the statute expressly states which official is to exercise the Ministerial power, no other official may exercise the power.[194] If the Act intends that the power be exercised by the Minister personally, it may not be exercised by an official. This legislative intention is indicated by statutory expressions such as "in the Minister's sole discretion".[195] A party, who has a right of appeal from a Ministry official to the Minister, is entitled to have the appeal decided by the Minister and not by another official.[196] Approval of by-laws and regulations may require the personal attention of the Minister.[197] Even where the Minister must exercise the power personally, the "leg work" may be done by staff.[198]

An official who exercises express authority to delegate should define the scope of the delegate's discretion and establish guidelines for the exercise of discretion. Unlimited discretion should not be conferred on a delegate.[199] Supervisory control over the delegate should be retained. The

---

[190] *R. v. Harrison*, [1976] S.C.J. No. 22. A Minister may be granted express authority to delegate: Canada *Interpretation Act*, R.S.C. 1985, c. I-21, s. 24 [as am.]; *Interpretation Act, 1995*, S.S. 1995, c. I-11.2, ss. 23, 23.1, 23.2 [as am].

[191] *R. v. NDT Ventures Ltd.*, [2001] N.J. No. 363 (Nfld. C.A.).

[192] *Searles v. Alberta (Health and Wellness)*, [2010] A.J. No. 602 (Alta. Q.B.), affd [2011] A.J. No. 521 (Alta. C.A.).

[193] *Dubé v. Lepage*, [1997] F.C.J. No. 616 (F.C.T.D.).

[194] *Ramawad v. Canada (Minister of Manpower and Immigration)*, [1977] S.C.J. No. 121. See for example, *Interpretation Act*, C.C.S.M. c. I80, s. 31, which defines who may exercise Ministerial authority.

[195] *Québec (Attorney General) v. Carriéres Ste.-Therese Ltée.*, [1985] S.C.J. No. 37; *R. v. NDT Ventures Ltd.*, [2001] N.J. No. 363 (Nfld. C.A.); *Edgar v. Canada (Attorney General)*, [1999] O.J. No. 4561 (Ont. C.A.).

[196] *Canadian Bronze Co. v. Canada (Deputy Minister of National Revenue, Customs and Excise)*, [1985] F.C.J. No. 75 (F.C.A.).

[197] *Horton v. St. Thomas Elgin General Hospital*, [1982] O.J. No. 3506 (Ont. H.C.J.).

[198] *R. v. NDT Ventures Ltd.*, [2001] N.J. No. 363 (Nfld. C.A.); *CAE Metal Abrasive Division of Canadian Bronze Co. v. Canada (Deputy Minister of National Revenue, Customs and Excise)*, [1985] F.C.J. No. 75 (F.C.A.).

[199] *Law Society of New Brunswick v. Pelletier*, [1989] N.B.J. No. 34 (N.B.C.A.); *C.E. Jamieson & Co. (Dominion) Ltd. v. Canada (Attorney General)*, [1987] F.C.J. No. 826 (F.C.T.D.); *Western Canada Wilderness Committee v. British Columbia (Minister of Environment and Parks)*, [1988] B.C.J. No. 436 (B.C.S.C.). But see: *International Brotherhood of Electrical Workers, Local 1739 v. International Brotherhood of Electrical Workers*, [2007] O.J. No. 2460 at paras. 36-40 (Ont. Div. Ct.); *Ngo v. Canada (Attorney General)*, [2005] F.C.J. No. 71 (F.C.).

delegate must comply with any duty inherent in the delegated power such as a duty of procedural fairness.[200] A delegate may not sub-delegate.[201]

Where a public officer has express authority to delegate and, separately, a regulation designates certain officers as having delegated authority, the public officer is not precluded from delegating to another person pursuant to the statutory authority.[202]

Delegation requires some express act of delegation. Abstention while another body acts is not sufficient.[203]

H.   TERRITORIAL JURISDICTION

A provincial tribunal does not have the power to make decisions regarding persons, activities, or things wholly outside the province.[204] If there is a real and substantial connection between the subject matter and the province, the provincial tribunal may regulate it.[205] A provincial tribunal, when considering the fitness of a person for registration in the province, may consider that person's conduct outside the province.[206] A province or provincial entity that engages in activities in another province may be regulated by the regulator of that other province.[207]

Likewise a city may regulate an activity outside its territorial limits only where it acts for the benefit of the inhabitants of the city.[208]

Those tribunals, such as securities commissions, which regulate in an international market, often work together with regulators of other countries reciprocating in collecting and sharing information with each other. If statutory powers are used to gather evidence on behalf of a foreign regulator, express statutory authority is required.[209]

---

[200]   *Theriault v. Nova Scotia (Marketing Board)*, [1981] N.S.J. No. 481 (N.S.T.D.).

[201]   *Murphy v. Canada (Minister of National Revenue)*, [2009] F.C.J. No. 1599 (F.C.).

[202]   *Regina (City) Police v. Saskatchewan (Human Rights Commission)*, [1992] S.J. No. 547 (Sask. C.A.).

[203]   *Hanson v. Ontario Universities Athletic Assn.*, [1975] O.J. No. 2557 (Ont. H.C.J.).

[204]   *British Airways Board v. British Columbia (Workers' Compensation Board)*, [1985] B.C.J. No. 2253 (B.C.C.A.), leave to appeal refused [1985] S.C.C.A. No. 63.

[205]   *Atlantic Shrimp Co. v. Newfoundland and Labrador (Labour Relations Board)*, [2006] N.J. No. 219 (N.L.T.D.); *Ayangma v. Canada Health Infoway Inc.*, [2009] P.E.I.J. No. 40 (P.E.I.S.C.); *Lawson v. Accusearch Inc.*, [2007] F.C.J. No. 164 (F.C.).

[206]   *Underwood, McLellan and Associates Ltd. v. Assn. of Professional Engineers*, [1979] S.J. No. 561 (Sask. C.A.), leave to appeal refused (1979), 1 Sask. R. 179n.

[207]   *Québec (Sa Majesté du Chef) v. Ontario (Securities Commission)*, [1992] O.J. No. 2232 (Ont. C.A.), leave to appeal refused [1992] S.C.C.A. No. 580.

[208]   *Shell Canada Products Ltd. v. Vancouver (City)*, [1994] S.C.J. No. 15.

[209]   *Global Securities Corp. v. British Columbia (Securities Commission)*, [2000] S.C.J. No. 5.

In marketing, transportation, and liquor control, Parliament has conferred on provincial tribunals power over interprovincial and international movement of goods,[210] resulting in overlapping provincial jurisdiction over interprovincial transportation. Co-operation is expected, as anyone wishing to transport goods must get a licence from the tribunal of each province it intends to pass through. If one provincial tribunal has licensed an interprovincial undertaking, the other tribunals should not refuse a licence without strong reasons.[211] A provincial tribunal, when considering an application for an interprovincial licence, should consider factors relevant to interprovincial transportation, rather than factors relevant to transportation within the province.[212] When conducting a hearing into complaints, a tribunal may exercise both its federal and provincial powers in a single hearing[213] and need not specify in its decision whether it is exercising its provincial or its federal powers or both.[214] The scope of a provincial tribunal's jurisdiction to exercise a federally delegated power is limited by the scope of the delegation.[215]

I.   THE CONSTITUTION AND HUMAN RIGHTS

A tribunal has no greater powers than has its legislature. A legislature may confer upon a tribunal only those powers that it may itself exercise. Section 91 of the *Constitution Act, 1982*[216] defines the powers conferred on Parliament and s. 92 of the Constitution defines the powers conferred on provincial legislatures. (For further discussion of this issue, see textbooks on constitutional law.)

An adjudicative tribunal, which has authority to decide questions of law, may decide constitutional questions, including *Charter* questions, that arise in the course of proceedings that are properly before it, and it may grant a remedy within its statutory authority[217] (unless the statute indicates

---

[210] *Fédération des producteurs de volailles du Québec v. Pelland*, [2005] S.C.J. No. 19.

[211] *Transports D. Drouin and Frères Ltée. v. McLaine's Transfer Ltd.*, [1978] P.E.I.J. No. 92 (P.E.I.C.A.).

[212] *Transports D. Drouin and Frères Ltée. v. McLaine's Transfer Ltd.*, [1978] P.E.I.J. No. 92 (P.E.I.C.A.).

[213] *Purolator Courier Ltd. v. Manitoba (Motor Transport Board)*, [1981] S.C.J. No. 88.

[214] *British Columbia (Milk Board) v. Grisnich*, [1995] S.C.J. No. 35.

[215] *Nadeau Poultry Farm Ltd. v. New Brunswick Farm Products Commission*, [2009] N.B.J. No. 277 (N.B.C.A.); *Sincennes v. Alberta (Energy and Utilities Board)*, [2009] A.J. No. 477 (Alta. C.A.), leave to appeal refused [2009] S.C.C.A. No. 300.

[216] Schedule B of the *Canada Act 1982* (U.K.), 1982, c. 11.

[217] *R. v. Conway*, [2010] S.C.J. No. 22. Example where no authority: *Covarrubias v. Canada (Minister of Citizenship and Immigration)*, [2006] F.C.J. No. 1682 (F.C.A.).

an intention that the tribunal not have this authority[218]). This includes authority to refuse to give effect to a statutory provision that it finds to be unconstitutional.[219] A tribunal may not decide a constitutional issue unless the party raising it has delivered a notice of constitutional question to the appropriate Attorneys General, the tribunal and the other parties.[220] The tribunal should decline to consider the constitutional issue unless the notice of constitutional question is delivered early enough in the proceeding to fairly enable all parties to present a proper evidentiary record for the examination of the constitutional issue.[221]

The *Charter of Rights and Freedoms* applies to every tribunal that exercises statutory powers or implements a government policy or program, even if it is otherwise independent of government. Discretion should be exercised consistently with *Charter* values.[222] A statutory power may not be exercised so as to infringe a *Charter* right, though, as a practical matter, very few *Charter* provisions apply to tribunals.

A tribunal has no role in the consultation of Aboriginal people under section 35 of the *Charter*, except to the extent granted by statute, but if it has jurisdiction to base its decision on the public interest, it may consider whether the Crown complied with its duty to consult.[223]

A tribunal may refuse to apply a statutory provision that conflicts with the human rights statute and its discretion must be exercised consistently with the human rights statute.[224] A tribunal that provides services, facilities, accommodation or employment may not discriminate against a person on a ground prohibited by the human rights statute.[225] The filing of

---

[218] See for example, B.C. *Administrative Tribunals Act*, S.B.C. 2004, c. 45, ss. 44-46; Alberta *Administrative Procedures and Jurisdiction Act*, R.S.A. 2000, c. A-3, s. 11 [as am.].

[219] *Nova Scotia (Workers' Compensation Board) v. Martin*, [2003] S.C.J. No. 54.

[220] *Federal Courts Act*, R.S.C. 1985, c. F-7, s. 57 [as am.]; *Constitutional Question Act*, R.S.B.C. 1996, c. 68, s. 8; *Administrative Procedures and Jurisdiction Act*, R.S.A. 2000, c. A-3, s. 12 [as am.]; *Constitutional Questions Act*, C.C.S.M. c. C180, s. 7; *Courts of Justice Act*, R.S.O. 1990, c. C.43, s. 109 [as am.]; *Constitutional Questions Act*, R.S.N.S. 1989, c. 89, s. 10 [as am.].

[221] *Costello v. Ontario (Securities Commission)*, [2004] O.J. No. 2972 (Ont. Div. Ct.), leave to appeal to C.A. refused December 7, 2004.

[222] *Slaight Communications Inc. v. Davidson*, [1989] S.C.J. No. 45; *Eldridge v. British Columbia (Attorney General)*, [1997] S.C.J. No. 86; *Blencoe v. British Columbia (Human Rights Commission)*, [2000] S.C.J. No. 43; *Greater Vancouver Transportation Authority v. Canadian Federation of Students – British Columbia Component*, [2009] S.C.J. No. 31.

[223] *Rio Tinto Alcan Inc. v. Carrier Sekani Tribal Council*, [2010] S.C.J. No. 43.

[224] *Tranchemontagne v. Ontario (Director, Disability Support Program)*, [2006] S.C.J. No. 14; *Siadat v. Ontario College of Teachers*, [2007] O.J. No. 65 (Ont. Div. Ct.). But see *Administrative Tribunals Act*, S.B.C. 2004, c. 45, ss. 46.1-46.3.

[225] *Insurance Corp. of British Columbia v. Heerspink*, [1982] S.C.J. No. 65; *British Columbia (Workers' Compensation Board) v. British Columbia (Council of Human Rights)*, [1990] B.C.J. No. 1367 (B.C.C.A.).

a complaint with a human rights commission does not prevent a tribunal from proceeding or from enforcing an order it has made.[226]

J. POWERS EXERCISED BY SUPERIOR COURTS

A provincial legislature cannot confer on a tribunal powers that are within the authority of the Superior Courts. If it could, it would be able to take powers away from independent judges and give them to tribunals over which it has greater control. This would defeat the independence of the superior courts established by the constitution. Section 92(14) of the *Constitution* confers on provincial legislatures the power to establish and administer superior courts, while s. 96 confers on the Governor General (who acts on the advice of the federal Cabinet) the power to appoint judges to those courts. This separation is designed to ensure the independence of the courts. Neither the federal nor the provincial governments have any control over decisions of the superior courts. Tribunals are not so independent. They may be subject to the direction of the government that appointed them.

To protect the jurisdiction of the superior courts, s. 96 of the *Constitution* has been interpreted to prevent provincial legislatures from conferring on provincial tribunals powers normally exercised by superior courts. A three-step test[227] has evolved to determine whether the powers conferred on the tribunal are normally exercised by superior courts.

(1) Does the challenged power or jurisdiction broadly conform to the power or jurisdiction exercised by superior, district, or county courts at the time of Confederation?

The focus here is on the type of dispute involved, on the subject matter, rather than on the apparatus of adjudication.[228] If the answer to this question is no, then the power may be validly conferred on a provincial tribunal and the other two steps of the test need not be considered. If the historical evidence indicates that the power is analogous to a power exercised by superior courts at the time of Confederation, then the second set of questions must be considered.[229]

(2) Is the function of the provincial tribunal a judicial function? Is the tribunal concerned with a private dispute, which it is called

---

[226] *Lodge v. Canada (Minister of Employment and Immigration)*, [1979] F.C.J. No. 10 (F.C.A.).

[227] *Reference re Residential Tenancies Act (Nova Scotia)*, [1996] S.C.J. No. 13; *Massey-Ferguson Industries Ltd. v. Saskatchewan*, [1981] S.C.J. No. 90.

[228] *Reference re Amendments to the Residential Tenancies Act (Nova Scotia)*, [1996] S.C.J. No. 13.

[229] *Re Residential Tenancies Act (Ontario)*, [1981] S.C.J. No. 57.

upon to adjudicate through the application of a recognized body of rules, in a manner consistent with fairness and impartiality?

The tribunal's power is not to be viewed in isolation from its context, but rather within its regulatory setting.[230] If the tribunal is primarily concerned with deciding questions of law or adjudicating private disputes between opposing parties, it may be regarded as exercising judicial powers but, if deciding private disputes is only a part of a mandate of a different nature, the questions may be answered in the negative.[231] If it does not exercise such judicial powers, the inquiry ends. If it does, the inquiry proceeds to step 3.

(3)   If the power or jurisdiction of the provincial tribunal is exercised in a judicial manner, does its function as a whole in its entire institutional context violate s. 96?

All the powers of the tribunal are reviewed. If the judicial power is incidental to its administrative powers, s. 96 is not violated. If the judicial or adjudicative function is the sole or central function of the tribunal, the power is invalid.[232]

The federal Parliament may be subject to the same constraints as provincial legislatures in that it too may be prevented from conferring s. 96 powers on administrative tribunals.[233]

K.   TRIBUNAL MUST COMPLY WITH ORDERS

A tribunal must obey a court order directing it to do or to abstain from doing something. If a tribunal fails to comply with a court order it may be found in contempt and compelled to implement the order.[234] It is not immune from judicial sanction. A tribunal's criticism of the court decision is not contempt unless it is accompanied by defiance of the court order.[235] Failure to imple-

---

[230]   *Tomko v. Nova Scotia (Labour Relations Board)*, [1975] S.C.J. No. 111.

[231]   *Crevier v. Québec (Attorney General)*, [1981] S.C.J. No. 80; *Farrah v. Quebec (Attorney General)*, [1978] S.C.J. No. 24; *Reference Re Residential Tenancies Act 1979 (Ontario)*, [1981] 1 S.C.J. No. 57.

[232]   *Re Residential Tenancies Act (Ontario)*, [1981] S.C.J. No. 57; *Farrah v. Quebec (Attorney General)*, [1978] S.C.J. No. 24.

[233]   *Canadian Imperial Bank of Commerce v. Rifou*, [1986] F.C.J. No. 454 (F.C.A.).

[234]   *Freedom Villages Inc. v. Gander (Town)*, [2008] N.J. No. 180 (N.L.T.D.); *Burstyn v. Canada (Revenue Agency)*, [2007] F.C.J. No. 1074 (F.C.); *Axelrod v. Toronto (City)*, [1984] O.J. No. 3391 (Ont. H.C.J.), vard [1985] O.J. No. 2664 (Ont. H.C.J.); *Royal Hotel Ltd. v. St. John (City) (No. 2)*, [1982] N.B.J. No. 356 (N.B.Q.B.).

[235]   *Canada (Commissioner of Competition) v. Superior Propane Inc.*, [2003] F.C.J. No. 151 (F.C.A.).

ment a court decision may expose an official to an award of costs or to liability in tort.[236]

Likewise, an inferior tribunal must implement an order of an appeal tribunal. If it disagrees with the order, it must appeal or apply for judicial review and may not simply ignore the appellate order.[237]

---

[236] *Holland v. Saskatchewan*, [2008] S.C.J. No. 43; *Bageerathan v. Canada (Minister of Citizenship and Immigration)*, [2009] F.C.J. No. 980 (F.C.); *Matusiak v. Canada (Attorney General)*, [2006] F.C.J. No. 835 (F.C.).

[237] *Burtsyn v. Canada (Customs and Revenue Agency)*, [2006] F.C.J. No. 954 (F.C.); *Hallingham v. Newfoundland (Workers' Compensation Commission)*, [1997] N.J. No. 259 (Nfld. C.A.); *Lee v. Alberta (Workers' Compensation Board)*, [1999] A.J. No. 306 (Alta. Q.B.); *Murphy v. Newfoundland (Workers' Compensation Commission)*, [1995] N.J. No. 359 (Nfld. T.D.); *Thompson v. Nova Scotia (Workers' Compensation Board)*, [1996] N.S.J. No. 44 (N.S.S.C.); *Smith v. Nova Scotia (Department of Community Services)*, [2009] N.S.J. No. 121 (N.S.S.C.).

Chapter 5

RULE-MAKING POWERS

A. INTRODUCTION

Canadian legislatures often delegate legislative powers to subordinate authorities. It is not uncommon to enact a statute to provide generally for the regulation of a sphere of activity and empower a regulatory authority to enact rules filling in the details of the regulatory scheme. Thus Cabinet, ministers, and tribunals acquire power to "create original law".[1] Obligations imposed by such rules are as binding as obligations imposed by statute. Delegates have made subordinate legislation in the nature of regulations, orders-in-council, rules, by-laws, orders, designations, directions and directives.

A decision to make a subordinate law is an exercise of judgment based on considerations of policy and the public interest, which are informed by the purposes of the statute and experience regulating in the field. Factors considered relate to questions of morality, politics, economics, international obligations or national defence and security, or to concerns of a social, scientific or technical nature.

B. TYPES OF RULES AND REGULATIONS

Types of subordinate legislation are varied. Typical forms of legally binding subordinate legislation include regulations, rules, by-laws and orders. These are distinguished from directives, policy statements and guidelines, which are not legally enforceable,[2] unless the statute that

---

[1] *British Columbia (Milk Board) v. Crowley*, [1954] B.C.J. No. 127 (B.C.S.C.).

[2] *Thamotharem v. Canada (Minister of Citizenship and Immigration)*, [2007] F.C.J. No. 734 (F.C.A.). The analysis for the purpose of determining whether a policy is legally enforceable is different from the analysis of whether a policy is "prescribed by law" for the purpose of ensuring that a limit on a Charter right is not arbitrary under s. 1: *Greater Vancouver Transportation Authority v. Canadian Federation of Students*, [2009] S.C.J. No. 31.

authorizes them expressly states that they are binding.[3] A regulation is a "law" which must be complied with, while a policy is not.[4]

The most formal type of subordinate legislation is a regulation. The statutory power to pass a regulation must be clearly granted to the enacting authority. The procedure to be followed before most regulations can become law is prescribed by Regulations Acts. "Regulation" is defined in Regulations Acts[5] and in most Interpretation Acts.[6] Essentially it is any document of a legislative nature, made pursuant to statutory authority, which imposes rules of conduct that are of general application and are legally binding. It includes anything that is called a regulation by any statute. It may also include any rule, order, by-law, or proclamation of a legislative nature made pursuant to statutory authority, unless explicitly excepted by the Regulations Act or by the authorizing statute.

However, not all decisions of a general nature made pursuant to statutory authority are regulations. Only those of a "legislative nature" qualify. Decisions of an administrative nature do not. Examples of administrative powers to which the Regulations Act procedures do not apply include statutory provisions which state that a Minister may designate, approve or exempt[7] or which mandate certain calculations using a base date fixed by an official.[8]

The word "order" is a general term that may mean a decision, direction or regulation. An order of general application may be a regulation. A regulation establishes the criteria to be applied to all cases. An order that

---

[3] *Bell Canada v. Canadian Telephone Employees Assn.*, [2003] S.C.J. No. 36; *Friends of the Oldman River Society v. Canada (Minister of Transport)*, [1992] S.C.J. No. 1; *Guy v. Nova Scotia (Workers' Compensation Appeals Tribunal)*, [2008] N.S.J. No. 1 (N.S.C.A.); *Toronto (City) v. R & G Realty Management Inc.*, [2009] O.J. No. 3358 (Ont. Div. Ct.); *Georgetown (Town) v. Eastern School District*, [2009] P.E.I.J. No. 25 (P.E.I.S.C.); *Skyline Roofing Ltd. v. Alberta (Workers' Compensation Board)*, [2001] A.J. No. 985 (Alta. Q.B.).

[4] *Martineau v. Matsqui Institution*, [1977] S.C.J. No. 44.

[5] *Statutory Instruments Act*, R.S.C. 1985, c. S-22, s. 2(1) [as am.]; *Regulations Act*, R.S.B.C. 1996, c. 402, s. 1; *Regulations Act*, R.S.A. 2000, c. R-14, s. 1(1)(*f*); *Regulations Act, 1995*, S.S. 1995, c. R-16.2, s. 2; *Regulations Act*, C.C.S.M. c. R60, s. 1; *Legislation Act, 2006*, S.O. 2006, c. 21, Sch. F, s. 17; *Regulations Act*, R.S.Q. c. R-18.1, s. 1; *Regulations Act*, S.N.B. 1991, c. R-7.1, s. 1 [as am.]; *Regulations Act*, R.S.N.S. 1989, c. 393, s. 2(*g*); *Regulations Revision Act*, R.S.P.E.I. 1988, c. R-11, s. 1(*b*); *Statutes and Subordinate Legislation Act*, R.S.N.L. 1990, c. S-27, s. 9(1)(*e*). Hereafter all these statutes will be referred to collectively as Regulations Acts.

[6] *Interpretation Act*, R.S.C. 1985, c. I-21, s. 2(1) [as am.]; *Interpretation Act*, R.S.B.C. 1996, c. 238, s. 1; *Interpretation Act*, R.S.A. 2000, c. I-8, s. 1(1)(*c*); *Interpretation Act*, 1995, S.S. 1995, c. I-11.2, s. 2; *Interpretation Act*, C.C.S.M. c. I80, s. 1; *Interpretation Act*, R.S.N.S. 1989, c. 235, s. 7(3) [as am.]; *Interpretation Act*, R.S.P.E.I. 1988, c. I-8, s. 1(*e*); *Interpretation Act*, R.S.N.L. 1990, c. I-19, s. 2(1)(*b*).

[7] *Canada (Attorney General) v. Prism Helicopters Ltd.*, [2007] F.C.J. No. 1736 (F.C.), affd [2008] F.C.J. No. 1554 (F.C.A.); *Alberta Union of Provincial Employees v. Alberta*, [2002] A.J. No. 455 (Alta. Q.B.).

[8] *Nova Scotia (Director of Assessment) v. Canada Trustco Mortgage Co.*, [1997] N.S.J. No. 105 (N.S.C.A.).

resolves a dispute between two or more persons or applies to a specific set of facts or to specific parties is not a regulation.[9]

Some tribunals have statutory authority to make rules on substantive matters, which are as legally binding as regulations. Typically the statutory authority excepts these rules from Regulations Act procedure and prescribes a different procedure for making them. Codes which are agreed to by regulated persons but not made pursuant to the statutory procedure, might not be binding law.[10] Similarly, legally binding municipal by-laws are made pursuant to authority and procedures explicitly prescribed by Municipal Acts.

The government makes many decisions of general application without express statutory authority. Often they involve spending government money on policy initiatives and special projects. These are very common in health care and social welfare. Like any private philanthropist, the Crown has the capacity to establish programs for public benefit and to define or restrict the distribution of benefits. These programs are not regulations and neither the creation nor the cancellation of these programs gives rise to legal rights. There are few restrictions on the government. If a statute already occupies the field, the matter cannot be dealt with by policy initiative. In addition, a policy cannot interfere with the legal rights, duties and liberties of persons without legal authority.[11]

C. SOURCE AND SCOPE OF POWER TO MAKE REGULATIONS

The power to make legally binding subordinate legislation is derived solely from statute.[12] However, it is not necessary to specify on the face of the regulation or rule the statutory authority for its enactment.[13]

---

[9] *Canadian Pacific Ltd. v. Canada (Transport Commission)*, [1985] 2 F.C. 136 (F.C.A.); *Mosher v. Nova Scotia (Department of Environment and Labour)*, [2006] N.S.J. No. 249 (N.S.S.C.); *Alberta Cement Corp. v. Alberta Environmental Protection*, [1997] A.J. No. 893 (Alta. Q.B.), affd [1999] A.J. No. 796 (Alta. C.A.); *Skyline Roofing Ltd. v. Alberta (Workers' Compensation Board)*, [1996] A.J. No. 690 (Alta. Q.B.).

[10] *Council of Canadians with Disabilities v. Via Rail Canada Inc.*, [2007] S.C.J. No. 15 at para. 346 (dissent).

[11] *Pharmaceutical Manufacturers Assn. v. British Columbia (Attorney General)*, [1997] B.C.J. No. 1902 (B.C.C.A.), leave to appeal refused [1997] S.C.C.A. No. 529; *Associated Respiratory Services Inc. v. British Columbia (Purchasing Commission)*, [1994] B.C.J. No. 14 (B.C.C.A.), leave to appeal refused [1994] S.C.C.A. No. 437; *Simon v. Metropolitan Toronto (Municipality)*, [1993] O.J. No. 101 (Ont. Div. Ct.); *Independent Contractors and Business Assn. v. British Columbia*, [1995] B.C.J. No. 777 (B.C.S.C.).

[12] *114957 Canada Ltée v. Hudson (Town)*, [2001] S.C.J. No. 42. Implied authority may be sufficient: *Giant Grosmont Petroleums Ltd. v. Gulf Canada Resources Ltd.*, [2001] A.J. No. 864 (Alta. C.A.), leave to appeal refused [2001] S.C.C.A. No. 484.

A regulation may not violate the Constitution.[14]

A regulation may not conflict with any statute.[15] If there is a conflict between a regulation and a statute, the statute, being paramount, prevails. A conflict exists only if one enactment compels what the other forbids. A valid municipal by-law may impose higher standards than are imposed by a federal or provincial statute,[16] but may not conflict with that statute.[17] A valid regulation and a valid municipal by-law may both regulate the same matter unless one prohibits what the other compels. If one prohibits what the other permits, but does not compel, there is no operational conflict.[18]

A regulation that is authorized by statute and does not violate the Constitution is valid and may not be attacked on any other ground.[19] Municipal by-laws may be subject to attack on other grounds.[20]

A Cabinet or Minister's regulation may not be attacked on the grounds of bad faith. Government may be moved by any number of political, economic, social or partisan considerations. Because of Cabinet secrecy, the motives of government in making a regulation may not be known. Even when known, the motives of Cabinet are irrelevant to the question of whether a regulation is authorized. Even if it can be proven that the regulation was motivated by partisan politics, lobbying by a special interest group and the government's desire to be re-elected, these are not grounds for it to be struck down. If regulation-making authority is abused, the only remedy is an appeal to the electors.[21] A regulation may not be attacked for being unreasonable or for being based on poor

---

[13] *British Columbia (Milk Board) v. Grisnich*, [1995] S.C.J. No. 35.

[14] *Beauchemin v. Blainville (Town)*, [2003] J.Q. no 10048 (Que. C.A.); *Canadian Civil Liberties Assn. v. Ontario (Minister of Education)*, [1990] O.J. No. 104 (Ont. C.A.); *Charter*, s. 2(b): *Rocket v. Royal College of Dental Surgeons*, [1990] S.C.J. No. 65; *Peterborough (City) v. Ramsden*, [1993] S.C.J. No. 87; *Canadian Charter of Rights and Freedoms*, s. 6: *Mia v. British Columbia (Medical Services Commission)*, [1985] B.C.J. No. 2920 (B.C.S.C.).

[15] *Friends of the Oldman River Society v. Canada (Minister of Transport)*, [1992] S.C.J. No. 1; *British Columbia Teachers' Federation v. British Columbia (Attorney General)*, [1985] B.C.J. No. 2517 (B.C.C.A.), leave to appeal refused March 5, 1987; *FCT Insurance Co. (c.o.b. First Canadian Title) v. Law Society of New Brunswick*, [2009] N.B.J. No. 122 (N.B.C.A.).

[16] *114957 Canada Ltée v. Hudson (Town)*, [2001] S.C.J. No. 42.

[17] *Cash Converters Canada Inc. v. Oshawa (City)*, [2007] O.J. No. 2613 (Ont. C.A.).

[18] *British Columbia Lottery Corp. v. Vancouver (City)*, [1999] B.C.J. No. 79 (B.C.C.A.); *Law Society of Upper Canada v. Barrie (City)*, [2000] O.J. No. 9 (Ont. S.C.J.).

[19] *Ontario Federation of Anglers and Hunters v. Ontario (Ministry of Natural Resources)*, [2002] O.J. No. 1445 (Ont. C.A.), leave to appeal refused [2002] S.C.C.A. No. 252; *R. v. Wonderland Gifts Ltd.*, [1996] N.J. No. 146 (Nfld. C.A.).

[20] But maybe not: see concurring opinion of LeBel J. in *Chamberlain v. Surrey School District No. 36*, [2002] S.C.J. No. 87.

[21] *Thorne's Hardware Ltd. v. Canada*, [1983] S.C.J. No. 10; *Ontario Federation of Anglers and Hunters v. Ontario (Ministry of Natural Resources)*, [2002] O.J. No. 1445 (Ont. C.A.); *Ontario Black Bear/Ontario Sportsmen and Resource Users Assn. v. Ontario*, [2000] O.J. No. 263 (Ont. S.C.J.).

business sense or misguided notions.[22] Substantive law made by a regulatory authority may be attacked on the ground that it was made for an improper purpose.[23]

A municipal by-law may be attacked only if patently unreasonable, that is, made in bad faith, arbitrarily, for an improper purpose or without following normal process.[24] Bad faith on the part of an individual councillor is not evidence that the Council as a whole acted in bad faith.[25]

A regulation is not invalid on the grounds that it is vague or uncertain. Ambiguity is not fatal. The language of a regulation must be interpreted and applied. It is not void for uncertainty, even if those regulated by it are uncertain as to what it means.[26] However, a vague municipal by-law may be invalid. Whether a by-law is vague depends on whether those regulated by it can determine its meaning.[27] Merely because a by-law is difficult to interpret does not mean it is vague.[28]

A regulation may differentiate among different classes of regulated people. A power to make regulations includes implicitly a power to establish categories of regulated persons,[29] unless the statute expressly requires equal treatment.[30] A municipal by-law may not differentiate among different classes without express or implied authority to do so[31] because such discrimination may be regarded as evidence of bad faith.[32]

---

[22] *UL Canada Inc. v. Québec (Procureur Général)*, [2003] J.Q. no 13505 (Que. C.A.), affd [2005] S.C.J. No. 11; *Aerlinte Eireann Teoranta v. Canada*, [1987] F.C.J. No. 145 (F.C.T.D.), affd [1990] F.C.J. No. 170 (F.C.A.).

[23] *FCT Insurance Co. (c.o.b. First Canadian Title) v. Law Society of New Brunswick*, [2009] N.B.J. No. 122 (N.B.C.A.).

[24] *Nanaimo (City) v. Rascal Trucking Ltd.*, [2000] S.C.J. No. 14; *Chamberlain v. Surrey School District No. 36*, [2002] S.C.J. No. 87, per LeBel J.; *Toronto Livery Assn. v. Toronto (City)*, [2009] O.J. No. 2725 (Ont. C.A.); *Barrick Gold Corp. v. Ontario (Minister of Municipal Affairs and Housing)*, [2000] O.J. No. 4426 (Ont. C.A.); *Grosvenor v. East Luther Grand Valley (Township)*, [2007] O.J. No. 241 (Ont. C.A.).

[25] *Consortium Developments (Clearwater) Ltd. v. Sarnia (City)*, [1998] S.C.J. No. 26; *MacMillan Bloedel Ltd. v. Galiano Island Trust Committee*, [1995] B.C.J. No. 1763 (B.C.C.A.), leave to appeal refused [1995] S.C.C.A. No. 439.

[26] *R. v. Wonderland Gifts Ltd.*, [1996] N.J. No. 146 (Nfld. C.A.).

[27] *Arcade Amusements Inc. v. Montreal (City)*, [1985] S.C.J. No. 16.

[28] *Montreal (Ville) v. 2952-1366 Québec Inc.*, [2005] S.C.J. No. 63; *Rolling Lands Ltd. v. Hamilton-Wentworth (Regional Municipality)*, [1980] O.J. No. 3884 (Ont. Div. Ct.).

[29] *Canada (Attorney General) v. Compagnie de publication la Presse Ltée*, [1966] S.C.J. No. 60; *Moresby Explorers Ltd. v. Canada (Attorney General)*, [2007] F.C.J. No. 1116 (F.C.A.), leave to appeal refused [2007] S.C.C.A. No. 536.

[30] *Canada v. St. Lawrence Cruise Lines Inc.*, [1997] F.C.J. No. 866 (F.C.A.).

[31] *114957 Canada Ltée v. Hudson (Town)*, [2001] S.C.J. No. 42; *R. v. Sharma*, [1993] S.C.J. No. 18; *Lemoyne (Ville) v. Bessette*, [1995] A.Q. no 739, 129 D.L.R. (4th) 697 (Que. C.A.).

[32] *H.G. Winton Ltd. v. North York (Borough)*, [1978] O.J. No. 3488 (Ont. Div. Ct.).

A regulation may not impose penalties or create offences without express statutory authority.[33] Statutory offence and penalty provisions typically authorize the prosecution of violations of regulations.

A municipality's authority to regulate an activity by by-law may be used to restrict the activity but not to prohibit it completely.[34] Statutory authority to regulate or prohibit a specific activity cannot be extended, by by-law, to other similar activities not listed in the statute.[35] A municipality may regulate activities within its territorial limits, including those of businesses operating from premises outside the territory.[36]

A statute which authorizes regulations "respecting" or "governing" a subject grants broad authority to make regulations which establish general policy and to delegate the administrative details to public officials.[37] Authority to make regulations "prescribing" things does not permit delegation. A power to pass regulations establishing the policies or standards applicable to a situation does not authorize a regulation delegating authority to prescribe them in some other way. A repetition of the words of the statute is not a valid exercise of regulation-making power.[38] Similarly, a municipal by-law should not merely repeat the words of the empowering statute.[39] This evades the exercise of the power and amounts to a delegation of the power to regulate that was not contemplated by the statute.

Statutory authority to make regulations is discretionary. There is no duty to make them. Where the same matter is within the scope of authority to make a regulation, to issue a directive or to make a decision in an individual case, the regulator may choose how best to deal with it.[40]

---

[33] *R. v. Abitibi Price Inc.*, [1995] N.J. No. 151 (N.S.C.A.).

[34] *United Taxi Drivers' Fellowship of Southern Alberta v. Calgary (City)*, [2004] S.C.J. No. 19; *114957 Canada Ltée v. Hudson (Town)*, [2001] S.C.J. No. 42.

[35] *R. v. Wassilyn*, [1999] O.J. No. 907 (Ont. C.A.).

[36] *1254582 Alberta Ltd. v. Edmonton (City)*, [2009] A.J. No. 1 (Alta. C.A.), leave to appeal refused [2009] S.C.C.A. No. 80; *Halifax (Regional Municipality) v. Ed DeWolfe Trucking Ltd.*, [2007] N.S.J. No. 333 (N.S.C.A.).

[37] *Jackson v. Ontario (Minister of Natural Resources)*, [2009] O.J. No. 5166 (Ont. C.A.); *Peralta v. Ontario*, [1985] O.J. No. 2304 (Ont. C.A.), affd [1988] S.C.J. No. 92; *Vrabec v. College of Physicians and Surgeons (B.C.)*, [2009] B.C.J. No. 1000 (B.C.S.C.).

[38] *Brant Dairy Co. Ltd. v. Ontario (Milk Commission)*, [1972] S.C.J. No. 82; *Canada (Attorney General) v. Brent*, [1956] S.C.J. No. 10; *Gallant v. New Brunswick*, [1998] N.B.J. No. 161 (N.B.C.A.), leave to appeal refused [1998] S.C.C.A. No. 376.

[39] *Canadian Institute of Public Real Estate Companies v. Toronto (City)*, [1979] S.C.J. No. 20; *Air Canada v. Dorval (City)*, [1985] S.C.J. No. 42.

[40] *Mercier v. Canada (Correctional Services)*, [2010] F.C.J. No. 816 (F.C.A.), leave to appeal refused [2010] S.C.C.A. No. 331; *Pim v. Ontario (Minister of Environment)*, [1978] O.J. No. 3672 (Ont. Div. Ct.); *Marchment and MacKay Ltd. v. Ontario (Securities Commission)*, [1997] O.J. No. 2575 (Ont. Div. Ct.); *Canadian Parks and Wilderness Society v. Canada (Minister of Canadian Heritage)*, [2003] F.C.J. No. 703 (F.C.A.); *Vaziri v. Canada (Minister of Citizenship and Immigration)*, [2006] F.C.J. No. 1458 (F.C.).

D. PROCEDURE

Regulations must be enacted in accordance with the formal requirements of the Regulations Act. As Regulations Acts in Canada are not uniform, readers are advised to read the applicable Regulations Act, but the typical rules are described in the following paragraphs.

Many Regulations Acts provide for review by a Registrar, Deputy Attorney General or other authority, of a regulation before it is enacted or before it is accepted for filing. That authority may review it to determine whether it is a "regulation", whether the enacting authority had the power to enact it, whether it is within the scope of that power, that it does not constitute an unusual or unexpected use of the power, and that it is clear and unambiguous in its terms. Most reviewing authorities have only some of these powers of review. There may be optional or periodic review of regulations by the legislature. Some Acts provide that failure to review a regulation before it came into force does not render it invalid.

All Regulations Acts require that regulations be filed or registered with a Clerk or Registrar. A regulation that is not filed or registered has no force or effect.[41] Regulations Acts require the publication of most regulations in an official gazette or on a government website. This requirement is intended to bring the regulation to the attention of those affected by it.[42] Most Acts require that published regulations be judicially noticed and deem that publication of a regulation is actual notice to all persons affected by it. Failure to publish a regulation does not render it invalid, but no person may be convicted of an offence against an unpublished regulation unless the person was given notice of it directly.

The duty of procedural fairness does not apply. When enacting subordinate legislation, there is no duty to permit persons affected to make representations before the enactment, unless expressly required by statute.[43]

---

[41] *Mosher v. Nova Scotia (Department of Environment and Labour)*, [2006] N.S.J. No. 249 (N.S.S.C.).

[42] *Butler Metal Products Co. v. Canada (Employment and Immigration Commission)*, [1982] F.C.J. No. 181 (F.C.A.).

[43] *Canada (Attorney General) v. Inuit Tapirisat of Canada*, [1980] S.C.J. No. 99; *Apotex Inc. v. Canada (Attorney General)*, [2000] F.C.J. No. 634 (F.C.A.), leave to appeal refused [2000] S.C.C.A. No. 379; *Vanderkloet v. Leeds and Grenville County Board of Education*, [1985] O.J. No. 2605 (Ont. C.A.), leave to appeal refused (1986), 54 O.R. (2d) 352*n*; *Groupe des Éléveurs de Volailles de l'Est de l'Ont. v. Canadian Chicken Marketing Agency*, [1984] F.C.J. No. 251 (F.C.T.D.). The *Administrative Procedures and Jurisdiction Act*, R.S.A. 2000, c. A-3, s. 1(*c*), and the *Statutory Powers Procedure Act*, R.S.O. 1990, c. S.22, s. 3(2)(*h*) [as am.], do not apply to the enactment of regulations.

Some regulations are exempted from Regulations Acts. Typically, these are regulations that apply to only a few parties who can be notified directly, or they are concerned with national defence and security.

Municipal Acts prescribe procedures for the enactment of by-laws, but little or no procedure for passing resolutions.[44] Failure to follow prescribed procedure may result in a by-law being declared illegal or not, depending on the seriousness of the default and other circumstances.[45]

Some rule-making powers permit the swift enactment of rules in emergency situations by excepting those rules from the formal procedural requirements. The circumstances may be scrutinized by a court to determine whether there was in fact an emergency.[46]

E. ENACTMENT, AMENDMENT AND REPEAL

1. Enabling Statute

Most Interpretation Acts provide that no regulation comes into force until its enabling statute is proclaimed in force.[47] These provisions are declaratory of the common law.[48] There is no power to enforce a regulation if the statute under which it is enacted is not in force. However, if the statute expressly authorizes retroactive regulations, a regulation may be made after the statute comes into force to be effective on a prior date.[49]

If a statute is amended or repealed and replaced by another statute, Interpretation Acts state that all regulations and rules made under the former statute remain in effect insofar as they are not inconsistent with the new or amended Act.[50] If the statutory amendment grants new or

---

[44] *Air Canada v. Dorval (City)*, [1985] S.C.J. No. 42.

[45] *London (City) v. RSJ Holdings Inc.*, [2007] S.C.J. No. 29; *Canadian Pacific Railway Co. v. Vancouver (City)*, [2006] S.C.J. No. 5; *Immeubles Port Louis Ltée v. Lafontaine (Village)*, [1991] S.C.J. No. 14.

[46] *Kuypers v. Langley (Township)*, [1992] B.C.J. No. 113 (B.C.S.C.); *Plante v. Québec (Procureur-Général)*, [1991] R.J.Q. 465 (C.S.).

[47] *Interpretation Act*, R.S.C. 1985, c. I-21, s. 7; *Interpretation Act*, R.S.B.C. 1996, c. 238, s. 5; *Interpretation Act*, R.S.A. 2000, c. I-8, s. 7; *Interpretation Act*, C.C.S.M. c. I80, s. 12; *Legislation Act, 2006*, S.O. 2006, c. 21, Sch. F, s. 10; *Interpretation Act*, R.S.N.B. 1993, c. I-13, s. 5(2); *Interpretation Act*, R.S.N.S. 1989, c. 235, s. 8; *Interpretation Act*, R.S.P.E.I. 1988, c. I-8, s. 6.

[48] *Scarborough (City) v. Ontario (Attorney General)*, [1997] O.J. No. 701 (Ont. Gen. Div.).

[49] *Alpha Laboratories Inc. v. Ontario*, [1999] O.J. No. 552 (Ont. Div. Ct.), leave to appeal refused April 27, 1999 (Ont. C.A.), leave to appeal refused [1999] S.C.C.A. No. 365.

[50] *Interpretation Act*, R.S.C. 1985, c. I-21, s. 44(g); *Interpretation Act*, R.S.B.C. 1996, c. 238, s. 36(1)(e); *Interpretation Act*, R.S.A. 2000, c. I-8, s. 36(1)(e); *Interpretation Act, 1995*, S.S. 1995, c. I-11.2, s. 35(1)(g) [as am.]; *Interpretation Act*, C.C.S.M. c. I80, s. 47(6); *Legislation Act, 2006*, S.O. 2006, c. 21, Sch. F, s. 52(6); *Interpretation Act*, R.S.N.B. 1993, c. I-13, s. 9; *Interpretation Act*,

expanded regulation-making powers and authorizes retroactive regulations, a regulation made under this new power may be made retroactive to take effect before the statutory authority for it was enacted.[51]

Many old statutes prescribed detailed and specific regulation-making powers. The trend in new statutes is to prescribe generally-worded authority to regulate or govern in a sphere of activity. The repeal and replacement of a specific regulation-making authorization with general authority to regulate should not be interpreted as a repeal of authority over the specific matter.[52]

Where a statute is repealed and no other statute has been enacted to replace it, all regulations and rules enacted under it are also repealed.[53]

2. Regulations and Rules

Regulations Acts state that a regulation comes into effect on the date it is filed or published, or on a later date specified in the regulation.[54] Most Regulations Acts provide that no regulation may come into effect before it is filed, unless the Act under which it is enacted permits a regulation to come into effect on an earlier date.[55] Many statutes that grant regulation-making authority do contain a provision to the effect that a regulation is, if it so provides, effective with reference to a period before it is filed.[56] If the Regulations Act is silent, a regulation, once filed or published, may take effect retroactively without express statutory authority. All that is

R.S.N.S. 1989, c. 235, s. 24(1)(*a*); *Interpretation Act*, R.S.P.E.I. 1988, c. I-8, s. 33(1)(*e*); *Interpretation Act*, R.S.N.L. 1990, c. I-19, s. 30(1)(*a*).

[51] *Alpha Laboratories Inc.*, [1999] O.J. No. 552 (Ont. Div. Ct.), leave to appeal refused April 27, 1999 (Ont. C.A.), leave to appeal refused [1999] S.C.C.A. No. 365.

[52] *United Taxi Drivers' Fellowship of Southern Alberta v. Calgary (City)*, [2004] S.C.J. No. 19; *Giant Grosmont Petroleums Ltd. v. Gulf Canada Resources Ltd.*, [2001] A.J. No. 864 (Alta. C.A.), leave to appeal refused [2001] S.C.C.A. No. 484.

[53] *Stocker v. Fredericton (City)*, [1978] N.B.J. No. 99 (N.B.Q.B.).

[54] *Statutory Instruments Act*, R.S.C. 1985, c. S-22, s. 9; *Regulations Act*, R.S.B.C. 1996, c. 402, s. 4; *Regulations Act*, R.S.A. 2000, c. R-14, s. 2(2); *Regulations Act, 1995*, S.S. 1995, c. R-16.2, s. 5; *Regulations Act*, C.C.S.M. c. R60, s. 3; *Legislation Act, 2006*, S.O. 2006, c. 21, Sch. F, ss. 22-23; *Regulations Act*, R.S.Q. c. R-18.1, s. 17; *Regulations Act*, S.N.B. 1991, c. R-7.1, s. 3; *Regulations Act*, R.S.N.S. 1989, c. 393, s. 3(6) [as am.]; *Statutes and Subordinate Legislation Act*, R.S.N.L. 1990, c. S-27, s. 10(2) [as am.].

[55] *Statutory Instruments Act*, R.S.C. 1985, c. S-22, s. 9; *Regulations Act*, R.S.B.C. 1996, c. 402, s. 4(1); *Regulations Act, 1995*, S.S. 1995, c. R-16.2, ss. 4(1) and 5; *Regulations Act*, C.C.S.M. c. R60, s. 3; *Regulations Act*, S.N.B. 1991, c. R-7.1, s. 3; *Regulations Act*, R.S.N.S. 1989, c. 393, s. 3(6) [as am.]; *Statutes and Subordinate Legislation Act*, R.S.N.L. 1990, c. S-27, s. 10(2) [as am.]. In Alberta and Quebec, no regulation may have retroactive effect: *Regulations Act*, R.S.A. 2000, c. R-14, s. 2(2); *Regulations Act*, R.S.Q. c. R-18.1, s. 17.

[56] *Alpha Laboratories Inc.*, [1999] O.J. No. 552 (Ont. Div. Ct.), leave to appeal refused April 27, 1999 (Ont. C.A.), leave to appeal refused [1999] S.C.C.A. No. 365.

required is an express provision in the regulation that it is to take effect on an earlier date.[57]

Interpretation Acts provide that the power to make regulations includes the power to amend and repeal the regulations. The procedure for enacting a regulation must be followed when amending or repealing it.[58]

Interpretation Acts provide that the repeal of a regulation does not affect any right accrued or liability incurred under the regulation, but that the procedure established by an amending regulation, insofar as it can be adapted, shall be followed in all proceedings, whether commenced before or after the regulation was amended.[59] An accrued right is one that has vested, not one that is hoped for or expected. For example, when a permit is granted, the right to it has vested. If a regulation prescribing new eligibility criteria is made effective on a date after an application for a permit was filed but before it is granted, the new criteria may be applied to the application. The filing of an application does not create a vested right to have the old eligibility criteria applied.[60]

A court declaration that a regulation is invalid is effective in respect of all persons subject to the regulation, not just the parties to the court proceeding.[61] However, after a declaration of invalidity, the legislature may, by statute, reinstate the regulation and may make it effective retroactively to the date it was first made.[62]

---

[57] *Canada (Attorney General) v. Compagnie de publication la Presse Ltée*, [1966] S.C.J. No. 60.

[58] *Interpretation Act*, R.S.C. 1985, c. I-21, s. 31(4) [as am.]; *Interpretation Act*, R.S.B.C. 1996, c. 238, s. 27(4); *Interpretation Act, 1995*, S.S. 1995, c. I-11.2, s. 25(d); *Interpretation Act, C.C.S.M.* c. I80, s. 34; *Legislation Act, 2006*, S.O. 2006, c. 21, Sch. F, s. 54; *Interpretation Act*, R.S.N.B. 1993, c. I-13, s. 26; *Interpretation Act*, R.S.N.S. 1989, c. 235, s. 19(f); *Interpretation Act*, R.S.P.E.I. 1988, c. I-8, s. 24(4); *Interpretation Act*, R.S.N.L. 1990, c. I.19, s. 22(e).

[59] *Interpretation Act*, R.S.C. 1985, c. I-21, ss. 43 and 44; *Interpretation Act*, R.S.B.C. 1996, c. 238, ss. 35 and 36; *Interpretation Act*, R.S.A. 2000, c. I-8, ss. 35-36; *Interpretation Act, 1995*, S.S. 1995, c. I-11.2, ss. 34 and 35 [as am.]; *Interpretation Act, C.C.S.M.* c. I80, ss. 46-47; *Legislation Act, 2006*, S.O. 2006, c. 21, Sch. F, ss. 51-52; *Interpretation Act*, R.S.Q., c. I-16, ss. 12 and 13; *Interpretation Act*, R.S.N.B. 1993, c. I-13, s. 8; *Interpretation Act*, R.S.N.S. 1989, c. 235, s. 23; *Interpretation Act*, R.S.P.E.I. 1988, c. I-8, s. 32; *Interpretation Act*, R.S.N.L. 1990, c. I-19, s. 29.

[60] *Apotex Inc. v. Canada (Attorney General)*, [2000] F.C.J. No. 634 (F.C.A.), leave to appeal refused [2000] S.C.C.A. No. 379; *Alpha Laboratories Inc.*, [1999] O.J. No. 552 (Ont. Div. Ct.), leave to appeal refused April 27, 1999 (Ont. C.A.), leave to appeal refused [1999] S.C.C.A. No. 365.

[61] *Emms v. Canada (Minister of Indian Affairs and Northern Development)*, [1979] S.C.J. No. 91.

[62] *Barbour v. University of British Columbia*, [2010] B.C.J. No. 219 (B.C.C.A.), leave to appeal refused [2010] S.C.C.A. No. 135; *Nanaimo (Regional District) v. Spruston Enterprises Ltd.*, [1998] B.C.J. No. 2323 (B.C.C.A.).

Part II

Review of the Tribunal's Action

Chapter 6

APPEALS FROM TRIBUNAL DECISIONS

A. RIGHT OF APPEAL

Any right to appeal a tribunal's decision must be found in the statute governing that tribunal. If none is found, the tribunal's decisions cannot be appealed.[1] A tribunal cannot create a right to appeal its decisions.[2]

Most statutes grant a right of appeal from a "decision" or "order". This permits only appeals of final decisions. Interim rulings on bias or on jurisdictional, procedural or evidentiary issues may not be appealed,[3] nor may a refusal to initiate a proceeding.[4] A decision is regarded as final if it finally decides the merits of the case, even though methods of implementation remain to be decided,[5] or if it finally disposes of the case, even if it does not decide the merits.[6] A party who was successful in the result may not appeal even though dissatisfied with the tribunal's reasons.[7]

B. PARTIES TO AN APPEAL

Who may appeal a tribunal decision? Persons who had standing before the tribunal may appeal the matters decided that affect their legal interests.[8] A

---

[1] *Maritime Natural Gas Pipeline Contractors Assn. Inc. v. New Brunswick (Board of Commissioners of Public Utilities)*, [2002] N.B.J. No. 299 (N.B.C.A.); *Newfoundland Transport Ltd. v. Newfoundland (Public Utilities Board)*, [1983] N.J. No. 92 (Nfld. C.A.).

[2] *Medora v. Dental Society*, [1984] N.B.J. No. 236 (N.B.C.A.).

[3] *Syncrude Canada Ltd. v. Alberta (Human Rights and Citizenship Commission)*, [2008] A.J. No. 614 (Alta. C.A.); *Mary and David Goodine Dairy Farm v. New Brunswick (Milk Marketing Board)*, [2002] N.B.J. No. 177 (N.B.C.A.); *Newfoundland Transport Ltd. v. Newfoundland (Public Utilities Board)*, [1983] N.J. No. 92 (Nfld. C.A.); *Maritime Natural Gas Pipeline Contractors Assn. Inc. v. New Brunswick (Board of Commissioners of Public Utilities)*, [2002] N.B.J. No. 299 (N.B.C.A.); *CHC Global Operations, a division of CHC Helicopters International Inc. v. Global Helicopter Pilots Assn.*, [2008] F.C.J. No. 1579 (F.C.A.).

[4] *Communications, Energy and Paperworkers Union of Canada v. CanWest MediaWorks Inc.*, [2008] F.C.J. No. 1155 (F.C.A.); *Graywood Investments Ltd. v. Ontario (Energy Board)*, [2005] O.J. No. 345 at para. 28 (Ont. Div. Ct.).

[5] *Ontario (Human Rights Commission) v. Ontario Teachers' Federation*, [1994] O.J. No. 1585 (Ont. Gen. Div.).

[6] *Prince Albert (City) v. Riocan Holdings Inc.*, [2004] S.J. No. 337 (Sask. C.A.).

[7] *Gauvin v. New Brunswick (Workplace Health, Safety and Compensation Commission)*, [2010] N.B.J. No. 266 (N.B.C.A.).

[8] *Berg v. British Columbia (Police Complaint Commissioner)*, [2006] B.C.J. No. 1027 at § VI (B.C.C.A.), leave to appeal refused [2006] S.C.C.A. No. 300; *Assn. of Architects v. Assn. of*

right of appeal granted to any person "directly affected" or "aggrieved" by the tribunal's decision permits appeals by persons who were not parties before the tribunal, but who can show adverse effect. One who is "directly affected" is affected by the decision to a greater extent than the community at large.[9] A "person aggrieved" is one against whom a decision has been made which prejudicially affects the person's interests.[10] A right of appeal granted to "any interested person" requires a legal interest in the subject matter of the tribunal decision, which turns on whether the person was entitled to be a party before the tribunal.[11] A witness who was not a party may not appeal adverse findings.[12]

Every party in the proceeding under appeal is entitled to receive notice of the appeal and to standing as a respondent in the appeal.[13]

Most statutes are silent as to the tribunal's status in an appeal of its decision. Even when the statute grants the tribunal a right to be heard, the issues on which it may present submissions may be restricted in the same way as on judicial review.[14] These restrictions do not apply to an agency whose mandate is to manage a regulatory scheme, particularly in a further appeal of a decision of an appellate tribunal.[15] A regulator may not appeal a decision of its committee.[16]

Architectural Technologists, [2002] F.C.J. No. 813 (F.C.A.), leave to appeal refused [2002] S.C.C.A. No. 316; *Partington v. Complaints Inquiry Committee*, [2005] A.J. No. 787 (Alta. C.A.).

9   *Canadian Union of Public Employees, Local 30 v. Alberta (Public Health Advisory and Appeal Board)*, [1996] A.J. No. 48 (Alta. C.A.); *Friends of the Athabasca Environmental Assn. v. Alberta (Public Health Advisory and Appeal Board)*, [1996] A.J. No. 47 (Alta. C.A.); *Morguard Investments Ltd. v. British Columbia (Assessor of Area No. 12 – Coquitlam)*, [2006] B.C.J. No. 106 (B.C.C.A.).

10   *Allen v. College of Dental Surgeons (B.C.)*, [2007] B.C.J. No. 221 (B.C.C.A.); *Halifax Atlantic Investments Ltd. v. Halifax (City)*, [1978] N.S.J. No. 574 (N.S.C.A.).

11   For example, *Canadian Broadcasting League v. Canada (Canadian Radio-Television and Telecommunications Commission)*, [1979] F.C.J. No. 169 (F.C.A.); *Victoria Wood Development Corp. v. Jan Davies Ltd.*, [1979] O.J. No. 4352 (Ont. C.A.), leave to appeal refused (1979), 25 O.R. (2d) 774n.

12   *Becker v. Ontario (Director of Arbitrations, Financial Services Commission)*, [2000] O.J. No. 210 (Ont. Div. Ct.).

13   *TransCanada Pipeline Ventures Ltd. v. Alberta (Utilities Commission)*, [2009] A.J. No. 756 (Alta. C.A.); *Buena Vista (Village) v. Regina Beach (Town)*, [1997] S.J. No. 459 (Sask. Q.B.).

14   *British Columbia (Securities Commission) v. Pacific International Securities Inc.*, [2002] B.C.J. No. 1480 (B.C.C.A.); *Air Canada v. Canada (Canadian Transportation Agency)*, [2008] F.C.J. No. 708 (F.C.A.). See the discussion of tribunal standing in chapter 7 "F.4. The Tribunal".

15   *Prince Edward Island (Workers' Compensation Board) v. MacDonald*, [2007] P.E.I.J. No. 14 (P.E.I.C.A.); *Sarcee Gravel Products Inc. v. Alberta (Workers' Compensation Board)*, [2002] A.J. No. 927 (Alta. Q.B.).

16   *Bahcheli v. Alberta Securities Commission*, [2007] A.J. No. 520 (Alta. C.A.).

If there is no respondent to defend the tribunal's decision, the Attorney General should be notified of the appeal.[17] The Attorney General always has standing to defend decisions of statutory tribunals.

C. LEAVE TO APPEAL

Some statutes permit appeals only with leave. An applicant for leave must establish a fairly arguable case of substance and importance, and show reason to doubt the correctness of the decision.[18] An applicant may be required to show that the appeal raises a question of public importance, which may be demonstrated by affidavit evidence, filed with leave.[19] An applicant need not show that success on the merits is likely. Leave may be more difficult to obtain if the standard of review on appeal is whether the decision was reasonable rather than whether it was correct.[20] If the grounds for appeal are restricted by statute, the appellant must show that the appeal is on permitted grounds. For example, if the statute permits appeals only on questions of law, a question of law must be raised.[21]

Even if the test for leave to appeal is met, leave may be refused for any reason that the appeal could be dismissed without a decision on the merits. Thus leave may be refused where the decision appealed is not final[22] or time limits for appealing have not been met. If the statute requires leave to appeal and imposes a time limit for filing a notice of appeal, the leave to appeal application must be decided and the notice of appeal filed within the time limit. If not, leave will be refused.[23]

---

[17] *Castel v. Manitoba (Criminal Injuries Compensation Board)*, [1978] M.J. No. 48 (Man. C.A.); *Re Nova Scotia (Workmen's Compensation Board)*, [1976] N.S.J. No. 370 (N.S.C.A.).

[18] *Greyhound Lines Inc. v. Transport Adirondack Inc.*, [1996] A.Q. no 425 (Que. C.A.); *Milner Power Inc. v. Alberta (Energy and Utilities Board)*, [2009] A.J. No. 989 (Alta. C.A.); *McEwan v. British Columbia (Securities Commission)*, [2006] B.C.J. No. 3060 (B.C.C.A.); *Elliott v. Manitoba (Director of Social Services)*, [1982] M.J. No. 102 (Man. C.A.); *Rosedale Golf Assn. Ltd. v. Degasperis*, [2004] O.J. No. 1153 (Ont. Div. Ct.).

[19] *Canada Mortgage and Housing Corp. v. Iness*, [2002] O.J. No. 4334 (Ont. C.A.).

[20] *Gelco Express Ltd. v. Douglas*, [1990] M.J. No. 510 (Man. C.A.).

[21] *Vinogradov v. University of Calgary*, [1990] A.J. No. 809 (Alta. C.A.), leave to appeal refused [1991] 1 S.C.R. xv; *Saskatoon (City) v. Boardwalk Reit Properties Holding Ltd.*, [2007] S.J. No. 262 (Sask. C.A.).

[22] *Big Loop Cattle Co. Ltd. v. Alberta (Energy Resources Conservation Board)*, [2009] A.J. No. 988 (Alta. C.A.); *Avion Services Corp. v. Unicity Taxi Ltd.*, [2009] M.J. No. 174 (Man. C.A.); *Bennett v. British Columbia (Superintendent of Brokers)*, [1994] B.C.J. No. 2168 (B.C.C.A.).

[23] *Wilbur-Ellis Co. of Canada Ltd. v. Canada (Deputy Minister of National Revenue, Customs and Excise)*, [1995] F.C.J. No. 1435 (F.C.A.).

D. NOTICE OF APPEAL AND TIME LIMITS

The procedure to be followed on appeal is prescribed by the statute granting the right of appeal or by the rules of practice of the court or appeal tribunal to which the appeal is made.

Notice of appeal must be served on all other parties and on the tribunal. It must identify the decision or order that is the subject of the appeal. The grounds of appeal should be concisely stated but failure to identify the grounds or to provide other information may be remedied.[24]

Time limits of 30 days or less are typically prescribed for serving and filing a notice of appeal.[25] This time limit usually begins to run on the date that the appellant receives notice of the tribunal decision.[26] If the tribunal issues its decision in parts, the time limit begins to run when notice of the final part of the decision is given.[27] An appeal is out of time if the notice of appeal is not filed with the appellate body in time, even if it was mailed in time.[28] If notice of appeal is delivered on time, the appeal is not defeated by the failure of the tribunal to state a case in time.[29]

An appellate body may not waive or extend the time limit without express statutory authority.[30] Where the statute permits an extension of the time limit, it will be granted only if the appellant can show that a genuine intention to appeal existed at the time the right to appeal existed, that failure to meet the time limit was caused by a special circumstance that justifies the failure, that the other parties are not prejudiced by the delay,

---

[24] *Roses's Well Services Ltd. v. Troyer*, [2006] A.J. No. 73 (Alta. Q.B.); *Luigi Stornelli Ltd. v. Centre City Capital Ltd.*, [1985] O.J. No. 2495 (Ont. Div. Ct.); *Wolek v. Herzog*, [1984] O.J. No. 3227 (Ont. Div. Ct.).

[25] See for example *Administrative Tribunals Act*, S.B.C. 2004, c. 45, s. 24.

[26] *Pacific National Investments Ltd. v. British Columbia (Assessor of Area No. 01 — Saanich/Capital)*, [1994] B.C.J. No. 1298 (B.C.C.A.); *Coventry Homes Inc. v. Beaumont (Town)*, [2001] A.J. No. 219 (Alta. C.A.); *Thomas v. Assn. of New Brunswick Registered Nursing Assistants*, [2002] N.B.J. No. 202 (N.B.C.A.); *Booth v. Island Regulatory and Appeals Commission*, [2004] P.E.I.J. No. 72 (P.E.I.C.A.).

[27] *Thomas v. Assn. of New Brunswick Registered Nursing Assistants*, [2002] N.B.J. No. 202 (N.B.C.A.); *Gough v. Peel Regional Police Service*, [2006] O.J. No. 803 (Ont. Div. Ct.); *Brighton v. Nova Scotia (Minister of Agriculture and Fisheries)*, [2002] N.S.J. No. 298 (N.S.S.C.).

[28] *Glow-Worm Investments Ltd. v. Atlantic Shopping Centres Ltd.*, [1981] N.S.J. No. 415 (N.S.C.A.), leave to appeal refused [1981] S.C.C.A. No. 119; *Re Dunnett*, [1979] F.C.J. No. 1138 (F.C.T.D.); *Re Kelly*, [1979] F.C.J. No. 1137 (F.C.T.D.).

[29] *Canada (Attorney General) v. Giroux*, [1979] F.C.J. No. 49 (F.C.A.).

[30] *Kirchmeir v. Edmonton Chief of Police*, [2001] A.J. No. 1507 (Alta. C.A.); *Wascana Energy Inc. v. Gull Lake No. 139 (Rural Municipality)*, [1998] S.J. No. 346 (Sask. C.A.); *Thomas v. Assn. of New Brunswick Registered Nursing Assistants*, [2002] N.B.J. No. 202 (N.B.C.A.); *Pagee v. Director (Winnipeg Central)*, [2000] M.J. No. 180 (Man. C.A.).

and that the appeal has a reasonable chance of success.[31] A timely but unsuccessful request to the tribunal for reconsideration might not meet the requirement to show a genuine intention to appeal.[32]

E. STAY OF TRIBUNAL ORDER

A tribunal order takes effect immediately unless the statute grants a stay of the order upon the delivery of a notice of appeal.[33] A stay suspends the order, but not the legislative requirements that were applied by it.[34]

A statute may expressly empower the appellate body, or the tribunal whose order is under appeal, to stay the enforcement of the order pending the outcome of the appeal. If the right of appeal is to a superior court, the court has inherent authority to grant a stay[35] unless the statute expressly precludes it.[36] If both the tribunal and the appellate body have power to grant a stay, application should first be made to the tribunal.[37]

As a stay is in the nature of an interlocutory injunction, the same common law principles apply. The appellant must demonstrate a *prima facie* case on appeal or, at least, a serious issue to be tried. Balance of convenience and irreparable harm to the parties are weighed.[38] Also, the public interest in having the decision take effect without delay may be weighed against any irreparable harm that may be suffered by a party if the decision takes effect before the appeal is decided.[39] Harm is irreparable

---

[31] *Cook v. College of Physical Therapists*, [1998] A.J. No. 99 (Alta. C.A.); *Antigonish (Town) v. Antigonish (County)*, [1997] N.S.J. No. 282 (N.S.C.A.).

[32] *Canada (Minister of Human Resources Development) v. Hogervorst*, [2007] F.C.J. No. 37 (F.C.A.); *Dene Tha' First Nation v. Alberta (Energy and Utilities Board)*, [2003] A.J. No. 1051 (Alta. C.A.).

[33] See generally *Administrative Tribunals Act*, S.B.C. 2004, c. 45, s. 24, s. 25; *Statutory Powers Procedure Act*, R.S.O. 1990, c. S.22, s. 25(1) [as am.] (*"SPPA"*); *Administrative Justice Act*, R.S.Q. c. J-3, s. 107.

[34] *Denby v. Agriculture, Food and Rural Affairs Appeal Tribunal*, [2006] O.J. No. 1968 (Ont. Div. Ct.).

[35] *Irving Oil Ltd. v. Prince Edward Island (Public Utilities Commission)*, [1984] P.E.I.J. No. 43 (P.E.I.C.A.); *New Brunswick (Electric Power Commission) v. Maritime Electric Co.*, [1985] F.C.J. No. 93 (F.C.A.), leave to appeal refused [1985] S.C.C.A. No. 314.

[36] *College of Physicians and Surgeons v. Arnold*, [1999] O.J. No. 693 (Ont. Div. Ct.); *contra*: *Kooner v. College of Physicians and Surgeons*, [2002] O.J. No. 1594 (Ont. Div. Ct.).

[37] *Rose v. Registrar of Collection Agencies*, [1982] O.J. No. 3401 (Ont. Div. Ct.).

[38] *Dudzic v. Law Society of Upper Canada*, [1990] O.J. No. 35 (Ont. Div. Ct.); *Irving Oil Ltd. v. Prince Edward Island (Public Utilities Commission)*, [1984] P.E.I.J. No. 43 (P.E.I.C.A.); *New Brunswick (Electric Power Commission) v. Maritime Electric Co. Ltd.*, [1985] F.C.J. No. 93 (F.C.A.), leave to appeal refused [1985] S.C.C.A. No. 314.

[39] *Manitoba (Attorney General) v. Metropolitan Stores (MTS) Ltd.*, [1987] S.C.J. No. 6.

if it cannot be undone or cured, or if it will render the appeal moot.[40] Tardiness in launching the appeal is grounds for refusing a stay. See also the discussion of stays pending judicial review in chapter 7.

If a stay is granted but the appellant fails to perfect the appeal within reasonable time, the stay may be removed.[41]

F.   RECORD

Appeals are heard on the record that was before the tribunal. Usually it is the tribunal's responsibility to prepare and file the record with the appellate body.[42] A statute may prescribe the contents of the record.[43] Generally, it includes the order or decision under appeal, the reasons for the decision, if any, relevant interlocutory orders, the application or notice of hearing by which the proceeding was commenced, the documentary evidence and the transcript, if any. The appellant must pay the cost of producing the transcript.[44] The record should not include the transcript of argument before the tribunal, the cases relied upon by counsel[45] nor the notes of tribunal members.[46] If the full record is large and cumbersome, parties should agree to omit parts that are not relevant to the appeal. If the "hearing" was conducted by way of an exchange of correspondence, that correspondence should be included in the record.[47] If a tribunal's record of an informal proceeding is a messy set of notes, the tribunal need only provide a good quality photocopy of the record to the appellant who must produce legible copies of the parts of the record that are relevant to the appeal.[48] If it is necessary to preserve confidentiality of parts of the record, a sealing order may be obtained by way of a motion to the appellate body.[49]

---

[40] *O'Connor v. Nova Scotia*, [2001] N.S.J. No. 90 (N.S.C.A.); *Gaudet v. Ontario (Securities Commission)*, [1990] O.J. No. 689 (Ont. Div. Ct.).

[41] *Frost v. Alberta Assn. of Architects*, [1995] A.J. No. 521 (Alta. C.A.).

[42] *Milner Power Inc. v. Alberta Energy and Utilities Board*, [2007] A.J. No. 919 at para. 41 (Alta. C.A.).

[43] For example, the Ont. *Statutory Powers Procedure Act*, R.S.O. 1990, c. S.22, s. 25(1) [as am.], s. 20.

[44] *Storey v. Saskatchewan (Municipal Inspector, Property Maintenance Appeals Committee)*, [1998] S.J. No. 515 (Sask. Q.B.).

[45] *Flamborough (Town) v. Canada (National Energy Board)*, [1984] F.C.J. No. 526 (F.C.A.), leave to appeal refused [1984] 2 S.C.R. vii.

[46] *Storey v. Saskatchewan (Municipal Inspector, Property Maintenance Appeals Committee)*, [1998] S.J. No. 515 (Sask. Q.B.).

[47] *Gallant v. New Brunswick (Workers' Compensation Board)*, [1987] N.B.J. No. 1168 (N.B.Q.B.).

[48] *Stewart v. New Brunswick (Workplace Health, Safety and Compensation Commission)*, [1996] N.B.J. No. 226 (N.B.C.A.).

[49] *Osif v. College of Physicians and Surgeons of Nova Scotia*, [2008] N.S.J. No. 539 (N.S.C.A.).

See also the discussion of the record in chapter 7.

G. APPEAL ON THE RECORD OR BY WAY OF A NEW HEARING

Most appeals are decided upon a review of the record and after hearing submissions. Essentially, the question is whether the tribunal made a reviewable error. An appeal to a court is on the record,[50] unless the statute prescribes a new hearing. If the parties had a full oral hearing before the first tribunal, an appeal to another tribunal should be heard by way of submissions on the record of the first tribunal because the right to an oral hearing is a right to one hearing.[51] If the first tribunal did not hold an oral hearing, but delivers a record of its written proceeding, the appellate tribunal may consider the record in the context of conducting the appeal by way of a new hearing.[52] If there is no record of the proceeding before the first tribunal, the appeal can be only by way of a new hearing.[53] An appellate tribunal with the power to summons witnesses may hold a new hearing but is not required to do so.[54] An appeal provision that permits parties to supplement the record with additional evidence does not mandate a new hearing but may warrant a less deferential standard of review of the decision of the lower tribunal.[55]

If the appeal is on the record, when and to what extent may the record be supplemented by additional evidence? Fresh evidence is admissible on appeal only if the party submitting it can demonstrate that it could not have been obtained with reasonable diligence for use at the hearing below, that it will probably have an important influence on the result of the case, and that

---

[50] *College of Physicians and Surgeons v. K.*, [1987] O.J. No. 168 (Ont. C.A.); *Haugen v. Camrose (County)*, [1979] A.J. No. 543 (Alta. C.A.); *Dupras v. Mason*, [1994] B.C.J. No. 2456 (B.C.C.A.).

[51] *St-Pie (Municipalité de) c. Commission de protection du territoire agricole du Québec*, [2009] J.Q. no 15512 (Que. C.A.), leave to appeal refused [2010] S.C.C.A. No. 54.

[52] *British Columbia Chicken Marketing Board v. British Columbia Marketing Board*, [2002] B.C.J. No. 1930 (B.C.C.A.); *Kwan v. Canada (Minister of Citizenship and Immigration)*, [2001] F.C.J. No. 1333 (F.C.T.D.); *McLeod v. Alberta Securities Commission*, [2006] A.J. No. 939 (Alta. C.A.), leave to appeal refused [2006] S.C.C.A. No. 380.

[53] *Kawartha Pine Ridge District School Board v. Grant*, [2010] O.J. No. 1093 (Ont. Div. Ct.); *Calgary General Hospital Board v. Williams*, [1982] A.J. No. 700 (Alta. C.A.); See also *Harelkin v. University of Regina*, [1979] S.C.J. No. 59.

[54] *Newfoundland (Workers' Compensation Commission) v. Breen*, [1997] N.J. No. 70 (N.B.C.A.); *Calgary General Hospital v. Williams*, [1982] A.J. No. 700 (Alta. C.A.); *Westcoast Transmission Co. v. Husky Oil Operations Ltd.*, [1980] A.J. No. 854 (Alta. C.A.).

[55] *Novopharm Ltd. v. AstraZeneca AB*, [2001] F.C.J. No. 1580 (F.C.A.), leave to appeal refused [2001] S.C.C.A. No. 646.

it is credible.[56] If the lower tribunal has authority to reconsider its decision, the appellate tribunal should refer the case back to the lower tribunal for reconsideration in light of the fresh evidence.[57]

In an appeal by way of a new hearing, the burden of proof is on the appellant.[58] The appellate body may consider the record of evidence that was before the lower tribunal, because it is not expected to start from scratch,[59] and it may accord considerable weight to the reasons.[60] The lower decision maker may testify if the decision below was based on that person's knowledge of facts.[61] New evidence, that was not available at the time of the hearing before the lower tribunal, should be admitted.[62] Other evidence that was not presented to the tribunal of first instance may be admitted before the appellate tribunal but, if it was deliberately withheld from the first tribunal, it should be approached with caution.[63]

H.   SCOPE OF APPEAL

What matters may be the subject of an appeal? The scope of an appeal is confined by the statute granting the right of appeal. The appellate body has no mandate to go beyond that.[64] The parties cannot, by agreement, confer jurisdiction on the appellate body that it does not have.[65] A right to appeal questions of law permits appeal on grounds of procedural unfairness[66] but does not permit appeal of questions of fact or evidence, except a material finding of fact which is not supported by any evidence. This exception is characterized as an error of law and has been stated more broadly to include errors of process relating to evidence so as to permit

---

[56]   *Ryan v. Law Society of New Brunswick*, [2000] N.B.J. No. 540 (N.B.C.A.); *Higgins v. Canada (Attorney General)*, [2009] F.C.J. No. 1420 (F.C.A.).

[57]   *Bonavista (Town) v. Bonavista Local Board of Appeal*, [1995] N.J. No. 212 (Nfld. C.A.); *Ambellidis v. Québec (Commission d'appel en matières de lésions professionelles)*, [1999] J.Q. no 224 (Que. C.A.); *Newfoundland (Workers' Compensation Commission) v. Breen*, [1997] N.J. No. 70 (N.B.C.A.).

[58]   *Nova Scotia (Director of Assessment) v. Knickle*, [2007] N.S.J. No. 449 (N.S.C.A.).

[59]   *R.D.R. Construction Ltd. v. Nova Scotia (Rent Review Commission)*, [1982] N.S.J. No. 546 (N.S.C.A.).

[60]   *Lamb v. Canadian Reserve Oil and Gas Ltd.*, [1976] S.C.J. No. 35; *Whitehouse v. Sun Oil Co.*, [1982] A.J. No. 656 (Alta. C.A.); *Tuplin v. Canada (Registrar of Indian and Northern Affairs)*, [2001] P.E.I.J. No. 113 (P.E.I.T.D.).

[61]   *Austin v. Ontario (Racing Commission)*, [2007] O.J. No. 3249 (Ont. C.A.).

[62]   *Chan v. Orenbach*, [1986] O.J. No. 690 (Ont. Div. Ct.).

[63]   *St-Pie (Municipalité de) c. Commission de protection du territoire agricole du Québec*, [2009] J.Q. no 15512 (Que. C.A.), leave to appeal refused [2010] S.C.C.A. No. 54; *Chieftain Development Co. v. Lachowich*, [1981] A.J. No. 605 (Alta. Q.B.).

[64]   *British Columbia (Attorney General) v. Winter*, [1982] B.C.J. No. 1648 (B.C.S.C.).

[65]   *Newfoundland (Minister of Justice) v. Hanlon*, [2000] N.J. No. 10 (Nfld. C.A.).

[66]   *Foster v. Alberta (Transportation and Safety Board)*, [2006] A.J. No. 1263 (Alta. C.A.).

appeal on the ground that material evidence was disregarded, overlooked or mischaracterized or that unreasonable inferences were drawn from evidence, but not so as to permit appeal of substantive errors as to the sufficiency or weight given to evidence.[67]

An appellate body has no greater authority than that of the lower tribunal. At most it may consider only those matters within the jurisdiction of the lower tribunal, and make only those orders that that tribunal had power to make.[68] Authority granted to the appellate body to substitute its opinion for that of the lower tribunal should be exercised only where the lower tribunal's decision contravenes law or policy, and not where the appellate body simply disagrees with the decision.[69]

Regardless how broad the scope of appeal appears to be from the wording of the appeal provision, the extent of deference shown by the appellate body to the decision of the lower tribunal may depend on a number of other factors, including the extent to which the issue under appeal is within the special expertise of the lower tribunal. These factors are more fully discussed in chapter 8. In appeals from lower tribunals to appellate tribunals, the greater expertise is often possessed by the lower tribunal because of its practical experience gained in its daily regulation in the field. For that reason, its exercise of discretion should be given deference by the appellate tribunal.[70] This approach to determining the standard of review described in chapter 8 may be supplanted by a statutory test that the appeal tribunal must apply.[71]

---

[67] *Professional Salon Services Inc. v. Saskatchewan (Human Rights Commission)*, [2007] S.J. No. 675 (Sask. C.A.), leave to appeal refused [2008] S.C.C.A. No. 69; *Young v. Nova Scotia (Workers' Compensation Appeals Tribunal)*, [2009] N.S.J. No. 157 (N.S.C.A.); *Alberta (Workers' Compensation Board) v. Alberta (Appeals Commission)*, [2005] A.J. No. 1012 (Alta. C.A.).

[68] *Furnival v. Calgary (City)*, [1979] A.J. No. 621 (Alta. C.A.); *Woodglen and Co. v. North York (City)*, [1984] O.J. No. 3320 (Ont. Div. Ct.).

[69] *Newfoundland (Workers' Compensation Commission) v. Breen*, [1997] N.J. No. 70 (Nfld. C.A.).

[70] *St-Pie (Municipalité de) c. Commission de protection du territoire agricole du Québec*, [2009] J.Q. no 15512 (Que. C.A.), leave to appeal refused [2010] S.C.C.A. No. 54; *Plimmer v. Calgary (City) Chief of Police*, [2004] A.J. No. 616 (Alta. C.A.); *Budhai v. Canada (Attorney General)*, [2002] F.C.J. No. 1089 (F.C.A.); *College of Physicians and Surgeons v. Payne*, [2002] O.J. No. 3574 (Ont. Div. Ct.); *Brousseau v. Barreau du Québec*, [2001] J.Q. no 258, 200 D.L.R. (4th) 470 at 492-500 (Que. C.A.), leave to appeal refused [2001] C.S.C.R. no 142; *Walker v. Québec (Régie des alcools, des courses et des jeux)*, [2001] J.Q. no 70 (Que. C.A.).

[71] *Midtown Tavern & Grill Ltd. v. Nova Scotia (Utility and Review Board)*, [2006] N.S.J. No. 418 (N.S.C.A.).

I. STATED CASE OR REFERENCE

Some statutes provide for appeal by way of a stated case. In these situations, the tribunal states the facts as found by it, the applicable law and its reasons for decision. In addition, it poses the questions to be answered by the appellate court. If the statute permits a party to require that a case be stated, the tribunal may refuse to do so if the question is not a question of law or is a question that the court has previously decided. The tribunal is not a mere conduit of the questions and may ensure that the questions are properly framed.[72] If the statute permits a party to request that a case be stated, the tribunal cannot be made to state a case.[73] If not satisfied with the questions posed by the stated case, a party may ask the court to remit it to the tribunal for amendment.[74] The court may not consider a question that the tribunal did not state.[75] A tribunal cannot be required to state a case on an issue not raised in the proceeding before it.[76]

As the courts prefer not to decide hypothetical or academic questions, the stated case must describe the facts of a live case before the tribunal and must be necessary to resolve issues concerning the law applicable to those facts.[77] Prior to stating a case, the tribunal should hold a hearing and make findings of the relevant facts or obtain agreement from all parties as to the facts. A court may refuse to decide a stated case without the necessary findings of fact or where the facts are in dispute. All facts relevant to the question must be found in the stated case and the court may not substitute findings of its own nor look beyond the stated case for additional or different facts. However, the court may review information not found in the stated case if a party alleges that there is no evidence to support a finding of fact (in which case reference may be made to the transcript and exhibits to determine if there was any evidence), or it is argued that the tribunal lacked authority and that the facts in support of that allegation do not appear in the stated case.[78] If a relevant fact was inadvertently omitted from the stated case, the court may admit that fact on the consent of the parties.[79]

---

[72] *Saskatchewan (Municipal Board) v. First City Trust Co.*, [1996] S.J. No. 277 (Sask. C.A.); *Agpro Grain Inc. v. Moose Jaw (City)*, [1997] S.J. No. 112 (Sask. Q.B.).

[73] *R.D.R. Construction Ltd. v. Nova Scotia (Rent Review Commission)*, [1982] N.S.J. No. 546 (N.S.C.A.).

[74] *Saskatchewan (Municipal Board) v. First City Trust Co.*, [1996] S.J. No. 277 (Sask. C.A.).

[75] *Broadway Properties Ltd. v. Vancouver (Assessor) Area #09*, [2007] B.C.J. No. 1227 (B.C.C.A.).

[76] *British Columbia (Assessment Commissioner) v. Woodwards Stores Ltd.*, [1982] B.C.J. No. 1661 (B.C.S.C.).

[77] *Re Prince Edward Island (Labour Relations Board)*, [1997] P.E.I.J. No. 24 (P.E.I.C.A.).

[78] *Caldwell v. Stuart*, [1984] S.C.J. No. 62.

[79] *Pacific National Investments Ltd. v. British Columbia (Assessor of Area No. 01 — Saanich/Capital)*, [1994] B.C.J. No. 1298 (B.C.C.A.).

Some statutes permit tribunals to refer questions of law to a superior court.[80] The question of law should be one that the tribunal must decide for the purpose of dealing with the matter before it, and one of the possible answers to the question must dispose of the matter. The reference should contain findings of fact that are relevant to the question of law, because a court will not consider an academic question.[81] The court may refuse to decide questions involving disputed facts.[82]

Most statutes which authorize stated cases state that the "court shall decide". However, the court may refuse to decide the question if it is of the opinion that it is not appropriate to do so.[83]

J. APPEALS TO CABINET

Some statutes permit parties to petition the Lieutenant Governor or Governor General in Council or a Minister to review a decision of an administrative tribunal. Cabinet and its Ministers, unlike the courts, are not concerned with questions of law. They apply their view of the public interest to the matters in dispute[84] and make what is essentially a political decision, responding to the political, economic and social concerns of the moment.[85]

K. COSTS

Appellate courts have an inherent power to award the costs of an appeal. Appellate tribunals cannot award costs unless they are empowered by statute to do so. Neither may award costs of the hearing before the inferior tribunal unless that tribunal had the power to award costs.[86] If the statute grants power to award costs of the proceeding before the inferior tribunal, the appellate court must apply the rules governing costs under which the lower tribunal operates.[87]

---

[80] See, for example, *Federal Courts Act*, R.S.C. 1985, c. F-7, s. 18.3 [as am.]; *Administrative Tribunals Act*, S.B.C. 2004, c. 45, s. 43.

[81] *Re Rosen*, [1987] F.C.J. No. 320 (F.C.A.); *Re Canada Post Corp.*, [1989] F.C.J. No. 239 (F.C.A.); *contra: Ottawa (City) v. Ontario (Attorney General)*, [2002] O.J. No. 2501 (Ont. C.A.), leave to appeal refused [2002] S.C.C.A. No. 361.

[82] *Canada (Registrar, Indian Register) v. Sinclair*, [2003] F.C.J. No. 1967 (F.C.A.).

[83] *Re Prince Edward Island (Labour Relations Board)*, [1997] P.E.I.J. No. 24 (P.E.I.C.A.).

[84] *Islands Protection Society v. British Columbia (Environmental Appeal Board)*, [1988] B.C.J. No. 654 (B.C.S.C.); *Davisville Investment Co. v. Toronto (City)*, [1977] O.J. No. 2193 (Ont. C.A.).

[85] *Inuit Tapirisat of Canada v. Canada (Attorney General)*, [1980] S.C.J. No. 99.

[86] *Ontario (Minister of Mines and Northern Affairs) v. Sheridan Geophysics*, [1976] S.C.J. No. 76.

[87] *DCA Employees Pension Committee v. Ontario (Superintendent of Financial Services)*, [2007] O.J. No. 2176 at paras. 177-184 (Ont. C.A.), affd [2009] S.C.J. No. 39.

Chapter 7

JUDICIAL REVIEW PROCEDURE

A. INTRODUCTION

Application to the court for review of a tribunal decision should be made only as a last resort. Parties should take advantage of internal procedures available to a tribunal to correct its errors and of rights of appeal granted by statute. These other ways of correcting tribunal errors tend to be more satisfactory especially as an application for judicial review may be dismissed for failure to pursue other processes.[1] Only when those routes are unavailable, or have been tried without success, should parties resort to judicial review. That said, how does a party apply for judicial review of a tribunal's decision? The procedure varies across Canada.

Not everything that a public official does is reviewable. A court may decline to review a communication that does not involve an exercise of authority, such as a letter expressing an opinion, warning the recipient to comply with requirements, proposing a meeting, or refusing a request to do something in the absence of an obligation to do it.[2]

B. FEDERAL COURT OR PROVINCIAL SUPERIOR COURT?

A party applying for judicial review must first decide which court has authority to supervise the tribunal in question, the Federal Court or a provincial superior court. Generally, tribunals created by Parliament are supervised by the Federal Court while tribunals established by provincial statute are supervised by their respective provincial superior court.

---

[1] See discussion in Chapter 9 concerning the court's discretion to dismiss an application.

[2] *1099065 Ontario Inc. (c.o.b. Outer Space Sports) v. Canada (Minister of Public Safety and Emergency Preparedness)*, [2008] F.C.J. No. 177 (F.C.A.); *Democracy Watch v. Canada (Conflict of Interest and Ethics Commissioner)*, [2009] F.C.J. No. 34 (F.C.A.), leave to appeal refused [2009] S.C.C.A. No. 139; *Sex Party v. British Columbia (General Manager, Liquor Control and Licensing Branch)*, [2006] B.C.J. No. 1210 (B.C.C.A.); *Cassiar Watch v. Canada (Minister of Fisheries and Oceans)*, [2010] F.C.J. No. 282 (F.C.); *Nguyen v. Alberta (Alberta Workers' Compensation Appeals Commission)*, [2008] A.J. No. 1222 (Alta. Q.B.); *Ranger v. Board of Examiners of the Assn. of Social Workers*, [2000] N.S.J. No. 301, 186 N.S.R. (2d) 332 (N.S.S.C.); *Sandiford v. Canada (Attorney General)*, [2009] F.C.J. No. 1026 (F.C.); *contra: Larny Holdings Ltd. v. Canada (Minister of Health)*, [2002] F.C.J. No. 1026 (F.C.T.D.); *Air Canada v. Toronto Port Authority*, [2010] F.C.J. No. 942 (F.C.).

Section 18 of the *Federal Courts Act*[3] gives the Federal Court exclusive original jurisdiction over federal tribunals. The provincial courts do not have authority to supervise federal tribunals by way of judicial review.[4] Even if a province is a party affected by the decision of the federal tribunal, the Federal Court has jurisdiction.[5]

There are two exceptions to this general rule. When a person is detained by order of a federal tribunal, an application for a writ of *habeas corpus* (to have the detention order judicially reviewed) may be made to a provincial superior court because the federal court does not have authority to issue a writ of *habeas corpus*. For that review to be effective, the provincial superior court may issue to the federal tribunal a writ of *certiorari* (simply, a command to deliver up the tribunal's record so that it may be reviewed by the court). Thus, the person who is detained has a choice of applying to the Federal Court for judicial review or to the provincial Superior Court for a writ of *habeas corpus*. However, either court may exercise its discretion to refuse to review the detention where Parliament has put in place a complete, comprehensive and expert procedure for review of the detention decision.[6]

Both the provincial superior courts and the federal courts have authority to declare a federal statute or regulation to be unconstitutional, even when it relates to a federal tribunal.[7] Provincial superior courts are not obliged to execute an invalid federal statute or regulation.[8] However, as a provincial superior court may not review a federal tribunal's exercise of power nor grant any remedy other than a declaration that a statutory provision is invalid, constitutional challenges to the actions of federal tribunals should be brought in the Federal Court.[9]

Some tribunals created by one government exercise powers conferred upon them by another government. For example, the provincial marketing and transportation boards exercise powers conferred upon them by federal

---

[3] R.S.C. 1985, c. F-7 [as am.].

[4] *Groupe des Eléveurs de Volailles de l'Est de l'Ont. v. Canadian Chicken Marketing Agency*, [1984] F.C.J. No. 251 (F.C.T.D.). But see: *Canada (Attorney General) v. TeleZone Inc.*, [2010] S.C.J. No. 62.

[5] *Friends of the Oldman River Society v. Canada (Minister of Environment)*, [1993] F.C.J. No. 316 (F.C.A.).

[6] *May v. Ferndale Institution*, [2005] S.C.J. No. 84.

[7] *Canada (Labour Relations Board) v. Paul l'Anglais Inc.*, [1983] S.C.J. No. 12.

[8] *Canada (Attorney General) v. Law Society (B.C.)*, [1982] S.C.J. No. 70; *Groupe des Eléveurs de Volailles de l'Est de l'Ont. v. Canadian Chicken Marketing Agency*, [1984] F.C.J. No. 251 (F.C.T.D.); *Bassett v. Canada*, [1987] S.J. No. 9 (Sask. C.A.).

[9] *State Farm Mutual Automobile Insurance Co. v. Canada (Privacy Commissioner)*, [2009] N.B.J. No. 10 (N.B.C.A.); *Canada (Attorney General) v. Prince Edward Island*, [2006] P.E.I.J. No. 65, leave to appeal refused [2007] S.C.C.A. No. 97; *Mousseau v. Canada (Attorney General)*, [1993] N.S.J. No. 382 (N.S.C.A.).

statutes. This inter-delegation of powers is necessary to create one integrated national system of regulation. A provincial tribunal, even when exercising powers conferred upon it pursuant to a federal statute, is supervised by its provincial superior court.[10] The definition of "federal board, commission or other tribunal" in section 2(1) of the *Federal Courts Act* does not include tribunals established by provincial law nor federal officials when they exercise provincial statutory powers.[11] A tribunal created by a federal-provincial agreement is supervised by provincial superior courts.[12] A federally incorporated self-regulatory organization is supervised by a provincial superior court when exercising provincial regulatory powers,[13] but by Federal Court when exercising federal authority.[14]

Tribunals of the Yukon, Northwest and Nunavut Territories are not federal tribunals, even though Parliament has ultimate responsibility to govern the territories. These tribunals are established by Territorial Ordinance and are supervised by the superior courts of the territories.[15]

C. FEDERAL COURT

The Federal Court hears all applications for judicial review of federal tribunals,[16] except for the tribunals listed in s. 28 of the *Federal Courts Act* which are reviewed by the Federal Court of Appeal. There need not be a decision or order of the tribunal before the court's power of review may be invoked. Any act of a federal tribunal or official affecting the applicant's legal rights may be reviewed.[17] As the date and details of the matter must be clearly set out in the originating notice of motion, there cannot be judicial review of a general pattern of conduct without identification of

---

[10] *Groupe des Eléveurs de Volailles de l'Est de l'Ont. v. Canadian Chicken Marketing Agency*, [1984] F.C.J. No. 251 (F.C.T.D.); *Bicknell Freighters Ltd. v. Manitoba (Highway Transport Board)*, [1977] M.J. No. 40 (Man. C.A.); *9037-9694 Québec Inc. v. Canada (Procureur général)*, [2002] F.C.J. No. 1132 (F.C.T.D.).

[11] R.S.C. 1985, c. F-7, s. 2(1) [as am.]; *Anisman v. Canada (Border Services Agency)*, [2010] F.C.J. No. 221 (F.C.A.).

[12] *Canadian Restaurant and Foodservices Assn. v. Canada (Dairy Commission)*, [2001] F.C.J. No. 179 (F.C.T.D.).

[13] *Rosenbush v. National Dental Examining Board*, [1992] F.C.J. No. 423 (F.C.A.); *Kass v. Canada (Attorney General)*, [1998] F.C.J. No. 1448 (F.C.T.D.).

[14] *Onuschak v. Canadian Society of Immigration*, [2009] F.C.J. No. 1596 (F.C.).

[15] *Pfeiffer v. Northwest Territories (Commissioner)*, [1977] N.W.T.J. No. 8 (N.W.T.S.C.); *Smith v. Canada*, [1977] F.C.J. No. 180 (F.C.T.D.).

[16] *Federal Courts Act*, R.S.C. 1985, c. F-7, s. 18 [as am.].

[17] *Krause v. Canada*, [1999] F.C.J. No. 179 (F.C.A.); *Khadr v. Canada (Attorney General)*, [2006] F.C.J. No. 888 (F.C.); *Larny Holdings Ltd. v. Canada (Minister of Health)*, [2002] F.C.J. No. 1026 (F.C.T.D.). Except policy decisions: *Alberta v. Canada (Wheat Board)*, [1997] F.C.J. No. 1484 (F.C.T.D.), affd [1998] F.C.J. No. 1747 (F.C.A.).

specific incidents.[18] The court rarely grants preliminary motions to quash applications for judicial review. Parties are expected to argue applications on their merits.[19]

The procedural rules to be followed on all applications for judicial review are listed starting at s. 18.1 of the *Federal Courts Act* and in Part V of the *Federal Court Rules*. Applications for judicial review are to be heard in a summary way.[20] The court is given broad powers to order a tribunal to do any act or thing, to prohibit a tribunal from proceeding, to declare invalid and quash any tribunal decision, and to refer the matter back to the tribunal for reconsideration in accordance with directions made by the court.[21] The court may also make interim orders.[22] Grounds are listed upon which relief may be granted but, where there has been no substantial wrong or miscarriage of justice, relief may be refused and the tribunal's decision validated.[23]

D.   PROVINCIAL SUPERIOR COURTS

1.   British Columbia, Ontario and Prince Edward Island

Ontario, British Columbia and Prince Edward Island have enacted statutes, that prescribe the procedure to be followed on applications for judicial review.[24] As these enactments are similar but not identical, be careful when applying a judicial interpretation of a provision of one province to a similar provision of another.

Under the British Columbia and Ontario Acts, two general categories of relief are available:[25]

(1)   application may be made for an order in the nature of *mandamus* (an order requiring a public official to exercise statutory

---

[18]   *Conféderation des Syndicats Nationaux v. Canada (Commission de l'assurance-emploi)*, [1998] F.C.J. No. 144 (F.C.T.D.).

[19]   *Bull (David) Laboratories (Canada) Inc. v. Parmacia Inc.*, [1994] F.C.J. No. 1629 (F.C.A.); *Schwarz Hospitality Group Ltd. v. Canada (Minister of Canadian Heritage)*, [1999] F.C.J. No. 747 (F.C.T.D.).

[20]   R.S.C. 1985, c. F-7, s. 18.4 [as am.]; *Federal Court Rules, 1998*, SOR/98-106; *Merck Frosst Canada Inc. v. Canada (Minister of National Health and Welfare)*, [1994] F.C.J. No. 1707 (F.C.T.D.).

[21]   *Federal Courts Act*, R.S.C. 1985, c. F-7, s. 18.1(3) [as am.].

[22]   *Federal Courts Act*, R.S.C. 1985, c. F-7, s. 18.2 [as am.].

[23]   *Federal Courts Act*, R.S.C. 1985, c. F-7, s. 18.1(4), (5) [as am.].

[24]   *Judicial Review Procedure Act*, R.S.B.C. 1996, c. 241; *Judicial Review Procedure Act*, R.S.O. 1990, c. J.1; *Judicial Review Act*, R.S.P.E.I. 1988, c. J-3.

[25]   *Judicial Review Procedure Act*, R.S.B.C. 1996, c. 241, s. 2(2); *Judicial Review Procedure Act*, R.S.O. 1990, c. J.1, s. 2(1).

authority), prohibition (an order prohibiting a public official from exceeding statutory authority), or *certiorari*[26] (an order requiring an inferior tribunal to deliver up its record so that its decision may be reviewed and, if appropriate, set aside); or

(2) application may be made for an injunction or a declaration in relation to the exercise, refusal to exercise, or proposed or purported exercise of a statutory power.

"Statutory power" is a defined term.[27] It includes powers conferred by or under a statute to make a decision or perform an act that affects a person's legal interest, to impose requirements on a person, or to make rules. It does not include powers conferred by or under a statute to investigate and report,[28] nor to contract or to manage property.[29] It does not include actions of government which do not involve the exercise of a "statutory power",[30] nor an exercise of prerogative power.[31] The issuance of a notice of hearing is not an exercise of a "statutory power".[32]

A statutory power may be challenged under category (2) only if the authorized person exercises the power, refused to exercise it, or proposes or purports to exercise it. A declaration or injunction is not available in respect of a statutory power that merely exists and has a potential to be exercised. It is the exercise or non-exercise of the statutory power that may be challenged, not its existence. For there to be a proposed exercise of a power, there must be a clear intention to exercise the power in respect of a particular matter. For there to be a purported exercise of a statutory power, there must be an actual attempt to exercise the power that for some reason falls short of an actual exercise of the power.[33] The constitutionality

---

[26] Latin: "to be better informed".

[27] *Judicial Review Procedure Act*, R.S.B.C. 1996, c. 241, s. 1; *Judicial Review Procedure Act*, R.S.O. 1990, c. J.1, s. 1.

[28] *Taser International Inc. v. British Columbia (Commissioner)*, [2010] B.C.J. No. 1578 (B.C.S.C.).

[29] *Eagleridge Bluffs and Wetlands Preservation Society v. British Columbia (Ministry of Transportation)*, [2006] B.C.J. No. 1504 (B.C.C.A.); *Midnorthern Appliances Industries Corp. v. Ontario Housing Corp.*, [1977] O.J. No. 2395 (Ont. Div. Ct.); *Cordsen v. Greater Victoria Water District*, [1982] B.C.J. No. 1584 (B.C.S.C.); *Paine v. University of Toronto*, [1981] O.J. No. 3187 (Ont. C.A.), leave to appeal refused [1982] 1 S.C.R. x.

[30] *Greene v. Law Society (British Columbia)*, [2005] B.C.J. No. 586 (B.C.S.C.); *Hospital Employees Union v. Northern Health Authority*, [2003] B.C.J. No. 1173 (B.C.S.C.); *Blaber v. University of Victoria*, [1995] B.C.J. No. 558 (B.C.S.C.); *Masters v. Ontario*, [1993] O.J. No. 3091 (Ont. Gen. Div.); *Ayerst, McKenna and Harrison Inc. v. Ontario (Attorney General)*, [1992] O.J. No. 173 (Ont. Div. Ct.).

[31] *Cook v. Canada (Minister of Aboriginal Relations and Reconciliation)*, [2007] B.C.J. No. 2556 (B.C.S.C.).

[32] *Pierce v. Law Society of British Columbia*, [1993] B.C.J. No. 1031 (B.C.S.C.).

[33] *Service Employees International Union, Local 204 v. Broadway Manor Nursing Home*, [1984] O.J. No. 3360 (Ont. C.A.), leave to appeal refused (1985), 8 O.A.C. 320n; *Culhane v. British Columbia (Attorney General)*, [1980] B.C.J. No. 1556 (B.C.C.A.).

of the statutory power cannot be challenged on judicial review because it is a challenge to the existence of the power rather than its exercise.[34]

To obtain relief in the nature of *mandamus*, prohibition, or *certiorari* under category (1), there need not be an exercise, refusal to exercise, or proposed or purported exercise of a statutory power.[35] Prerogative writs were historically issued on behalf of the Sovereign to compel public officials to do their duty and obey the law. They may not be used to review an exercise of the Crown's prerogative, but can be used to review an exercise by public officials of power delegated to them pursuant to the prerogative.[36] Only the actions of public officials are reviewable. Private tribunals, such as unions or real estate boards, may be challenged only by way of action for an injunction or a declaration,[37] though their exercise of statutory powers may be challenged under category (2).

The Prince Edward Island Act has substituted for these two categories of relief, orders that would nullify or prohibit acts of a tribunal, direct a tribunal to act, declare rights of a person, or refer a matter back to a tribunal for further consideration.[38] "Tribunal" is defined to mean a person upon whom an enactment confers authority to make a decision and includes the Lieutenant Governor in Council and a Minister.[39] This Act provides a procedure for review of only those tribunals that exercise statutory powers and only in respect of their decisions, not preliminary matters such as a notice of hearing.[40]

---

[34] *Keewatin v. Ontario (Minister of Natural Resources)*, [2003] O.J. No. 2937 (Ont. Div. Ct.).

[35] *Service Employees International Union, Local 204 v. Broadway Manor Nursing Home*, [1984] O.J. No. 3360 (Ont. C.A.), leave to appeal refused (1985), 8 O.A.C. 320n.

[36] *Cook v. Canada (Minister of Aboriginal Relations and Reconciliation)*, [2007] B.C.J. No. 2556 (B.C.S.C.).

[37] *Mohr v. Vancouver, New Westminster and Fraser Valley District Council of Carpenters*, [1988] B.C.J. No. 2075 (B.C.C.A.); *Vinogradov v. University of Calgary*, [1987] A.J. No. 164 (Alta. C.A.); *Ireland v. Victoria Real Estate Board*, [1987] B.C.J. No. 821 (B.C.S.C.); *Peg-Win Real Estate Ltd. v. Winnipeg Real Estate Board*, [1985] M.J. No. 339 (Man. Q.B.), affd [1985] M.J. No. 461 (Man. C.A.); contra: *Rees v. United Assn. of Journeymen and Apprentices of the Plumbing and Pipefitting Industry of the United States and Canada, Local 527*, [1983] O.J. No. 3152 (Ont. Div. Ct.); *Fawcett v. Canadian Chiropractic Examining Board*, [2010] O.J. No. 3955 (Ont. S.C.J.). See also *Cimolai v. Children's and Women's Health Centre*, [2003] B.C.J. No. 1313 (B.C.C.A.), which finds a hospital to be a public body.

[38] *Judicial Review Act*, R.S.P.E.I. 1988, c. J-3, ss. 2 and 3(3) [as am.].

[39] *Judicial Review Act*, R.S.P.E.I. 1988, c. J-3, s. 1(h) [as am.]; *Summerside Seafood Supreme Inc. v. Prince Edward Island (Minister of Fisheries, Aquaculture and Environment)*, [2006] P.E.I.J. No. 32 at para. 68 (P.E.I.C.A.); *Greenisle Environmental Inc. v. Prince Edward Island*, [2005] P.E.I.J. No. 41 (P.E.I.S.C.).

[40] *Prince Edward Island v. Burge*, [1995] P.E.I.J. No. 148 (P.E.I.C.A.); *K.J.G.W. Holdings Inc. v. Prince Edward Island (Liquor Control Commission)*, [1995] P.E.I.J. No. 35 (P.E.I.C.A.).

While the British Columbia and Ontario Acts require that applications for prerogative writs be dealt with as applications for judicial review,[41] the Prince Edward Island Act does not, leaving applicants with the option of applying outside the Act for a prerogative writ.[42]

An application for judicial review in British Columbia and Prince Edward Island is made to a single judge of the Supreme Court.[43] In Ontario, an application for judicial review is normally made to the Divisional Court, comprising three judges but, if the case is urgent and the delay required for an application to the Divisional Court is likely to involve a failure of justice, the application may be made to a single judge, with leave.[44] If the application, on its face, lacks merit, a motion to quash the application may be brought before a single judge.[45]

In British Columbia, the detailed procedural rules are set out primarily in Rule 16-1 of the *Supreme Court Civil Rules*, which prescribes the form and content of the petition and its service on all persons whose interests may be affected by the order sought. One new requirement is that a respondent must deliver a response stating their response on the issues.

In Ontario and Prince Edward Island, rule 68 of the *Rules of Civil Procedure* prescribes the form of the notice of application and fixes time limits for the filing of the record and factums. Rule 68.06 empowers the Registrar to dismiss an application for delay. An application for judicial review may not be made pursuant to rule 14.05.[46]

In Ontario, a tribunal must file its record forthwith and in Prince Edward Island within ten days, while in British Columbia the court may direct that the record be filed.

---

[41] *Judicial Review Procedure Act*, R.S.B.C. 1996, c. 241, s. 12; *Judicial Review Procedure Act*, R.S.O. 1990, c. J.1, s. 7.

[42] *National Farmers Union v. Prince Edward Island (Potato Marketing Council)*, [1989] P.E.I.J. No. 14 (P.E.I.S.C.).

[43] *Judicial Review Procedure Act*, R.S.B.C. 1996, c. 241, s. 2(1); *Judicial Review Act*, R.S.P.E.I. 1988, c. J-3, ss. 1(*f*) and 3(1) [as am.].

[44] *Judicial Review Procedure Act*, R.S.O. 1990, c. J.1, s. 6.

[45] *Keewatin v. Ontario (Minister of Natural Resources)*, [2003] O.J. No. 2937 (Ont. Div. Ct.); *East Luther Grand Valley (Township) v. Ontario (Minister of Environment and Energy)*, [2000] O.J. No. 1424 (Ont. S.C.J.); *Geneen v. Toronto (City)*, [1999] O.J. No. 149 (Ont. Div. Ct.).

[46] *Canada Post Corp. v. Canadian Union of Postal Workers*, [1989] O.J. No. 1583 (Ont. H.C.J.); *Law Society of Prince Edward Island v. MacKinnon*, [2001] P.E.I.J. No. 63 (P.E.I.S.C.).

2. Alberta, Saskatchewan, Manitoba, New Brunswick, Nova Scotia, Newfoundland / Labrador and the Territories

Alberta, Nova Scotia and the Yukon Territory have recently amended their rules. As in the new British Columbia rules, the Nova Scotia and Yukon Rules now require a respondent to deliver a written response stating the respondent's position on the issues.

Part 3 (Subdivision 2) of the Alberta *Rules of Court*, Rule 54 of Newfoundland and Labrador *Rules of the Supreme Court* and Part 44 of the *Rules of the Supreme Court* of the Northwest and Nunavut Territories provide that application may be made to the Court by way of originating application for orders in the nature of the prerogative remedies of *certiorari*, prohibition, *mandamus* and *quo warranto*. The tribunal must file its record as soon as practicable, though the Alberta rule permits the tribunal, instead, to provide an explanation why this cannot be done.

Part 52 of the Saskatchewan *Rules of Practice and Procedure* permits an application for judicial review to be made by notice of motion. The remedies include orders in the nature of the prerogative writs as well as a declaration, injunction or damages as collateral relief. The tribunal must deliver its record forthwith.

Rule 68 of the Manitoba *Rules of Practice* provides that *mandamus*, prohibition, *certiorari*, and *quo warranto* may be granted on application. The court may require that notice be given to any person who may be affected by the order sought.

Rule 54 of the Yukon *Rules of Court* permits an originating application for an order in the nature of a prerogative remedy. As in the Federal Court, each application is limited to review of a single decision. As in Nova Scotia, a respondent must deliver a response. The Rule explicitly provides for case management. The court may order the decision maker to deliver the record. A process is prescribed for a party to request the record and for the tribunal to object.

Rule 69 of the New Brunswick *Rules of Court* provides that *certiorari*, *mandamus*, prohibition, *quo warranto*, and orders to set aside or remit an award may be obtained by way of notice of application for judicial review. The date for hearing the application must be fixed by a judge who may refuse to fix a date if not satisfied that there is a ground for relief.[47] If grounds are shown, the judge may fix a date before the Court of Queen's

---

[47] *Canadian Union of Public Employees, Local 1253 v. New Brunswick (Board of Management)*, [2006] N.B.J. No. 122 (N.B.C.A.).

Bench, or direct that the application be returnable before the Court of Appeal. The court may direct the tribunal to file its record.

Rule 7 of the Nova Scotia *Civil Procedure Rules* has replaced the prerogative writs with a notice of judicial review. A respondent must deliver a notice of participation stating the respondent's position on the issues. The applicant must bring a motion for directions to obtain a hearing date. Within five days of being notified, the tribunal must deliver the record or undertake to appear at the motion to seek directions with respect to the record.

3.   Quebec

Article 846 of the *Code of Civil Procedure* empowers a Superior Court, at the request of a party, to evoke a decision or pending decision of a tribunal if grounds for review listed in art. 846 are established. The writ of evocation is the equivalent of *certiorari* and prohibition combined.[48] It is available only with respect to statutory tribunals.[49] A court may refuse to evoke an interlocutory ruling of a tribunal if the tribunal is free to reverse its ruling before making its final decision.[50] Interim decisions that have final effect may be reviewed.[51] Recommendations of an investigator, that will not be implemented without a hearing, are not subject to evocation.[52] Evocation pursuant to art. 846 is the preferred procedure for review of decisions by tribunals that exercise quasi-judicial powers.[53] The exercise of other statutory powers may be reviewed in an action under art. 33 requesting the Superior Court to exercise its superintending power over inferior tribunals.[54]

Article 844 permits any person interested to apply to a Superior Court for an order commanding a tribunal to perform an act that it is by law bound to perform, but that it has omitted, neglected, or refused to perform. This is the equivalent of the prerogative writ of *mandamus*.[55]

---

[48]   *Québec (Attorney General) v. Canada (Attorney General)*, [1978] S.C.J. No. 84.

[49]   *Theoret v. Cholette*, [1980] C.S. 643 (Que.).

[50]   *College d'Enseignement General et Professionel de Valleyfield v. Gauthier-Cashman*, [1984] C.A. 633 (Que.).

[51]   *Brault v. Comité d'Inspection Professionnelle de la Corporation Professionnelle des Ergothera-peutes*, [1985] C.S. 209 (Que.).

[52]   *Cote Saint-Luc (Cité) v. Québec (Commission des Droits de la Personne)*, [1981] C.S. 27 (Que.).

[53]   *Noël v. Société d'énergie de la Baie James*, [2001] S.C.J. No. 41.

[54]   *Immeubles Port Louis Ltée v. Lafontaine (Village)*, [1991] S.C.J. No. 14; *Lacelle c. Bureau des services financiers*, [2005] J.Q. no 2751 (Que. S.C.), leave to appeal refused [2005] J.Q. no 20328 (Que. C.A.).

[55]   *Canadian Newspaper Co. v. Québec (City) (Director of Public Road and Traffic Service)*, [1987] R.J.Q. 1078, 36 D.L.R. (4th) 641 (Que. S.C.).

Articles 834.1 to 837 set out the procedure to be followed. A petition for these orders is made by motion and must be supported by an affidavit setting out all the necessary facts. The motion and supporting documents must be served on the tribunal and on adverse parties. A motion must be commenced within a reasonable time after the impugned decision or event. A petition will not be dismissed solely because the petitioner mistakenly applied under art. 846 instead of under art. 844.[56]

E.   CHOICE OF APPLICATION OR ACTION

The prerogative writs of *certiorari*, prohibition and *mandamus* may be obtained only by way of judicial review.[57] A decision made in the exercise of a statutory power may be set aside only on judicial review.[58] The choice of proceeding by way of action arises when other relief such as a declaration, injunction or damages is sought instead of a prerogative remedy or other order setting aside the decision.[59] An action, for a declaration that a decision made pursuant to statute is invalid, may be dismissed as an abuse of process for failure to follow the statutory process for review of the decision.[60] The decisions of tribunals that do not have legal capacity to be sued may not be challenged in an action.[61]

The federal, Northwest Territories and Nunavut courts may direct that an application for judicial review be continued as an action where appropriate.[62] A court may order this conversion if satisfied that a trial is necessary to establish facts that cannot adequately be established by the record supplemented by affidavits, to facilitate access to justice and avoid unnecessary cost and delay, to determine constitutional questions, and to permit an award of damages.[63] On the same grounds the Ontario Divisional Court may

---

[56] *Brazeau v. Comité d'Arbitrage de Comptes Professionnels*, [1981] C.S. 333 (Que.).

[57] *Judicial Review Procedure Act*, R.S.O. 1990, c. J.1, s. 7; *Judicial Review Procedure Act*, R.S.B.C. 1996, c. 241, s. 12; *Auton (Guardian ad litem of) v. British Columbia (Minister of Health)*, [1999] B.C.J. No. 718 (B.C.S.C.).

[58] *Canada (Attorney General) v. TeleZone Inc.*, [2010] S.C.J. No. 62.

[59] *Canada (Attorney General) v. TeleZone Inc.*, [2010] S.C.J. No. 62.

[60] *Shuswap Lake Utilities Ltd. v. British Columbia (Comptroller of Water Rights)*, [2008] B.C.J. No. 716 (B.C.C.A.).

[61] *Ontario v. Gratton-Masuy Environmental Technologies Inc. (c.o.b. EcoFlo Ontario)*, [2010] O.J. No. 2935 (Ont. C.A.).

[62] *Federal Courts Act*, R.S.C. 1985, c. F-7, s. 18.4(2) [as am.]; *Rules of the Supreme Court of the Northwest Territories*, N.W.T. Reg. 010-96, r. 605(2); *Rules of the Supreme Court of Nunavut*, N.W.T. Reg. 010-96, r. 605(2).

[63] *Association des crabiers acadiens inc. v. Canada (Attorney General)*, [2009] F.C.J. No. 1567 (F.C.A.).

dismiss an application without prejudice to the right of the applicant to commence an action.[64]

Where a decision pursuant to statutory authority affects a large number of people, an application for judicial review is preferable to a class proceeding because it is less expensive and more expeditious and because a declaration of invalidity applies with respect to everyone affected.[65]

Some decision makers are not subject to judicial review. To be subject to judicial review, the decision maker must be a public official, be established by statute, be a decision maker to whom parties are required by statute to resort to settle their differences, or exercise powers conferred by statute.[66] Only one of these factors need be present. The exercise of statutory powers delegated by way of privatization of government services to private entities is subject to judicial review.[67] An arbitration board appointed pursuant to a collective agreement is regarded as a statutory tribunal because it draws its powers from statute.[68]

Non-statutory bodies with powers to discipline members include unions, real estate boards, stock exchanges, clubs and associations. Non-statutory bodies may be challenged only by an action for a declaration or injunction which may include a claim for damages.[69]

In British Columbia, Ontario and Prince Edward Island, a declaration or injunction may be sought in an application for judicial review but only against

---

[64] *Seaway Trust Co. v. Ontario (Attorney General)*, [1983] O.J. No. 2210 (Ont. C.A.); *Keewatin v. Ontario (Minister of Natural Resources)*, [2003] O.J. No. 2937 (Ont. Div. Ct.).

[65] *Marcotte v. Longueuil (City)*, [2009] S.C.J. No. 43; *Auton (Guardian ad litem of) v. British Columbia (Minister of Health)*, [1999] B.C.J. No. 718 (B.C.S.C.); *Gray v. Ontario*, [2005] O.J. No. 4221 (Ont. S.C.J.); *S.R. Gent (Canada) Inc. v. Ontario (Workplace Safety and Insurance Board)*, [1999] O.J. No. 3362 (Ont. S.C.J.).

[66] *Roberval Express Ltd. v. Transport Drivers, Warehousemen and General Workers Union, Local 106*, [1982] S.C.J. No. 106; *Ontario Nurses' Assn. v. Rouge Valley Health System*, [2008] O.J. No. 4566 (Ont. Div. Ct.); *Scheerer v. Waldbillig*, [2006] O.J. No. 744 (Ont. Div. Ct.); *Freeman-Maloy v. Marsden*, [2006] O.J. No. 1228 (Ont. C.A.), leave to appeal refused [2006] S.C.C.A. No. 201.

[67] Reviewable: *Luzak v. Real Estate Council*, [2003] O.J. No. 4494 (Ont. Div. Ct.). Not reviewable: *A.I. Enterprises Ltd. v. Joyce Avenue Apartments Ltd.*, [2002] N.B.J. No. 8 (N.B.Q.B.).

[68] *Roberval Express Ltd. v. Transport Drivers, Warehousemen and General Workers Union, Local 106*, [1982] S.C.J. No. 106.

[69] *Knox v. Conservative Party of Canada*, [2007] A.J. No. 1046 (Alta. C.A.), leave to appeal refused [2007] S.C.C.A. No. 567; *Warren v. Hampton Country Club Inc.*, [1995] N.B.J. No. 608 (N.B.C.A.); *Mohr v. Vancouver, New Westminster and Fraser Valley District Council of Carpenters*, [1988] B.C.J. No. 2075 (B.C.C.A.); *Vinogradov v. University of Calgary*, [1987] A.J. No. 164 (Alta. C.A.); *Ireland v. Victoria Real Estate Board*, [1987] B.C.J. No. 821 (B.C.S.C.); *Peg-Win Real Estate Ltd. v. Winnipeg Real Estate Board*, [1985] M.J. No. 339 (Man. Q.B.), affd [1985] M.J. No. 461 (Man. C.A.). The Saskatchewan rules may permit applications for judicial review against non-statutory bodies: *Chyz v. Appraisal Institute of Canada*, [1985] S.J. No. 820 (Sask. C.A.).

statutory bodies.[70] The rules of other jurisdictions authorize the remedies of declaration or injunction on judicial review.[71] In British Columbia, Ontario, the Northwest Territories and Nunavut, any party to an action for a declaration or injunction in relation to an exercise of statutory power may apply to court for an order that the action be disposed of as if it were an application for judicial review,[72] unless a trial is necessary to fully address the issues.[73]

Damages may be claimed in an action but not in an application for judicial review,[74] except in Saskatchewan.[75] However, a mandatory order requiring a party to return funds received pursuant to a tribunal order may be made on application.[76] (See discussion of damages in chapter 9.)

Subordinate law such as a regulation may not be challenged by way of *certiorari.*[77] In jurisdictions that have expanded the matters that are subject to judicial review to include any exercise of statutory power, a challenge to a regulation may be made by application for judicial review.[78]

Commercial decisions of the Crown are not reviewable pursuant to prerogative writs,[79] but the Crown's breach of a contract may be the subject of an action by a party to the contract.[80]

---

[70] *Judicial Review Procedure Act*, R.S.B.C. 1996, c. 241, s. 2(2)(*b*); *Judicial Review Procedure Act*, R.S.O. 1990, c. J.1, s. 2(1)2; *Judicial Review Act*, R.S.P.E.I. 1988, c. J-3, ss. 2 and 3(3) [as am.].

[71] *Rules of Court*, Alta. Reg. 124/2010, r. 3.15(1)(*b*); *Queen's Bench Rules*, R.S.S. 1978, c. Q-1, r. 664(2); *Rules of the Supreme Court of the Northwest Territories*, N.W.T. Reg. 010-96, r. 592(2)(*b*); *Rules of the Supreme Court of Nunavut*, r. 592(2)(*b*).

[72] *Judicial Review Procedure Act*, R.S.B.C. 1996, c. 241, s. 13; *Judicial Review Procedure Act*, R.S.O. 1990, c. J.1, s. 8; *Rules of the Supreme Court of the Northwest Territories*, N.W.T. Reg. 010-96, r. 605; *Rules of the Supreme Court of Nunavut*, N.W.T. Reg. 010-96, r. 605.

[73] *South-West Oxford (Township) v. Ontario (Attorney General)*, [1983] O.J. No. 3272 (Ont. H.C.J.).

[74] *Seaway Trust Co. v. Ontario (Attorney General)*, [1983] O.J. No. 2210 (Ont. C.A.); *Lussier v. Collin*, [1984] F.C.J. No. 195 (F.C.A.).

[75] R.S.S. 1978, c. Q-1, *Queen's Bench Rules*, r. 664(2)(b).

[76] *Collins v. Ontario (Pension Commission)*, [1986] O.J. No. 769 (Ont. Div. Ct.); *contra*: *Haagsman v. British Columbia (Minister of Forests)*, [1998] B.C.J. No. 2735 (B.C.S.C.).

[77] *Brown v. Alberta Dental Assn.*, [2002] A.J. No. 142 (Alta. C.A.).

[78] *Saskatchewan Government Employees' Union v. Saskatchewan*, [1997] S.J. No. 123 (Sask. Q.B.); affd [1997] S.J. No. 277 (Sask. C.A.); *Eli Lilly Canada Inc. v. Novopharm Ltd.*, [2009] F.C.J. No. 566 (F.C.A.); *contra*: *Carrier-Sekani Tribal Council v. Canada (Minister of Environment)*, [1992] F.C.J. No. 405 (F.C.A.), leave to appeal refused [1992] S.C.C.A. No. 360.

[79] *Labrador Airways Ltd. v. Canada Post Corp.*, [2001] N.J. No. 28 (Nfld. T.D.); *St. Lawrence Cement Inc. v. Ontario (Minister of Transportation)*, [1991] O.J. No. 438 (Ont. Gen. Div.). But see: *Bot Construction Ltd. v. Ontario (Ministry of Transportation)*, [2009] O.J. No. 5309 (Ont. C.A.).

[80] *Chiasson v. Canada (Attorney General)*, [2009] F.C.J. No. 1268 (F.C.A.).

F. PARTIES

1. Applicants and Respondents

Who may be heard on judicial review? Only parties before the tribunal and persons who are directly affected by the tribunal decision have a statutory right to apply for judicial review.[81] Rules require that every party, and any person who appears to be interested or likely to be affected by the application for judicial review, should be served as a respondent.[82] In the absence of a statutory right, at common law, any person who was a party before the tribunal or is directly affected by the tribunal decision may apply for judicial review and has a right to be served with notice of an application brought by another party.[83] A person, who will be affected if the application is successful, may apply for standing as a respondent.[84] If an applicant fails to name and serve a respondent, any order obtained may be set aside.[85] The issues raised must concern the applicant's legal interests. A party has no standing to apply for judicial review of the tribunal's lack of procedural fairness to another person.[86] Commercial interests do not meet the test of "directly affected".[87]

---

[81] *Federal Courts Act*, R.S.C. 1985, c. F-7, s. 18.1(1) [as am.]: *Friends of the Canadian Wheat Board v. Canada (Attorney General)*, [2011] F.C.J. No. 297 (F.C.A.); *Code of Civil Procedure*, R.S.Q. c. C-25, art. 846 (*Hotte v. Bombardier Ltée.*, [1981] C.A. 376 (Que.)); *Queen's Bench Rules*, r. 665; *Judicial Review Act*, R.S.P.E.I. 1988, c. J-3, s. 5(*b*) [as am.]; *Rules of the Supreme Court of the Northwest Territories*, N.W.T. Reg. 010-96, r. 603, *Rules of the Supreme Court of Nunavut*, N.W.T. Reg. 010-96, r. 603.

[82] *Supreme Court Civil Rules*, B.C. Reg. 297/2001, r. 16-1(3); *Rules of Court*, Alta. Reg. 390/68, r. 3.15(3)(c); *Queen's Bench Rules*, R.S.S. 1978, c. Q-1, r. 667; *Court of Queen's Bench Rules*, Man. Reg. 553/88, r. 68.02; *Civil Procedure Rules*, R.S.N.S. 1989, c. 240, r. 7.07; *Rules of the Supreme Court, 1986*, S.N.L. 1986, c. 42, Sch. D, r. 54.03; *Rules of the Supreme Court of the Northwest Territories*, N.W.T. Reg. 010-96, r. 597, *Rules of the Supreme Court of Nunavut*, N.W.T. Reg. 010-96, r. 597; *Rules of Court*, Y.O.I.C. 2009/65, r. 54(5).

[83] *Appleton v. Eastern Provincial Airways Ltd.*, [1983] F.C.J. No. 906 (F.C.A.); *Hartwig v. Saskatoon (City) (Stonechild Inquiry)*, [2007] S.J. No. 337 at para. 68 (Sask. C.A.); *Alberta Liquor Store Assn. v. Alberta (Gaming and Liquor Commission)*, [2006] A.J. No. 1597 (Alta. Q.B.). See the discussion in chapter 2 on parties before the tribunal, at J.

[84] *Friends of the Oldman River Society v. Canada (Minister of Transport)*, [1992] S.C.J. No. 1; *Edmonton Friends of North Environmental Society v. Canada (Minister of Western Economic Diversification)*, [1990] F.C.J. No. 871 (F.C.A.); *Facility Assn. v. Newfoundland and Labrador (Board of Commissioners of Public Utilities)*, [2003] N.J. No. 280 (Nfld. T.D.); *Brokenhead Ojibway Nation v. Canada (Attorney General)*, [2008] F.C.J. No. 929 (F.C.).

[85] *Nu-Pharm Inc. v. Canada (Attorney General)*, [1999] F.C.J. No. 1313 (F.C.A.).

[86] *Bell Canada v. Allstream Corp.*, [2004] F.C.J. No. 1491 (F.C.A.); *American Barrick Resources Corp. v. United Steelworkers of America*, [1991] O.J. No. 132 (Ont. Div. Ct.).

[87] *Island Timberlands LP v. Canada (Minister of Foreign Affairs)*, [2009] F.C.J. No. 1563 (F.C.A.); *CanWest MediaWorks Inc. v. Canada (Minister of Health)*, [2008] F.C.J. No. 944 (F.C.A.); contra: *Alberta Liquor Store Assn. v. Alberta (Gaming and Liquor Commission)*, [2006] A.J. No. 1597 (Alta. Q.B.); *Ridgeview Restaurant Ltd. v. Canada (Attorney General)*, [2010] F.C.J. No. 613 (F.C.), affd [2011] F.C.J. No. 186 (F.C.A.).

Witnesses, whose legal interests are not affected by the decision, may not apply for judicial review of negative comments made about them in the reasons for decision.[88] Whether a complainant may apply for judicial review of a decision dismissing the complaint depends on the complainant's statutory rights and role in the tribunal proceeding.[89] A unionized employee may not apply for judicial review of an arbitration decision because the union has a monopoly on representation.[90]

If there is no person directly or adversely affected, any person may apply for public interest standing to challenge a tribunal decision upon demonstrating that the challenge raises a serious issue, that the challenger has a genuine interest in the matter, and there is no other reasonable and effective way to bring the issue before the court.[91] An applicant will not be heard to argue that the rights of others have been adversely affected by an administrative decision.[92] Persons who are adversely affected should themselves file the application for review. The courts are reluctant to grant public interest standing unless they are satisfied that the parties will bring to the court's attention all of the relevant facts.[93]

2. Intervenors

If an application raises an important point of law but all sides of the argument are not represented, leave may be granted to an intervenor to ensure that the point is fully argued. However, if all sides are adequately represented, leave may be refused.[94] Those permitted to intervene before the tribunal are usually permitted to intervene on judicial review.

---

[88] *Hurd v. Hewitt*, [1994] O.J. No. 2552 (Ont. C.A.); *Becker v. Ontario (Director of Arbitrations, Financial Services Commission)*, [2000] O.J. No. 210 (Ont. Div. Ct.).

[89] *Mitten v. College of Alberta Psychologists*, [2010] A.J. No. 545 (Alta. C.A.); *British Columbia (Police Complaints Commissioner) v. Murphy*, [2003] B.C.J. No. 399 (B.C.S.C.); *Allen v. College of Dental Surgeons (B.C.)*, [2007] B.C.J. No. 221 (B.C.C.A.); *Canada (Human Rights Commission) v. Eldorado Nuclear Ltd.*, [1980] F.C.J. No. 156 (F.C.A.); *Emerman v. Association of Professional Engineers and Geoscientists of British Columbia*, [2008] B.C.J. No. 1663 (B.C.S.C.).

[90] *Noël v. Société d'énergie de la Baie James*, [2001] S.C.J. No. 41.

[91] *Canada (Minister of Finance) v. Finlay*, [1986] S.C.J. No. 73; *Canada (Minister of Justice) v. Borowski*, [1981] S.C.J. No. 103; *League for Human Rights of B'Nai Brith Canada v. Canada*, [2010] F.C.J. No. 1424 (F.C.A.).

[92] *604598 Saskatchewan Ltd. v. Saskatchewan (Liquor and Gaming Licensing Commission)*, [1998] S.J. No. 73 (Sask. C.A.), leave to appeal refused [1998] S.C.C.A. No. 146; *CanWest MediaWorks Inc. v. Canada (Minister of Health)*, [2008] F.C.J. No. 944 (F.C.A.).

[93] *604598 Saskatchewan Ltd. v. Saskatchewan (Liquor and Gaming Licensing Commission)*, [1998] S.J. No. 73 (Sask. C.A.), leave to appeal refused [1998] S.C.C.A. No. 146; *Pharmaceutical Manufacturers Assn. of Canada v. British Columbia (Attorney General)*, [1997] B.C.J. No. 1902 (B.C.C.A.), leave to appeal refused [1997] S.C.C.A. No. 529.

[94] *Amnesty International Canada v. Canada (Canadian Forces)*, [2008] F.C.J. No. 1629 (F.C.A.); *Mr. Pawn Ltd. v. Winnipeg (City)*, [1998] M.J. No. 509 (Man. Q.B.).

Intervenors may not introduce issues not raised by the parties especially if a new issue would make complex an otherwise straightforward hearing. Intervenors are not permitted to file evidence or cross-examine witnesses and must present their arguments on the evidence filed by the parties. The court may prevent repetitive submissions on any issue that has been adequately dealt with by a party, and may refuse to award costs to intervenors. Also intervenors have no right of appeal.[95]

3.   The Attorney General

The Attorney General has broader interests than an ordinary litigant. The Attorney General is guardian of the public interest and is responsible for the interpretation and application of all statutes and regulations and for the supervision of all who exercise statutory authority.[96] For this reason, the rules of most jurisdictions require the applicant to serve notice of the application on the Attorney General and the Attorney General may be a party as of right to any application for judicial review.[97]

Where the application challenges the validity of a regulation or other decision made by Cabinet, the Attorney General (not Her Majesty the Queen) is the proper respondent.[98]

The Attorney General may apply for judicial review of any exercise of statutory power and is most likely to do so where a tribunal has acted beyond its statutory authority and public rights are affected.[99] Historically,

---

[95]   *Faculty Association of the University of British Columbia v. University of British Columbia*, [2008] B.C.J. No. 1823 (B.C.C.A.); *Johnson v. Alberta (Director of Vital Statistics)*, [2008] A.J. No. 2 (Alta. C.A.); *Merck Frosst Canada Inc. v. Canada (Minister of National Health and Welfare)*, [1997] F.C.J. No. 155 (F.C.T.D.); *Al Yamani v. Canada (Solicitor General)*, [1995] F.C.J. No. 1453 (F.C.T.D.); *Brewer v. Fraser Milner Casgrain LLP*, [2008] A.J. No. 460 at paras. 40-49 (Alta. C.A.), leave to appeal refused [2008] S.C.C.A. No. 290.

[96]   *Sutcliffe v. Ontario (Minister of the Environment)*, [2004] O.J. No. 277 (Ont. C.A.).

[97]   *Federal Court Rules*, SOR/98-106, rr. 303(2), 304(1)(b)(iii); *Judicial Review Procedure Act*, R.S.B.C. 1996, c. 241, s. 16; *Rules of Court*, Alta. Reg. 390/68, r. 3.17; *Queen's Bench Rules*, R.S.S. 1978, c. Q-1, r. 667(2); *Judicial Review Procedure Act*, R.S.O. 1990, c. J.1, s. 9(4); *Rules of Court*, N.B. Reg. 82-73, r. 69.05(1)(a); *Civil Procedure Rules*, r. 7.07; *Judicial Review Act*, R.S.P.E.I. 1988, c. J-3, s. 9; *Rules of the Supreme Court, 1986*, S.N.L. 1986, c. 42, Sch. D, r. 54.03(3)(a); *Rules of the Supreme Court of the Northwest Territories*, N.W.T. Reg. 010-96, r. 597(1)(b); *Rules of the Supreme Court of Nunavut*, N.W.T. Reg. 010-96, r. 597(1)(b); *Rules of Court*, Y.O.I.C. 2009/65, r. 54(6); *Fry v. Doucette*, [1980] N.S.J. No. 465 (N.S.C.A.).

[98]   *Canada (Attorney General) v. Inuit Tapirisat of Canada*, [1980] S.C.J. No. 99; *Lang v. British Columbia (Superintendent of Motor Vehicles)*, [2005] B.C.J. No. 906 (B.C.C.A.).

[99]   *Federal Courts Act*, R.S.C. 1985, c. F-7, s. 18.1(1) [as am.]; *Queen's Bench Rules*, R.S.S. 1978, c. Q-1, r. 665(2); *Alberta (Attorney General) v. Beaver (County) No. 9*, [1984] A.J. No. 1034 (Alta. C.A.).

prerogative writs could be obtained, even by private citizens, only on behalf of and with the consent of the Attorney General as applicant.[100]

Where a tribunal decision affects the public interests of another jurisdiction, the Attorney General of the latter jurisdiction, or a tribunal with a mandate to protect the public interest in that jurisdiction, may apply for judicial review of the tribunal decision,[101] but must meet the test for standing applicable to a public interest applicant.[102]

Government and public interests need not be represented by the Attorney General in all cases. Where a government Ministry is a party directly affected by the tribunal decision, or will be directly affected if the application for judicial review is successful, the Minister may be a party to the application for judicial review.[103]

4.   The Tribunal

The rules of most jurisdictions require that notice of an application be served on the tribunal whose exercise of power is challenged.[104] The primary purpose of this requirement is to require the tribunal to deliver the record to the court for review. The tribunal may be named as a respondent except in the federal courts[105] (or as *mis en cause* in Quebec).[106] The tribunal should be named by its statutory title.[107] An applicant who names the individual tribunal members

---

[100] *Lang v. British Columbia (Superintendent of Motor Vehicles)*, [2005] B.C.J. No. 906 (B.C.C.A.); *Alberta (Attorney General) v. Beaver (County) No. 9*, [1984] A.J. No. 1034 (Alta. C.A.).

[101] *Nova Scotia (Attorney General) v. Ultramar Canada Inc.*, [1995] F.C.J. No. 1160 (F.C.T.D.); *Régie des rentes du Québec v. Commission des régimes de retraite de l'Ontario*, [2000] O.J. No. 2845 (Ont. Div. Ct.).

[102] *Alberta v. Canada (Wheat Board)*, [1997] F.C.J. No. 1484 (F.C.T.D.), affd [1998] F.C.J. No. 1747 (F.C.A.).

[103] *Manitoba v. Christie, MacKay and Co.*, [1992] M.J. No. 618 (Man. C.A.).

[104] *Federal Court Rules*, SOR/98-106, r. 304 (1)(b)(i); *Judicial Review Procedure Act*, R.S.B.C. 1996, c. 241, s. 15; *Rules of Court*, Alta. Reg. 390/68, r. 3.15(3)(a); *Queen's Bench Rules*, R.S.S. 1978, c. Q-1, r. 669(1); *Judicial Review Procedure Act*, R.S.O. 1990, c. J.1, s. 9(2); *Rules of Court*, N.B. Reg. 82-73, r. 69.05(1)(b); *Judicial Review Act*, R.S.P.E.I. 1988, c. J-3, s. 7(4); *Rules of the Supreme Court*, 1996, S.N.L. 1986, c. 42, Sch. D, r. 54.03(3)(b); *Rules of the Supreme Court of the Northwest Territories*, N.W.T. Reg. 010-96, r. 597(1)(a); *Rules of the Supreme Court of Nunavut*, N.W.T. Reg. 010-96, r. 597(1)(a); *Rules of Court*, Y.O.I.C. 2009/65, r. 54(6)(b).

[105] Federally, a tribunal is not named as a respondent and, if it wishes to participate, it must apply for leave to intervene: *Federal Court Rules*, SOR/98-106, r. 303; *Maple Leaf Foods Inc. v. Consorzio Del Prosciutto Di Parma*, [2010] F.C.J. No. 528 (F.C.A.).

[106] The historical designation of the tribunal as "mis-en-cause" is no longer used, except in Quebec: *Syndicat des journalists de Radio-Canada (CSN) v. Surintendant des Institutions Financières*, [1997] F.C.J. No. 69 (F.C.T.D.).

[107] *Judicial Review Procedure Act*, R.S.B.C. 1996, c. 241, s. 15(2); *Queen's Bench Rules*, R.S.S. 1978, c. Q-1, r. 666(2); *Judicial Review Procedure Act*, R.S.O. 1990, c. J.1, s. 9(3); *Judicial Review Act*, R.S.P.E.I. 1988, c. J-3, s. 7; *Midgley v. Law Society of Alberta*, [1980] A.J. No. 608 (Alta. Q.B.); *Canada (Attorney General) v. Canada (Canadian Human Rights Commission)*,

may be suspected of attempting to intimidate them.[108] If the challenged action was done by a government department, the Minister responsible for that department is the proper respondent.[109] Other government officials or agencies involved in the decision-making process should not be named unless their decision is to be reviewed.[110]

Even if the statute states that a tribunal is a party or is "entitled to be heard", the court has discretion to refuse to hear submissions from the tribunal and often does restrict tribunal standing to certain issues.[111] The courts across Canada are widely divergent in their views, though each jurisdiction appears to be internally consistent. The Federal and Alberta Courts are the strictest in denying standing to tribunals, though the Federal Court might be relaxing its stance somewhat.[112] The Ontario courts tend to be the most lenient, being willing to hear tribunals on all issues.[113] Most other courts attempt to find a middle ground. The Supreme Court of Canada has not recently addressed this issue.[114]

The argument for opposing tribunal standing[115] is that participation by the tribunal may give rise to a reasonable apprehension of bias. Independence is lost when the tribunal descends into the arena to take sides between the

---

[1979] F.C.J. No. 145, [1980] 1 F.C. 142 (F.C.A.). Except when the tribunal is *ad hoc* and does not have a formal name: *Sunshine Village Corp. v. Canada (Minister of Canadian Heritage)*, [1995] F.C.J. No. 767 (F.C.T.D.). If the tribunal has been legislated out of existence, the Attorney General is the proper respondent: *West Van Cab Ltd. v. British Columbia*, [2009] B.C.J. No. 248 (B.C.C.A.).

[108] *Petrie v. Rothesay (Town)*, [2002] N.B.J. No. 168 (N.B.C.A.).

[109] *Mahmood v. Canada*, [1998] F.C.J. No. 1345 (F.C.T.D.).

[110] *Anderson v. Canada (Operations Officer, Fourth Maritime Operations Group)*, [1996] F.C.J. No. 1370 (F.C.A.); *Taser International Inc. v. British Columbia (Commissioner)*, [2010] B.C.J. No. 802 (B.C.S.C.); *Coote v. Assante Corp.*, [2007] O.J. No. 1902 (Ont. Div. Ct.).

[111] *Brewer v. Fraser Milner Casgrain LLP*, [2008] A.J. No. 460 (Alta. C.A.), leave to appeal refused [2008] S.C.C.A. No. 290; *United Brotherhood of Carpenters and Joiners of America, Local 1386 v. Bransen Construction Ltd.*, [2002] N.B.J. No. 114 (N.B.C.A.); *British Columbia Teachers' Federation v. British Columbia (Information and Privacy Commissioner)*, [2005] B.C.J. No. 2394 (B.C.S.C.).

[112] *Canada (Human Rights Commission) v. Canada (Attorney General)*, [1994] F.C.J. No. 26 (F.C.A.); *Brewer v. Fraser Milner Casgrain LLP*, [2008] A.J. No. 460 (Alta. C.A.), leave to appeal refused [2008] S.C.C.A. No. 290; *Canada (Attorney General) v. Quadrini*, [2010] F.C.J. No. 1204 (F.C.A.).

[113] *Children's Lawyer for Ontario v. Goodis*, [2005] O.J. No. 1426 (Ont. C.A.). But see *United Food and Commercial Workers International Union v. Rol-Land Farms Ltd.*, [2008] O.J. No. 682 at paras. 78-82 (Ont. Div. Ct.).

[114] Not since *Northwestern Utilities Ltd. v. Edmonton (City)*, [1978] S.C.J. No. 107; *Canadian Assn. of Industrial, Mechanical and Allied Workers, Local 14 v. Paccar of Canada Ltd.*, [1989] S.C.J. No. 107.

[115] *Northwestern Utilities Ltd. v. Edmonton (City)*, [1978] S.C.J. No. 107; *Canada (Human Rights Commission) v. Canada (Attorney General)*, [1994] F.C.J. No. 26 (F.C.A.); *United Brotherhood of Carpenters and Joiners of America, Local 1386 v. Bransen Construction Ltd.*, [2002] N.B.J. No. 114 (F.C.A.); *Brewer v. Fraser Milner Casgrain LLP*, [2008] A.J. No. 460 (Alta. C.A.), refused [2008] S.C.C.A. No. 290; *Canada (Attorney General) v. Quadrini*, [2010] F.C.J. No. 1204 (F.C.A.).

parties. "Such active and even aggressive participation can have no other effect than to discredit the impartiality of an administrative tribunal."[116] The tribunal had its opportunity to explain its decision in its reasons and for it to provide more reasons in its factum aimed at bolstering reasons that are otherwise materially deficient is unacceptable bootstrapping. A judge never appears in appellate court to explain the judgment. This is particularly a concern if the matter may be referred back to the tribunal for reconsideration.

The argument for tribunal standing rests on the view that a tribunal has something to contribute beyond that expected of the parties.[117] The tribunal's special expertise may be of assistance to the court.[118] The tribunal plays the role of friend of the court who seeks only to enrich the legal debate.[119] In a challenge to tribunal procedure, the tribunal may be able to explain the policy behind its procedural choices. In some cases, there is no other party to defend the tribunal decision.[120]

Some have suggested a context-specific approach that focuses on the different mandate and structure of various tribunals,[121] though this approach will likely be refined further. The concern of bias is greater if the tribunal's primary role is to adjudicate between opposing parties than if the regulator's mandate is to govern a field of activity in the public interest. There is a difference between a tribunal to whom parties resort to resolve their disputes and a tribunal that actively starts the process that results in the order under review.[122] The former is expected to be disinterested while the latter is expected to have an interest. An inquisitorial tribunal may be permitted a more active role than an adjudicative tribu-

---

[116] *Northwestern Utilities Ltd. v. Edmonton (City)*, [1978] S.C.J. No. 107.

[117] *United Brotherhood of Carpenters and Joiners of America, Local 1386 v. Bransen Construction Ltd.*, [2002] N.B.J. No. 114 (N.B.C.A.).

[118] *Canadian Assn. of Industrial, Mechanical and Allied Workers, Local 14 v. Paccar of Canada Ltd.*, [1989] S.C.J. No. 107; Though, in *Ferguson Bus Lines Ltd. v. Amalgamated Transit Union, Local 1374*, [1990] F.C.J. No. 274 (F.C.A.), the court said that, "it is only when its expertise may cast some light imperceptible to ordinary mortals on the subject that participation so potentially damaging to it should be countenanced". See also, *United Brotherhood of Carpenters and Joiners of America, Local 1386 v. Bransen Construction Ltd.*, [2002] N.B.J. No. 114 (N.B.C.A.); *Brewer v. Fraser Milner Casgrain LLP*, [2008] A.J. No. 460 (Alta. C.A.), refused [2008] S.C.C.A. No. 290.

[119] However, a tribunal is not a true friend of the court because it is not disinterested: *United Brotherhood of Carpenters and Joiners of America, Local 1386 v. Bransen Construction Ltd.*, [2002] N.B.J. No. 114 (N.B.C.A.).

[120] *Children's Lawyer for Ontario v. Goodis*, [2005] O.J. No. 1426 (Ont. C.A.); *Canada (Attorney General) v. Quadrini*, [2010] F.C.J. No. 1204 (F.C.A.).

[121] *United Brotherhood of Carpenters and Joiners of America, Local 1386 v. Bransen Construction Ltd.*, [2002] N.B.J. No. 114 (N.B.C.A.); *Children's Lawyer for Ontario v. Goodis*, [2005] O.J. No. 1426 (Ont. C.A.); *Imperial Oil Ltd. v. Alberta (Minister of the Environment)*, [2003] A.J. No. 721 (Alta. Q.B.); *Canada (Attorney General) v. Quadrini*, [2010] F.C.J. No. 1204 (F.C.A.).

[122] *Imperial Oil Ltd. v. Alberta (Minister of the Environment)*, [2003] A.J. No. 721 (Alta. Q.B.).

nal.[123] The concern that there will be no one to defend the tribunal decision is greater in those cases, such as professional discipline, where there is no opposing party, than in those cases where the opposing party simply chooses not to show up.[124]

A contextual approach would also take into account the nature of the issues that the tribunal seeks standing to address.[125] The concern that active tribunal participation would give rise to a reasonable apprehension of bias is greatest when the tribunal presents argument on the merits of the case that the tribunal decided. This concern is not so great when the tribunal simply explains the record and the tribunal's process and structure. Many would permit a tribunal to speak to the standard of review to be applied to its decision but whether the tribunal should be permitted to speak on questions of statutory interpretation, including those that define the tribunal's jurisdiction, continues to be debated. These issues are close to the merits. In contrast, some courts would permit tribunals to argue questions of jurisdiction but not procedure.[126]

A tribunal that is not granted full party standing has no right of appeal, except with leave to protect its jurisdiction.[127] The Attorney General is the proper party on judicial review and has a right of appeal.

Where a superior tribunal has reviewed a decision of a subordinate official or tribunal, after a hearing in which one of the opposing parties was the subordinate, that subordinate may participate as a party in an application for judicial review of the superior tribunal's decision.[128] A committee, to which some of a tribunal's powers have been delegated, may not apply for judicial review of a decision of another committee, to which other powers have been delegated. Disputes between committees should be settled by the

---

[123] *British Columbia Teachers' Federation v. British Columbia (Information and Privacy Commissioner)*, [2005] B.C.J. No. 2394 (B.C.S.C.).

[124] *Elizabeth Métis Settlement v. Larocque*, [1998] A.J. No. 654 (Alta. C.A.); *Canada (Attorney General) v. Canada (Human Rights Tribunal)*, [1994] F.C.J. No. 300 (F.C.T.D.); *Skyline Roofing Ltd. v. Alberta (Workers' Compensation Board)*, [2001] A.J. No. 985 (Alta. Q.B.).

[125] *United Brotherhood of Carpenters and Joiners of America, Local 1386 v. Bransen Construction Ltd.*, [2002] N.B.J. No. 114 (N.B.C.A.); *Ontario (Registrar, Motor Vehicle Dealers Act) v. C. (J.G.)* (2004), 73 O.R. (3d) 141 (Ont. Div. Ct.).

[126] *Northwestern Utilities v. Edmonton (City)*, [1978] S.C.J. No. 107; *British Columbia Securities Commission v. Pacific International Securities Inc.*, [2002] B.C.J. No. 1480 (B.C.C.A.); *Children's Lawyer for Ontario v. Goodis*, [2005] O.J. No. 1426 (Ont. C.A.).

[127] *Brewer v. Fraser Milner Casgrain LLP*, [2008] A.J. No. 460 (Alta. C.A.), leave to appeal refused [2008] S.C.C.A. No. 290.

[128] *Commission des transports du Québec c. Villeneuve*, [2009] J.Q. no 8351 (Que. C.A.); *Imperial Oil Ltd. v. Alberta (Minister of the Environment)*, [2003] A.J. No. 721 (Alta. Q.B.); *Skyline Roofing Ltd. v. Alberta (Workers' Compensation Board)*, [2001] A.J. No. 985 (Alta. Q.B.); *Receveur v. Saskatchewan (Acting Deputy Superintendent of Insurance)*, [1993] S.J. No. 453 (Sask. Q.B.).

governing body of the tribunal.[129] A professional body, that does not have statutory authority to review its committee's decision, does not have standing to apply for judicial review of the committee's decision.[130] The fact that tribunal staff may have been a party before the tribunal does not give them standing on judicial review.[131]

A tribunal that participates in a judicial review application should be represented by counsel independent of the litigants[132] and should formally authorize its participation.[133]

G. FORM

Court rules prescribe the form by which an application for judicial review is commenced. It is called a petition, a notice of application, a notice of motion or an originating notice. The persons who commence the application are called applicants, petitioners or requérantes, and all other parties are named as respondents or intimés. All persons to be bound by the court order should be named. (See the discussion above regarding parties.) Parties must be identified by their real names unless leave of the court is obtained to identify them by initials or pseudonyms.[134]

The decision or action to be reviewed is identified by date and by a description of a few words. All relief requested should be specified, because a court may refuse to award relief not requested,[135] though an application for judicial review will not fail for an imperfect description of the relief sought if its nature is sufficiently described to put the respondent on notice.[136] Usually an application may be amended to include additional claims for relief.[137] The grounds upon which the applicant asserts a claim to that relief must be listed as these are the only grounds

---

[129] *Re Law Society of Manitoba*, [1990] M.J. No. 191 (Man. C.A.).

[130] *Bahcheli v. Alberta Securities Commission*, [2007] A.J. No. 520 (Alta. C.A.); *Watson v. Catney*, [2007] O.J. No. 231 (Ont. C.A.); *Manitoba Chiropractors Assn. v. Alevizos*, [2003] M.J. No. 206 (Man. C.A.); contra: *Assn. of Professional Engineers and Geoscientists v. Visser*, [2004] B.C.J. No. 1053 (B.C.S.C.).

[131] *ICN Pharmaceuticals Inc. v. Canada (Staff of the Patented Medicine Prices Review Board)*, [1996] F.C.J. No. 1065 (F.C.A.); contra: *Real Estate Council (Alta.) v. Henderson*, [2007] A.J. No. 1068 (Alta. C.A.), leave to appeal refused [2007] S.C.C.A. No. 588.

[132] *Casavant v. Saskatchewan Teachers' Federation*, [2005] S.J. No. 257 at para. 62 (Sask. C.A.); *British Columbia Government Employees Union v. British Columbia (Public Service Commission)*, [1979] B.C.J. No. 2078 (B.C.S.C.).

[133] *Bateman v. Assn. of Professional Engineers*, [1984] M.J. No. 195 (Man. C.A.).

[134] *Monsieur A v. Canada (Attorney General)*, [2008] F.C.J. No. 1407 (F.C.); *V.F. v. E.B.*, [2011] B.C.J. No. 962 (B.C.C.A.).

[135] *Janis Realty Ltd. v. Shediac (Town)*, [2006] N.B.J. No. 347 (N.B.Q.B.).

[136] *Parsons v. Nova Scotia Boxing Authority*, [1984] N.S.J. No. 408 (N.S.T.D.).

[137] *Fortin v. Royal Canadian Mounted Police Commissioner*, [1985] F.C.J. No. 155 (F.C.T.D.).

that the court will consider.[138] Some rules require the parties to submit written argument.[139] When any of these requirements are not met, leave to amend is usually granted.[140] An application for judicial review is rarely dismissed on a technicality.

The rules of some provinces now prescribe a form to be delivered by each respondent stating their response to the issues raised in the applicant's notice.[141]

H. TIME LIMITS

In most jurisdictions, short time limits are imposed on applicants for judicial review. Applications in the Federal, Prince Edward Island, Northwest Territories and Nunavut courts must be brought within 30 days of the decision or order.[142] In Nova Scotia, a notice of judicial review must be delivered within the earlier of 25 days after the decision is communicated to the applicant or six months after the decision is made.[143] In British Columbia, the application must be brought within 60 days of the date the final decision is issued.[144] In New Brunswick, an application for *certiorari* must be made within three months of the date of the order.[145] In Alberta, an originating application for judicial review must be made within six months of the date of the decision.[146] Newfoundland's six-month limitation period was repealed

---

[138] *Canada (Human Rights Commission) v. Pathak*, [1995] F.C.J. No. 555 (F.C.A.), leave to appeal refused [1995] S.C.C.A. No. 306; *Sackville (Town) v. Canadian Union of Public Employees, Local 1188*, [2007] N.B.J. No. 97 at para. 29 (N.B.C.A.).

[139] *Federal Court Rules*, SOR/98-106, r. 309(2)(h); *Rules of Civil Procedure*, R.R.O. 1990, Reg. 194, r. 68.04 [as am.]; *Rules of Court*, N.B. Reg. 82-73, r. 69.08; *Rules of Civil Procedure*, R.S.P.E.I. 1988, c. S-10, r. 68.04.

[140] *Saanich Inlet Preservation Society v. Cowichan Valley (Regional District)*, [1983] B.C.J. No. 873 (B.C.C.A.); *Saskatoon Criminal Defence Lawyers Assn. v. Saskatchewan*, [1984] S.J. No. 319 (Sask. Q.B.).

[141] *Supreme Court Civil Rules*, B.C. Reg. 168/2009, r. 16-1(5); *Civil Procedure Rules*, R.S.N.S. 1989, c. 240, r. 7.08; *Rules of Court*, Y.O.I.C. 2009/65, r. 54(10).

[142] *Federal Courts Act*, R.S.C. 1985, c. F-7, s. 18.1(2) [as am.]. The period begins to run the date the party is notified, not the date his lawyer is notified of the decision: *Opisbo v. Canada (Minister of Employment and Immigration)*, [1985] F.C.J. No. 206 (F.C.A.). *Judicial Review Act*, R.S.P.E.I. 1988, c. J-3, s. 3(1.1); *Rules of the Supreme Court of the Northwest Territories*, N.W.T. Reg. 010-96, r. 596(1); *Rules of the Supreme Court of Nunavut*, N.W.T. Reg. 010-96, r. 596(1): The period begins to run on the date of the decision.

[143] *Civil Procedure Rules*, R.S.N.S. 1989, c. 240, r. 7.05(1).

[144] *Administrative Tribunals Act*, S.B.C. 2004, c. 45, s. 57 (if the tribunal's enabling Act states that this provision applies).

[145] *Rules of Court*, N.B. Reg. 82-73, r. 69.03.

[146] *Rules of Court*, Alta. Reg. 390/68, r. 3.15(2); *Athabasca Chipewyan First Nation v. Alberta (Minister of Energy)*, [2009] A.J. No. 1143 (Q.B.), affd [2011] A.J. No. 70 (Alta. C.A.).

after the court ruled that it was not authorized by statute.[147] These time limits apply even where the applicant alleges that the tribunal order is a nullity.[148] In Quebec, the application must be brought within a reasonable time from the decision or event, which is generally interpreted as 30 days.[149]

The time limit to challenge rulings, made prior to the final decision on the merits, does not begin to run until the final decision is made. Then, all rulings that affect the result may be challenged in one application.[150] If the decision is issued in parts, the time limit begins to run when the last part of the decision is released.[151] A time limit begins to run on the date of receipt of the decision, not on the date of receipt of reasons for decision.[152]

When the tribunal is asked to reconsider its decision, the time limit begins to run from the date of the original decision, unless the tribunal is persuaded on reconsideration to change the decision, in which case, the time limit begins to run when the second decision is released.[153]

If the matter under review is not a decision or order but, rather, a continuing failure to act in respect of which there is no specific date, the prescribed time limit does not apply.[154] Likewise, the prescribed time limit does not apply to an application for prohibition to prevent a future act.[155]

In Saskatchewan, Manitoba, Ontario, Newfoundland and the Yukon Territory, a general time limit is not prescribed but applicants are advised to check whether a time limit is prescribed by the statute that governs the tribunal. The British Columbia *Judicial Review Procedure Act* expressly states that an application for judicial review is not barred by the passage

---

[147] *Rules of the Supreme Court*, S.N.L. 1986, c. 42, Sch. D, r. 54.06; *Batstone v. Newfoundland and Labrador (Workplace Health, Safety and Compensation Review Division)*, [2010] N.J. No. 199 (N.L.T.D.).

[148] *Telus Communications Inc. v. Opportunity No. 17 (Municipal District)*, [1998] A.J. No. 1182 (Alta. Q.B.); *contra: Alberta Union of Provincial Employees v. Alberta*, [2002] A.J. No. 455 (Alta. Q.B.).

[149] *Code of Civil Procedure*, R.S.Q. c. C-25, art. 835.1; *Loyer c. Québec (Commission des Affaires sociales)*, [1999] J.Q. no 1728 (Que. C.A.).

[150] *Emery v. Alberta (Workers' Compensation Board, Appeals Commission)*, [2000] A.J. No. 1189 (Alta. Q.B.).

[151] *Pelican Spruce Mills Ltd. v. Pelican Spruce Mills Employees Assn.*, [1988] A.J. No. 231 (Alta. Q.B.).

[152] *Chen v. Canada (Minister of Citizenship and Immigration)*, [2010] F.C.J. No. 1096 (F.C.).

[153] *Molineaux v. Alberta (Workers' Compensation Board)*, [2001] A.J. No. 1501 (Alta. Q.B.); *Independent Contractors and Business Assn. v. Canada (Minister of Labour)*, [1998] F.C.J. No. 352 (F.C.A.); *McPhee v. Nova Scotia (Pulpwood Marketing Board)*, [1986] N.S.J. No. 4 (N.S.S.C.); *Manyluk v. Alberta (Municipal Government Board)*, [2010] A.J. No. 326 (Alta. Q.B.); *Vause v. British Columbia (Mediation and Arbitration Board)*, [2009] B.C.J. No. 1345 (B.C.S.C.).

[154] *Krause v. Canada*, [1999] F.C.J. No. 179 (F.C.A.).

[155] *Whitechapel Estates Ltd. v. British Columbia (Ministry of Transportation and Highways)*, [1998] B.C.J. No. 1931 (B.C.C.A.).

of time unless another statute expressly imposes a time limit or substantial prejudice or hardship will result to any person by reason of the delay.[156]

Since judicial review is discretionary, relief may be refused where there has been unreasonable delay in making the application.[157]

The Federal Court of Appeal and the British Columbia, Ontario, New Brunswick, Nova Scotia and Prince Edward Island courts are expressly empowered to extend time limits.[158] To obtain leave to commence an application late, an applicant must provide a reasonable explanation for the delay and must demonstrate that the intention to apply for judicial review existed before the time limit expired, the existence of an arguable case and that no person will suffer prejudice by reason of the delay.[159] In Alberta the time limits may not be extended.[160]

An application commenced within the time limit must be served on all parties within a reasonable time.[161] An application commenced in time may be dismissed for delay in prosecuting it or for failure to meet the time limits for perfecting it.[162] Some court rules impose time limits for the delivery of the tribunal record[163] or respondent's materials.[164]

---

[156] *Judicial Review Procedure Act*, R.S.B.C. 1996, c. 241, s. 11. Section 57 of the *Administrative Tribunals Act*, S.B.C. 2004, c. 45, imposes a 60-day time limit if the tribunal's enabling Act says it applies: *Speckling v. British Columbia (Labour Relations Board)*, [2008] B.C.J. No. 627 (B.C.C.A.).

[157] *Immeubles Port Louis Ltée v. Lafontaine (Village)*, [1991] S.C.J. No. 14; *Pearlman v. Winnipeg (City)*, [1977] M.J. No. 26 (Man. C.A.); *MacLean v. University of British Columbia Appeal Board*, [1993] B.C.J. No. 2755 (B.C.C.A.); *Faulkner v. Stony Mountain Institution*, [1986] F.C.J. No. 439 (F.C.T.D.); *Carpenter v. Vancouver (City) Police Commissioner*, [1986] B.C.J. No. 1216 (B.C.C.A.), leave to appeal refused [1987] S.C.C.A. No. 92; *Queen's Bench Rules*, R.S.S. 1978, c. Q-1, r. 675(1); *Henry v. Saskatchewan (Workers' Compensation Board)*, [1999] S.J. No. 114 (Sask. C.A.); *Heynen v. Yukon Territory*, [2008] Y.J. No. 68 (Y.T.C.A.); *Green v. Ontario (Human Rights Commission)*, [2010] O.J. No. 2058 (Ont. Div. Ct.); *Rules of the Supreme Court*, S.N.L. 1986, c. 42, Sch. D, r. 54.06.

[158] *Federal Courts Act*, R.S.C. 1985, c. F-7, s. 18.1(2) [as am.]; *Administrative Tribunals Act*, S.B.C. 2004, c. 45, s. 57(2); *Judicial Review Procedure Act*, R.S.O. 1990, c. J.1, s. 5; *Rules of Court*, N.B. Reg. 82-73, r. 69.03; *Civil Procedure Rules*, R.S.N.S. 1989, c. 240, r. 2.03; *Judicial Review Act*, R.S.P.E.I. 1988, c. J-3, s. 3(1.1) [as am.].

[159] *Zenner v. College of Optometrists*, [2004] P.E.I.J. No. 28 (P.E.I.C.A.), revd on other grounds [2005] S.C.J. No. 80; *Independent Contractors and Business Assn. v. Canada (Minister of Labour)*, [1998] F.C.J. No. 352 (F.C.A.).

[160] *Rules of Court*, Alta. Reg. 390/68, r. 3.15(2); *Canadian Broadcasting Corp. v. Canadian Media Guild*, [1998] A.J. No. 886 (Alta. Q.B.).

[161] *Alberta (Union of Provincial Employees) v. Alberta*, [1986] A.J. No. 124 (Alta. C.A.).

[162] *Day v. Canada (Attorney General)*, [2004] F.C.J. No. 2027 (F.C.); *Ontario Provincial Conference of the International Union of Bricklayers and Allied Craftworkers v. International Union of Bricklayers and Allied Craftworkers*, [2003] O.J. No. 2044 (Ont. Div. Ct.); *Rules of Civil Procedure*, R.R.O. 1990, Reg. 194, r. 68.06.

[163] *Federal Court Rules, 1998*, SOR 98-106, r. 317; *Abaev v. Canada (Minister of Citizenship and Immigration)*, [1999] F.C.J. No. 322 (F.C.T.D.); *Civil Procedure Rules*, R.S.N.S. 1989, c. 240, r. 7.09; *Rules of Court*, Y.O.I.C. 2009/65, r. 54(22).

I. STAY OF TRIBUNAL ORDER OR PROCEEDING

The commencement of an application for judicial review does not prevent the tribunal's order from taking effect nor stop proceedings in progress.[165] While the application is pending, the order must be obeyed and the proceedings may, at the discretion of the tribunal, continue. A regulator may continue normal regulatory activities.[166]

The applicant for judicial review may ask the tribunal to adjourn its proceeding pending the outcome of the application for judicial review but the tribunal is not required to do so.[167] The applicant may apply to court for an order prohibiting the tribunal from continuing its proceeding or an order staying the tribunal order until the application is decided. Provincial superior courts have an inherent power to grant a stay.[168] This power is expressly granted to the Federal Court and to superior courts in British Columbia, Alberta, Saskatchewan, Ontario, Quebec, New Brunswick, Nova Scotia, Prince Edward Island, the Northwest Territories and Nunavut.[169]

The court applies the three-part test for obtaining an interlocutory injunction.[170] First, the applicant must persuade the court that the application discloses a *prima facie* case or, at least, a serious issue to be tried. The obstacle presented by this test turns on the nature of the issue and the

---

[164] *Federal Court Rules, 1998*, SOR 98-106, r. 310; *Supreme Court Civil Rules*, B.C. Reg. 168/2009, r. 16-1(4); *Rules of Civil Procedure*, R.R.O. 1990, Reg. 194, r. 68.04(4) [as am.]; *Civil Procedure Rules*, R.S.N.S. 1989, c. 240, r. 7.08; *Rules of Civil Procedure*, R.S.P.E.I. 1988, c. S-10, r. 68.04(4).

[165] *Queen's Bench Rules*, R.S.S. 1978, c. Q-1, r. 668(2); *Statutory Powers Procedure Act*, R.S.O. 1990, c. S.22, s. 25(2); *Code of Civil Procedure*, R.S.Q. c. C-25, art. 834.1 [as am.]; *Judicial Review Act*, R.S.P.E.I. 1988, c. J-3, s. 8(3); *Cedarvale Tree Services Ltd. v. Labourers' International Union of North America, Local 183*, [1971] O.J. No. 1719 at para. 27 (Ont. C.A.); *Barrys Ltd. v. Fishermen, Food and Allied Workers' Union*, [1993] N.J. No. 280 (Nfld. C.A.), leave to appeal refused [1993] S.C.C.A. No. 501; *Montreal (Ville) v. Québec (Commission des droits de la personne et droits de la jeunesse)*, [1999] S.C.J. No. 42.

[166] *Jesse v. Vermilion River No. 24 (County)*, [2004] A.J. No. 1377 at para. 52 (Alta. Q.B.).

[167] *Cedarvale Tree Services Ltd. v. Labourers' International Union of North America, Local 183*, [1971] O.J. No. 1719 at para. 27 (Ont. C.A.).

[168] *Manitoba (Attorney General) v. Metropolitan Stores (MTS) Ltd.*, [1987] S.C.J. No. 6.

[169] *Federal Courts Act*, R.S.C. 1985, c. F-7, s. 18.2 [as am.]; *Judicial Review Procedure Act*, R.S.B.C. 1996, c. 241, s. 10; *Rules of Court*, Alta. Reg. 390/68, r. 3.23; *Queen's Bench Rules*, R.S.S. 1978, c. Q-1, r. 668(1); *Judicial Review Procedure Act*, R.S.O. 1990, c. J.1, s. 4; *Code of Civil Procedure*, R.S.Q. c. C-25 art. 834.1; *Rules of Court*, N.B. Reg. 82-73, r. 69.06; *Civil Procedure Rules*, R.S.N.S. 1989, c. 240, r. 7.28; *Judicial Review Act*, R.S.P.E.I. 1988, c. J-3, s. 3(4); *Rules of the Supreme Court of the Northwest Territories*, N.W.T. Reg. 010-96, r. 604; *Rules of the Supreme Court of Nunavut*, N.W.T. Reg. 010-96, r. 604.

[170] *Manitoba (Attorney General) v. Metropolitan Stores (MTS) Ltd.*, [1987] S.C.J. No. 6; *RJR-Macdonald Inc. v. Canada (Attorney General)*, [1994] S.C.J. No. 17. These cases were decided under the *Charter of Rights and Freedoms*. Except under the *Charter*, an injunction is not available as against the Crown and its servants: see discussion in chapter 9 "B.2. Prohibit Tribunal from Proceeding".

standard of review applicable to it.[171] The order requested by the applicant must not be inconsistent with a statute.[172] Second, the applicant must show that it will suffer irreparable harm if the stay is not granted. "Irreparable" refers to the nature of the harm suffered rather than its magnitude. It is harm which cannot be quantified in monetary terms or which cannot be cured.[173] The time and expense that may be incurred in continuing with the tribunal hearing, pending judicial review, is not regarded as irreparable harm.[174] Irreparable harm must be proven with explicit and detailed evidence.[175] Third, the court may balance the competing interests of the parties before the tribunal and the public interest served by the tribunal. Irreparable harm to the public interest is presumed in all cases where the tribunal has a public interest mandate and made its decision in pursuit of that mandate.[176] If refusal of the stay would deprive the applicant of a meaningful right to be heard by the court, a stay may be granted,[177] provided the stay is not detrimental to the public interest.[178]

If an application is truly urgent, an early hearing date may be obtained from the court. In Ontario, pursuant to s. 6(2) of the *Judicial Review Procedure Act*, if the case is one of urgency and the delay involved in an application to Divisional Court is likely to involve a failure of justice, an urgent application for judicial review may be made to a single judge instead of to a three-judge panel of the Divisional Court.[179] Under s. 6(2), the single

---

[171] *Grand Council of the Crees (Eeyou Istchee) v. Quebec (Attorney General)*, [2009] Q.J. No. 3986 (Que. C.A.); *National Waste Services Inc. v. National Automobile, Aerospace, Transportation and General Workers' Union of Canada*, [2009] O.J. No. 4485 (Ont. Div. Ct.).

[172] *E.g.*, an expired licence cannot be reinstated by the court pending judicial review: *9101-9380 Québec Inc. (Tabacs Galaxy) v. Canada (Customs and Revenue Agency)*, [2005] F.C.J. No. 1167 (F.C.).

[173] *RJR-Macdonald Inc. v. Canada (Attorney General)*, [1994] S.C.J. No. 17; *Suresh v. Canada (Minister of Citizenship and Immigration)*, [1999] F.C.J. No. 1180 (F.C.A.); *Brookfield Lumber Co. v. Nova Scotia (Minister of the Environment)*, [1995] N.S.J. No. 175 (N.S.S.C.).

[174] *Bell Canada v. Communications, Energy and Paperworkers Union of Canada*, [1997] F.C.J. No. 207 (F.C.T.D.); *Newfoundland and Labrador Association of Public and Private Employees v. Western Regional Integrated Health Authority*, [2008] N.J. No. 41 (N.L.T.D.). If the motion is to stay an ongoing tribunal proceeding, see chapter 9 "B.2. Prohibit Tribunal from Proceeding and C.1. Application is Premature".

[175] *Biathlon Canada v. Canada (Minister of National Revenue)*, [2010] F.C.J. No. 1305 (F.C.).

[176] *RJR-Macdonald Inc. v. Canada (Attorney General)*, [1994] S.C.J. No. 17; *David Hunt Farms Ltd. v. Canada (Minister of Agriculture)*, [1994] F.C.J. No. 164 (F.C.A.); *Algonquin Wildlands League v. Ontario (Minister of Natural Resources)*, [1996] O.J. No. 3355 (Ont. Div. Ct.).

[177] *Suresh v. Canada (Minister of Citizenship and Immigration)*, [1999] F.C.J. No. 1180 (F.C.A.).

[178] *Manitoba (Attorney General) v. Metropolitan Stores (MTS) Ltd.*, [1987] S.C.J. No. 6; *Mazerolle v. School Board District No. 7*, [1987] N.B.J. No. 1180 (N.B.C.A.); Alta. *Rules of Court*, Alta. Reg. 390/68, r. 3.23.

[179] A judge may refuse to hear an application on an urgent basis even when all parties consent: *Communications, Energy and Paperworkers Union, Local 774 v. Beachville Lime Ltd.*, [2001] O.J. No. 67 (Ont. Div. Ct.). The six-month delay for a case to be heard by the Divisional Court

judge has jurisdiction to render a final decision on the application. If unsuccessful under s. 6(2), the applicant may request that the judge grant a stay pending the hearing by the Divisional Court.

J. THE RECORD AND OTHER EVIDENCE

The record that was before the tribunal is the evidence on which a court bases its review of the tribunal's action or decision. In some jurisdictions the contents of the record are prescribed.[180] The record must include the document that initiated the proceedings before the tribunal and the tribunal order or decision.[181] If relevant to the issues raised in the application for judicial review, the record may include the tribunal's reasons (including dissenting reasons)[182] interim rulings made by the tribunal,[183] the exhibits filed with the tribunal, and, if an oral hearing was held and transcribed, the transcript.[184] The record does not include communications for the purpose of settlement[185] nor documents protected by deliberative secrecy or privilege such as drafts of the tribunal decision,[186] notes made by members of the tribunal[187] legal opinions given to the tribunal by its counsel[188] or other analyses done by tribunal staff to assist the tribunal in its deliberations.[189] The record does not include briefs of authorities filed with the tribunal.[190]

---

outside of Toronto is not sufficient grounds under s. 6(2): *Simpson v. Henderson*, [1976] O.J. No. 2206 (Ont. H.C.J.).

[180] *Judicial Review Procedure Act*, R.S.B.C. 1996, c. 241, s. 1; *Rules of Court*, Alta. Reg. 390/68, r. 3.18; *Queen's Bench Rules*, R.S.S. 1978, c. Q-1, r. 669; *Statutory Powers Procedure Act*, R.S.O. 1990, c. S.22, s. 20; *Judicial Review Act*, R.S.P.E.I. 1988, c. J-3, s. 1(g) [as am.]; *Rules of the Supreme Court*, S.N.L. 1986, c. 42, Sch. D, r. 54.08.

[181] *Canadian Union of Public Employees, Local 301 v. Montreal (City)*, [1997] S.C.J. No. 39 at para. 75.

[182] *Calgary Health Region v. United Nurses of Alberta*, [2008] A.J. No. 1429 (Alta. Q.B.); *Saskatchewan Wheat Pool v. Grain Services Union*, [1987] S.J. No. 556 (Sask. Q.B.).

[183] *Pyramid Corp. v. International Brotherhood of Electrical Workers, Local 529*, [2004] S.J. No. 276 (Sask. Q.B.).

[184] *Canadian Union of Public Employees, Local 301 v. Montreal (City)*, [1997] S.C.J. No. 39 at para. 75; *Hartwig v. Saskatoon (City) Police Assn. (Stonechild Inquiry)*, [2007] S.J. No. 337 (Sask. C.A.).

[185] *Inter-Leasing Inc. v. Ontario (Minister of Finance)*, [2009] O.J. No. 4714 (Ont. Div. Ct.).

[186] *Consolidated Bathurst Packaging Ltd. v. International Woodworkers of America, Local 2-69*, [1985] O.J. No. 2597 (Ont. Div. Ct.), revd on other grounds [1986] O.J. No. 828 (Ont. C.A.), affd [1990] S.C.J. No. 20.

[187] *156621 Canada Ltd. v. Ottawa (City)*, [2004] O.J. No. 1003 (Ont. S.C.J.); *Yorke v. Northside-Victoria District School Board*, [1992] N.S.J. No. 167 (N.S.C.A.); *Canada (Privacy Commissioner) v. Canada (Labour Relations Board)*, [2000] F.C.J. No. 617 (F.C.A.); *Apotex Inc. v. Alberta*, [2006] A.J. No. 435 (Alta. C.A.), leave to appeal refused [2006] S.C.C.A. No. 250.

[188] *Pritchard v. Ontario (Human Rights Commission)*, [2004] S.C.J. No. 16; *Scarcella v. Canada (Attorney General)*, [2009] F.C.J. No. 1614 (F.C.).

[189] *Maax Bath Inc. v. Almag Aluminum Inc.*, [2009] F.C.J. No. 725 (F.C.A.).

[190] *Construction Assn. Management Labour Bureau Ltd. v. International Brotherhood of Electrical Workers, Local 625*, [1983] N.S.J. No. 31 (N.S.T.D.).

The tribunal is not obliged to create new documents as the record contains only existing documents in the possession of the tribunal[191] that were used in making the decision.[192]

In most jurisdictions, the tribunal, upon being served with the application for judicial review, is required to file the record with the court.[193] Federal tribunals need file a record only if served with a request to do so and no objection is made to the request.[194] In British Columbia and New Brunswick, the record need not be filed unless the court orders that it be filed.[195] These procedures replace the historical two-step process, which required that the applicant first satisfy the court on affidavit evidence that there were grounds for review. If persuaded, the court would issue a writ of *certiorari* requiring the tribunal to deliver its record for review by the court. In most jurisdictions, the requirement that the tribunal file the record before the applicant has established grounds for review has combined the two steps into one, but tribunals have successfully resisted filing the record where the application disclosed no grounds for judicial review or was premature.[196] Some rules of court prescribe a procedure for the tribunal to object to filing all or part of the record.[197]

The court may give directions as to the contents of the record and may dispense with any part of the record that is not relevant to the issues raised in the application. If the record is voluminous, the parties should endeavour to agree on the omission of parts that are not relevant to the

---

[191] *Terminaux portuaires du Québec v. Conseil canadien des relations du travail*, [1993] F.C.J. No. 421 (F.C.A.).

[192] *Maax Bath Inc. v. Almag Aluminum Inc.*, [2009] F.C.J. No. 725 (F.C.A.); *Stevens v. Conservative Party of Canada*, [2004] F.C.J. No. 451 (F.C.); *Hamilton v. Board of Education of Wild Rose School Division No. 66*, [2002] A.J. No. 772 at paras. 71-77 (Alta. Q.B.); *Select Brand Distributors Inc. v. Canada (Attorney General)*, [2010] F.C.J. No. 33 (F.C.A.).

[193] *Rules of Court*, Alta. Reg. 390/68, r. 3.18; *IMS Health Canada, Ltd. v. Alberta (Information and Privacy Commissioner)*, [2005] A.J. No. 1293 (Alta. C.A.); *Queen's Bench Rules*, R.S.S. 1978, c. Q-1, r. 669; *Judicial Review Procedure Act*, R.S.O. 1990, c. J.1, s. 10: This requirement applies only in judicial review of an exercise of a "statutory power of decision", not an exercise of any "statutory power" nor an interim ruling: *Jacko v. Ontario (Chief Coroner)*, [2008] O.J. No. 5376 (Ont. Div. Ct.); *Civil Procedure Rules*, R.S.N.S. 1989, c. 240, r. 7.09; *Judicial Review Act*, R.S.P.E.I. 1988, c. J-3, s. 8(1); *Rules of the Supreme Court*, S.N.L. 1986, c. 42, Sch. D, r. 54.08; *Rules of the Supreme Court of the Northwest Territories*, N.W.T. Reg. 010-96, r. 598; *Rules of the Supreme Court of Nunavut*, N.W.T. Reg. 010-96, r. 598; *Rules of Court*, Y.O.I.C. 2009/65, r. 54(22).

[194] *Federal Court Rules, 1998*, SOR/98-106, rr. 317, 318. The applicant's evidence must be filed within the time limit prescribed by rule 306 regardless whether or when the tribunal delivers its record: *Pfeiffer v. Canada (Superintendent of Bankruptcy)*, [2004] F.C.J. No. 902 (F.C.A.).

[195] *Judicial Review Procedure Act*, R.S.B.C. 1996, c. 241, s. 17; *Rules of Court*, N.B. Reg. 82-73, r. 69.10.

[196] *Nova Scotia (Securities Commission) v. Potter*, [2006] N.S.J. No. 147 (N.S.C.A.); *Medhurst v. Medhurst*, [1984] O.J. No. 3140 (Ont. H.C.J.); *Engineering Students Society, University of Saskatchewan v. Saskatchewan (Human Rights Commission)*, [1983] S.J. No. 274 (Sask. Q.B.).

[197] *Rules of Court*, Alta. Reg. 390/68, r. 3.18(3); *Rules of the Supreme Court*, N.B. Reg. 82-73, r. 54.08(5); *Civil Procedure Rules*, R.S.N.S. 1989, c. 240, r. 7.10; *Rules of Court*, Y.O.I.C. 2009/65, r. 54(23).

application.[198] The tribunal may exclude from the record anything that is not relevant to the application for judicial review,[199] but only with leave of the court in those jurisdictions where the tribunal is required to deliver, as part of the record, all exhibits and transcripts.[200] Confidential or privileged parts of the record may be sealed with leave of the court,[201] or the court may ban publication of certain information in the record.[202] A right to a court hearing in one of Canada's official languages does not include a right to have the record translated.[203]

Some rules of court require the applicant to file an Application Record, which is not the same as the tribunal record. It should contain the notice of application for judicial review and only the portions of the tribunal record that serve to define and focus the issues raised in the application for judicial review.[204] The respondent similarly may file a Respondent's Record.

Only material that was considered by the tribunal in coming to its decision is relevant on judicial review because it is not the role of the court to decide the matter anew. The court simply conducts a review of the tribunal decision. For this reason, the only evidence that is admissible before the court is the record that was before the tribunal. Evidence that was not before the tribunal is not admissible without leave of the court. If the issue to be decided on the application involves a question of law, or concerns the tribunal's statutory authority, the court will refuse leave to file additional evidence.[205] Evidence challenging the wisdom of the decision is not admissible.[206] The tribunal's findings of fact may not be challenged with evidence that was not

---

[198] *Hartwig v. Saskatoon (City) Police Assn. (Stonechild Inquiry)*, [2007] S.J. No. 337 at paras. 70-72 (Sask. C.A.).

[199] *Canada (Human Rights Commission) v. Pathak*, [1995] F.C.J. No. 555 (F.C.A.), leave to appeal refused [1995] S.C.C.A. No. 306; *Canadian Union of Public Employees, Local 88 v. St. Elizabeth's Hospital*, [1996] S.J. No. 323 (Sask. Q.B.).

[200] *Daciuk v. Manitoba (Labour Board)*, [1984] M.J. No. 518 (Man. Q.B.); *Trans Qué. and Maritimes Pipeline Inc. v. Canada (National Energy Board)*, [1984] F.C.J. No. 165 (F.C.A.).

[201] *Goodis v. Ontario (Ministry of Correctional Services)*, [2006] S.C.J. No. 31; *Segasayo v. Canada (Minister of Public Safety and Emergency Preparedness)*, [2007] F.C.J. No. 529 (F.C.); *Wilson v. Bourbeau*, [2009] O.J. No. 1841 (Ont. Div. Ct.); *Smyth v. Edmonton (City) Police Service*, [2005] A.J. No. 1216 (Alta. Q.B.); *EpiCept Corp. v. Canada (Minister of Health)*, [2010] F.C.J. No. 133 (F.C.).

[202] *Menon v. College of Physicians and Surgeons (New Brunswick)*, [2007] N.B.J. No. 257, [2008] N.B.J. No. 124 (N.B.Q.B.).

[203] *Caron v. Alberta (Chief Commissioner of the Alberta Human Rights and Citizenship Commission)*, [2007] A.J. No. 378 (Alta. Q.B.).

[204] *Merck Frosst Canada Inc. v. Canada (Minister of National Health and Welfare)*, [1994] F.C.J. No. 1707 (F.C.T.D.).

[205] *AOV Adults Only Video Ltd. v. Manitoba (Labour Board)*, [2003] M.J. No. 201 (Man. C.A.).

[206] *Mr. Shredding Waste Management Ltd. v. New Brunswick (Minister of Environment and Local Government)*, [2004] N.B.J. No. 353 (N.B.C.A.); *Vancouver Island Peace Society v. Canada*, [1992] F.C.J. No. 324 (F.C.T.D.); *Association des crabiers acadiens inc. v. Canada (Attorney General)*, [2005] F.C.J. No. 1591 (F.C.).

before the tribunal.[207] Fresh evidence, discovered since the tribunal made its decision, is not admissible on judicial review.[208] The tribunal may not file additional evidence to buttress its decision.[209] Correspondence from the tribunal subsequent to its decision is not admissible except to the extent that it contains supplementary reasons for decision or concerns reconsideration or amendment of the decision.[210] If the applicant alleges bias,[211] use of statutory power for an improper purpose,[212] fraud on the tribunal,[213] absence of evidence to support a material finding of fact[214] or failure to follow fair procedure,[215] the court may grant leave to file evidence proving these allegations. Affidavits describing the testimony given before the tribunal, in the absence of a transcript or tribunal summary, are not admissible.[216] If a transcript is available, the audio recording is not admissible.[217]

The additional evidence is usually filed by way of affidavit. *Viva voce* evidence may not be called without leave of the court, which is

---

[207] *Keeprite Workers' Independent Union v. Keeprite Products Ltd.*, [1980] O.J. No. 3691 (Ont. C.A.); *Morlacci v. British Columbia (Minister of Energy, Mines and Petroleum Resources)*, [1997] B.C.J. No. 2045 (B.C.C.A.); *Hartwig v. Saskatoon (City) (Stonechild Inquiry)*, [2007] S.J. No. 337 at § B (Sask. C.A.); *Alberta Liquor Store Assn. v. Alberta (Gaming and Liquor Commission)*, [2006] A.J. No. 1597 (Alta. Q.B.).

[208] *Beci v. Canada (Minister of Citizenship and Immigration)*, [1997] F.C.J. No. 584 (F.C.T.D.). See record filed on appeal in chapter 6 "F. Record" and the tribunal's power to reconsider its decision in chapter 4 "D. Post-Decision Powers".

[209] *Waverley (Village Commissioners) v. Kerr*, [1994] N.S.J. No. 84 (N.S.C.A.), leave to appeal refused [1994] S.C.C.A. No. 411; *United Food and Commercial Workers International Union v. Rol-Land Farms Ltd.*, [2008] O.J. No. 682 (Ont. Div. Ct.); *Dragage F.R.P.D. Ltée v. Bouchard*, [1994] F.C.J. No. 1259 (F.C.T.D.).

[210] *Canada Life Assurance Co. v. Nova Scotia (Minister of Municipal Affairs)*, [1996] N.S.J. No. 194 (N.S.C.A.).

[211] *Tremblay v. Québec (Commission des affaires sociales)*, [1992] S.C.J. No. 20, but the record may not be supplemented if the allegation of bias was raised before the tribunal: *Hoechst Marion Roussel Canada v. Canada (Attorney General)*, [2004] F.C.J. No. 633 (F.C.).

[212] *Mr. Shredding Waste Management Ltd. v. New Brunswick (Minister of Environment and Local Government)*, [2004] N.B.J. No. 353 (N.B.C.A.).

[213] Evidence that a witness committed perjury: *St. John's Transportation Commission v. Amalgamated Transit Union, Local 1662*, [1998] N.J. No. 35 (Nfld. T.D.).

[214] *Windsor Board of Education v. Windsor Women Teachers' Assn.*, [1991] O.J. No. 2148 (Ont. C.A.). But see: *Ontario Secondary School Teachers' Federation v. Thames Valley District School Board*, [2004] O.J. No. 4784 (Ont. S.C.J.).

[215] *R. v. Miller*, [1985] S.C.J. No. 79.

[216] *142445 Ontario Ltd. (c.o.b. Utilities Kingston) v. International Brotherhood of Electrical Workers, Local 636*, [2009] O.J. No. 2011 (Ont. Div. Ct.); *United Food and Commercial Workers Union, Local 401 v. Westfair Foods Ltd.*, [2010] A.J. No. 386 (Alta. C.A.); *1254582 Alberta Ltd. (c.o.b. Airport Taxi Service) v. Miscellaneous Employees Teamsters Local Union 987 of Alberta*, [2009] A.J. No. 205 (Alta. Q.B.). B.C.C.A. has granted leave to appeal on this issue: *SELI Canada Inc. v. Construction and Specialized Workers' Union, Local 1611*, [2010] B.C.J. No. 1583 (B.C.C.A.). The S.C.C. has referred to such affidavits but not addressed the question of their admissibility: *Canadian Union of Public Employees, Local 301 v. Montreal (City)*, [1997] S.C.J. No. 39.

[217] *Chen v. Canada (Minister of Citizenship and Immigration)*, [1999] F.C.J. No. 551 (F.C.A.).

rarely given.[218] An affidavit should be restricted to the personal knowledge of the witness.[219] It may include hearsay evidence that is reliable and necessary, only if there is no other witness with personal knowledge.[220]

In exceptional circumstances, applicants may be permitted to obtain evidence by questioning the decision makers or tribunal registrar as to the process by which the tribunal made its decision, but no inquiries may be made into the deliberations of the decision makers, which are protected by deliberative secrecy.[221] In one case, a recording made with a hidden tape recorder by the applicant of the deliberations of the tribunal was admitted as evidence when it revealed bias even though the recording contravened the criminal law wiretap prohibitions.[222]

K. COSTS

As with civil actions, the costs of taking or defending an application are normally awarded to the winning party and paid by the losing party, except in exceptional circumstances. Costs may be awarded only for the court proceeding, not for the proceeding before the tribunal.[223] Costs are calculated on the lower partial-indemnity scale and may be fixed by the court in an amount that is reasonable in the circumstances of the case.[224] Substantial-indemnity costs are awarded only where there has been reprehensible, scandalous or outrageous conduct by a party.[225] Costs are not normally awarded to or against a tribunal, except in exceptional cases, such as where

---

[218] *Copeland v. McDonald*, [1978] F.C.J. No. 67 (F.C.T.D.).

[219] *MacDonald v. Nova Scotia (Worker's Compensation Board)*, [1995] N.S.J. No. 445 (N.S.S.C.); *Prajapati v. Canada (Minister of Citizenship and Immigration)*, [1995] F.C.J. No. 1463 (F.C.T.D.).

[220] *Éthier v. R.C.M.P. Commissioner*, [1993] F.C.J. No. 183 (F.C.A.).

[221] *Ellis-Don Ltd. v. Ontario (Labour Relations Board)*, [2001] S.C.J. No. 5; *Milner Power Inc. v. Alberta Energy and Utilities Board*, [2007] A.J. No. 919 at paras. 40-62 (Alta. C.A.); *Cherubini Metal Works Ltd. v. Nova Scotia (Attorney General)*, [2007] N.S.J. No. 133 (N.S.C.A.); *Payne v. Ontario (Human Rights Commission)*, [2000] O.J. No. 2987 (Ont. C.A.); *Waverley (Village Commissioners) v. Kerr*, [1994] N.S.J. No. 84 (N.S.C.A.), leave to appeal refused [1994] S.C.C.A. No. 411; *Tremblay v. Québec (Commission des affaires sociales)*, [1992] S.C.J. No. 20. In B.C. a tribunal member or staff person may not be subpoenaed: *Administrative Tribunals Act*, S.B.C. 2004, c. 45, s. 55.

[222] *Touat v. Montréal (Ville de)*, [1992] J.Q. no 2556 (C.S.).

[223] *Poulton v. Ontario (Racing Commission)*, [1999] O.J. No. 3152 (Ont. C.A.); *Eggertson v. Alberta Teachers' Assn.*, [2003] A.J. No. 384 (Alta. C.A.).

[224] *McDonald v. Anishinabek Police Service*, [2007] O.J. No. 424 at para. 29 (Ont. Div. Ct.).

[225] *Baker v. Canada (Minister of Citizenship and Immigration)*, [1999] S.C.J. No. 39 at para. 77; *Sawridge Band v. Canada*, [2006] F.C.J. No. 842 (F.C.); *Brown v. Metropolitan Authority*, [1996] N.S.J. No. 146 (N.S.C.A.); *Hollinger Farms No. 1 Inc. v. Ontario (Minister of the Environment)*, [2007] O.J. No. 3712 (Ont. Div. Ct.); *Taser International Inc. v. British Columbia (Commissioner)*, [2010] B.C.J. No. 802 (B.C.S.C.); *College of Physicians and Surgeons (Alta.) v. J.H.*, [2009] A.J. No. 99 (Alta. Q.B.).

judicial review was necessary because of tribunal misconduct or the tribunal aggressively argued the merits of the application.[226]

L. OMBUDSMAN

Judicial review is not the only option available to a person adversely affected by action of a statutory tribunal or government official. The ombudsman[227] is an independent official with power to scrutinize governmental abuses affecting members of the public. Also, the ombudsman's services are free (unlike judicial review, which can be quite expensive). With powers to summons documents and question officials and others under oath, the ombudsman can dig up information not available to the courts and litigants. He or she has access to confidential government files, which are not open to ordinary litigants. Unlike the courts on judicial review, the ombudsman may review the merits of a public official's decision, and is not restricted to assessing its legality. If maladministration is uncovered, the ombudsman can recommend but not order a governmental official to remedy the wrong. An ombudsman can and does report bureaucratic abuses to the legislature, which may then correct the problem. Ombudsmen's recommendations are usually adopted. However, one disadvantage of using the services of an ombudsman is that the complainant loses control over the review. If the complaint is accepted, the ombudsman takes charge of the matter. Also, unlike a court, the ombudsman does not have authority to set aside the decision.

---

[226] *Blencoe v. British Columbia (Human Rights Commission)*, [2000] S.C.J. No. 43; *Lang v. British Columbia (Superintendent of Motor Vehicles)*, [2005] B.C.J. No. 906 (B.C.C.A.); *Court v. Alberta (Environmental Appeal Board)*, [2003] A.J. No. 1376 (Alta. Q.B.); *Matusiak v. Canada (Attorney General)*, [2006] F.C.J. No. 835 (F.C.).

[227] *British Columbia Development Corp. v. British Columbia (Ombudsman)*, [1984] S.C.J. No. 50, [1984] 2 S.C.R. 447; *Newfoundland (Office of the Citizens' Representative) v. Newfoundland and Labrador Housing Corp.*, [2009] N.J. No. 208 (N.S.S.C.); *Alberta (Ombudsman) v. Alberta (Human Rights and Citizenship Commission)*, [2008] A.J. No. 283 (Alta. Q.B.).

Chapter 8

SCOPE OF JUDICIAL REVIEW

A. INTRODUCTION

The purpose of determining which standard of review to apply in each case is to respect the constitutional roles of the court, the legislature and the executive. In keeping with its role to uphold the rule of law, the court exercises its power of review so as to ensure that the tribunal does not overstep its legal authority, while respecting the intentions of the democratically elected legislature by giving deference to the wisdom of the tribunal decision on the merits.[1]

The court's power of review is applied to the result of the tribunal process. A person who is content with the result cannot complain about comments made by the tribunal in its reasons, nor about an interim ruling. The tribunal's reasons for decision may be considered to ascertain whether its decision was arrived at by reviewable error but the reasons alone cannot be quashed leaving the result in effect.[2]

A court may decline to consider an issue that was not raised before the tribunal, unless it is purely a question of legal analysis which would not require any additional evidence or it concerns the jurisdiction of the tribunal to decide the matter.[3] The nature of a review presumes the tribunal decided the issue to be reviewed. In the absence of a tribunal decision on an issue, there is nothing to which a standard of review can be applied. The legislative intention that the tribunal have the first say is respected by declining judicial review especially if the new issue may be raised before the tribunal by way of a request for reconsideration.

---

[1] *Dunsmuir v. New Brunswick*, [2008] S.C.J. No. 9 at paras. 27-30, 49, 159.

[2] *Libby, McNeill & Libby of Canada Ltd. v. United Automobile, Aerospace and Agricultural Implement Workers of America*, [1978] O.J. No. 3542 (Ont. C.A.); *United Brotherhood of Carpenters and Joiners of America, Local 1023 v. Laviolette*, [1998] N.B.J. No. 130 (N.B.C.A.).

[3] *Johnson v. British Columbia (Workers' Compensation Board)*, [2008] B.C.J. No. 1080 (B.C.C.A.), [2009] B.C.J. No. 1313 (B.C.S.C.); *Ulmer v. British Columbia Society for the Prevention of Cruelty to Animals*, [2010] B.C.J. No. 2277 (B.C.C.A.), leave to appeal refused [2011] S.C.C.A. No. 33; *Nabors Canada Ltd. v. Alberta (Appeals Commission for Alberta Workers' Compensation)*, [2010] A.J. No. 1097 (Alta. C.A.); *Public Service Alliance of Canada v. Canadian Corp. of Commissionaires*, [2004] A.J. No. 1132 at paras. 29-32 (Alta. Q.B.); *Kainth v. Canada (Minister of Citizenship and Immigration)*, [2009] F.C.J. No. 134 at paras. 24-28 (F.C.); *Rodrigues v. Canada (Minister of Citizenship and Immigration)*, [2008] F.C.J. No. 108 (F.C.).

B.   THE STANDARDS OF REVIEW

The Supreme Court of Canada has articulated two standards for the review of the merits of a tribunal decision:[4]

(1)   Reasonableness: A court will not interfere with a tribunal decision that is reasonable. This is a deferential standard that recognizes the legislative intention to grant discretion to the tribunal. Reasonableness is concerned with the existence of justification, transparency and intelligibility within the decision-making process, as well as whether the decision falls within a range of possible, acceptable outcomes which are defensible in respect of the facts and law.[5] The ambit of reasonable outcomes is informed by the context including the statutory purposes, the nature and expertise of the decision maker, and the nature of the issue.[6]

(2)   Correctness: The tribunal's interpretation of the question of law must be correct. The court may undertake its own legal analysis to arrive at the correct interpretation.[7]

Even when the standard of review is correctness, well-articulated reasons of an expert tribunal may persuade a court that its decision is correct, and may also provide policy analysis that influences the court to avoid an impractical interpretation.

Some statutes prescribe a standard of review of patent unreasonableness, without defining it. The courts interpret this standard consistently with the court's reasonableness standard.[8]

There are two approaches to the analysis of tribunal reasons.[9] The first, discussed in chapter 2, concerns procedural fairness, asking whether

---

[4]   *Dunsmuir v. New Brunswick*, [2008] S.C.J. No. 9.

[5]   *Dunsmuir v. New Brunswick*, [2008] S.C.J. No. 9 at paras. 47-49.

[6]   *Dunsmuir v. New Brunswick*, [2008] S.C.J. No. 9, concurring opinions at paras. 135-139, 144, 149-153, 167; *Canada (Citizenship and Immigration) v. Khosa*, [2009] S.C.J. No. 12 at paras. 28, 33, 59; *Mills v. Ontario (Workplace Safety and Insurance Appeals Tribunal)*, [2008] O.J. No. 2150 at para. 22 (Ont. C.A.).

[7]   *Dunsmuir v. New Brunswick*, [2008] S.C.J. No. 9 at para. 50.

[8]   *Canada (Citizenship and Immigration) v. Khosa*, [2009] S.C.J. No. 12 at paras. 50-51; *Victoria Times Colonist, a Division of Canwest Mediaworks Publications Inc. v. Communications, Energy and Paperworkers Union of Canada, Local 25-G*, [2009] B.C.J. No. 1022 (B.C.C.A.); *Viking Logistics Ltd. v. British Columbia (Workers' Compensation Board)*, [2010] B.C.J. No. 1874 (B.C.S.C.); *Audmax Inc. v. Ontario (Human Rights Tribunal)*, [2011] O.J. No. 210 (Ont. Div. Ct.).

[9]   *Newfoundland and Labrador (Treasury Board) v. Newfoundland and Labrador Nurses' Union*, [2010] N.J. No. 63 at paras. 36-38 (C.A. dissent), leave to appeal granted [2010] S.C.C.A. No. 137; *Burke v. Newfoundland and Labrador Assn. of Public and Private Employees*, [2010] N.J. No. 62 (N.L.C.A.).

the tribunal must give reasons for decision and, if so, whether the reasons are adequate to explain why the tribunal reached its conclusion.[10] The second, discussed here, applies the reasonableness standard of review to the tribunal decision.[11]

When the reasonableness standard of review is applied, conflicting interpretations of a question of law may be upheld by the courts if both are reasonable,[12] though an interpretation may be held to be unreasonable if it is inconsistent with the prevailing interpretation.[13] However, when the test of correctness is applied, it is not likely that different interpretations of the law will be upheld, because there can be only one correct interpretation, while there can be several reasonable interpretations.[14] Given that most statutes are not ambiguous and do not permit more than one reasonable interpretation, there will not often be different interpretations that may both be upheld as reasonable.

However, where two tribunals make orders that impose conflicting obligations on a party, so that compliance with one order results in a violation of the other order, a court must decide which order takes precedence. To do so, the court first reviews each decision separately applying the applicable standard of review. If, as a result of this review, both decisions are upheld, then the court reviews them to determine if they truly conflict, in that one requires a party to do what the other prohibits. If it does, then the court determines which should be given precedence.[15]

C. WHICH STANDARD OF REVIEW APPLIES?

The standard of review may be prescribed by statute.[16] If not, it may have already been determined by the courts. It is not necessary to re-determine

---

[10] *Baker v. Canada (Minister of Citizenship and Immigration)*, [1999] S.C.J. No. 39 at paras. 43-44. See chapter 2 "W.6. Sufficiency of Reasons".

[11] *Dunsmuir v. New Brunswick*, [2008] S.C.J. No. 9 at para. 47.

[12] *Domtar Inc. v. Québec (Commission d'appel en matière de lésions professionnelles)*, [1993] S.C.J. No. 75. This approach to questions of statutory interpretation is being questioned as inconsistent with the rule of law: *Taub v. Investment Dealers Assn. of Canada*, [2009] O.J. No. 3552 at paras. 65-67 (Ont. C.A.).

[13] *United Brotherhood of Carpenters and Joiners of America, Local 1985 v. Graham Construction and Engineering Ltd.*, [2008] S.J. No. 319 (Sask. C.A.), leave to appeal refused [2008] S.C.C.A. No. 343.

[14] *Essex County Roman Catholic School Board v. Ontario English Catholic Teachers' Assn.*, [2001] O.J. No. 3602 (Ont. C.A.).

[15] *British Columbia Telephone Co. v. Shaw Cable Systems (B.C.) Ltd.*, [1995] S.C.J. No. 54.

[16] See for example, *Administrative Tribunals Act*, S.B.C. 2004, c. 45, ss. 58-59; *Federal Courts Act*, R.S.C. 1985, c. F-7, s. 18.1 [as am.]; *Canada (Citizenship and Immigration) v. Khosa*, [2009] S.C.J. No. 12; *Lavender Co-Operative Housing Assn. v. Ford*, [2011] B.C.J. No. 401 (B.C.C.A.).

this question in every case.[17] If the standard of review has not been determined for the type of question at issue, the Supreme Court of Canada has developed an analytical approach to determine which standard of review should be applied to the tribunal decision under review. This requires the consideration and weighing of four factors for the purpose of determining how much deference is owed to the tribunal decision:

(1) The presence or absence of a privative clause or statutory right of appeal.

(2) The nature of the issue decided by the tribunal.

(3) On that issue, the expertise of the tribunal relative to that of the reviewing court.

(4) The purposes of the legislation and the provision in particular.[18]

The purpose of this approach is to ascertain how much deference the legislature intended that a reviewing court give to this decision made by this tribunal. In the circumstances of the case, how much freedom to manoeuvre without court supervision did the legislature intend to confer on the tribunal? Underpinning the analysis is the constitutional separation of the powers and roles accorded to the court and to the legislature and executive (of which tribunals form a part). The court's constitutional role is to protect the rule of law.[19] Policy is the exclusive realm of the legislature which may by statute delegate the power to make policy choices. The court does not have authority to make policy. Its role is to supervise those who exercise statutory power to ensure that they act lawfully, within the authority delegated to them by the legislature. The court must defer to the intention of the legislature as expressed in the statute.[20]

The four factors should not be applied in a technical or mechanistic way. They do overlap and their interplay determines the level of deference owed to the tribunal decision.[21] If there is more than one clearly delineated question at issue on judicial review, the appropriate standard of review should be separately determined for each question. However care should

---

[17] *Dunsmuir v. New Brunswick*, [2008] S.C.J. No. 9 at paras. 57, 62.

[18] *Dunsmuir v. New Brunswick*, [2008] S.C.J. No. 9 at para. 64; *Pushpanathan v. Canada (Minister of Citizenship and Immigration)*, [1998] S.C.J. No. 46.

[19] *Dunsmuir v. New Brunswick*, [2008] S.C.J. No. 9 at paras. 27-30, 48, 123-131, 159.

[20] *Ocean Port Hotel Ltd. v. British Columbia (General Manager, Liquor Control and Licensing Branch)*, [2001] S.C.J. No. 17 at para. 22; *Canada (Citizenship and Immigration) v. Khosa*, [2009] S.C.J. No. 12 at paras. 19, 50.

[21] *Canada (Citizenship and Immigration) v. Khosa*, [2009] S.C.J. No. 12 at para. 54.

be taken not to parse a tribunal decision into myriad parts in order to reduce the level of deference accorded by the court.[22]

The standard of review is a question of law to be decided by the court. Agreement between the parties cannot determine the standard to be applied by the reviewing court.[23]

On appeal from a decision of a lower court, the role of the Court of Appeal is to determine whether the lower court correctly chose and applied the appropriate standard of review. If not, the appellate court should choose the appropriate standard and then review the tribunal decision on that basis.[24]

1.   The Presence or Absence of a Privative Clause or Statutory Right of Appeal

If there is a statutory right of appeal that is restricted to questions of law or jurisdiction and leave to appeal must be obtained, the standard of review is likely to be correctness.[25] Appeal provisions that permit appeal on all issues and permit the court to substitute its decision for that of the tribunal attract this standard of reasonableness except for questions of jurisdiction and precedent-setting questions of law, which attract a standard of correctness.[26]

A privative clause indicates a legislative intention to restrict court review of the tribunal's decisions. The stronger the privative clause, the more deference is generally due.[27] The extent to which a privative clause shields a tribunal's decisions from judicial review depends on the language of the clause as well as the other three factors.[28] Typically, three kinds of privative clauses are found in statutes that govern administrative

---

[22] *Lévis (City), Fraternité des policiers de Lévis Inc.*, [2007] S.C.J. No. 14 at para. 19; *Council of Canadians with Disabilities v. Via Rail Canada Inc.*, [2007] S.C.J. No. 15 at paras. 100, 278.

[23] *Monsanto Canada Inc. v. Ontario (Superintendent of Financial Services)*, [2004] S.C.J. No. 51 at para. 6.

[24] *Dr. Q v. College of Physicians and Surgeons*, [2003] S.C.J. No. 18 at para. 43.

[25] *Chieu v. Canada (Minister of Citizenship and Immigration)*, [2002] S.C.J. No. 1; *Pushpanathan v. Canada (Minister of Citizenship and Immigration)*, [1998] S.C.J. No. 46.

[26] *Pezim v. British Columbia (Superintendent of Brokers)*, [1994] S.C.J. No. 58; *Canada (Director of Investigation and Research, Competition Act) v. Southam Inc.*, [1996] S.C.J. No. 116.

[27] *Dr. Q v. College of Physicians and Surgeons*, [2003] S.C.J. No. 18 at para. 27; *Pushpanathan v. Canada (Minister of Citizenship and Immigration)*, [1998] S.C.J. No. 46. Section 58 of the *Administrative Tribunals Act*, S.B.C. 2004, c. 45, imposes a standard of review of patently unreasonable to decisions protected by a "privative clause" as defined in s. 1.

[28] *Ross v. New Brunswick School District No. 15*, [1996] S.C.J. No. 40; *United Brotherhood of Carpenters and Joiners of America, Local 579 v. Bradco Construction Ltd.*, [1993] S.C.J. No. 56; *Dayco v. Canadian Auto Workers*, [1993] S.C.J. No. 53.

tribunals. The weakest states that a tribunal's decision is "final and conclusive". Somewhat stronger is a provision that grants the tribunal "exclusive jurisdiction" over the issue to be decided. Some clauses allow review only of specified issues, such as whether the tribunal acted within jurisdiction or followed fair procedure. Others prohibit review by the courts except within a specified time period, typically 30 days. The strongest precludes judicial review of the tribunal's decision by the courts. However, not even an absolute privative clause may prevent a court from reviewing whether the tribunal acted within its statutory mandate. While none of these clauses completely shield a tribunal's decision from judicial review, they do indicate the level of deference that the legislature expects the court to give to the tribunal decision.[29]

Deference may be given by the court even in the absence of a legislative indication, by way of a privative clause or a circumscribed right of appeal. The most important factors in determining the standard of review are the nature of the issue and the relative expertise of the court and the tribunal with respect to that issue.[30]

2.   The Nature of the Issue Decided by the Tribunal

Different issues decided by the same tribunal may attract different standards of review.

Statutory provisions that define the scope of a tribunal's jurisdiction attract a standard of review of correctness because a tribunal that exceeds its authority acts unlawfully.[31] Likewise, the tribunal's interpretation and application of the *Constitution* must be correct.[32]

The most difficult type of issue for which to determine the standard of review is a question of statutory interpretation that is within the tribunal's jurisdiction. Judges of the Supreme Court of Canada do not agree on the appropriate degree of deference. From 2003 until 2008, a less deferential approach prevailed which gave preference to the constitutional role of the court as the guardian of the rule of law. Questions of statutory interpretation

---

[29]   *Dunsmuir v. New Brunswick*, [2008] S.C.J. No. 9 at paras. 31, 52, 67, 143, 163; *Pasiechnyk v. Saskatchewan (Workers' Compensation Board)*, [1997] S.C.J. No. 74; *Royal Oak Mines Inc. v. Canada (Labour Relations Board)*, [1996] S.C.J. No. 14.

[30]   *Canada (Citizenship and Immigration) v. Khosa*, [2009] S.C.J. No. 12 at paras. 4, 25-26 (dissent: 74-98).

[31]   *Dunsmuir v. New Brunswick*, [2008] S.C.J. No. 9 at paras. 28-29, 50, 59; *ATCO Gas and Pipelines Ltd. v. Alberta (Energy and Utilities Board)*, [2006] S.C.J. No. 4; *Toronto Hydro-Electric System Ltd. v. Ontario (Energy Board)*, [2010] O.J. No. 1594 (Ont. C.A.), leave to appeal refused [2010] S.C.C.A. No. 225.

[32]   *Multani v. Commission scolaire Marguerite-Bourgeoys*, [2006] S.C.J. No. 6; *Westcoast Energy Inc. v. Canada (National Energy Board)*, [1998] S.C.J. No. 27.

were regarded by the majority of the Court as pure questions of law within the domain of the court, subject to review on a standard of correctness.[33] The only exception was the rare statutory provision which required special technical expertise to interpret, which could be reviewed on a standard of reasonableness.[34] Since 2008, a more deferential approach has prevailed which respects the greater familiarity that a tribunal is presumed to have with its home statute and the circumstances governed by it. The majority of the Court have applied a reasonableness standard to questions of statutory interpretation within a tribunal's jurisdiction, except those questions of interpretation which set a precedent for future cases.[35] These competing approaches continue to vex the Court.

On other questions of law, including questions of common law, the interpretation of statutes other than the tribunal's home statute, and the reconciling of conflicting statutes, the standard of review is more likely to be correctness.[36]

When a labour arbitrator interprets a collective agreement to resolve a grievance or a dispute between the parties to the agreement, the interpretation need only be reasonable.[37] Although an arbitrator may, without interference, choose from among several reasonable interpretations of a clause of a collective agreement, an arbitrator may not change the meaning of the clause to something that the parties did not bargain for,[38] for that is an unreasonable interpretation. An arbitrator's decision that a grievance is arbitrable is reviewable only if patently unreasonable.[39]

If the issue is one of public policy or requires the weighing of factors or balancing of competing interests it will attract a more deferential standard of review. The determination of what is in the public interest is a polycentric question that is hard to review. Deference is given to decisions on social,

---

[33] *Monsanto Canada, Inc. v. Ontario (Superintendent of Financial Services)*, [2004] S.C.J. No. 51 at para. 8; *Barrie Public Utilities v. Canadian Cable Television Assn.*, [2003] S.C.J. No. 27 at para. 16; *Canada (Deputy Minister of National Revenue) v. Mattel Canada Inc.*, [2001] S.C.J. No. 37; *SOCAN v. Canadian Assn. of Internet Providers*, [2004] S.C.J. No. 44.

[34] E.g., "material change" in *Pezim v. British Columbia (Superintendent of Brokers)*, [1994] S.C.J. No. 58; *Barrie Public Utilities v. Canadian Cable Television Assn.*, [2003] S.C.J. No. 27 at para. 16.

[35] *Dunsmuir v. New Brunswick*, [2008] S.C.J. No. 9 at paras. 54-55, 60, 124, 128, 163. The dissents in *Smith v. Alliance Pipeline Ltd.*, [2011] S.C.J. No. 7, and *Canada (Citizenship and Immigration) v. Khosa*, [2009] S.C.J. No. 12 at paras. 94-95, question whether a tribunal's expertise and familiarity with its home statute may be presumed or should be demonstrated.

[36] *Dunsmuir v. New Brunswick*, [2008] S.C.J. No. 9 at paras. 124, 128, 163; *Lévis (City) v. Fraternité des policiers de Lévis Inc.*, [2007] S.C.J. No. 14 at paras. 21-23.

[37] *Voice Construction Ltd. v. Construction and General Workers' Union, Local 92*, [2004] S.C.J. No. 2.

[38] *Douglas Aircraft Co. of Canada Ltd. v. McConnell*, [1979] S.C.J. No. 106.

[39] *Parry Sound (District) Social Services Administration Board v. Ontario Public Service Employees Union, Local 324*, [2003] S.C.J. No. 42.

economic, technical and scientific questions. A tribunal's choice of orders from a variety of orders permitted by the statute is entitled to deference.[40] The review of policy decisions and the exercise of discretion is discussed more below.

Findings of fact receive the highest deference, especially if they turn on the credibility of witnesses who testified before the tribunal. The review of findings of fact is discussed more below. Questions of mixed fact and law may receive less deference. The difference between a pure question of fact and a question of mixed fact and law is determined by asking whether a decision on the issue will set a precedent for future cases. An example is the meaning of the word "discrimination" which turns on the facts but sets a precedent for future cases. These questions may be subject to a standard of review of reasonableness or even correctness.[41]

3. On that Issue, the Expertise of the Tribunal Relative to that of the Reviewing Court

This is the most important factor. Who has more expertise on the question that the court is asked to review; the tribunal or the court? The fact that the tribunal is generally regarded as an "expert tribunal" is not determinative. What matters is its expertise on the question at issue. On that question, the tribunal must have more expertise than the court to be accorded deference.[42]

The rationale behind this factor is the recognition that tribunal decisions are often influenced by the tribunal's knowledge and experience in the field it regulates. Each time a court interferes with a decision of the tribunal, confidence and respect for its work may be lost. Routine interference in tribunal decisions by the courts would give victory to the parties better able to afford delay and fund litigation. Deference gives expert tribunals the respect they deserve, while maintaining a salutary degree of court supervision.[43]

---

[40] *Dr. Q v. College of Physicians and Surgeons*, [2003] S.C.J. No. 18 at para. 31; *Dunsmuir v. New Brunswick*, [2008] S.C.J. No. 9 at paras. 47, 53, 123, 130, 137; *Canadian Union of Public Employees, Local 301 v. Montreal (City)*, [1997] S.C.J. No. 39 at para. 45; *Royal Oak Mines Inc. v. Canada (Labour Relations Board)*, [1996] S.C.J. No. 14.

[41] *Canada (Director of Investigation and Research, Competition Act) v. Southam Inc.*, [1996] S.C.J. No. 116; *Harvard College v. Canada (Commissioner of Patents)*, [2002] S.C.J. No. 77 at para. 150; *Chamberlain v. Surrey School District No. 36*, [2002] S.C.J. No. 87 at para. 11.

[42] *Pushpanathan v. Canada (Minister of Citizenship and Immigration)*, [1998] S.C.J. No. 46; *ATCO Gas and Pipelines Ltd. v. Alberta (Energy and Utilities Board)*, [2006] S.C.J. No. 4 at paras. 26-27. Section 58 of the *Administrative Tribunals Act*, S.B.C. 2004, c. 45, deems every tribunal whose decision is protected by a "privative clause", as defined, to be an expert tribunal.

[43] *Canada (Attorney General) v. Public Service Alliance of Canada*, [1993] S.C.J. No. 35; *Dunsmuir v. New Brunswick*, [2008] S.C.J. No. 9 at para. 49.

A number of factors are considered in determining a tribunal's expertise on the question in issue. More deference is shown to tribunals given broad powers than to those with circumscribed powers. An adjudicative tribunal whose only role is to apply law to facts or to resolve disputes between parties may be regarded as having less expertise than a tribunal that is involved in policy development.[44] To the extent that a tribunal has a role in policy development, this factor is relevant only to the extent that this role was engaged in deciding the matter in issue.[45] The extent of the tribunal's experience or institutional expertise in dealing with similar problems may be relevant.[46] A tribunal that has developed a body of jurisprudence to guide it in making its decisions is presumed to have greater expertise.[47] A statutory requirement that members of the panel appointed to hear the case have special expertise in the subject matter may be indicative of a higher level of expertise.[48] An appellate tribunal whose only role is to hear and decide appeals in a variety of regulated fields may have less expertise than a tribunal that regulates in one of those fields.[49]

Also a higher level of deference is accorded to decisions of tribunals exercising a statutory mandate to protect the public,[50] or with remedial powers that confer on the tribunal the flexibility to address a wide variety of problems in the field they regulate.[51] A discipline panel comprising peers in the profession are regarded as having a higher level of expertise with respect to the generally accepted standards of the profession. They also have greater expertise in the choice of remedy appropriate to protect the public interest.[52]

Who wields the statutory power is important. Statutory power is conferred on a Minister or on Cabinet with the intention that the decision be influenced by policy considerations. These are elected officials who are expected to take into account the political, economic and social concerns of the moment. The court's supervisory role is limited to determining

---

[44]   *Monsanto Canada, Inc. v. Ontario (Superintendent of Financial Services)*, [2004] S.C.J. No. 51 at para. 11.

[45]   *Canada (Deputy Minister of National Revenue) v. Mattel Canada Inc.*, [2001] S.C.J. No. 37 at para. 31.

[46]   *Dr. Q v. College of Physicians and Surgeons*, [2003] S.C.J. No. 18 at para. 29; *Canada (Deputy Minister of National Revenue) v. Mattel Canada Inc.*, [2001] S.C.J. No. 37 at para. 30.

[47]   *Canada (Attorney General) v. Mossop*, [1993] S.C.J. No. 20; *Canadian Union of Public Employees, Local 963 v. New Brunswick (Liquor Corp.)*, [1979] S.C.J. No. 45.

[48]   *Monsanto Canada, Inc. v. Ontario (Superintendent of Financial Services)*, [2004] S.C.J. No. 51 at para. 11; *Dr. Q v. College of Physicians and Surgeons*, [2003] S.C.J. No. 18 at para. 29.

[49]   *Monsanto Canada, Inc. v. Ontario (Superintendent of Financial Services)*, [2004] S.C.J. No. 51 at para. 11.

[50]   *Pezim v. British Columbia (Superintendent of Brokers)*, [1994] S.C.J. No. 58.

[51]   *Royal Oak Mines v. Canada (Labour Relations Board)*, [1996] S.C.J. No. 14.

[52]   *Ryan v. Law Society of New Brunswick*, [2003] S.C.J. No. 17 at para. 31; *Pearlman v. Manitoba Law Society Judicial Committee*, [1991] S.C.J. No. 66 at para. 39; *Association des courtiers et agents immobiliers du Québec v. Proprio Direct inc.*, [2008] S.C.J. No. 32 at para. 21.

whether the decision was made within the confines of the statutory mandate.[53] A high degree of deference continues to be given.[54]

Elected bodies, such as municipalities and school boards, are given deference, not because of their expertise, but because they are elected and are expected to base their decisions on political considerations and their understanding of community concerns. They must balance complex and divergent interests to arrive at a decision in the public interest.[55] The standard of review analysis is not applied to a review of an exercise of legislative powers by an elected body. Such decisions are reviewable only to determine whether they acted within their statutory mandate.[56]

4. The Purposes of the Legislation and of the Provision in Particular

Where the purpose of the legislation is the protection of vulnerable groups, the court is not inclined to give deference because that is a role that has traditionally been played by the courts. However, complex administrative schemes that require the balancing of competing interests and the public interest are traditionally given to expert regulators. If the statute contains an elaborate framework to regulate a highly specialized activity, it is presumed to require a high level of knowledge and expertise in the tribunal. This legislative purpose is substantially different from the normal role of the courts, suggesting greater deference.[57]

If the statutory purpose requires the tribunal to select from a range of remedial choices, to consider policy issues or to balance multiple interests or considerations, a court may show greater deference.[58] These types of issues are characterized as "polycentric".[59] Statutory provisions that call

---

[53] *Canada (Attorney General) v. Inuit Tapirisat of Canada*, [1980] S.C.J. No. 99; *Ontario Federation of Anglers and Hunters v. Ontario (Ministry of Natural Resources)*, [2002] O.J. No. 1445 (Ont. C.A.), leave to appeal refused [2002] S.C.C.A. No. 252.

[54] *Lake v. Canada (Minister of Justice)*, [2008] S.C.J. No. 23; *Suresh v. Canada (Minister of Citizenship and Immigration)*, [2002] S.C.J. No. 3; *Mount Sinai Hospital Center v. Quebec (Minister of Health and Social Services)*, [2001] S.C.J. No. 43; *Dunsmuir v. New Brunswick*, [2008] S.C.J. No. 9 at paras. 135-137.

[55] *Nanaimo (City) v. Rascal Trucking Ltd.*, [2000] S.C.J. No. 14; *Chamberlain v. Surrey School District No. 36*, [2002] S.C.J. No. 87 at para. 11.

[56] *United Taxi Drivers' Fellowship of Southern Alberta v. Calgary (City)*, [2004] S.C.J. No. 19; Justice LeBel suggests that this approach should be applied to all decisions of elected bodies: *Chamberlain v. Surrey School District No. 36*, [2002] S.C.J. No. 87 at para. 11. The pragmatic and functional approach is useful in reviewing adjudicative and quasi-judicial decisions made pursuant to statutory authority. It should not be applied in other contexts.

[57] *Monsanto Canada Inc. v. Ontario (Superintendent of Financial Services)*, [2004] S.C.J. No. 51; *Dr. Q v. College of Physicians and Surgeons*, [2003] S.C.J. No. 18.

[58] *Dr. Q v. College of Physicians and Surgeons*, [2003] S.C.J. No. 18.

[59] *Pushpanathan v. Canada (Minister of Citizenship and Immigration)*, [1998] S.C.J. No. 46.

upon a decision maker to exercise its discretion "in the public interest" or "in its opinion" invite the consideration of policy in light of the purposes of the Act attract a more deferential standard of review.[60] However, when an expert regulator adjudicates a dispute or determines a question of law that is not polycentric, less deference may be shown.[61]

If the statutory purpose is the resolution of disputes or the determination of rights between parties, less deference may be shown. A statutory mandate that is similar to the traditional adjudicative role of the courts may invite less deference.[62] A statutory purpose requiring that decisions be made expeditiously invites more deference so as to discourage court intervention that may cause unacceptable delays.[63]

D. ERRORS OF FACT

Some statutes prescribe the standard of review of errors of fact.[64] In the absence of statutory direction, deference is given to tribunal findings of fact, which may be set aside only if unreasonable.[65] An unreasonable finding of fact is one that is not supported by any evidence.[66] So long as there was some evidence to support a material finding of fact, a court will not review the evidence considered by the tribunal to determine whether it was sufficient. Only essential findings of fact upon which the decision of the tribunal turns are reviewable.

The weight given to evidence is reviewable only if unreasonable.[67] The choice as to which evidence is important and the weight given to each

---

[60] *Cartaway Resources Corp. (Re)*, [2004] S.C.J. No. 22; *Dr. Q v. College of Physicians and Surgeons*, [2003] S.C.J. No. 18. *Association des courtiers et agents immobiliers du Québec v. Proprio Direct inc.*, [2008] S.C.J. No. 32 at paras. 17-19.

[61] *Barrie Public Utilities v. Canadian Cable Television Assn.*, [2003] S.C.J. No. 27 at para. 16; *ATCO Gas and Pipelines Ltd. v. Alberta (Energy and Utilities Board)*, [2006] S.C.J. No. 4.

[62] *Dr. Q v. College of Physicians and Surgeons*, [2003] S.C.J. No. 18.

[63] *Starson v. Swayze*, [2003] S.C.J. No. 33 at para. 87.

[64] See for example, *Federal Courts Act*, R.S.C. 1985, c. F-7, s. 18.1 [as am.]; *Canada (Citizenship and Immigration) v. Khosa*, [2009] S.C.J. No. 12; *Judicial Review Procedure Act*, R.S.O. 1990, c. J.1, s. 2(3).

[65] *Ross v. New Brunswick School District No. 15*, [1996] S.C.J. No. 40, 133 D.L.R. (4th) 1; *Blanchard v. Control Data Canada Ltd.*, [1984] S.C.J. No. 51; *Suresh v. Canada (Minister of Citizenship and Immigration)*, [2002] S.C.J. No. 3, 208 D.L.R. (4th) 1 at para. 29. A different standard may be prescribed by statute. For example, see *Federal Courts Act*, R.S.C. 1985, c. F-7, s. 18.1(4)(*d*) [as am.]: *Mugesera v. Canada (Minister of Citizenship and Immigration)*, [2005] S.C.J. No. 39 at para. 38; *Administrative Tribunals Act*, S.B.C. 2004, c. 45, s. 59(2).

[66] *W.W. Lester (1978) Ltd. v. United Assn. of Journeymen and Apprentices of the Plumbing and Pipefitting Industry, Local 740*, [1990] S.C.J. No. 127 at para. 94; *McInnes v. Simon Fraser University*, [1982] B.C.J. No. 1779 (B.C.S.C.), affd [1983] B.C.J. No. 2187 (B.C.C.A.); *Douglas Aircraft Co. of Canada Ltd. v. McConnell*, [1979] S.C.J. No. 106.

[67] *Haché v. Lunenberg County District School Board*, [2004] N.S.J. No. 120 (N.S.C.A.).

item of evidence is based, in part, on the tribunal's expertise. The failure to mention an item of evidence in the tribunal's reasons is not proof of a failure to consider it but only proof that the tribunal did not regard it as being of sufficient importance as to require mention.[68]

A court may review whether the tribunal's refusal to admit evidence tendered by a party was reasonable only if the evidence is both relevant and crucial to a material issue decided by the tribunal.[69] The admission of irrelevant evidence is not reviewable unless it influenced a material finding.[70]

A tribunal may draw inferences from primary facts. An inference may be reviewed if it is not reasonably supported by any primary facts.[71] The reasonableness standard of review recognizes that some inferences are based in part upon a tribunal's expertise and knowledge in the field.[72]

It is rare for a court to set aside a finding on credibility, because the tribunal, having heard the witnesses, was in the best position to assess credibility.[73] Findings on credibility may be set aside if the reasons given by the tribunal are not adequate to permit the court to assess the reasonableness of the findings,[74] and for any of the reasons noted above.[75]

If there is a right of appeal on questions of fact and the tribunal possesses no special expertise, the court may examine the evidence and substitute its own findings of fact for those made by the tribunal.[76] A court may be more willing to substitute its opinion as to inferences that may be drawn from the primary facts.[77]

Where the tribunal decision is based on agreed or admitted facts and there were no questions of credibility or choices between conflicting evidence, a court may give less deference to the tribunal's findings.[78]

---

[68] *Stelco Inc. v. British Steel Canada Inc.*, [2000] F.C.J. No. 286 (F.C.A.).

[69] *Université du Québec à Trois-Rivières v. Larocque*, [1993] S.C.J. No. 23.

[70] *Kelly v. Nova Scotia (Police Commission)*, [2006] N.S.J. No. 78 at § 2 (N.S.C.A.).

[71] *Toronto (City) Board of Education v. Ontario Secondary School Teachers' Federation, District 15*, [1997] S.C.J. No. 27; *Pasqua Hospital v. Harmatiuk*, [1983] S.J. No. 545 (Sask. Q.B.), affd [1987] S.J. No. 314 (Sask. C.A.).

[72] *Ross v. New Brunswick School District No. 15*, [1996] S.C.J. No. 40.

[73] *Dr. Q v. College of Physicians and Surgeons*, [2003] S.C.J. No. 18; *Cyanamid Canada Inc. v. Canada (Deputy Minister of National Revenue, Customs and Excise)*, [1983] F.C.J. No. 603 (F.C.A.); *Pierce v. Law Society of British Columbia*, [2002] B.C.J. No. 840 (B.C.C.A.).

[74] *Law Society of Upper Canada v. Neinstein*, [2010] O.J. No. 1046 (Ont. C.A.).

[75] *P.S.S. Professional Salon Services Inc. v. Saskatchewan (Human Rights Commission)*, [2007] S.J. No. 675 (Sask. C.A.), leave to appeal refused [2008] S.C.C.A. No. 69.

[76] *Dickason v. University of Alberta*, [1992] S.C.J. No. 76.

[77] *Ontario (Human Rights Commission) v. Zurich Insurance Co.*, [1992] S.C.J. No. 63 at para. 16.

[78] *Gould v. Yukon Order of Pioneers*, [1996] S.C.J. No. 29.

E.   PROCEDURAL ERRORS

The question of procedural fairness is concerned with the process followed by the tribunal resulting in its final decision. The standard of review analysis discussed above applies only to the merits of the decision. It does not apply to the question of whether fair procedure was followed.[79]

A court will interfere with a tribunal decision because of procedural errors committed by the tribunal only if those errors resulted in manifest unfairness or actual prejudice to the applicant's right to be heard. Minor procedural lapses are not grounds to set aside a decision. What is required is a fair procedure, not perfection.[80]

There is a presumption that fair procedure was followed. The onus is on the complaining party to satisfy the court that the tribunal committed a serious procedural error that resulted in unfairness.[81] An actual violation of the duty of fairness must be proven. A reasonable apprehension of a violation is not sufficient for judicial review.[82]

Courts generally do not devise the procedure to be followed by tribunals. That task is left to the tribunal, which is better able to create procedure that is fair to the parties while carrying out its mandate effectively and efficiently. Courts merely supervise tribunals to ensure that no person's right to be heard is seriously prejudiced by unfair procedure.[83]

Procedure which violates the duty of fairness, but which is prescribed by statute, is not reviewable by the courts because they have no authority to overturn a statutory provision, absent a violation of the Constitution.[84]

---

[79]   *Ha v. Canada (Minister of Citizenship and Immigration)*, [2004] F.C.J. No. 174 (F.C.A.).

[80]   *Uniboard Surfaces Inc. v. Kronotex Fussboden GmbH and Co. KG*, [2006] F.C.J. No. 1837 (F.C.A.); *Society Promoting Environmental Conservation v. Canada (Attorney General)*, [2003] F.C.J. No. 861 (F.C.A.); *Bridgeland Riverside Community Assn. v. Calgary (City)*, [1982] A.J. No. 692 at para. 28 (Alta. C.A.); *Edmonton Police Association v. Edmonton (City)*, [2007] A.J. No. 584 (Alta. C.A.); *Judicial Review Procedure Act*, R.S.B.C. 1996, c. 241, s. 9; *Rules of Court*, Alta. Reg. 390/68, r. 3.24(3); *Judicial Review Procedure Act*, R.S.O. 1990, c. J.1, s. 3; *Judicial Review Act*, R.S.P.E.I. 1988, c. J-3, s. 6.

[81]   *Kupeyan v. Royal College of Dental Surgeons*, [1982] O.J. No. 3376 at para. 33 (Ont. Div. Ct.); *Little v. Cowichan Valley (Regional District)*, [1977] B.C.J. No. 1048 at para. 35 (B.C.S.C.), affd [1978] B.C.J. No. 1293 (B.C.C.A.).

[82]   *Ellis-Don Ltd. v. Ontario (Labour Relations Board)*, [2001] S.C.J. No. 5.

[83]   *Prassad v. Canada (Minister of Employment and Immigration)*, [1989] S.C.J. No. 25; *Council of Canadians with Disabilities v. Via Rail Canada Inc.*, [2007] S.C.J. No. 15 at paras. 230-245; *Mensinger v. Canada (Minister of Employment and Immigration)*, [1987] 1 F.C. 59 (F.C.T.D.).

[84]   *Ocean Port Hotel Ltd. v. British Columbia (General Manager, Liquor Control and Licensing Branch)*, [2001] S.C.J. No. 17.

F. POLICY AND THE EXERCISE OF DISCRETION

Courts review neither the wisdom nor the merits of discretionary decisions made by tribunals pursuant to statutory authority. Nor do they review whether government policy accomplishes its intended purpose. A court should not substitute its own decision for that of the tribunal just because it would have exercised the discretion differently had it been charged with the responsibility. A discretionary decision of a tribunal made in good faith, within the scope of its statutory authority and pursuant to fair procedure will be permitted to stand.[85]

The restricted authority of the courts to review the exercise of discretion is rooted in the fundamental theory of the separation of powers between parliament, the executive and the courts. Parliament and the executive make policy. The courts apply the law. It is not the role of the courts to question the wisdom or folly of the government's policy choices. If a court were to determine a question of policy, then the ability of the government to change the court-established policy, to accord with a new scientific, social or political understanding, would be severely circumscribed. Government by judges is not democracy. Accordingly, the court has no power to review the merits of discretionary decisions.[86]

Correctness is never applied as a standard of review of an exercise of discretion. The broader the discretion, the greater will be the reluctance of the courts to interfere with the decision maker's choices. A discretionary power to develop a policy applicable to the regulated community is accorded a high level of deference. The same standard is applied to a decision made by a Minister in the public interest even when deciding an individual case. A discretionary decision that is reviewable is, essentially, one that is beyond the scope of the statutory authority, is an abuse of the

---

[85] *Baker v. Canada (Minister of Citizenship and Immigration)*, [1999] S.C.J. No. 39; *Maple Lodge Farms Ltd. v. Canada*, [1982] S.C.J. No. 57, [1982] 2 S.C.R. 2; *Oakwood Development Ltd. v. St. François Xavier (Rural Municipality)*, [1985] S.C.J. No. 49; *Apotex Inc. v. Ontario (Minister of Health)*, [2004] O.J. No. 4360 (Ont. C.A.), leave to appeal refused [2005] S.C.C.A. No. 8.

[86] *Friends of the Earth v. Canada (Minister of the Environment)*, [2008] F.C.J. No. 1464 (F.C.), affd [2009] F.C.J. No. 1307 (F.C.A.), leave to appeal refused [2009] S.C.C.A. No. 497; *Vancouver Island Peace Society v. Canada*, [1992] F.C.J. No. 324 (F.C.T.D.); *TransCanada Pipelines Ltd. v. Beardmore (Township)*, [2000] O.J. No. 1066 (Ont. C.A.), leave to appeal refused [2000] S.C.C.A. No. 264; *UL Canada Inc. v. Québec (Procureur Général)*, [2003] J.Q. no 13505 (Que. C.A.), affd [2005] S.C.J. No. 11; *Lachine General Hospital Corp. v. Quebec (Attorney General)*, [1996] A.Q. no 3406, 142 D.L.R. (4th) 659 at 674-77 (Que. C.A.); *Carpenter Fishing Corp. v. Canada*, [1997] F.C.J. No. 1811 (F.C.A.), leave to appeal refused [1999] S.C.C.A. No. 349; *Newfoundland (Minister of Justice) v. Hanlon*, [2000] N.J. No. 10 (Nfld. C.A.); *R. v. Wonderland Gifts Ltd.*, [1996] N.J. No. 146 (Nfld. C.A.); *Canadian Assn. of Regulated Importers v. Canada (Attorney General)*, [1994] F.C.J. No. 1 (F.C.A.), leave to appeal refused [1994] S.C.C.A. No. 99; *Newfoundland and Labrador (Consumer Advocate) v. Newfoundland and Labrador (Public Utilities Board)*, [2005] N.J. No. 83 (N.L.T.D.).

power or is a violation of a constitutional right.[87] The extent of deference may decrease as the scope of discretion narrows, is exercised by a lower-level decision maker and is concerned with options applicable in the adjudication of an individual case, but the standard of review remains reasonableness.[88]

Query whether the standard of review analysis should apply at all to the merits of discretionary decisions by elected officials, such as Cabinet or a Minister. Elected officials are accountable to the legislature and, ultimately, to the ballot box.[89] Historically their decisions were reviewable only if they acted outside the terms of the enabling statute or abused their powers. Their motives are not justiciable.[90]

The Supreme Court of Canada has ruled that the standard of review analysis does not apply to legislative decisions made by municipalities and that these decisions are reviewable only to determine whether they are authorized by statute. However, the court did state that the standard of review analysis continues to apply to adjudicative and policy decisions made by municipalities.[91] It will be difficult to draw a line between legislative and policy decisions. It would make more sense to draw the line between adjudicative decisions on one side and policy and legislative decisions on the other.

---

[87] *Lake v. Canada (Minister of Justice)*, [2008] S.C.J. No. 23; *Mount Sinai Hospital Center v. Quebec (Minister of Health and Social Services)*, [2001] S.C.J. No. 43; *Suresh v. Canada (Minister of Citizenship and Immigration)*, [2002] S.C.J. No. 3; *Canadian Union of Public Employees v. Ontario (Minister of Labour)*, [2003] S.C.J. No. 28; *TransCanada Pipelines Ltd. v. Beardmore (Township)*, [2000] O.J. No. 1066 (Ont. C.A.), leave to appeal refused [2000] S.C.C.A. No. 264; *St. Anthony Seafoods Ltd. Partnership v. Newfoundland and Labrador (Minister of Fisheries and Aquaculture)*, [2004] N.J. No. 336 (N.L.C.A.), leave to appeal refused [2004] S.C.C.A. No. 548; *Moresby Explorers Ltd. v. Canada (Attorney General)*, [2007] F.C.J. No. 1116 (F.C.A.), leave to appeal refused [2007] S.C.C.A. No. 536; *Quebec (Attorney General) v. Germain Blanchard ltée*, [2005] J.Q. no 7953 (Que. C.A.), leave to appeal refused [2005] C.S.C.R. no 384; *Vosters v. Canada (Agriculture and Agri-Food)*, [2009] F.C.J. No. 1351 (F.C.).

[88] *Baker v. Canada (Minister of Citizenship and Immigration)*, [1999] S.C.J. No. 39; *Dunsmuir v. New Brunswick*, [2008] S.C.J. No. 9 at paras. 53, 151, 165.

[89] *Ontario Federation of Anglers and Hunters v. Ontario (Ministry of Natural Resources)*, [2002] O.J. No. 1445 (Ont. C.A.), leave to appeal refused [2002] S.C.C.A. No. 252; *Canadian Parks and Wilderness Society v. Canada (Minister of Canadian Heritage)*, [2003] F.C.J. No. 703 (F.C.A.); *Canadian Union of Public Employees v. Canada (Minister of Health)*, [2004] F.C.J. No. 1582 (F.C.).

[90] *Thorne's Hardware Ltd. v. Canada*, [1983] S.C.J. No. 10; *Canada (Attorney General) v. Inuit Tapirisat of Canada*, [1980] S.C.J. No. 99; *Ontario Federation of Anglers and Hunters v. Ontario (Ministry of Natural Resources)*, [2002] O.J. No. 1445 (Ont. C.A.), leave to appeal refused [2002] S.C.C.A. No. 252.

[91] *United Taxi Drivers' Fellowship of Southern Alberta v. Calgary (City)*, [2004] S.C.J. No. 19. Justice LeBel suggests that this should also be the approach to decisions by elected school boards: *Chamberlain v. Surrey School District No. 36*, [2002] S.C.J. No. 87.

Government policy initiatives and programs, which are established without statutory authority, are not reviewable by the courts, except to the extent that there exists a statute, which already occupies the field, or they interfere with the legal rights, duties or liberties of a person.[92] Government decisions with respect to project funding are not reviewable at all. The disbursement of public funds is within the authority of Parliament alone. "The appropriation, allocation or disbursement of such funds by a court is offensive to principle."[93]

Similarly, decisions pursuant to the royal prerogative are not reviewable unless they violate the *Charter* or important individual rights are at stake.[94] There now exist some statutes and regulations concerning matters within the royal prerogative, such as pardons, mercy and honours. These are now reviewable for compliance with the statutory and regulatory requirements but otherwise remain non-justiciable.[95]

G.   REVIEW OF LAW-MAKING

Regulations are presumed valid. The onus is on the challenger to establish that a regulation was made without authority. Many of the principles that apply to the review of tribunal decisions do not apply to the review of regulations. A regulation may be struck down only if it was not authorized by statute or it violates the *Constitution*.[96]

Regulations are not subject to attack on the grounds of bad faith or improper purpose. Government may be moved by any number of political,

---

[92] *Pharmaceutical Manufacturers Assn. of Canada v. British Columbia (Attorney General)*, [1997] B.C.J. No. 1902 (B.C.C.A.), leave to appeal refused [1997] S.C.C.A. No. 529.

[93] *Hamilton-Wentworth (Regional Municipality) v. Ontario (Minister of Transportation)*, [1991] O.J. No. 439 (Ont. Div. Ct.), leave to appeal refused [1991] O.J. No. 3201 (Ont. C.A.); *Arsenault v. Canada (Attorney General)*, [2009] F.C.J. No. 1306 (F.C.A.), leave to appeal refused [2009] S.C.C.A. No. 543.

[94] *Canada (Prime Minister) v. Khadr*, [2010] S.C.J. No. 3; *Operation Dismantle Inc. v. Canada*, [1985] S.C.J. No. 22; *Black v. Canada (Prime Minister)*, [2001] O.J. No. 1853 (Ont. C.A.); *Samson v. Canada (Attorney General)*, [1998] F.C.J. No. 1208 (F.C.T.D.); *Dixon v. Canada (Somalia Inquiry Commission)*, [1997] F.C.J. No. 985 (F.C.A.), leave to appeal refused [1997] S.C.C.A. No. 505; *Copello v. Canada (Minister of Foreign Affairs)*, [2003] F.C.J. No. 1056 (F.C.A.); *Ganis v. Canada (Minister of Justice)*, [2006] B.C.J. No. 3139 (B.C.C.A.), leave to appeal refused [2007] S.C.C.A. No. 111; *Smith v. Canada (Attorney General)*, [2009] F.C.J. No. 234 (F.C.).

[95] *Chiasson v. Canada*, [2003] F.C.J. No. 477 (F.C.A); *Bonamy v. Canada (Attorney General)*, [2001] F.C.J. No. 1158 (F.C.T.D.); *Khadr v. Canada (Attorney General)*, [2006] F.C.J. No. 888 (F.C.).

[96] *Ontario Federation of Anglers and Hunters v. Ontario (Ministry of Natural Resources)*, [2002] O.J. No. 1445 (Ont. C.A.), leave to appeal refused [2002] S.C.C.A. No. 252; *R. v. Wonderland Gifts Ltd.*, [1996] N.J. No. 146 (Nfld. C.A.); *Saputo Inc. v. Canada (Attorney General)*, [2009] F.C.J. No. 1225 (F.C.), affd [2011] F.C.J. No. 291 (F.C.A.); *Brown v. Dental Assn.*, [2002] A.J. No. 142 (Alta. C.A.); *Enbridge Gas Distribution Inc. v. Ontario Energy Board*, [2005] O.J. No. 33 (Ont. C.A.).

economic, social or partisan considerations. Because of Cabinet secrecy, the motives of government in making a regulation are generally not known. Even when known, Cabinet's motives are irrelevant to the question of whether a regulation is authorized by statute. Even if it can be proven that the regulation was motivated by partisan politics, lobbying by a special interest group or the government's desire to be re-elected, these are not reasons for it to be struck down. If regulation-making authority is abused, the only remedy is an appeal to the electors.[97]

The failure or refusal to make regulations is not justiciable because regulation-making authority is permissive, not mandatory.[98] Similarly, neither Royal Assent given to a Bill enacted by the legislature nor its proclamation into effect is reviewable.[99]

---

[97] *Thorne's Hardware Ltd. v. Canada*, [1983] S.C.J. No. 10; *Ref. re: Validity of Regulations in Relation to Chemicals*, [1943] S.C.J. No. 1; *Ontario Federation of Anglers and Hunters v. Ontario (Ministry of Natural Resources)*, [2002] O.J. No. 1445 (Ont. C.A.), leave to appeal refused [2002] S.C.C.A. No. 252; *Vancouver Island Peace Society v. Canada*, [1992] F.C.J. No. 324 (F.C.); *Ontario Black Bear/Ontario Sportsmen and Resource Users Assn. v. Ontario*, [2000] O.J. No. 263 (Ont. S.C.J.); *UL Canada Inc. v. Québec (Procureur Général)*, [2003] J.Q. no 13505 (Que. C.A.), affd [2005] S.C.J. No. 11.

[98] *Canadian Union of Public Employees v. Canada (Minister of Health)*, [2004] F.C.J. No. 1582 (F.C.).

[99] *Babineau v. Ontario (Lieutenant Governor)*, [2009] O.J. No. 4230 (Ont. Div. Ct.); *Beauchamp v. Canada (Attorney General)*, [2009] F.C.J. No. 437 (F.C.).

Chapter 9

JUDICIAL REMEDIES

A. INTRODUCTION

This chapter describes the types of remedies that a court may award on judicial review and the discretionary nature of these remedies. A court may be requested to quash a decision of a tribunal, to prohibit the tribunal from taking contemplated action or to require the tribunal to take action it refuses to take. It may also simply define the rights of parties and the powers of the tribunal. In rare cases, a court may award damages.

In deciding whether to grant a remedy, courts consider not only the legal and factual merits of the case, but also a number of other factors. Firstly a court's powers to remedy a situation are no broader than the powers of the tribunal. A court may not award a remedy that was not within the tribunal's power to award.[1] Secondly, even if the merits of the case warrant a remedy, the court has discretion to refuse to grant it. The latter half of this chapter discusses the factors relevant to the exercise of the court's discretion when deciding whether to award a remedy. Thirdly, given the public law nature of judicial review, consent of the parties is not sufficient to obtain a remedy setting aside a tribunal decision. A cogent reason for the remedy must also be given.[2]

B. TYPES OF REMEDIES

1. Quash the Order or Decision of the Tribunal

If a test described in chapter 8 is met, a court may quash a tribunal decision or order. This relief may be obtained if there is a statutory right of appeal (see chapter 6). If not, this relief may be obtained pursuant to a statutory right to apply for judicial review or pursuant to the prerogative writ of *certiorari* (in Quebec, evocation) (see chapter 7).

On judicial review, a court's power is limited to quashing the decision. It may not issue the order the tribunal should have made had it not erred, because a court does not have statutory authority to exercise the discretion

---

[1] *Murdoch v. Canada (Royal Canadian Mounted Police)*, [2005] F.C.J. No. 522 (F.C.).

[2] *Johnson v. Canada (Minister of Citizenship and Immigration)*, [2005] F.C.J. No. 1523 (F.C.).

conferred on the tribunal.[3] In contrast, on appeal a court may substitute its decision for that of the tribunal,[4] but should not do so where the decision requires application of the tribunal's policy expertise.[5]

If the tribunal error affects only part of its order, the entire order need not be quashed. The defective part may be severed from the order. This should be done only where the remaining order can stand on its own as a complete and enforceable order not crippled by the loss of one of its components. This turns on the effect that the tribunal intended to achieve when issuing the order. If the order could not achieve that effect without the impugned part, it should not be severed. Would the tribunal, knowing that it could not include the invalid part, have issued the order without it?[6]

In addition to quashing an order, a court may refer the matter back to the tribunal to be reconsidered. If the court issues directions to be followed on reconsideration, the directions must clearly state what the tribunal may or may not do. A direction is too vague if it simply requires the tribunal to reconsider the matter in accordance with the court's reasons.[7] Directions may be given to avert unfair procedure or excess of power, but not to direct the result of the tribunal's reconsideration on the merits.[8]

All Superior Courts have an inherent power to refer a matter back to a tribunal. In some provinces this authority is granted expressly.[9] The Alberta Rules permit the court to direct the person who made the decision to reconsider it.[10] This does not preclude the court from referring the matter back to a different panel of the tribunal in appropriate circumstances.[11] The British Columbia *Judicial Review Procedure Act* requires that, when a court refers a matter back to a tribunal, the court must advise the tribunal of its reasons and give such directions as it considers appropriate, and the tribunal

---

[3]   *Congrégation des témoins de Jéhovah de St-Jérôme-Lafontaine v. Lafontaine (Village)*, [2004] S.C.J. No. 45; *Edgar v. Canada (Attorney General)*, [1999] O.J. No. 4561 (Ont. C.A.). However, in one case the S.C.C. has, without explanation, made the order the tribunal should have made: *Renaud v. Québec (Commission des affaires sociales)*, [1999] S.C.J. No. 70; This was followed in *Canadian Civil Liberties Assn. v. Ontario (Civilian Commission on Police Services)*, [2002] O.J. No. 3737 (Ont. C.A.).

[4]   *Commission de protection du territoire agricole du Québec c. Tremblay*, [2007] J.Q. no 9983 (Que. C.A.).

[5]   *Ontario (Registrar, Motor Vehicle Act) v. Jacobs*, [2004] O.J. No. 189 (Ont. Div. Ct.).

[6]   *United Automart Ltd. v. Kamloops (City)*, [1981] B.C.J. No. 1770 (B.C.S.C.), revd on other grounds [1983] B.C.J. No. 1526 (B.C.C.A.); *R. v. Varga*, [1979] O.J. No. 4494 (Ont. C.A.); *Medora v. New Brunswick Dental Society*, [1984] N.B.J. No. 236 (N.B.C.A.).

[7]   *University of British Columbia v. College of Teachers*, [2002] B.C.J. No. 1039 (B.C.C.A.).

[8]   *Testa v. British Columbia (Workers' Compensation Board)*, [1989] B.C.J. No. 665 (B.C.C.A.).

[9]   *Queen's Bench Rules*, R.S.S. 1978, c. Q-1, r. 674; *Rules of Court*, N.B. Reg. 82-73, r. 69.13; *Judicial Review Act*, R.S.P.E.I. 1988, c. J-3, s. 3(3)(*e*).

[10] *Rules of Court*, Alta. Reg. 390/68, r. 3.24(2).

[11] *Foothills Provincial General Hospital v. United Nurses of Alberta, Local 115*, [1994] A.J. No. 24 (Alta. Q.B.).

is required to pay heed to those reasons and directions.[12] The *Federal Courts Act* permits the court to refer the matter back to the tribunal for determination in accordance with such directions as the court considers appropriate.[13] This provision has been interpreted to permit the court to direct a specific decision on the merits where none of the facts are in dispute.[14] The power to refer a matter back to the tribunal for reconsideration, does not give the court authority to supervise the tribunal's reconsideration.[15] Errors by the tribunal on reconsideration may be the subject of a new application for review.

An order quashing a decision or order, without a reference back, does not preclude a tribunal from dealing with the matter. Its proceedings may be continued as if the part of the proceeding that was quashed had not yet taken place.[16] Where only one step in a proceeding has been quashed, the tribunal remains seized of the matter and, upon doing that step again (without the error that resulted in it being quashed),[17] may continue the proceeding to its conclusion. It need not start from scratch, ignoring all that went before.[18] Even where all steps in a proceeding are quashed, the tribunal may continue the proceeding, although it must start again at the beginning. If there is a statutory time limit on the commencement of proceedings, provided the original proceeding was commenced within the time limit, the continuation of the proceeding after it has been quashed, even if it must start again from the beginning, is not out of time.[19] In an exceptional case, the court may prohibit the tribunal from re-hearing the matter.[20]

It is efficient to have the same tribunal members conduct the re-hearing, since they are familiar with the matter[21] but, if there is a reasonable

---

[12] R.S.B.C. 1996, c. 241, ss. 5, 6.

[13] R.S.C. 1985, c. F-7, s. 18.1(3)(*b*) [as am.].

[14] *Turanskaya v. Canada (Minister of Citizenship and Immigration)*, [1997] F.C.J. No. 254 (F.C.A.); *Canada (Attorney General) v. Georgian College of Applied Arts and Technology*, [2004] F.C.J. No. 1454 (F.C.A.).

[15] *Teva Neuroscience G.P.-S.E.N.C. v. Canada (Attorney General)*, [2010] F.C.J. No. 1499 (F.C.).

[16] *Al Yamani v. Canada (Minister of Citizenship and Immigration)*, [2002] F.C.J. No. 1550 (F.C.), affd [2003] F.C.J. No. 1931 (F.C.A.), leave to appeal refused [2004] S.C.C.A. No. 62.

[17] But, absent the violation of an express direction from the court, a repetition of the error is not contempt: *Pelishko v. Canada (Minister of Citizenship and Immigration)*, [2003] F.C.J. No. 129 (F.C.T.D.).

[18] *Nova Scotia (Labour Relations Board) v. Little Narrows Gypsum Co.*, [1977] N.S.J. No. 603 (N.S.C.A.); *Watko v. St. Clements (Municipality)*, [1979] M.J. No. 280 (Man. Q.B.).

[19] *Nicholson v. Haldimand-Norfolk (Regional Municipality) Commissioners of Police*, [1980] O.J. No. 3845 (Ont. C.A.), leave to appeal refused [1981] S.C.C.A. No. 254; *Webb v. Ontario (Securities Commission)*, [1987] O.J. No. 161 (Ont. Div. Ct.).

[20] *Stetler v. Ontario Flue-Cured Tobacco Growers' Marketing Board*, [2009] O.J. No. 1050 (Ont. C.A.).

[21] *Canada (Attorney General) v. Basra*, [2010] F.C.J. No. 76 at para. 30 (F.C.A.); *Compagnie des Transformateurs Philips Ltée v. Metallurgistes Unis*, [1985] C.A. 684 (Que. C.A.);

apprehension that these tribunal members no longer have an open mind on the merits of the case, a court may direct that the matter be decided by a different panel,[22] if available. If the court does not specify whether the re-hearing is to be before the same or a different panel, the re-hearing may be before any quorum of the tribunal.[23] If the decision maker who originally heard the matter is no longer in office, the matter must be heard anew by the incumbent.[24] Where reconsideration does not change the result, the tribunal need not demonstrate in its reasons that it has given regard to the court's reasons for quashing the first order.[25]

2.   Prohibit Tribunal from Proceeding

Where a tribunal is about to take a specific action that is not authorized by statute, a court, on judicial review, may issue a writ of prohibition[26] (in Quebec, evocation). This is a drastic order that will be made by a court only where a tribunal clearly lacks authority to proceed. If the existence of authority is debatable or turns on findings of fact that have yet to be made by the tribunal, an order of prohibition may be refused. It must be clear and beyond doubt that the tribunal lacks authority to proceed.[27] A tribunal acting within authority will not be prohibited from embarking upon what may be regarded as unnecessary, unwise, or fruitless pursuits.[28] An advisory body will not be prohibited from conducting proceedings, simply because there is no certainty that the decision maker will follow its advice and recommendations.[29]

International Longshoremen's and Warehousemen's Union, Local 500 v. British Columbia Maritime Employers Assn., [1987] F.C.J. No. 725 (F.C.A.).

[22]   *Elk Valley Coal Corp. v. United Mine Workers of America, Local 1656*, [2009] A.J. No. 1400 (Alta. C.A.); *Eastern Provincial Airways Ltd. v. Canada (Labour Relations Board)*, [1983] F.C.J. No. 907 (F.C.A.).

[23]   *Re Singh*, [1978] F.C.J. No. 180 (F.C.A.).

[24]   *Floris v. Nova Scotia (Director of Livestock Services)*, [1987] N.S.J. No. 106 (N.S.S.C.); *Ayangma v. Eastern School Board*, [2009] P.E.I.J. No. 33 (P.E.I.C.A.).

[25]   *Lee v. Canada (Minister of Citizenship and Immigration)*, [2003] F.C.J. No. 977 (F.C.T.D.), affd [2004] F.C.J. No. 602 (F.C.A.).

[26]   *Ontario v. Gratton-Masuy Environmental Technologies Inc. (c.o.b. EcoFlo Ontario)*, [2010] O.J. No. 2935 at paras. 55-56 (Ont. C.A.).

[27]   *Halifax (Regional Municipality) v. Nova Scotia (Human Rights Commission)*, [2010] N.S.J. No. 54 (N.S.C.A.), leave to appeal granted [2010] S.C.C.A. No. 132; *New Brunswick School District No. 15 v. New Brunswick (Human Rights Board of Inquiry)*, [1989] N.B.J. No. 844 (N.B.C.A.), leave to appeal to S.C.C. refused [1989] S.C.C.A. No. 432; *Citizens for a Southern Bypass Committee v. Pasadena (Town Council)*, [1995] N.J. No. 341 (Nfld. C.A.).

[28]   *Nova Scotia (Labour Relations Board) v. Little Narrows Gypsum Co.*, [1977] N.S.J. No. 603 (N.S.C.A.).

[29]   *Swampy Cree Tribunal Council v. Manitoba (Clean Environment Commission)*, [1994] M.J. No. 747 (Man. Q.B.).

A court may be reluctant to entertain an application for an order prohibiting a tribunal from proceeding if the tribunal has not been offered an opportunity to decide whether it has authority to proceed. If the tribunal lacks authority, it may, upon being advised, agree to halt its proceeding. One must not assume in advance that a tribunal will intentionally act illegally. As discussed in chapter 4, tribunals have a duty to decide whether they have statutory authority to proceed and, before interfering, courts permit them to consider the issue.

In very rare cases, a tribunal may be prohibited from proceeding where it has statutory authority to proceed, but refuses to follow fair procedure or is guilty of some other serious irregularity. The tribunal should be given an opportunity to rectify the problem before an application to the court is made. In these circumstances, an order of limited duration may be issued so as to expire when the defects are cured.[30]

In a few jurisdictions, a writ of *quo warranto* may be issued to prohibit the exercise of powers by persons who do not validly hold office. This order requires office holders to prove that they have a lawful right to their office. This order is available only if the office is of a public nature created by the Crown, by a Royal Charter or by legislative Act (rather than the office of a deputy or public servant) and the holder has exercised the office (a mere claim to office is not enough).[31]

In some cases a tribunal, acting without authority, may be stopped by injunction. Some courts are expressly empowered to issue injunctions in respect of the exercise of statutory powers.[32] However, statutes governing proceedings against the Crown prohibit the issuance of injunctions against the Crown and its servants.[33] The combined effect of these statutes is to permit the issuance of injunctions against entities that exercise statutory power but are not part of the Crown (such as self-regulatory

---

[30] *Elliott v. Burin Peninsula School Board District No. 7*, [1998] N.J. No. 128 (Nfld. C.A.); *Chyz v. Appraisal Institute of Canada*, [1985] S.J. No. 820 (Sask. C.A.).

[31] *Jock v. Canada*, [1991] F.C.J. No. 204 (F.C.T.D.); *Comité de surveillance de l'Association des intermediaries en assurance de personnes du Québec c. Murphy*, [2007] J.Q. no 3655 (Que. C.A.); *Union canadienne des travailleurs en communication c. Papiccio*, [2005] J.Q. no 1324 (Que. C.A.).

[32] *Federal Courts Act*, R.S.C. 1985, c. F-7, s. 18 [en. S.C. 1990, c. 8, s. 5]; *Judicial Review Procedure Act*, R.S.B.C. 1996, c. 241, s. 2; *Rules of Court*, Reg. 390/68, r. 3.15(1)(b); *Queen's Bench Rules*, R.S.S. 1978, c. Q-1, r. 664; *Judicial Review Procedure Act*, R.S.O. 1990, c. J.1, s. 2; *Civil Procedure Rules*, R.S.N.S. 1989, c. 240, r. 7.11(c); *Judicial Review Act*, R.S.P.E.I. 1988, c. J-3, s. 2(1)(b).

[33] *Crown Liability and Proceedings Act*, R.S.C. 1985, c. C-50, s. 22 [as am.]; *Crown Proceeding Act*, R.S.B.C. 1996, c. 89, s. 11; *Proceedings Against the Crown Act*, R.S.A. 2000, c. P-25, s. 17; *Proceedings Against the Crown Act*, R.S.S. 1978, c. P-27, s. 17; *Proceedings Against the Crown Act*, C.C.S.M., c. P140, s. 14; *Proceedings Against the Crown Act*, R.S.O. 1990, c. P.27, s. 14; *Proceedings Against the Crown Act*, R.S.N.B. 1973, c. P-18, s. 14; *Proceedings Against the Crown Act*, R.S.N.S. 1989, c. 360, s. 16; *Crown Proceedings Act*, R.S.P.E.I. 1988, c. C-32, s. 13; *Proceedings Against the Crown Act*, R.S.N.L. 1990, c. P-26, s. 15.

bodies, municipal authorities and school boards) but to preclude the courts from issuing injunctions to prevent the lawful exercise of statutory authority by Ministers and other servants of the Crown.[34] Regardless, in all cases involving the illegal exercise of statutory authority, a writ of prohibition is the preferred remedy.[35]

If an order prohibiting or enjoining the tribunal from proceeding is refused at this stage and the tribunal is permitted to proceed, an application to quash may be commenced after the tribunal decision is issued.

3.   Mandamus: Order the Tribunal to Act

A court, on judicial review, may order a tribunal to perform a specific act, but only if:

(1)   the applicant has a legal right to have the act performed in the manner and at the time the request that it be performed is made;

(2)   the tribunal is under a corresponding legal duty to so act; and

(3)   the tribunal has been requested to act and has refused to do so.[36]

The legal right and corresponding duty must be found in a statute, regulation or order made under statute. *Mandamus* is not available to enforce policy[37] or a contractual right.[38] The tribunal should be allowed a reasonable amount of time to consider the request before application is made to court.[39] If there has been unreasonable delay in processing the request, the court may impose a deadline by which the tribunal must make a decision.[40]

---

[34]   *Douglas v. Saskatchewan (Minister of Learning)*, [2005] S.J. No. 401 (Sask. Q.B.); *Summerside Seafood Supreme Inc. v. Prince Edward Island (Minister of Fisheries, Aquaculture and Environment)*, [2006] P.E.I.J. No. 32 (P.E.I.C.A.); *Loomis v. Ontario (Ministry of Agriculture and Food)*, [1993] O.J. No. 2788 (Ont. Div. Ct.); *Aroland First Nation v. Ontario*, [1996] O.J. No. 557 (Ont. Gen. Div.).

[35]   *Bingo Enterprises Ltd. v. Manitoba (Lotteries and Gaming Licensing Board)*, [1983] M.J. No. 57 (Man. C.A.).

[36]   *Karavos v. Toronto (City)*, [1948] O.W.N. 17 at 18 (Ont. C.A.); *Khalil v. Canada (Secretary of State)*, [1999] F.C.J. No. 1093 (F.C.A.).

[37]   *Arsenault v. Canada (Attorney General)*, [2009] F.C.J. No. 1306 (F.C.A.), leave to appeal refused [2009] S.C.C.A. No. 543; *Hassum v. Contestoga College Institute of Technology and Advanced Learning*, [2008] O.J. No. 1141 (Ont. S.C.J.).

[38]   *Devil's Gap Cottagers (1982) Ltd. v. Rat Portage Band No. 38B*, [2008] F.C.J. No. 1018 (F.C.).

[39]   *Austin v. Canada (Minister of Consumer and Corporate Affairs)*, [1986] F.C.J. No. 696 (F.C.T.D.).

[40]   *Ben-Musa v. Canada (Minister of Citizenship and Immigration)*, [2005] F.C.J. No. 942 (F.C.); *Douze v. Canada (Minister of Citizenship and Immigration)*, [2010] F.C.J. No. 1680 (F.C.).

If a tribunal refuses even to consider whether to act, a court may order it to consider the issue.[41] A court may order a tribunal to exercise its statutory discretion, but not which way to decide.[42] Where the exercise of discretion cannot be done without investigation, a court will not order the tribunal to exercise its discretion prior to completing its investigation, provided the investigation is being actively undertaken.[43] A court will not direct how a tribunal is to exercise its discretion, unless the discretion has in fact been exercised and all that remains is the implementation of the decision,[44] or if it is clear that the tribunal would have granted the request but for the one improper consideration.[45] As *mandamus* is by nature a final order, it may not be granted as interlocutory relief.[46]

4. Enforce the Statute and Orders of the Tribunal

When a party refuses to obey an order of a tribunal, many statutes empower the tribunal or other parties to apply to a court for an order requiring obedience. Then, if the court order is not obeyed, the court may fine or imprison the miscreant. Tribunals rarely have the power to enforce their orders and must request a court's assistance.[47]

One common statutory procedure for enforcing an order of a tribunal is as follows. First, the tribunal issues an order requiring the person to do or refrain from doing a particular act. Then, if that person disobeys the order, the tribunal may apply to the court for an order requiring the person to comply with it.[48] If the person did not take advantage of a right to appeal the tribunal order, or appealed and lost, the validity of the order is presumed.[49] The court should be satisfied, by affidavit evidence on a balance of probabilities, that the person has, in fact, disobeyed the tribunal

---

[41]   *Canada (Minister of Manpower and Immigration) v. Tsiafakis*, [1977] F.C.J. No. 26 (F.C.A.); *Corp. Brasserie Lakeport Inc. v. Québec (Régie des alcohols, des courses et des jeux)*, [1996] Q.J. No. 1638 (Que. S.C.).

[42]   *Apotex Inc. v. Canada (Minister of National Health and Welfare)*, [1999] F.C.J. No. 1978 (F.C.A.); *Ridge v. Assn. of Architects*, [1979] S.J. No. 419 (Sask. C.A.).

[43]   *Alouette Amusement Canada Inc. v. Atlantic Lottery Corp.*, [1991] N.B.J. No. 465 (N.B.Q.B.); *Conille v. Canada (Minister of Citizenship and Immigration)*, [1998] F.C.J. No. 1553 (F.C.T.D.).

[44]   *Mount Sinai Hospital Center v. Quebec (Minister of Health and Social Services)*, [2001] S.C.J. No. 43.

[45]   *Trinity Western University v. College of Teachers*, [2001] S.C.J. No. 32; *Mignault Perrault (Succession de) c. Hudson (Ville d')*, [2010] J.Q. no 11921 (Que. C.A.).

[46]   *Delisle v. Canada (Attorney General)*, [2004] F.C.J. No. 966 (F.C.C.).

[47]   One tribunal that does is the Competition Tribunal: *Chrysler Canada Ltd. v. Canada (Competition Tribunal)*, [1992] S.C.J. No. 64.

[48]   For example, see the *Statutory Powers Procedure Act*, R.S.O. 1990, c. S.22, s. 19 [as am.].

[49]   *British Columbia (Provincial Agricultural Land Commission) v. Pickell*, [1980] B.C.J. No. 145 (B.C.S.C.).

order. If the court order is disobeyed, another application may be made to court to punish for contempt.

Another common statutory procedure simply permits the tribunal order to be registered with the court and enforced as if it had been issued by the court.[50] The tribunal order must be clear and unambiguous to be enforced.[51] The court may refuse to enforce it until an appeal or application for judicial review is concluded,[52] after which, the tribunal order is presumed valid.[53] If the order is for the payment of money, the plaintiff may move for summary judgment and the defendant may not re-litigate the issues decided by the tribunal.[54] If leave of the court is required to register a tribunal order, it may be refused if no useful purpose would be served. If the tribunal order merely declares the rights of parties, leave to register it as a court order might be refused because there is no positive act to enforce, such as the payment of money or the performance of a specific act.[55] If leave is not required, a court may on the same grounds refuse to enforce an order that has been registered. Although an order of a tribunal, upon being registered, has the same force and effect as if it were an order made by the court, it may not be appealed pursuant to the rules that apply to appeals from court orders. It may be challenged only pursuant to provisions for appeal and judicial review that are available to challenge orders of the tribunal. If, after registration with the court, the order is violated, application may be made to the court for an order finding the violator in contempt.[56]

A court will not issue *mandamus* requiring a tribunal to commence a court proceeding to enforce its order because the tribunal has discretion.[57]

Absent statutory provision for court enforcement of tribunal orders, the Attorney General, or the tribunal if it has a mandate to protect the

---

[50] For a typical provision, see the *Administrative Tribunals Act*, S.B.C. 2004, c. 45, s. 54.

[51] *United Food and Commercial Workers, Local 1252 v. Western Star*, [1995] N.J. No. 334 (S.C.); *Toronto Transit Commission v. Ryan*, [1998] O.J. No. 51 (Ont. Gen. Div.); *Larocque v. Louis Bull Tribe*, [2008] F.C.J. No. 1817 (F.C.).

[52] *Boucher v. Logistik Unicorp Inc.*, [2001] J.Q. no 64 (Que. C.A.), leave to appeal refused [2001] C.S.C.R. no 115; *Citation Industries Ltd. v. United Brotherhood of Carpenters and Joiners of America, Local 1928*, [1988] B.C.J. No. 1795 (B.C.C.A.); *International Woodworkers of America v. Patchogue Plymouth, Hawkesbury Mills*, [1976] O.J. No. 1062 (Ont. H.C.J.).

[53] *United Nurses of Alberta v. Alberta (Attorney General)*, [1992] S.C.J. No. 37; *Fraser v. Victoria City Police*, [1990] B.C.J. No. 1617 (B.C.C.A.).

[54] *Durnford v. 2201336 Nova Scotia Ltd.*, [2003] N.S.J. No. 303 (N.S.S.C.); *British Columbia (Securities Commission) v. Hrappstead*, [2009] B.C.J. No. 1736 (B.C.S.C.).

[55] *Central and Eastern Trust Co. v. Seven Seas Restaurant Ltd.*, [1978] N.B.J. No. 37 (N.B.S.C.).

[56] *Citation Industries Ltd. v. United Brotherhood of Carpenters and Joiners of America, Local 1928*, [1988] B.C.J. No. 1795 (B.C.C.A.); *United Electrical, Radio and Machine Workers of America, Local 567 v. Milltronics Ltd.*, [1981] O.J. No. 276 (Ont. H.C.J.); *Alberta (Minister of Environment) v. Verbeek*, [2004] A.J. No. 269 (Alta. Q.B.).

[57] *Wnek v. Witless Bay (Town)*, [2003] N.J. No. 36 (N.S.S.C.).

public, may apply to court for an injunction.[58] Also a party whom the order benefits may bring an action against the disobedient party to enforce it.[59] Success may depend on whether the tribunal order is of a type that a court would enforce, and whether the court believes it should enforce the tribunal order in the absence of any statutory procedure for obtaining court assistance. If the party who refuses to obey the tribunal order is another tribunal over whom the first tribunal has power, the disobedient tribunal may be brought into line by a court order in the nature of *mandamus*.[60]

Many statutes provide for prosecution of persons who disobey tribunal orders. Validity of the order cannot be challenged in defence to the charge, if adequate alternate procedures for challenging the order were available.[61] In addition the *Criminal Code* makes it a criminal offence to disobey a lawful order made by any tribunal, federal or provincial.[62]

Some statutes authorize a tribunal to apply to court for an order requiring a person to comply with its statute, regulations and by-laws. The injunction may be granted upon proof of violation of the law without proof of harm to the public interest, and courts are reluctant to refuse an injunction on discretionary grounds.[63] The tribunal need not hold a hearing into whether the Act has been violated before applying to court.[64] The failure of the tribunal to enforce the statute against other violators is not a valid reason to refuse an injunction.[65]

Absent statutory authority, a tribunal with a mandate to protect the public, may apply to court for an injunction to enforce a statute. Proof that the person is violating the statute, without any other evidence of harm, may be sufficient proof of harm to the public to weigh the balance of convenience in favour of granting an injunction unless the injunction would interfere

---

[58] *Pharmascience Inc. v. Binet*, [2006] S.C.J. No. 48; *Toronto (Metropolitan) Police Force v. Lymer*, [1992] O.J. No. 2359 (Ont. Gen. Div.), leave to appeal refused (*sub nom. Metro. Toronto (Municipality) Police Services Board v. Metro. Toronto Police Assn.*), [1992] O.J. No. 2464 (Ont. Gen. Div.).

[59] *Melia v. Moose Jaw Roman Catholic Separate School District No. 22*, [1979] S.J. No. 568 (Sask. C.A.).

[60] *DeWolf v. Halifax (City)*, [1979] N.S.J. No. 711 (N.S.S.C.); *Lee v. Alberta (Workers' Compensation Board)*, [1999] A.J. No. 306 (Alta. Q.B.); *Hallingham v. Newfoundland (Workers' Compensation Commission)*, [1997] N.J. No. 259 (Nfld. C.A.).

[61] *R. v. Consolidated Maybrun Mines Ltd.*, [1998] S.C.J. No. 32; *R. v. Al Klippert Ltd.*, [1998] S.C.J. No. 33.

[62] R.S.C. 1985, c. C-46, s. 127 [as am.]; *United Nurses of Alberta v. Alberta (Attorney General)*, [1992] S.C.J. No. 37.

[63] *College of Opticians (B.C.) v. Coastal Contacts Inc.*, [2009] B.C.J. No. 2099 (B.C.C.A.); *British Columbia (Minister of Environment, Lands and Parks) v. Alpha Manufacturing Inc.*, [1997] B.C.J. No. 1989 (B.C.C.A.); *Maple Ridge (District) v. Thornhill Aggregates Ltd.*, [1998] B.C.J. No. 1485 (B.C.C.A.), leave to appeal refused [1998] S.C.C.A. No. 407.

[64] *Ontario (Board of Funeral Services) v. Blondell*, [1994] O.J. No. 2441 (Ont. Gen. Div.).

[65] *Polai v. Toronto (City)*, [1972] S.C.J. No. 73.

with a *Charter* right, in which case stronger proof would be required.[66] The court is not bound by the tribunal's interpretation of the statute even if the defendant has unsuccessfully appealed tribunal orders on the same issue.[67]

The Attorney General may also bring an action for an injunction to enforce a statutory requirement and, upon showing that there has been a clear and deliberate breach of the Act, an injunction is usually granted.[68]

Violation of a court order is civil contempt, which may be punished if proven beyond a reasonable doubt.[69] Evidence must establish that, after receiving notice of the court order,[70] the person intentionally did an act that is prohibited by the court order. Only proof of the intention to do the act is required. An intention to violate the court order need not be proven.[71]

5. Declaration: Define Powers, Rights and Duties

If there is a dispute as to the meaning of a legal power, right or duty prescribed by or under statute, a court may interpret it and declare its correct meaning. By this means, a court may define the scope of the powers of a tribunal or the legal rights or duties of a party. The purpose of requesting a declaration of the court is to clarify the law on a particular point. Declarations are not made on matters of morality, wisdom or policy.[72]

A declaration of rights, duties or powers is a part of every decision that grants other relief. A declaration alone may be sought by way of judicial review when other relief is unnecessary or unavailable in the circumstances.[73] As courts refuse to decide academic questions, declarato-

---

[66] *Canada (Human Rights Commission) v. Canadian Liberty Net*, [1998] S.C.J. No. 31; *Ordre des pharmaciens v. Meditrust Pharmacy Services Inc.*, [1994] A.Q. no 749, 122 D.L.R. (4th) 209 (Que. C.A.), leave to appeal refused [1994] S.C.C.A. No. 554; *Chicken Farmers of Ontario v. Drost*, [2005] O.J. No. 3973 (Ont. Div. Ct.); *Fraser Health Authority v. Jongerden (c.o.b. Home on the Range)*, [2010] B.C.J. No. 480 (B.C.S.C.); *St. Paul (County No. 19) v. Belland*, [2006] A.J. No. 152 (Alta. C.A.). But see: *British Columbia Assn. of Optometrists v. Clearbrook Optical Ltd.*, [2000] B.C.J. No. 934 (B.C.C.A.); *Law Society of Upper Canada v. Junger*, [1991] O.J. No. 2024 (Ont. Gen. Div.), affd [1996] O.J. No. 201 (Ont. C.A.).

[67] *International Alliance of Theatrical Stage Employees Moving Picture Technicians, Artists and Allied Crafts of the United States, its Territories and Canada, Stage Local 56 v. Société de la Place des Arts de Montréal*, [2004] S.C.J. No. 4.

[68] *Sault Ste. Marie (City) v. S.S. Kresge Co. Ltd.*, [1966] O.J. No. 1002 (Ont. H.C.J.); *Ontario (Attorney General) v. Paul Magder Furs Ltd.*, [1990] O.J. No. 63 (Ont. H.C.J.).

[69] *College of Optometrists of Ontario v. SHS Optical Ltd.*, [2008] O.J. No. 3933 (Ont. C.A.), leave to appeal refused [2008] S.C.C.A. No. 506.

[70] *Warman v. Tremaine*, [2010] F.C.J. No. 1376 (F.C.).

[71] *North Vancouver (District) v. Sorrenti*, [2004] B.C.J. No. 1130 (B.C.C.A.).

[72] *Dee v. Canada (Minister of Employment and Immigration)*, [1987] F.C.J. No. 1158 (F.C.T.D.).

[73] *Kelso v. Canada*, [1981] S.C.J. No. 19; *Ontario v. Gratton-Masuy Environmental Technologies Inc.*, [2010] O.J. No. 2935 (Ont. C.A.); *Shuswap Lake Utilities Ltd. v. British Columbia (Comptroller of Water Rights)*, [2008] B.C.J. No. 716 (B.C.C.A.).

ry relief must be necessary to determine a party's rights with respect to an actual exercise of statutory power. A declaration may also be refused if it would have no practical effect, if there is no one present in court with a true interest in presenting the opposing view,[74] or if the question could more appropriately be raised in proceedings before the tribunal.[75]

A declaration of the court does not order anyone to do anything or to refrain from doing anything. It is not enforceable as a mandatory or a compensatory order may be. However, a declaration of the court is traditionally respected.[76] A declaratory order is final in nature and will not be made on an interlocutory application.[77]

6. Award Compensation or Damages

A public officer may be sued for damages only for abuse of power. To establish this tort of "misfeasance in public office", the plaintiff must prove, first, that the public officer engaged in deliberate and unlawful conduct in his or her capacity as a public officer and, second, that the public officer must have been aware both that his or her conduct was unlawful and that it was likely to harm the plaintiff.[78] In the absence of bad faith, there is no liability in damages for the negligent exercise of statutory power, for the misinterpretation of statute or for the failure to follow proper procedures,[79] but there may be liability for negligent failure to implement a court order.[80]

Many statutes grant public officers immunity from suit for acts done in good faith in the performance of their duties. Bad faith may be proven with direct evidence of the public officer's words or conduct or by circumstantial evidence of acts that are so markedly inconsistent with the statutory mandate that a court cannot reasonably conclude that they were

---

[74] *Solosky v. Canada*, [1979] S.C.J. No. 130.

[75] *Ordre des opticians d'ordonnances v. Harrison*, [1993] A.Q. no 1416.

[76] *Lount Corp. v. Canada (Attorney General)*, [1983] F.C.J. No. 137 (F.C.T.D.), affd [1985] F.C.J. No. 139 (F.C.A.).

[77] *Loomis v. Ontario (Ministry of Agriculture and Food)*, [1993] O.J. No. 2788 (Ont. Div. Ct.); *Aroland First Nation v. Ontario*, [1996] O.J. No. 557 (Ont. Gen. Div.); *Bush v. Saskatchewan (Minister of Environment and Resource Management)*, [1994] S.J. No. 165 (Sask. Q.B.).

[78] *Odhavji Estate v. Woodhouse*, [2003] S.C.J. No. 74; *Roncarelli v. Duplessis*, [1959] S.C.J. No. 1.

[79] *Holland v. Saskatchewan*, [2008] S.C.J. No. 43; *Odhavji Estate v. Woodhouse*, [2003] S.C.J. No. 74; *Harris v. Law Society of Alberta*, [1936] S.C.J. No. 5; *Welbridge Holdings Ltd. v. Winnipeg (City)*, [1970] S.C.J. No. 102; *Cooper v. Hobart*, [2001] S.C.J. No. 76; *Roeder v. Lang Michener Lawrence & Shaw*, [2007] B.C.J. No. 501 (B.C.C.A.). But see *O'Dwyer v. Ontario (Racing Commission)*, [2008] O.J. No. 2219 (Ont. C.A.).

[80] *Holland v. Saskatchewan*, [2008] S.C.J. No. 43. But see *Courtiers JD & Associés ltée c. Québec (Procureur général)*, [2009] J.Q. no 3466 (Que. S.C.); *Chiasson v. Canada (Attorney General)*, [2009] F.C.J. No. 1268 (F.C.A.).

performed in good faith.[81] Facts supporting an allegation of bad faith must be pleaded.[82]

No action in libel or slander may succeed for comments made in a tribunal's reasons or in the course of its proceedings.[83]

A municipality or the Crown may be liable in damages for negligent performance by its servants of operational duties such as inspections.[84]

Entities, such as marketing boards, that have power to contract and to carry on a business may be ordered to pay damages for breach of contract, but not in respect of the exercise of statutory powers.[85]

Orders to pay fines and costs issued by private associations against their members may be collected by way of civil action for damages.[86]

A party who received money as a result of a tribunal order, that was later declared invalid, might not be able to rely on the order in defence to an action by the payors for recovery.[87]

An action designed to discourage parties from exercising their legal rights before a regulator may be struck as abusive.[88]

C.   DISCRETION

On judicial review there is no right to a remedy even if all the necessary criteria are met. A court may choose not to grant a remedy to an applicant who is otherwise entitled. Superior courts have discretion when exercising their power of judicial review.[89] The common grounds upon which the discretion to refuse a remedy is exercised are described below.

---

[81]   *Entreprises Sibeca Inc. v. Frelighsburg (Municipality)*, [2004] S.C.J. No. 57 at paras. 25-26; *McCullock-Finney v. (Barreau) Québec*, [2004] S.C.J. No. 31.

[82]   *Ontario v. Gratton-Masuy Environmental Technologies Inc. (c.o.b. EcoFlo Ontario)*, [2010] O.J. No. 2935 (Ont. C.A.).

[83]   *Morier v. Rivard*, [1985] S.C.J. No. 81; *Stark v. Auerbach*, [1979] B.C.J. No. 988 (B.C.S.C.).

[84]   *Ingles v. Tutkaluk Construction Ltd.*, [2000] S.C.J. No. 13; *Fullowka v. Pinkerton's of Canada Ltd.*, [2010] S.C.J. No. 5.

[85]   *B.G. Ranches v. Manitoba (Agricultural Lands Protection Board)*, [1983] M.J. No. 72 (Man. Q.B.).

[86]   *New Brunswick Association of Real Estate Appraisers v. Poitras*, [2005] N.B.J. No. 545 (N.B.C.A.); *contra*: *Brotherhood of Maintenance of Way Employees v. Litke*, [1999] M.J. No. 433 (Man. C.A.), leave to appeal refused [1999] S.C.C.A. No. 564.

[87]   *Garland v. Consumers' Gas Co.*, [2004] S.C.J. No. 21.

[88]   *Hunt Oil Co. of Canada, Inc. v. Galleon Energy Inc.*, [2010] A.J. No. 348 (Alta. Q.B.), colloquially labelled SLAPP: Strategic Litigation Against Public Participation.

[89]   *Mining Watch Canada v. Canada (Fisheries and Oceans)*, [2010] S.C.J. No. 2; *Harelkin v. University of Regina*, [1979] S.C.J. No. 59.

1.   Application is Premature

Applications for judicial review filed before the tribunal has completed its proceeding are usually dismissed as being premature. Applications to challenge notices to commence proceedings or interim rulings made by the tribunal, including rulings as to their authority to proceed and constitutional issues, may be dismissed by the courts, if made prior to the conclusion of the tribunal proceeding. Courts prefer to avoid ruling on constitutional issues until absolutely necessary. Even allegations of bias on the part of the tribunal may be dismissed as premature, especially if the allegations have not been put to the tribunal for its ruling, or there is a right of appeal to another tribunal that may not suffer the same bias.[90]

Premature applications are not encouraged because they have the effect of fragmenting and protracting proceedings before the tribunal. They defeat one of the purposes of tribunal proceedings, which is to provide expeditious and inexpensive proceedings to deal with certain types of issues or problems. Often by the end of the proceeding, preliminary complaints are no longer of importance. A party may succeed in the result after having lost a number of preliminary challenges. They also defeat the purpose of the standard of review if the application is brought before there is a tribunal decision to which deference may be accorded. Courts prefer to consider all issues at once, rather than piecemeal, on the basis of a full record of the proceeding before the tribunal and the reasons for decision of the tribunal.[91]

Therefore, to obtain judicial review of an interim or preliminary ruling, the applicant must show exceptional or special circumstances that cannot await the conclusion of the tribunal's proceeding.[92]

---

[90] *Mondesir v. Manitoba Assn. of Optometrists*, [1998] M.J. No. 336 (Man. C.A.), leave to appeal refused [1998] S.C.C.A. No. 405; *Turnbull v. Canadian Institute of Actuaries*, [1995] M.J. No. 424 (Man. C.A.); *Ontario College of Art v. Ontario (Human Rights Commission)*, [1993] O.J. No. 61 (Ont. Div. Ct.); *Zündel v. Canada (Human Rights Commission)*, [2000] F.C.J. No. 678 (F.C.A.), leave to appeal refused [2000] S.C.C.A. No. 323; *Sztern v. Canada (Superintendent of Bankruptcy)*, [2008] F.C.J. No. 351 (F.C.).

[91] *Québec (Procureur général) v. Bouliane*, [2004] J.Q. no 4883 at paras. 159-167 (Que. C.A.), leave to appeal refused [2004] C.S.C.R. no 290; *Howe v. Institute of Chartered Accountants*, [1994] O.J. No. 1803 (Ont. C.A.), leave to appeal refused [1994] S.C.C.A. No. 348; *Szczecka v. Canada (Minister of Employment and Immigration)*, [1993] F.C.J. No. 934 (F.C.A.); *Robertson v. Edmonton Police Service*, [2003] A.J. No. 1213 (Alta. C.A.); *Ontario College of Art v. Ontario (Human Rights Commission)*, [1993] O.J. No. 61 (Ont. Div. Ct.); *Nova Scotia (Securities Commission) v. Potter*, [2006] N.S.J. No. 147 (N.S.C.A.).

[92] *C.B. Powell Ltd. v. Canada (Border Services Agency)*, [2010] F.C.J. No. 274 (F.C.A.); *University of Toronto v. Canadian Union of Educational Workers, Local 2*, [1988] O.J. No. 988 (Ont. Div. Ct.); *New Brunswick School District No. 15 v. New Brunswick (Human Rights Board of Inquiry)*, [1989] N.B.J. No. 844 (N.B.C.A.), leave to appeal refused [1989] S.C.C.A. No. 432; *Insurance Corp. of British Columbia v. Yuan*, [2009] B.C.J. No. 1473 (B.C.C.A.).

2.   An Alternate Remedy is Available

Judicial review is regarded as a remedy of last resort. Applicants must exhaust other avenues of redress before seeking judicial review.[93] The typical alternative is an appeal to court or to an appellate tribunal. Others include arbitration or reconsideration by the same tribunal.

All circumstances of the alternative are considered to determine whether that form of review is adequate.[94] It may not be adequate if:

(1)   the appellate tribunal does not have statutory authority over or is unwilling to address the issue raised by the applicant,[95] or does not have statutory authority to grant the remedy requested;[96]

(2)   the appeal is on the record, which does not include the evidence relevant to the complaint,[97] or contains evidentiary errors that the appellate tribunal has no authority to correct;[98]

(3)   the procedure is slower, more expensive and cumbersome,[99] or

(4)   the issue is the constitutional validity of statutory provisions.[100]

An appeal to an appellate tribunal is generally considered adequate,[101] even where bias is alleged against the lower tribunal.[102] Courts pay no regard to speculation that the appellate tribunal will fail to provide a fair process.[103] The transfer of the burden to the appellant from the

---

[93]   *Addison & Leyen Ltd. v. Canada*, [2007] S.C.J. No. 33.

[94]   *Canadian Pacific Ltd. v. Matsqui Indian Band*, [1995] S.C.J. No. 1; *Harelkin v. University of Regina*, [1979] S.C.J. No. 59; *R. v. Consolidated Maybrun Mines Ltd.*, [1998] S.C.J. No. 32; *KCP Innovative Services Inc. v. Alberta (Securities Commission)*, [2009] A.J. No. 310 (Alta. C.A.); *Saskatchewan (Minister of Agriculture, Food and Rural Revitalization) v. Canada (Attorney General)*, [2006] F.C.J. No. 435 (F.C.).

[95]   *Violette v. New Brunswick Dental Society*, [2004] N.B.J. No. 5 (N.B.C.A.); *Kingsbury v. Heighton*, [2003] N.S.J. No. 277 (N.S.C.A.).

[96]   *Evershed v. Ontario*, [1985] O.J. No. 2473 (Ont. C.A.).

[97]   *V.S.R. Investments Ltd. v. Laczko*, [1983] O.J. No. 2955 (Ont. Div. Ct.); *Milner Power Inc. v. Alberta Energy and Utilities Board*, [2007] A.J. No. 919 (Alta. C.A.).

[98]   *Cimolai v. Children's and Women's Health Centre*, [2003] B.C.J. No. 1313 (B.C.C.A.).

[99]   *Violette v. New Brunswick Dental Society*, [2004] N.B.J. No. 5 (N.B.C.A.).

[100]   *Kelly v. Ontario*, [2008] O.J. No. 1901 (Ont. S.C.J.), leave to appeal refused [2008] O.J. No. 3196 (Ont. Div. Ct.).

[101]   *Harelkin v. University of Regina*, [1979] S.C.J. No. 59; *R. v. Consolidated Maybrun Mines Ltd.*, [1998] S.C.J. No. 32; *Toth Equity Ltd. v. Ottawa (City)*, [2011] O.J. No. 2128 (Ont. C.A.); *contra: Cimolai v. Children's and Women's Health Centre*, [2003] B.C.J. No. 1313 (B.C.C.A.).

[102]   *Merchant v. Law Society of Alberta*, [2008] A.J. No. 1211 (Alta. C.A.), leave to appeal refused [2009] S.C.C.A. No. 4; *Turnbull v. Canadian Institute of Actuaries*, [1995] M.J. No. 424 (Man. C.A.).

[103]   *Harelkin v. University of Regina*, [1979] S.C.J. No. 59.

respondent before the lower tribunal is not reason to find that the right of appeal is not an adequate form of review.[104]

Judicial review is not available to an applicant who missed the time limit to appeal,[105] who abandoned an appeal,[106] or who did not apply for or was denied leave to appeal.[107]

Even if the relief requested is a declaration interpreting a statutory provision applied by the tribunal, that declaration may be granted only in the context of an appeal from the tribunal decision or, if there is no right of appeal, by way of judicial review, and not by way of application under the rules of court for the interpretation of a statute or a civil action.[108]

The Ontario *Judicial Review Procedure Act* permits judicial review "notwithstanding any right of appeal",[109] as does the Prince Edward Island *Judicial Review Act* provided the applicant files a written waiver of the right of appeal.[110] Despite these provisions judicial review is refused where there is an adequate right of appeal.[111] Section 18.5 of the *Federal Courts Act* prohibits applications for judicial review to the extent that the tribunal decision may be appealed to the Federal Court.[112] Article 846 of the Quebec *Code of Civil Procedure* does not permit a superior court to evoke a tribunal decision that is susceptible of appeal unless the decision involved a lack or excess of statutory authority.[113]

The simultaneous launching of an appeal and an application for judicial review is discouraged.[114] An application for judicial review and an

---

[104]   *Rafuse v. Hambling*, [1979] N.S.J. No. 749 at para. 59 (N.S.S.C.).

[105]   *South Eastern Regional Shopping Centre Ltd. v. Steinbach (Town)*, [1983] M.J. No. 95 (Man. C.A.).

[106]   *Quigley v. Torbay (Town)*, [2010] N.J. No. 10 (N.L.C.A.).

[107]   *Rozander v. Alberta (Energy Resources Conservation Board)*, [1978] A.J. No. 674 (Alta. C.A.), leave to appeal refused (1979), 14 A.R. 540*n*.

[108]   *Ontario v. Gratton-Masuy Environmental Technologies Inc. (c.o.b. EcoFlo Ontario)*, [2010] O.J. No. 2935 (Ont. C.A.); *Shuswap Lake Utilities Ltd. v. British Columbia (Comptroller of Water Rights)*, [2008] B.C.J. No. 716 (B.C.C.A.); *Sebastian v. Saskatchewan*, [1978] S.J. No. 526 (Sask. C.A.); *Canada Post Corp. v. Canadian Union of Postal Workers*, [1989] O.J. No. 1583 (Ont. H.C.J.); *Canada (Attorney General) v. TeleZone Inc.*, [2010] S.C.J. No. 62 at para. 75.

[109]   *Judicial Review Procedure Act*, R.S.O. 1990, c. J.1, s. 2(1).

[110]   *Judicial Review Act*, R.S.P.E.I. 1988, c. J-3, s. 4(2).

[111]   *McKenna's Furniture Store v. Prince Edward Island (Fire Marshall)*, [1997] P.E.I.J. No. 33 (P.E.I.S.C.).

[112]   R.S.C. 1985, c. F-7, s. 18.5 [as am.]. See *Fast v. Canada (Minister of Citizenship and Immigration)*, [2000] F.C.J. No. 1116 (F.C.T.D.), affd [2001] F.C.J. No. 1776 (F.C.A.).

[113]   R.S.Q. c. C-25, art. 846. See *Commission des Accidents du Travail du Québec v. Valade*, [1981] C.A. 37, affd [1982] S.C.J. No. 55.

[114]   *Pronto Cabs Ltd. v. Toronto (Metropolitan Licensing Commission)*, [1982] O.J. No. 3536 (Ont. Div. Ct.); *Fleischhacker v. Saskatchewan (Minister of Environment)*, [1985] S.J. No. 403 (Sask. Q.B.).

appeal to the same court cannot be consolidated.[115] Where no time limit is prescribed for judicial review, an application may be commenced after the applicant has exhausted all other rights of appeal and review.[116]

See also the discussion in chapter 4 regarding attempts by a party to re-litigate, before another tribunal or the court, matters already decided.

The one exception to this principle is an application by a person, who is detained, for a writ of *habeas corpus*. A court should not decline to hear the application unless the alternative is a complete comprehensive and expert procedure for review of the detention decision.[117]

3. Remedy Would Have No Practical Effect; Issues are Moot

If a court remedy would have no practical effect, it may be refused. The court may decline to grant a remedy if the tribunal error did not affect its result[118] or if the facts or law would likely persuade the tribunal to make the same decision.[119] If to repeat the regulatory process would impose excessive burdens on parties and a decision maker who acted in good faith, a declaration as to the error may be made without further remedy.[120]

If circumstances have changed since the tribunal made the order reviewed by the court, so that it would be impractical to make a different order, the court may refuse a remedy.[121] Once a tribunal order has expired or no longer affects the applicant's interests, the application is moot unless it concerns recurring orders of short duration that are evasive of review.[122] If the applicant's present circumstances are such that the remedy, if granted, will not be of any use, a court may refuse to award it. For example, a

---

[115] *Boucher v. Public Accountants Council*, [2002] O.J. No. 288, 156 O.A.C. 386 (Ont. S.C.J.).

[116] *Jones v. British Columbia (Workers' Compensation Board)*, [2003] B.C.J. No. 2556 (B.C.C.A.).

[117] *May v. Ferndale Institution*, [2005] S.C.J. No. 84.

[118] *Uniboard Surfaces Inc. v. Kronotex Fussboden GmbH and Co. KG*, [2006] F.C.J. No. 1837 (F.C.A.).

[119] *Mobil Oil Canada Ltd. v. Canada-Nfld. Offshore Petroleum Board*, [1994] S.C.J. No. 14; *Mills v. Sobeys Inc.*, [2000] N.S.J. No. 244 (N.S.C.A.); *Cha v. Canada (Minister of Citizenship and Immigration)*, [2006] F.C.J. No. 491 at para. 67 (F.C.A.); *Murphy v. Newhook*, [1984] N.J. No. 152 (Nfld. S.C.); *contra: Cardinal v. Kent Institution*, [1985] S.C.J. No. 78 at para. 23.

[120] *MiningWatch Canada v. Canada (Fisheries and Oceans)*, [2010] S.C.J. No. 2.

[121] *Chuang v. Royal College of Dental Surgeons of Ontario*, [2007] O.J. No. 1677 (Ont. Div. Ct.); *Moose Jaw Central Bingo Assn. Inc. v. Saskatchewan (Liquor and Gaming Authority)*, [1994] S.J. No. 76 (Sask. C.A.); *R. v. Law Society of Saskatchewan*, [1984] S.J. No. 841 (Sask. C.A.); *Moore v. New Brunswick (Civil Service Commission)*, [1981] N.B.J. No. 140 at para. 23 (N.B.Q.B.).

[122] *Air Canada v. Canada (Commissioner of Competition)*, [2002] F.C.J. No. 424 (F.C.A.), leave to appeal refused [2002] S.C.C.A. No. 212.

wrongfully dismissed employee who has since found another job may no longer want the lost job returned by arbitration award.[123]

Courts dislike being asked to make academic pronouncements in the absence of a live controversy about a tribunal action that affects the applicant's interests. Courts refuse to render decisions where the dispute is over or has not yet arisen.[124] The factors to be considered in determining whether an issue is moot include judicial economy, the active participation of parties willing to argue all sides of the issue, and respect for the limits on the court's constitutional authority to declare the law in the absence of a live controversy.[125]

4. Failure of Party to Object Promptly[126]

If a tribunal commits a procedural error or demonstrates an appearance of bias, no party should sit silently and permit the tribunal to continue unaware of any objection. Objections should be stated to the tribunal immediately upon discovery of the impropriety to permit the tribunal to make appropriate corrections. Failure to object promptly may be interpreted as acquiescence and may cause a court to refuse a remedy.[127] Even silence, while another party objects, is regarded as acquiescence.[128] A party who chooses not to attend the hearing waives the right to challenge procedural errors, bias and the decision on the merits.[129] Acquiescence cannot confer on a tribunal powers it does not otherwise have, but it can forgive procedural errors.[130]

---

[123] *Fraser Lake Sawmills v. International Woodworkers of America, Local 1-424*, [1984] B.C.J. No. 2768 (B.C.S.C.).

[124] *Solosky v. Canada*, [1979] S.C.J. No. 130.

[125] *Borowski v. Canada (Attorney General)*, [1989] S.C.J. No. 14; *Tamil Co-operative Homes Inc. v. Arulappah*, [2000] O.J. No. 3372 (Ont. C.A.); *Canada (Minister of Citizenship and Immigration) v. Nemsila*, [1997] F.C.J. No. 630 (F.C.A.).

[126] See also chapter 2 "H. Has the Party Waived Procedural Rules?" and chapter 3 "B.7. Objection and Waiver".

[127] *263657 Alberta Ltd. v. Banff (Town) (Subdivision and Development Appeal Board)*, [2003] A.J. No. 1019 (Alta. C.A.); *Eckervogt v. British Columbia (Minister of Employment and Investment)*, [2004] B.C.J. No. 1492 at paras. 46-49 (B.C.C.A.); *Compagnie de taxi Laurentides inc. c. Commission des transport du Québec*, [2009] J.Q. no 1872 at paras. 52-53 (Que. C.A.); *Grain Workers' Union, Local 333 v. Prince Rupert Grain Ltd.*, [1987] F.C.J. No. 442 (F.C.A.); *Emerson v. Law Society of Upper Canada*, [1983] O.J. No. 3287 (Ont. H.C.J.); *La Presse v. Bouchard*, [2001] J.Q. no 2501 (Que. S.C.).

[128] *International Longshoremen's and Warehousemen's Union, Local 500 v. British Columbia Maritime Employers' Assn.*, [1987] F.C.J. No. 725 (F.C.A.).

[129] *Violette v. New Brunswick Dental Society*, [2004] N.B.J. No. 5 (N.B.C.A.).

[130] *F. Zormann and Co. Real Estate Ltd. v. Toronto Real Estate Board*, [1982] O.J. No. 3262 (Ont. Div. Ct.); *Regional Cablesystems Inc. v. Wygant*, [2003] F.C.J. No. 321 (F.C.T.D.).

A tribunal that is advised of the objection may agree with the objector and correct the problem, thus avoiding the need to apply to court. If it disagrees, the court may have the benefit of the tribunal's reasons.[131]

An application for judicial review should be commenced promptly after the release of the tribunal's final decision. Delay or lack of diligence may cause a court to exercise its discretion to refuse to grant a remedy.[132]

5.   Applicant is a Bad Actor

Those who seek equity must come to court with clean hands. A court may deny a remedy if it disapproves of an applicant's misconduct. A remedy may be refused if the applicant made a misrepresentation to the tribunal or to the court.[133] If the applicant took a confrontational approach in the tribunal proceeding or attempted to obstruct the tribunal from doing its public duty, a court may overlook unfair procedure that was followed by the tribunal to achieve a fair result on the merits. A party who flouts the law that the tribunal has a mandate to enforce may not complain when the tribunal does not itself observe every requirement of the law.[134] A party who made a tactical choice to withhold information from the tribunal cannot complain that the decision did not have an adequate evidentiary basis.[135] Where the remedy sought from the court would assist the applicant to profit from illegal conduct or obtain an unfair advantage, the remedy may be refused.[136]

---

[131] *F. Zormann and Co. Real Estate Ltd. v. Toronto Real Estate Board*, [1982] O.J. No. 3262 (Ont. Div. Ct.).

[132] *Immeubles Port Louis Ltée v. Lafontaine (Village)*, [1991] S.C.J. No. 14; *Canada (Human Rights Commission) v. Taylor*, [1990] S.C.J. No. 129; *Angus v. Canada*, [1990] F.C.J. No. 610 (F.C.A.). See chapter 7 "G. Time Limits".

[133] *Thanabalasingham v. Canada (Minister of Citizenship and Immigration)*, [2006] F.C.J. No. 20 (F.C.A.); *Hollinger Farms No. 1 Inc. v. Ontario (Minister of the Environment)*, [2007] O.J. No. 3712 (Ont. Div. Ct.).

[134] *Homex Realty and Development Co. v. Wyoming (Village)*, [1980] S.C.J. No. 109; *Khalil v. Canada (Secretary of State)*, [1999] F.C.J. No. 1093 (F.C.A.); *Pathak v. British Columbia (Public Service Commission)*, [1996] B.C.J. No. 2111 (B.C.C.A.); *Zinck's Bus Co. v. Canada*, [1998] F.C.J. No. 1093 (F.C.); *Hollinger Farms No. 1 Inc. v. Ontario (Minister of the Environment)*, [2007] O.J. No. 2405 at para. 101 (Ont. Div. Ct.).

[135] *Council of Canadians with Disabilities v. Via Rail Canada Inc.*, [2007] S.C.J. No. 15 at paras. 235-245.

[136] *Basu v. Canada*, [1991] F.C.J. No. 1272 (F.C.T.D.); *Cosman Realty Ltd. v. Winnipeg (City)*, [2001] M.J. No. 254 (Man. Q.B.), affd [2001] M.J. No. 420 (Man. C.A.).

INDEX